THE PROBLEM OF THE MEDIA

The Problem of the Media

U.S. COMMUNICATION POLITICS IN THE TWENTY-FIRST CENTURY

Robert W. McChesney

 MONTHLY REVIEW PRESS New York

LIBRARY OF CONGRESS CATALOGING-IN-PUBLICATION DATA

McChesney, Robert Waterman, 1952-

  The problem of the media : U.S. communication politics in the
twenty-first century / Robert W. McChesney.

        p. cm.

Includes bibliographical references (p.) and index.

    ISBN 1-58367-105-6 (pbk.) — ISBN 1-58367-106-4 (cloth)

    1. Mass media—Political aspects—United States. 2. United States—
Politics and government—2002- I. Title.

    P95.82.U6M378 2004

    302.23'0973—DC22

                                        2003026386

ISBN 1-58367-105-6 (pbk)

ISBN 1-58367-106-4 (cloth)

MONTHLY REVIEW PRESS

122 West 27th Street

New York, NY 10001

www.monthlyreview.org

Publication of this book was assisted by a contribution
from the Judy Ruben Outreach Fund.

Printed in Canada   10 9 8 7 6 5 4 3 2 1

CONTENTS

PREFACE

The purpose of this book is to shed light on how the media system works in the United States and to provide a basis for citizens to play a more active role in shaping the policies upon which that system is built. The corporate domination of both the media system and the policy-making process that establishes and sustains it causes serious problems for a functioning democracy and a healthy culture. Media are not the only factor in explaining the woeful state of our democracy, but they are a key factor. It is difficult to imagine much headway being made on the crucial social issues that face our nation given how poorly they are covered by the current U.S. media system. The democratic solution to this problem is to increase informed public participation in media policy making. The corporate media powers-that-be and their political surrogates oppose this prospect because they know that when the public understands that the media system is the result of explicit public policies and not natural law, the public will probably demand reforms. In this book I focus on the United States mostly for reasons of expedience and because media policy issues are generally national in scope. A book like this ideally should include a discussion of the U.S. role in the global media system, but that subject is so large that it requires its own book-length treatment.

The corporate-insider hegemony over media policy debates, and the lack of public participation, are encouraged and protected ideologically by eight myths surrounding media in the United States. This book addresses these myths because the case for democratic media policy making is weaker, if not implausible, if they are left standing. The first myth is that media do not matter that much—that they merely reflect reality, rather than shape it. In fact, media are a social force in their own right, and not just a reflection of other forces. These are complex relationships, often difficult to disentangle, because media are so interwoven into the fabric of our lives. It is noteworthy that the argument that media have little or no social effect became prominent precisely as commercial interests locked up their control over media industries in the mid-twentieth century.

Proponents of this argument would like us to overlook the fact that media sell billions of dollars worth of advertising on the belief that they, indeed, have tremendous influence. Chapter 1 discusses the power of media, and the entire book is an exercise in establishing the importance of media in our lives.

In chapter 1, I also address the second myth—that the corporate, commercial media system is "natural," the intent of the Founders, and the logical outgrowth of democracy. In fact, the vision of a free press held during the first few generations of the republic was diametrically opposed to the contemporary idea that a free press means letting media owners do whatever they can to maximize profit. The early republic provided lavish subsidies to support a diverse range of media the market would never have supported; these press policies were sometimes generated by widespread public debate. The notion that letting media owners maximize profit would necessarily generate a free press came much later, when powerful media owners with a decided self-interest propagated that view. Those of us who argue for informed policy making, for enlightened and proactive policies to enhance a vibrant free press, do not stand outside the historical tradition of freedom of the press in the United States. We *are* the tradition.

The third myth is that debates concerning media policy in the United States have accurately reflected the range of public opinion and public interests. In chapter 1, I reveal how important policy making has been *and still is* to the creation of the U.S. media system, and I chronicle how corrupt that process has become over time. By the late twentieth century, media policy making was the private playground of a handful of powerful corporate lobbies and trade associations. The public knew next to nothing about the crucial debates over policies that would set the terms for the media system and it played almost no role whatsoever in their development. Chapter 1 provides the basis for understanding why the resultant media system is so deeply flawed: it is set up to serve the needs of a relative handful of profit-seeking corporations and wealthy investors. In that sense our media system is a success because it does that very well. But lost in the shuffle are the requirements of a democratic and self-governing people.

The fourth myth is that commercial media unquestionably provide the highest quality journalism possible—the caliber of journalism a democracy necessitates for informed self-government. I
criticize this position in chapters 2 and 3. This is a curious myth
because on the surface the notion of subjecting journalism to commercial principles is a nonstarter. What sort of integrity can the
news have if it can be bought and sold like ... advertising? The inherent problem with commercial journalism is a major reason that professionalism in journalism emerged a century ago. Yet built within
the journalists' professional code are significant flaws that limit its
usefulness. Those flaws, combined with media owners' pressures on
journalism to generate maximum profit, offer a recipe for disaster. I
examine press coverage of the electoral system to highlight the limitations of contemporary journalism.

The fifth myth is that the news media in the United States today
have a "left-wing" bias. This is a peculiar myth, of recent vintage in
the United States, and not prevalent in very many other nations. I
deconstruct this myth in chapter 3 and show that the reason for its
prevalence has little to do with the intellectual strength of the arguments and a great deal to do with the right-wing political muscle
behind them, including conservative power within the mainstream
media. What this myth does, more than anything else, is reinforce
and accentuate the core problems with commercial journalism.
Right-wing media bashing and commercial journalism, rather than
being antagonistic, constitute a marriage made in heaven.

The sixth myth is that the commercial media, due to the competitive pressure for profit, "give the people what they want"—so the only
policy option is to unleash the market. Government policies that interfere with the market substitute the prerogatives of a bureaucrat, no
matter how well informed or intended, with the will of the people as
expressed in the market. Government actions therefore are antidemocratic and should be kept to a minimum, largely to protect private
property rights. If there is a problem with the media, it is not due to
the system or the policies that put the system in place but to "the people" who demand the content that the commercial media firms obedi-

ently provide. This may well be the most important myth of all, partly because it contains an element of truth. At a certain level it seems like it *must* be true; after all, why wouldn't profit-seeking firms try to satisfy the market? But upon close inspection, the argument has a number of flaws. I address it indirectly throughout the book and review the weaknesses of this hypothesis directly in chapters 4 and 5. Not only does the market not necessarily give us what we want, but it also gives us plenty of what we do *not* want. In particular, the commercial media system has generated a hyper-commercial carpet bombing of our culture that is decidedly unwelcome by much of the population.

The seventh myth is that technologies determine the nature of media. This is a long-standing position and it, too, contains a small element of truth; the nature of media technologies does indeed have distinct effects upon the nature of the media system and its content. This myth, which I address in chapters 6 and 7, has become much more prevalent with the rise of the Internet and digital communication technologies. The Internet, we are told, will set us free. All we have to do is let the technology work its magic. Long-standing and lucrative commercial media industries, such as network commercial television and the music recording industry, appear to be in the process of a radical transformation, if not an elimination, by these new technologies. Indeed, to a casual observer, these technologies are so extraordinary as to render public policies unimportant. But nothing of the kind is true. These satellite and the Internet technologies themselves are the direct result of policies and subsidies. How they are going to be developed is not predetermined. It has everything to do with explicit policies, and commercial pressures wrought by those policies. Indeed, powerful commercial interests use this myth to prevent the public from pursuing alternative policies.

Finally, there is the myth that no alternative to the status quo will improve matters. No matter how many flaws are present, the status quo offers the best of all possible media worlds. In shorthand, the options are usually presented as one of corporate control versus one of government control. Jefferson or Stalin. This framing is dubious; societies can and do have mixed systems all the time. Even a "market" system is based on layers of explicit government policies and laws that make it possible. The point of this claim is patently ideological—to retard the growing awareness among citizens that they can create a media system superior to the one that currently serves the needs of a handful of media corporations. In fact, as I discuss in chapter 6, there are rich traditions in media policy making from which citizens may draw guidance.

The logic of my argument is that a democratic media system—or a democratic solution to the problem of the media, as I put it—would necessitate a large, well-funded, structurally pluralistic, and diverse nonprofit and noncommercial media sector, as well as a more competitive and decentralized commercial sector. Where economics preclude competitive commercial markets, there must be transparent regulation in the public interest. The reforms I envision should be content neutral and viewpoint neutral. This does not mean they would generate bland content, but rather that the reforms would not favor a specific viewpoint over others. We need to think creatively, not be imprisoned by the myth that there can be no alternative to the status quo but the gulag. The exact contours of such a media system must be determined by informed and widespread public debate. Without that, media reform and a democratic media system are unthinkable.

Unless all eight of these myths are subjected to critical analysis, the prospects for energizing popular participation in media policy making are remote. That most of these myths are accepted as revealed truth in mainstream political culture helps explain why so many groups that have a stake in media policy debates and should be active in them—for example, environmentalists, civil rights activists, labor unions, working journalists—have generally not engaged in the fight.

In this book I highlight the core problems of the U.S. media system—inadequate journalism and hyper-commercialism—and I chronicle how they are linked to the commercial structures of the media and how these structures are directly and indirectly linked to explicit government policies. These policies have been made in the public's name but without the public's informed consent. That is the root of the media crisis in the United States today. Over the past two decades, the turn in media policy making toward neoliberalism, the political philosophy that dogmatically equates generating profits with generating maximum human happiness, has only exacerbated the crisis. All of this suggests that we are in very dark times, with little sign of hope, and that this will be yet another book chronicling how screwed up the media system is, leaving depressed readers looking for the nearest window to jump out of.

But wait. There may be light on the horizon. No longer is concern with the problem of the media an academic one or one limited to the political margins. In 2003 media politics entered the heart of the political culture as millions of Americans stunned the political establishment by joining and organizing protests against concentrated media ownership. In the concluding chapter I assess what may prove to be a renaissance of informed public participation in media policy making. We may be entering an era of profound public debate over the very nature of our media system. If this is the case, it will lead to new solutions to the problem of the media, with a clear change in the nature of the immediate media content people experience in their lives. In this sense, the burgeoning movement to reform media is a necessary, even indispensable, aspect of larger social movements to democratize our politics and society.

I write this book as a scholar who has spent two decades studying these issues, and it reflects arguments and analyses I have developed in discussion and debates with other scholars, activists, journalists, and the public at large. They are fire-tested. But nearly all the research in the book is of recent vintage. I also write this book as an active citizen. When one argues that the corporate media system is deeply flawed and a barrier to a decent and humane society and that the solution to the problem of the media is increased public participation, it is not enough to write books. There is an obligation to write popular articles, to give public lectures, to organize. This book is driven by that political project. Indeed, in 2002, along with Josh Silver and my dear friend John Nichols, I formed a group, Free Press, specifically to advance the cause of increasing popular participation in media policy making.

So the reader has reason to ask: Is this a work of scholarship or is it a partisan political pamphlet? The English historian A. J. P. Taylor once argued that the principal difference between the methodologies of the lawyer and those of the historian was that "the lawyer aims to make a case; the historian wishes to understand a situation." According to Taylor, the evidence amassed by the lawyer is "loaded" in ways that will maximize the chances of conviction or acquittal: "Anyone who relies on [this kind of evidence] finds it almost impossible to escape from the load with which they are charged." A historian, however, should allow a "detached and scholarly" examination of the evidence to direct a conclusion rather than take a stand and then, retrospectively, seek documents to support a case.

So, to use Taylor's formulation, is this the work of a historian or a lawyer?

It is the work of a historian, a scholar. The value of these arguments, if they have value, is that I have applied evidence to them, and I have weighed evidence that undermines my arguments, and I have changed and improved my arguments if the evidence pushed me in that direction. Otherwise my work would have little credibility. That said, when one ventures into the realm of contemporary media criticism and when one criticizes the corporate status quo, one goes up against a lot of "lawyers," both literal and figurative. Industry public relations offices churn out piles of surveys, studies, and documents that invariably point to one conclusion: this is the best possible media system in the best of all possible worlds. This material typically ignores or distorts evidence that undermines this euphoric vision. It is understandable for commercial interests to present such a perspective; it is unacceptable conduct for a scholar or a public servant. As I demonstrate in chapter 7, FCC chairman Michael Powell, who is a lawyer, has also distinguished himself as a lawyer in Taylor's sense of the term. In my view, he is also one of the most dishonorable public officials of our times.

I think there also is an important case to be made that scholarship that grows out of an engagement with real and immediate political struggles, rather than handcuffed by political bias and opportunism, can be the laboratory for breakthroughs in social theory and analysis.

One look at economics, a field in which many great theorists from Smith and Ricardo to Marx and Keynes generated their work by direct engagement with the politics of the day, makes that clear. This book is hardly a work of great theory or some sort of paradigm-busting intellectual breakthrough, but it grows out of a direct engagement with core political questions of our times. In fact, in U.S. media studies the removal of academics from the hurly-burly real world of media policy debates along with the ahistorical nature of much of this work arguably have contributed to the scholarship being unread and irrelevant; to its being . . . well . . . academic.

This book was written over the course of 2003, precisely as the battle over U.S. media ownership laws was in full swing. As I pulled the book together in the autumn, I drew upon a small coterie of fellow scholars and close friends for criticism and suggestions. Together we form a school of critical work in media studies, and I hope our ranks will grow because there is much work to be done. I drew from the trailblazing and brilliant historical work of Ben Scott and Inger Stole in chapters 2 and 4, respectively. Ben and Inger each gave a close reading to the entire manuscript and provided me with priceless comments. Inger's comments helped me reorganize the book, to make it more coherent than it would have been otherwise. Dan Schiller, my colleague at the University of Illinois at Urbana-Champaign, graciously read and commented upon several chapters. Dan's pioneering historical research on policy struggles surrounding U.S. telecommunications was foundational for me as I developed the model in chapter 1. My co-editor at *Monthly Review*, John Bellamy "Duke" Foster, worked with me on drafts of parts of chapters 3 and 4 and inspired the broader vision of the book with a loving and meticulous read. C. Edwin Baker, for my money the best legal scholar on free press issues in the nation, commented upon chapter 6. Sut Jhally, in whose path I follow as I do my work, graciously read and commented on chapter 4 under absurdly short notice—as in, "Hey, can you read this and give me comments by tomorrow, because it is due at the publisher in forty-eight hours?" Lawrence Lessig did the same with the discussion of copyright in chapter 6. Victor Pickard helped me tighten up several citations.

I also received invaluable help from several nonacademics. Jeff Cohen, the journalist and founder of Fairness & Accuracy In Reporting (FAIR), gave detailed comments on the entire book, line by line; I have never worked with a better editor or a smarter media critic. If this book is understandable, Jeff gets the lion's share of the credit. Janine Jackson, the program director at FAIR, read most of the book and helped me clarify some key points. Gene Kimmelman of the Consumers Union read chapter 7 and made several excellent suggestions. Jeff Chester provided some thoughts concerning my discussion of broadband policy issues in chapter 6. All these comrades get credit for the good in what follows; none of them gets blame for the flaws.

Most important, I leaned heavily on the journalist John Nichols, with whom I wrote two short books on this subject in 2000 and 2002 and several articles for *The Nation* over the course of 2002 and 2003. John's political knowledge and instincts are unmatched, and I have learned more from him about politics than I could have learned in a lifetime of graduate seminars.

During 2003, our organization Free Press grew from one paid staffer working in borrowed space in the corner of someone else's office to some ten activists working on a range of media reform issues and campaigns. In November 2003, Free Press sponsored the first-ever National Conference on Media Reform, held in Madison, Wisconsin, and drawing some two thousand people. The Free Press website these activists have assembled has become a comprehensive entrée to the U.S. media reform movement (www.mediareform.net). The work ethic, principles, and commitment of these young activists inspired and motivated me as I put the finishing touches on this book. To see tangible organizing actually work, to see people from a variety of backgrounds come together, to see social change leading to increased justice and human happiness is the most extraordinary feeling imaginable. It makes one feel *alive*. Another world is not only possible; it is there for the taking.

1

POLITICAL PROBLEM, POLITICAL SOLUTIONS

Mention "the problem of the media" and most people think of poor or inadequate media content that negatively affects our culture, politics, and society. If the media were doing a commendable job, there would be no problem. But there is another meaning for the word *problem*; its first definition in *Webster's Dictionary* is "a question raised for inquiry, consideration, or solution." Media systems of one sort or another are going to exist, and they do not fall from the sky. The policies, structures, subsidies, and institutions that are created to control, direct, and regulate the media will be responsible for the logic and nature of the media system. Whether their content is good, bad, or a combination, the media therefore present a political problem for any society, and an unavoidable one at that. In other words, the first problem with the media deals with its content; the second and larger problem deals with the structure that generates that content. Understood this way, the manner in which a society decides how to structure the media system, how it elects to solve the problem of the media in the second sense, becomes of paramount importance. Such policy debates will often determine the contours and values of the media system that then produces the media content that is visible to all. I address "the problem of the media" in all these dimensions in this book.

The problem of the media exists in all societies, regardless of their structure, but the range of available solutions for each society is influenced by its political and economic structures, cultural traditions, and communication technologies, among other things. In dictatorships and authoritarian regimes, those in power generate a media system that supports their domination and minimizes the possibility of effective opposition. The direct link between control over the media

and control over the society is self-evident. But in democratic societies, the same tension exists between those who hold power and
those who do not, only the battle assumes different forms. Media are
at the center of struggles for power and control in any society, and
they are arguably even more vital players in democratic nations.

The political nature of the problem of the media in democratic
societies is well-known; virtually all theories of self-government are
premised on having an informed citizenry, and the creation of such
an informed citizenry is the media's province. The measure of a
media system in political terms is not whether it creates a viable
democratic society—that would be too much of a burden to place
upon it. Instead, the measure is whether the media system, on balance and in the context of the broader social and economic situation, challenges antidemocratic pressures and tendencies or
reinforces them. Is the media system a democratic force? Much less
understood is the importance of the media to economics; this relationship with economics goes a long way toward shaping the media's
political role and their relationship with the dominant political and
economic forces in society. In the United States the starting point for
grasping the problem of the media is seeing where the media system
fits in the broader capitalist economic system. The crucial tension
lies between the role of the media as profit-maximizing commercial
organizations and the need for the media to provide the basis for
informed self-government. It is this tension that fuels much of the
social concern around media and media policy making.

In this chapter I will present a framework for understanding the
problem of the media in the second, broader definition of the word
problem. Only then can we make sense of problems with content. I will
debunk the myths that the U.S. media are inherently the province of
the "free market" and that the modern commercial media system is
the result of informed debate. In doing so, I will look at the origins of
the U.S. press system in the late eighteenth and early nineteenth centuries and the role media policies made in crafting it. I will also
explore the public debate surrounding radio broadcasting in the
1930s and that battle's consequences that shape our media policy

making to this day. This analysis leads directly to an overview of the
corrupt and decrepit state of media policy making as it has evolved
over the twentieth century. The United States has not satisfactorily
addressed the problem of the media in recent generations. As a result,
the media system has been set up to serve the interests of those who
make the policies behind closed doors—large profit-driven media corporations—while the broad and vital interests of the population have
been largely neglected. This system has contributed to a political crisis of the highest magnitude and unless it is confronted directly will
severely limit our ability to make progress on any of the other major
social and political problems that face the nation. On balance, the
media system has become—ironically, in view of the freedom of the
press clause in the First Amendment—a significantly antidemocratic
force. It is a political problem that requires a political solution.

MEDIA, MARKETS, AND POLICIES

The operating assumption in most discussions of the U.S. media system is that media are a natural province of the market. From this perspective, when governments regulate these markets, they represent
an outside intervening force. To the pro-corporate political right this
is dogma. As one *Wall Street Journal* columnist put it, "Man's natural
instinct is to choose free enterprise and free markets," so government
regulation certainly violates nature and, quite possibly, the intent of
God.[1] But even among liberals the same position holds, although the
prospect of government regulation can be more readily justified.[2] By
this logic, much of media policy making or regulation, to the extent
it exists, is merely to protect property rights in the free market systems that have naturally and inexorably emerged.

This framework is ideologically loaded. Looking at the situation
from the classical liberal and democratic assumption that society
selects the manner in which it wishes to regulate social behavior, the
procedure by which a society chooses from a range of options may be
democratic, autocratic, plutocratic, or some combination, but it is a
decision that a society makes. Thus, enacting laws, setting regulations, and using markets ultimately become policy decisions. Private

property and markets are employed to the extent that they are seen as superior regulatory mechanisms to other alternatives. In contemporary society, we can regulate social behavior through four general paths: markets, laws, architecture, and cultural norms.[3] Each has its strengths and weaknesses, and none can lay claim to being the natural or "default" position. It is from this palette that people create the world in which they live. The more democratic a society, the more likely the decisions about how best to regulate social life will be the result of widespread informed debate. The less democratic a society, the more likely those decisions will be made by powerful self-interested parties with a minimum of popular participation.

This dispute, then, is not about whether the market is the *natural* manner to organize media—and all of social life for that matter. It is about whether the market is the *superior* means, or *a* superior means among others, to regulate media. Just as capitalism is not the "natural" social system for humanity, so commercial media are not Nature's creation either. Our social system and our media system both require aggressive and explicit government activity to exist. Media policy, then, is a far broader and more significant historical phenomenon than that found in the conventional wisdom, which depicts it as something inherently tedious drawn up by bespectacled policy wonks and government bureaucrats addressing obscure technical issues. To the contrary, the U.S. media system—even its most "free market" sectors—is the direct result of explicit government policies and in fact would not exist without those policies. Most dominant media firms exist because of government-granted and government-enforced monopoly broadcasting licenses, telecommunication franchises, and rights to content (a.k.a. copyright). Competitive markets in the classic sense are rare; they were established or strongly shaped by the government.

So the real struggle is over whose interests the regulation will represent. And this is where media policy making, rather than being dull and tedious, oozes with the excitement of politics at its most enthralling. In this context, the term *deregulation* becomes somewhat misleading; it means, more often than not, government regulation that advances the interests of the dominant corporate players. To the dominant firms, when government allocates to them lucrative monopoly licenses or regulates on their behalf, it is not considered regulation. But to society, it is a serious form of control, and one that results from explicit media policies made in the public's name.

For a concrete example of the misuse of the term *deregulation* in media, consider radio broadcasting. In 1996 the Telecommunications Act eliminated the cap on the number of radio stations a single company could own nationally. It had been 40 prior to that, and for decades it had been much lower than that. Radio, it was said, was now "deregulated." The vast majority of U.S. radio stations were sold after 1996 and a few massive firms came to dominate the industry. Clear Channel alone soon owned more than 1,200 stations. So does it make sense, as is regularly proclaimed, to depict radio broadcasting as deregulated— or is it simply regulated differently for different ends serving different interests? For a test of the deregulation hypothesis, one need only go out and commence broadcasting a signal on an AM or FM frequency used by an existing broadcaster. Immediate arrest and possible incarceration would result. That is serious regulation. The government is still granting monopoly licenses to radio and TV channels and still enforcing those monopoly licenses. It is not open season for anyone to begin using the airwaves. The only difference the Telecommunications Act made is that today the largest corporations can possess more of these monopoly licenses than they could before. (It is worth noting that these firms do not pay the government a single penny for the right to have monopoly access to these valuable and scarce channels of the publicly owned spectrum.) There is every bit as much regulation by the government as before, only now it is more explicitly directed to serve large corporate interests.

Although there is no mandatory connection between having a profit-driven economy and having a profit-driven media system, it is understandable why one would make that assumption. In the past hundred years, media have become an important location for profit making. This process has been ongoing in the United States but the decisive era came in the early twentieth century when the modern capitalist film, music, advertising, and broadcasting industries emerged. This growth of the commercial media sector was part and parcel of the rise of modern corporate-based capitalism in the United States. The integration of media into the commanding heights of U.S. capitalism has only increased in recent decades. In terms of sales, the eight or nine largest media firms now rank among the two or three hundred largest corporations in the world. Less than thirty years ago, only two media companies were among the three hundred largest firms in the United States, not to mention worldwide.[4] In terms of market value, eleven of the world's two hundred largest corporations are media firms, another three do significant media business, and many more on the list are in the related software, Internet, and telecommunications industries.[5] Today the United States has a media system dominated by a small number of very large vertically integrated corporations.

Looking at lists of wealthiest Americans from the nineteenth century to the present time provides some sense of the change. It was well into the second half of the twentieth century before more than one or two media magnates rated among the thirty richest Americans or families. By 1992—before the media explosion of the late 1990s—nine of the largest thirty fortunes were made in media, and a couple others on the list had closely related holdings, such as software.[6] Since the early 1990s and through 2001, commercial media have become one of the three fastest-growing industries in the United States. Studies suggest that media may not remain among the top three but will still grow well above the national average deep into the first decade of the twenty-first century.[7] Put another way, media spending per household grew at twice the rate of inflation throughout the 1990s.[8] And in 2002, *Forbes* magazine calculated that over *one-third* of the fifty wealthiest Americans generated the preponderance of their fortunes through media and related industries.[9]

Our media, then, far from being on the sidelines of the capitalist system, are among its greatest beneficiaries. Research links media corporations with the largest investment banks and demonstrates how often media corporation board members sit on other Fortune 500 companies' boards.[10] The interconnection of media and capitalism grows that much stronger when one considers the role of advertising, which provides around one-third of all media revenues. The very largest corporations generate the preponderance of advertising.[11] Investment in media and expenditures on media appear to be central to macroeconomic growth in the overall economy.[12]

These connections suggest considerable tension if the media are also supposed to grease the wheels of democratic self-governance. A central issue in democratic theory has been how to reconcile social and economic inequality with political equality. For most of the nation's founders this was a vexing issue, and, perhaps because they were the beneficiaries of the existing unequal distribution of resources, many favored restricting the franchise to white male property owners to prevent social turmoil. Benjamin Franklin and Thomas Paine were the most radical and argued that democracy must trump inequality. Franklin supported a clause in the Pennsylvania constitution warning that "an enormous Proportion of Property vested in a few Individuals is dangerous to the Rights, and destructive of the Common Happiness, of Mankind; and therefore every free State hath a Right by its Laws to discourage the Possession of such Property."[13] Battles to extend suffrage were central to U.S. politics until well into the twentieth century. Invariably these were fights between the haves and the have-nots.[14] The media system, in democratic theory, was charged with providing information equally so that even poor citizens would have the capacity to be effective citizens, despite their unequal access to resources. As I will discuss shortly, policies put in place in the early republic made it far more likely that the press would not be dominated by the wealthy and powerful but would be accessible and of value to broad segments of the population.

The emergence of modern corporate capitalism alters the initial equation. For a variety of reasons, universal adult suffrage arises alongside it in the United States. But at the same time, without discounting the ways in which capitalism can promote self-government, it also by its very nature tends to generate social and economic inequality. To the extent that the contemporary media system answers to investors first and foremost, it may become a weaker democratic force. Commercial media also may be useful to capitalism in generating a political culture that is more enthusiastic about capitalism and suspicious of capitalism's critics. In short, a cursory analysis of the U.S. media industries suggests troubling implications for the classic notion of a free press—and therefore for democracy—in which everyone has a realistic opportunity to communicate with others. We would expect, instead, a media system that would serve the interests of the wealthy and denigrate the interests of those at the bottom of the social pecking order.

Hence, even if one accepts that the U.S. economy functions more effectively with a highly commercialized media system, it does not mean that democracy is best served by such a system. In liberal and democratic theory, democracy must be in the driver's seat, and the type of media system and economy that develop can be justified only to the extent that they best meet the needs of the people, not vice versa. Ultimately, one must hold to the conviction that the media system that best serves democratic values will contribute to generating an economic system most responsive to the genuine needs of the population. At the same time, if one accepts that it is proper for a society's economy to be capitalistic, commercial control of media might sound more acceptable, especially if there is little awareness of policy alternatives. In a capitalist society, the requirements of political democracy do not compete on an equal basis with the exigencies of the market. Rather, there is a bias toward the market.

But this bias in policy debates toward the existing economic structure does not mandate the turn to market control over media any more than it mandates market control over education systems, electoral systems, or religion. Even more important for our purposes, different shades of market-regulated media systems exist based upon different choices in policies. The very nature of markets is influenced, if not explicitly determined, by government policies. Capitalist economies have coexisted with media systems that have had significant noncommercial and nonprofit elements over the years. In many nations they have cohabited—if not exactly had a successful marriage—through a good portion of the twentieth century. Even in the context of contemporary capitalism, significant changes in the media system would not require a radical change in the economy's structure. While it may be self-evident that a socialist or a critic of capitalism would have severe reservations about media policies that generate a profit-driven media system, one can be a proponent of capitalism and deplore rabidly "pro-capitalist" media policies. The British actor John Cleese observes that "capitalism is the best system" only if its profit-obsessed logic is constrained. Cleese points to contemporary media as a prime example of "inferior" damn-the-torpedoes capitalism: "I would rather live in Czechoslovakia under Dubcek than work for a newspaper run by Rupert Murdoch."[15]

We need to bury the notions that media are "naturally" commercial and that government has been and is an innocent bystander (or nonproductive intruder) in the process of creating media systems. Moreover, if media are necessary institutions for a healthy democracy and if the nature and logic of the media system result from explicit government policies, then debates over the fundamental nature of media policies will determine the caliber of the media system. Therefore, I am as concerned with the caliber and nature of the public debates surrounding media policies as I am with the policies themselves.

In particular, I will devote most of the attention in this chapter to what are termed *critical junctures*, those historical moments when the policy-making options are relatively broad and the policies put in place will set the media system on a track that will be difficult to reroute for decades, even generations.[16] Critical junctures are another way to say that society holds a "constitutional convention" of sorts to deal with the problem of the media. At these points there tends to be much greater public criticism of media systems and policies and much more organized public participation than during less tumultuous periods. Critical junctures can come about when important new media technologies emerge, when the existing media system enters a crisis, or when the political climate changes sufficiently to call accepted policies into question or to demand new ones. When two or all three factors kick in, there is a high probability of a critical juncture; at these historical moments, opportunities to recast the media that would be nearly impossible under normal circumstances can materialize.

U.S. MEDIA SYSTEM NOT "NATURALLY" PROFIT DRIVEN

It is one thing to assert that the U.S. media system is not naturally the province of large profit-driven corporations; it is another thing to demonstrate it. History indicates that the idea that this nation was founded on what is erroneously called a "libertarian" theory of the press—that government should let business run media to maximize profit—does not hold up under scrutiny. Media policy making has always been of paramount importance in the United States. The Constitution and the Bill of Rights contain numerous passages that still directly and indirectly create and shape our media system, either on their own or through the legislation, regulations, and court decisions that were later made on their basis. Media-related concerns permeate the political discourse of the revolutionary and constitutional era, and many politicians of those times—most notably, Madison and Jefferson—understood the vital importance of astute media policies for laying the foundation for a viable republic. Three constitutional provisions in particular provide blueprints for the media system's construction.

First, Article 1, Section 8 of the Constitution authorizes Congress to establish copyright "to promote the Progress of Science and the useful Arts, by securing for limited Times to Authors and Inventors the exclusive Right to Distribute Writings and Discoveries."[17] Copyright addresses the "public good" nature of media property that distinguishes it from all other industries. When one consumes a public good, it does not diminish the ability of others to consume it as well. If I read a book, someone else can read the same book, or a copy of it and we can both enjoy it. Such is not the same for an automobile or a hamburger. In this context, the problem was that if anyone could publish a book without the author's permission, the price would be low and the public would benefit, but the author would not receive much or any compensation, so there would be no incentive to write books. Copyright was an explicit government intervention—an artificial government-created and government-enforced anti–free market mechanism—to give authors (or publishers) a legal monopoly over their books for a "limited" time period to ensure the incentive to produce books. In its best light, copyright was a policy implemented not just to throw a bone to authors but rather to benefit society by encouraging cultural production. In fact, commercial publishers were eager to see copyright put in place and provided a strong force behind its adoption. It is difficult to imagine how book publishing and many subsequent media industries could have existed as commercial institutions without copyright protection.[18]

Second, whereas copyright was a somewhat obscure topic in the Constitution until recently, the same cannot be said for what is generally understood as the main media policy plank in the Constitution's Bill of Rights, the First Amendment: "Congress shall make no law respecting an establishment of religion, or prohibiting the free exercise thereof; or abridging the freedom of speech, or of the press; or the right of the people peaceably to assemble, and to petition the government for a redress of grievances." In the context of the late eighteenth century, this was a revolutionary policy statement concerning liberal freedoms and democratic society; such freedoms were barely given even rhetorical support anywhere in the world at the time. Indeed, it remains a revolutionary statement in the twenty-first century. Numerous great thinkers have been so taken by the powerful ideas embedded in the First Amendment that they have proclaimed themselves First Amendment "absolutists." The question then becomes what is it, exactly, that the First Amendment absolutely protects? This is arguably most difficult when attempting to decipher the meaning of the free press clause, one of the five core freedoms listed in the First Amendment.

A common contemporary "absolutist" notion of the free press argues that the Founders meant that the government should never be involved with media, commercial or otherwise. A core problem that plagues much contemporary thinking about the free press clause is that the terms *free speech* and *free press* are used interchangeably.[19] And in this union of free speech with free press, the former gets almost all the attention, while the conclusions are often applied without qualification to the latter. In a representative example, a classic text on the First Amendment collapses its discussion of freedom of the press into its chapter on freedom of speech and never even mentions the press.[20] So if one holds that the government should not stop a person from speaking on a street corner, then, ipso facto, the government should not stop commercial media from doing whatever they wish to do. What these positions tend to neglect is that while free speech and free press are similar or even interchangeable on some matters, they are quite distinct on others. Unique problems accompany constitutional protection of a free press, its political economy if you will, and these tend to be shunted aside when the discussion is framed solely in terms of free speech. Both are separate concerns, otherwise *there would have been no need for both to be included in the First Amendment.*

Specifically, engaging in the free press (using the media) is typically an industrial enterprise requiring considerable resources. Unlike speech, it has not been open to everyone. Also unlike speech, how the press system is structured will go a long way toward determining what ideas get heard and what ideas get silenced, even before a government commissar brings down the heavy hand of censorship. The legal scholar Michael Kent Curtis calls these institutional factors "the second constitution" in view of their centrality for a free press.[21] It is difficult to extrapolate from the Constitution a sense of what "free press" means because the press system of the 1790s was so radically different from ours. But it is clear that the Founders understood the importance of industrial structure and subsidy to the formation of a viable free press. This was not an area to be left to the whims of investors or the market or, more broadly, to an unregulated, nongovernmental sector.

To be blunt, the press in the early republic was not seen as an engine of capital accumulation, as merely one of many areas in which investors might put their capital to generate maximum returns in the marketplace. The press was highly partisan and integrally linked to the political process. Government printing contracts were for generations used by federal and state governments explicitly to subsidize the dominant partisan newspapers in Washington, D.C., and across the nation. It was not until the establishment of the U.S. Government Printing Office in 1860 that the practice ended. Likewise, the U.S. State Department was authorized by Congress to issue printing contracts to as many as three newspapers in every state and territory, for the purpose of publishing the federal laws.[22] This program stopped only in the 1870s.

Even this capsule history does not do justice to the way in which the press system was consciously subsidized as a fourth estate in the first several generations of the republic. In many respects "newspaper politics" were the heart and soul of all politics in the first few generations of U.S. history.[23] By the 1790s, and for decades thereafter, editors were seen as politicians and were treated accordingly. The popular political movements of the period depended upon printing contracts to subsidize their presses. When Jefferson assumed office in 1801, he aggressively coordinated both federal and state printing contracts to subsidize a press to counteract the Federalists. He arranged for printing subsidies for Samuel Harrison Smith to establish the *National Intelligencer*, which would become the *New York Times* and *Washington Post* of its day, though expressly committed to support Jeffersonian politics. Entering the White House in 1829, Andrew Jackson "elevated patronage of the press to a new level." He devoted $25,000 per year to the editor of his Washington-based newspaper and assigned fifty-nine editors to "plush political appointments."[24]

This episode in U.S. press history is important for two reasons. First, the freedom of the press clause appears more directly concerned with a functioning democracy. If the party in power could outlaw the opposition press, it would effectively terminate its opposition. This was not an abstract concern. During the Adams administration, the Federalists used the Alien and Sedition Acts to muzzle the Jeffersonian press. Second, ordinary Americans, at least those of the literate white male variety, were unusually interested in politics compared to other eras. Perhaps the nature of the press system had something to do with that. Its success hinged on a variety of well-subsidized viewpoints, not just those of the party in power, and new political groups had a chance to enter the fray. The historian of the *National Intelligencer* concluded that the subsidized system produced a caliber of journalism "that in many ways has not since been equaled on an intellectual level."[25]

Recent research has again and again repudiated the notion that the intent of the free press clause in the First Amendment was to empower individuals in the marketplace to do as they pleased, regardless of the implications for society as a whole. Such a notion violated the tenor of the times *in toto*. "A mountain of historical research," the leading historian of the free press tradition in Colonial and Revolutionary America observes, "finds in early American political discourse a stress on civic virtue and public, rather than private, good." All who argued for press liberty "defended the right to press liberty not for individual expression in our current, increasingly self-indulgent sense but rather so that the community might hear and judge the merit of others' views."[26] Akhil Reed Amar suggests that the First Amendment, especially the free press clause, was motivated by popular opposition to the preponderantly antidemocratic nature of the federal government, as devised in the Constitution.[27]

The writings of Jefferson and Madison attest to the distinct social function of the free press.[28] Jefferson, in particular, saw freedom of the press as the foundation of popular democracy and as protection against elite rule. "If once they [the people] become inattentive to the public affairs," he wrote his friend Edward Carrington, "you and I, and Congress and Assemblies, Judges and Governors, shall all become wolves." Ironically, Jefferson's letter to Carrington is sometimes taken as arguing that the government should let private interests rule the press and let the chips fall where they may. Here is the most cited passage, but I include the follow-up sentence, which is sometimes omitted. "The basis of our governments being the opinion of people," Jefferson wrote, "the very first object should be to keep that right; and were it left to me to decide whether we should have a government without newspapers, or newspapers without government, I should not hesitate a moment to prefer the latter. *But I should mean that every man should receive those papers, and be capable of reading them.*" The implication of this final sentence is that it is not enough to negatively protect the press system. Active promotion is necessary to ensure universal distribution of public information to competent citizens. In other words, the public's right to hear a variety of voices and properly digest their messages is the central platform of a democracy.[29] On another occasion, Jefferson remarked, "An enlightened citizenry is indispensable for the proper functioning of a republic."[30] As Madison famously put it, "A popular Government without popular information or the means of acquiring it, is but a Prologue to a Farce or a Tragedy or perhaps both." And such a free press, they argued, came as the result of explicit government policies and subsidies that would create it; to think otherwise was nonsensical.

More broadly, as Richard John, the leading historian of government communication policy in the eighteenth and nineteenth centuries has emphasized, only in the 1840s did discussion of "private enterprise" became widespread in U.S. political discourse. The notions of entrepreneurs and free markets were almost entirely absent in the early republic, as was the idea that the press was or should be a commercial activity set up solely to meet the needs of press owners. It was an unthinkable idea. As John concludes, "A commitment to energetic government in service of the public good has long been recognized as one of the principal legacies of the American Revolution."[31]

My point is not to argue about the "original intent" of the First Amendment and urge the Supreme Court to radically revise its interpretation of the free press clause on that basis. My point is to discredit the position that freedom of the press means strictly the right of private individuals to do as they please in the realm of media—regardless of the social implications—to suit their own (invariably) commercial interests. That notion has almost nothing to do with the Founders' intent or with our press system's evolution. The turn to a more market-based notion of a "free press" came gradually with the emergence of powerful private, profit-driven media. Nothing in the First Amendment mandated this interpretation. Had the United States evolved in a different manner, we would have no doubt had a different interpretation of the First Amendment. Yet while freedom of the press is a malleable policy, it is not Silly Putty. Even today the First Amendment is not widely interpreted in the purely commercial terms that corporate media and its advocates proclaim. In the Supreme Court's seminal 1927 *Whitney v. California* case, Justice Louis Brandeis concluded: "Those who won our independence believed that the final end of the State was to make men free to develop their faculties; ...that the greatest menace to freedom is an inert people; that public discussion is a political duty; and that this should be a fundamental principle of American government."[32] Jefferson and Madison live, even if it appears at times that they are on life support.

The commercial interpretation of a free press has been in ascendance for much of the past quarter century, if not longer. Proponents assert that this right is absolute, because the First Amendment says "no law." Therefore capitalists can do as they please in the realm of media and they need answer only to their bottom lines; the market will prove to be a superior regulator of the press. If the journalism is atrocious and the culture hyper-commercialized, if the public is uninformed or misinformed, if self-governance is a sham, the fault is not the press system but the moronic citizens who demand such fare and reward those who provide it. The government can't do a damned thing about it except indirectly, through improving education so that the next generation will not be composed of idiots. (Yet advocates of this commercial version of the First Amendment tend to correlate highly with those who are opposed to expanding and enhancing education, so it is largely a rhetorical point.) From this perspective, the connection between a free press and democracy, which inspired this nation's founders, is dead.

This commercial interpretation of the free press clause does not go unchallenged. A much more progressive interpretation of the First Amendment has held its ground, inspired by the work of people such as Alexander Meiklejohn and Supreme Court Justice Hugo Black. Black was a legendary First Amendment "absolutist," but he was no commercialist when it came to a free press. Government censorship was not the only threat to a free press, and it was not the only legitimate public concern. In his famous opinion in the 1945 *Associated Press v. U.S.* case, Black defended the government's right to regulate media ownership: "The First Amendment, far from providing an argument against application of the Sherman Act, here provides powerful reasons to the contrary. That Amendment rests on the assumption that the widest possible dissemination of information from diverse and antagonistic sources is essential to the welfare of the public, that a free press is a condition of a free society.... Freedom to publish means freedom for all and not for some."[33] According to the progressive perspective, then, the right to a free press is a social right to a diverse and effective press system enjoyed by all Americans, not just media corporations or wealthy owners of commercial media. The First Amendment thus not only permits but indeed *requires* positive government activities to promote a free press, much as it has done with postal and printing subsidies.[34] As constitutional law professor Burt Neuborne puts it, otherwise you are left with a "First Amendment for the rich."[35] Prior restraint by the government should be opposed—and proponents of this perspective take a backseat to no one in their opposition to government censorship—but it is not to be seen as the sole government activity concerning the press.

Two distinct interpretations of the First Amendment for media have emerged over the course of the twentieth century. In the realm of broadcasting, the progressive interpretation holds; in 1969 the Supreme Court ruled in *Red Lion Broadcasting Co. v. FCC* that the First Amendment is a social right of the entire population to have a radio and television system that best serves its democratically determined needs. The First Amendment privileges of the commercial broadcasters are secondary and they must meet publicly determined public interest standards to keep their monopoly broadcasting licenses. With regard to print and most other media, the commercialist position is increasingly influential and treats the First Amendment as a license for the media to do as they please. A concerted campaign by progressives in the Meiklejohnian tradition to extend the social interpretation of the First Amendment from broadcasting to newspapers in the 1970s failed in the 1974 case *Miami Herald v. Tornillo*. Since then, commercial broadcasters have been working the court system to see that they get accorded the same First Amendment privileges as other media. That would, in effect, privatize the broadcast spectrum, remove broadcasting from public control, and constitute a gift of tens, even hundreds, of billions of dollars in public property to a small number of large private firms. Seen that way, the First Amendment becomes a policy with significant economic as well as political implications.

SUBSIDIZING THE PRESS

The third pertinent section of the Constitution regarding media policy gave Congress the power "to establish Post Offices and Post Roads."
The resulting Post Office Act of 1792 was arguably one of the most
significant pieces of legislation in the nation's history; as Richard R.
John observes, the post office was "rapidly transformed into a dynamic institution that would exert a major influence on American commerce, politics, and political thought."[36] Theda Skocpol notes that
"the postal system was the biggest enterprise of any kind in the pre-
industrial United States."[37] As John puts it, "For the vast majority of
Americans, the postal system was the central government." It was the
largest single employer in the country.

What makes this crucial for our discussion, and what is striking
upon review, is that the post office was primarily a medium of mass
communication. In 1794 newspapers made up 70 percent of post
office traffic; by 1832 the figure had risen to well over 90 percent. The
crucial debate in the 1792 Congress was how much to charge newspapers to be sent through the mails. All parties agreed that Congress
should permit newspapers to be mailed at a price well below actual
cost—to be subsidized—to encourage their production and distribution. Postal subsidies of newspapers would become perhaps the
largest single expenditure of the federal government. In Congress, the
range of debate was between those who wished to charge newspapers
a nominal fee for postage and those who wanted to permit newspapers the use of the mails absolutely free of charge. The latter faction
was supported by Benjamin Franklin's grandson, the editor Benjamin
Bache, who argued that any postal charge would open the door to
commercial pressures that would be unacceptable because they
would "check if not entirely put a stop to the circulation of periodical
publications." James Madison led the fight in Congress for completely
free mailing privileges, calling even a token fee a "tax" on newspapers
that was "an insidious forerunner of something worse."[38]

Although those favoring free delivery did not prevail, pressure
from both printers and the citizenry made the only relevant issue for
Congress for subsequent generations whether to eliminate the postal

charge. It was seen as a public subsidy for democracy. As John C. Cal-
houn put it, "the mail and the press are the nerves of the body
politic."[39] Abolitionists and dissident political groups led the fight to
maintain and extend the postal subsidy of newspapers. In 1851, Congress granted free postal privileges to weekly newspapers within its
home county. Within a year 20 percent of newspapers being mailed
qualified for free postage.[40] A version of this policy continued into the
twentieth century, and postal rates on newspapers were never raised
during the nineteenth century.

By the middle of the nineteenth century the consequences of the
large postal subsidy—the fee was "trifling," even to Bache—had been
the "almost illimitable circulation of newspapers through the mails,"
as one journalist remarked in 1851. As John concludes, the 1792 act
"transformed the role of the newspaper press in American public
life."[41] In his *Democracy in America*, Alexis de Tocqueville wrote with
astonishment of the "incredibly large" number of periodicals in the
United States.[42] This had nothing to do with some notion of a laissez-
faire, commercially driven newspaper market—presumed by modern-
day absolutists as the sine qua non of the Founders' notion of a free
press. As Timothy Cook concludes, "Public policy from the outset of
the American Republic focused explicitly on getting the news to a
wide readership, and chose to support news outlets by taking on costs
of delivery and, through printers' exchanges, of production."[43] This
was enlightened democratic policy making, and it was successful. As
with the First Amendment, the United States was leading the world.

The post office regulatory model was challenged when the telegraph became a competitor of sorts in the 1840s and 1850s. The idea
that the postal service should be "privatized" was rejected categorical-
ly.[44] At first there was considerable public demand that telegraphy be
made a government monopoly like the mails, but those favoring market regulation won the day. It was a measure, to some extent, of the
increasing power of capital and notions of private enterprise in the
political culture. By the end of the Civil War, however, telegraphy had
gone from a competitive industry to a booming private monopoly
under the control of Western Union. The private monopoly control

over telegraphy was one of the most incendiary issues of the Gilded Age: between 1866 and 1900 some seventy bills were proposed to reform the industry, usually calling for some sort of nationalization.[45] This private control, as opposed to the systems in Europe in which the government operated the monopoly telegraph service, meant that Western Union could use its "natural monopoly" to favor more lucrative accounts from large business customers over smaller businesses and individuals. As such, economic historians regard the growth of Western Union as a major factor in the dominance of big business in American life.[46] For radicals, populists, socialists, and labor, nationalizing the telegraph was right up there with nationalizing the railroads as a core demand. Telegraphy faded in importance with the rise of radio and, especially, telephony in the early twentieth century. A similar public outcry greeted the private monopoly of telephony under the aegis of AT&T in the early twentieth century. After decades of political struggle, a compromise of sorts was reached: the telephone system was a private monopoly but one that was, unlike Western Union, theoretically held to strict government regulation.

The control and regulation of telecommunication systems like telegraphy and telephony are important and underrated components of media policy making. As with the post office, they have significantly affected the press system. Western Union was instrumental in revolutionizing journalism, the media system, and the broader political economy. It used its monopoly power to collaborate in the development of the Associated Press, a monopoly news service run in cooperative fashion by the largest newspaper publishers. This relationship was mostly unknown to the public. With exclusive access to the wires—Western Union refused to let potential competitors use its wires—AP became the only wire news service in the nation. So as not to offend any of its thousands of clients, it encouraged a journalism that was seemingly nonpartisan—hence it contributed heavily to the rise of journalistic "objectivity." Because newspapers without access to the AP were at a decided competitive disadvantage, it also discouraged competition in local markets. Likewise, the AP had extraordinary influence in the way it covered national politics because it served as the main voice for most major newspapers. Needless to say, it invariably presented a voice that took the side of business interests.[47]

Not surprisingly, the news coverage provided by AP and the major newspapers of the late nineteenth century strongly advocated keeping telegraphy a private and unregulated monopoly.[48] Western Union's interests were well taken care of by major U.S. newspapers. It was the first clear example of how concentrated press power could shape public debates over media and communication policy. It also highlights how much the press had moved from being a feisty fourth estate in service to democracy—or, less grandly, a political institution devoted to a variety of partisan causes—to a commercial institution dedicated to the rule of big business. Some members of Congress who opposed Western Union noted the monopoly's effect on newspaper concentration and content and went so far as to characterize the struggle for a publicly owned or regulated telegraph system as a battle to preserve a free press.[49] Dan Schiller's pioneering research reveals the broad-based and radical movement between the 1880s and the 1910s for reconstructing the corporate telecommunications systems; a core organizing principle was to break the "infernal bondage" imposed by Western Union and the AP.[50] One can only imagine how the telegraph might have influenced the media system and journalism differently if it had been a national monopoly like the post office and had people like James Madison been in Congress arguing for a well-subsidized diverse press. Along similar lines in the 1920s, AT&T's telephone network was instrumental in getting the NBC national radio network off the ground. The implication of having a single monopoly control telephony and national radio broadcasting was such that AT&T was required by the government to divest its broadcasting interests.

Although it does not appear in the U.S. Constitution, one other crucial policy was common in state constitutions, and prescribed by Jefferson and John Adams: public education. The Northwest Ordinance of 1787 provided the sentiment, even the wording, for many state constitutions concerning state-funded public education: "Being necessary to good government and the happiness of mankind, schools and the means of education shall forever be encouraged" by the state legislatures.[51] In spirit, one can see the strong link between public education and a free press as democratic institutions. Moreover, public schools formed an important market for books by creating literate citizens. Public libraries, also funded by state government, offered another avenue for individual education. The commercial publishing industries would have been a shadow of themselves—and much of it would not have existed—without these massive public subsidies.[52]

These subsidies point to another crucial manner in which governments shape and influence media systems: as purchasers and as advertisers. During the 1950s and 1960s, aggressive purchasing by the federal government of nonfiction books for its overseas libraries subsidized a veritable golden age of book publishing. Controversial and experimental work that would never have met market criteria otherwise was published. The sharp decline in library purchases of university press books in the past decade—due in part to monopoly control of academic journals that has driven their prices beyond the means of university libraries—threatens to eliminate the publication of significant scholarly work that was routinely published in the past.[53] Furthermore, since its inception the government has developed into a major purchaser of many forms of commercial media content, not just books. During World War II, for example, federal government purchases counted for some 90 percent of the Disney Corporation's sales.[54] The government has also become a major advertiser.

In the twentieth century, government media policies and subsidies provided the basis for much of commercial and corporate media's growth. The value of monopoly licenses to scarce broadcast channels, monopoly cable TV franchises, and copyright protection—all granted and enforced by the government and all provided at no charge to commercial interests—runs into the hundreds of billions of dollars. This is no "natural" free market. It is a market created and shaped by the government.

Understood this way, the crucial issue then becomes how these media policies and subsidies are generated. What is the nature of the policy-making process? In the first generations of the republic, these

policies were subject to relatively widespread informed public participation and debate. The resulting policies reflected such public
involvement. Over the course of the nineteenth century and certainly
by the twentieth century, as large commercial interests began to
dominate media markets, the public's role began to shrink. Nevertheless, the transition to a corporate-controlled, advertising-supported
media system was not seamless; at certain moments core policy
fights burst onto the political stage. The most important juncture
was the emergence of radio broadcasting.

THE RISE OF BROADCASTING

In the United States, as elsewhere, controlling and structuring radio
broadcasting posed an immediate and unavoidable political problem. The pro-commercial policy model deployed for other new
media, like national magazines or motion pictures or recorded
music, was simple and followed the "small c" conservative impulse:
Let commercial interests figure out how to make the most money and
then write laws and regulations to protect their system. Policy making, from this perspective, should not protect public interests. But
this approach was a nonstarter for radio broadcasting. Even a stridently pro-market policy required explicit, aggressive regulation by
the government, and there was no consensus even among business
interests about how to do it. In broadcasting, the rhetorical notion of
laissez-faire media policy making was reduced to the absurd.

Four factors explain why broadcasting, far more than any other
new medium, generated such a critical juncture for policy that set
the terms for much of media policy making for subsequent generations. First and foremost, there were a limited number of frequencies
for broadcasting. Only a small portion of those who would like to
broadcast would be able to do so. When more than one broadcaster
used the same frequency in the same region it created interference
and static that made reception difficult, even impossible. The spectrum was in the public domain, and there was no sentiment, even
among capitalists, to privatize it, even if that was possible. It fell
upon governments, whether they liked it or not, to determine who

would be able to secure monopoly rights to the scarce number of frequencies and who would not. Second, when broadcasting emerged, there was still no consensus that private companies seeking to maximize their profits regardless of the social implications rightfully and unquestionably should dominate. A rich legacy of serving the public, not owners, still prospered. (Commercial broadcasters would acknowledge this sentiment in their self-regulation codes.) Third, the preceding concerns were magnified by the *power* of radio broadcasting. This revolutionary medium could bring voices from around the world into people's homes at all hours of the day. Space and time collapsed as had never been imagined. Fourth, the federal government's other concerns affected radio. The U.S. Navy in particular had been instrumental in developing the technology and public subsidies had fueled its invention. The government also wanted to use radio for its own purposes, such as military communication.

I have written a detailed history of this critical juncture elsewhere.[55] For our purposes the following is worth noting. The pioneers of U.S. radio broadcasting in the early 1920s included many nonprofit institutions. At this time there was no sense that radio broadcasting could be profitable. Government policy making never authorized commercial broadcasting because it did not yet exist. The Radio Act of 1927 was emergency legislation that established the Federal Radio Commission (FRC) to bring order to the airwaves. Because many more broadcasters were operating than the spectrum could possibly accommodate, the FRC was supposed to award licenses on the basis of the vague admonition to select those applicants that best served the "public interest." By the late 1920s the two main national networks, NBC and CBS, began to see potential profit in creating national chains of stations supported by the sale of advertising. The new FRC, acting with minimal oversight by Congress, basically implemented a plan drafted by commercial broadcasting engineers and lawyers to turn almost all of the best channels over to commercial broadcasters, especially those affiliated with NBC and CBS, and to acknowledge advertising as the only legitimate form of support for broadcasters. In just a few years, network commercial broadcasting became an enormous and highly profitable industry in the United States—during the Great Depression, no less. Nonprofit and noncommercial broadcasting, which accounted for roughly half the stations in 1924 or 1925, basically fell off the map. By 1934 nonprofit broadcasters had virtually ceased to exist for most Americans.

The Radio Act of 1927 was temporary legislation and the FRC had to be renewed by Congress annually, so these issues were debated until the passage of the Communications Act of 1934, which established the Federal Communications Commission (FCC) as a permanent regulatory body. During these seven years a feisty broadcast reform movement composed of displaced educational broadcasters, religious groups, organized labor, farmers, women's groups, journalists, and civil libertarians like the ACLU coalesced. Its existence reflected the profound public dissatisfaction with advertising-drenched radio broadcasting. The movement bitterly complained that commercial broadcasting demonstrated a grotesque misuse of a scarce and valuable public resource. Commercial interests had hijacked radio broadcasting. A genuine public debate about the radio broadcasting system was required. Proponents assumed that any public debate would inevitably lead to a system with a powerful nonprofit and noncommercial broadcasting sector and in which commercial broadcasters would play a subordinate role. The reformers were inspired by the British Broadcasting Corporation (BBC), which showed what well-funded public broadcasting could accomplish, though few favored a centralized and exclusively noncommercial radio system. The reformers were also inspired by a similar reform movement in Canada that halted a purely commercial radio system and forced the establishment of the public Canadian Broadcasting Corporation (CBC) in 1932.

Commercial broadcasters responded to this challenge as if their very lives were in danger. In the early 1930s advocates for nonprofit broadcasting got major reform bills to the floor of the House or the Senate, where they had significant support. Broadcasters wielded all their political skills to undercut their adversaries and became obsessed with minimizing or eliminating public participation in or awareness of broadcast policy debates. While they loudly spoke of the public's love of commercial radio, they knew they could not let the public express this love in a debate over how the industry should be structured. Indeed, the radio lobby was adamant that radio regulation was so "complex" that only experts, not even members of Congress, should be permitted to make policy. They argued that FRC members—many of whom would go on to lucrative careers in commercial broadcasting—should be solely permitted to make broadcasting a viable profit-generating industry. Through their trade association, the National Association of Broadcasters (NAB), the industry developed an elaborate public relations campaign to promote commercial broadcasting as an inherently democratic and American system. It would be difficult to exaggerate the power of the NAB as a lobby; in addition to having money it also controlled access to the airwaves for politicians.

The crucial political development came in December 1933 when the NAB reached an agreement with the American Newspaper Publishers Association: the broadcasters would not compete in providing news if the publishers would not support the broadcast reformers on Capitol Hill and, tacitly, in their pages. With the passage of the Communications Act and the formation of the FCC in 1934, the NAB accomplished its mission. Congress no longer debated the propriety of commercial broadcasting; it was now a system to be regulated by the FCC outside the light of public attention. With no sense of irony, as soon as the law passed and the system was entrenched, in a 180-degree reversal, the NAB began to characterize any government regulation as a violation of broadcasters' First Amendment rights. Commercial broadcasters, who received what would eventually total in the hundreds of billions of dollars in value through the grant of monopoly broadcast licenses at no charge, went from statists to libertarians almost overnight.

This outcome set the pattern for subsequent debates over new media technologies. FM radio, shortwave, and television all presented innovations threatening to engender a critical juncture, a public reappraisal of broadcasting that could lead to its reformation. But in each case only a whisper of the radio broadcasting policy debate resulted; policy makers simply assumed that the logic of the existing commercial broadcasting system would naturally dominate the new technologies. To the general public, not to mention members of Congress, there was no sense that a debate was even possible, so the matter was given no thought.[56] The FCC's plan for the development of television was a particularly shameful episode. FCC chairman Charles Denny pushed for a plan that basically gave NBC and CBS near monopoly control, and six months later Denny left the FCC to triple his salary as an NBC executive.[57] Later, cable television became a regulated monopoly service in local communities. The handful of firms that came to own most of the cable TV systems were able to parlay this market power into the eventual ownership of many successful cable TV channels.[58] To this day, most of the largest media firms have been built around government monopoly licenses to either broadcast channels or cable franchises.

If anything, the government played an even larger role in subsidizing subsequent communication technologies. The development of the Comsat communication satellite system by the government in the late 1950s and early 1960s was a monumental accomplishment; after the government had assumed all the risk and had gotten it off the ground, its takeover by private interests behind closed doors and with the assistance of government regulators reeked of corruption.[59] It barely raised an eyebrow in Washington, however, because it followed the pattern established in 1934.

But the Communications Act of 1934 did not totally deregulate and privatize broadcasting and telecommunication. To the contrary, the law made it clear that government monopoly rights to broadcasting and telecommunication licenses were to be granted with the condition that the commercial recipient serve the "public interest." In theory, recipients of these licenses were not to be regarded as pure profit-motivated firms but rather as public service firms. Broadcasters were therefore required to include some programming they would have ordinarily avoided if they were strictly profit-maximizing, and it was this less commercially viable public service programming that justified their possession of the valuable monopoly broadcast license. Cable TV systems, in a similar manner, were expected to make concessions to the public interest to justify their monopoly franchises, usually by setting aside channels for public access and noncommercial use.[60]

The caliber and intensity of public interest regulation of commercial broadcasters depended very much on the political temper of the times. During a brief period in the 1940s, when Clifford Durr was on the FCC and Dallas Smythe was its chief economist, the FCC proposed an aggressive regulatory regime typified by a report demanding real public service programming by commercial broadcasters, called *The Blue Book*.[61] Over the years consultants such as Charles Siepmann and FCC members such as Frieda Hennock, Newton Minow, and Nicholas Johnson used what leverage they could to up the public service ante for commercial broadcasters.[62] But the private and commercial domination of the broadcast system was inviolable. After the 1940s, the high water mark for broadcast regulation came in the late 1960s and early 1970s, when public interest groups associated with the likes of Ralph Nader began to work the corridors of regulatory agencies with mild success.

The FCC did place some regulations on commercial broadcasters. The most notable public service requirement was the Fairness Doctrine, inspired by *The Blue Book*, which required commercial broadcasters to give ample time to matters of public importance and to provide a range of viewpoints on controversial issues.[63] In addition, ownership restrictions limited the number of radio and television stations that a single broadcaster could own. The theory went that it would be improper to let individual firms possess too many of these monopoly licenses or use the profits generated from having a broadcast license to gobble up all the other non-broadcast media. While the commercial basis of the industry was beyond reproach, the FCC had political and popular support to keep ownership relatively diverse. (These policies also had the support of many advertisers as well as small station owners, who knew they would have a dubious future if ownership caps were lifted.) In 1975 the FCC prohibited a single firm from owning both a daily newspaper and a broadcast station in the same market.[64] Likewise, firms were not permitted to own a TV station and be the monopoly cable TV system provider in the same community. To prevent broadcast networks from using their monopoly power to dominate TV show production, the FCC adopted the "financial inter- est and syndication rules" that prevented the networks from owning prime-time programs, hence fostering an independent TV production sector.[65] Foreign ownership of U.S. broadcast stations is also prohibit- ed, on national security grounds.[66]

With the exception of the ownership restrictions, broadcast regula- tion in the public interest has largely been a failure in the United States, even in the relatively enlightened 1940s and 1970s. The Fair- ness Doctrine, for example, was never enforced to require commercial broadcasters to do ample public affairs and controversial program- ming; instead, broadcasters used its provision to include more than one side of an issue as an excuse to offer as little public affairs pro- gramming as possible.[67] The reason for broadcast regulation's failure is obvious: for the system to work effectively, the FCC would have to review licenses rigorously when they came up for renewal and assign them to different applicants if the existing licensee was found to have been negligent in the provision of public service or to superior appli- cants even if the existing broadcaster had been adequate. This penalty was almost never leveled against a commercially successful broadcast- er and was *never* used to punish a licensee for failing to meet the stan- dards of the Fairness Doctrine.[68]

In a classic example of just how reluctant the FCC has been to tamper with commercial broadcast licensees, in the 1960s it refused to withdraw the license of an explicitly white supremacist station in Jackson, Mississippi, which had a 45 percent African American popu- lation. Finally, the U.S. District Court in the District of Columbia over- turned the FCC, leaving Judge Warren Burger, later to be chief justice, to comment that the FCC was "beyond repair."[69] By 2003 FCC member Michael Copps characterized the license renewal process as a "farce," noting that it amounts to little more than mailing in a postcard.[70] The reason for this deplorable state was equally clear: commercial broadcasters represented such a powerful lobbying force that each effort by the FCC to enforce strict regulation—and there were only a few such cases—was met by howls of protest on Capitol Hill. Because there was no threat of losing a license for noncompliance, there was no reason to comply. It seemed far better for the NAB to trumpet the public service that stations provided voluntarily, almost none of which affected the stations' operations or bottom line in any appreciable manner.[71]

Today public service has degenerated into tragicomedy. By 2002, a study revealed that much of the do-gooder "public service" advertising—all that remained of broadcasters' public service activity—was relegated to the "wee hours of the night," when audiences were minuscule and it was impossible to sell much commercial advertising anyway.[72] An October 2003 survey of local TV stations in six markets determined that less than one-half of 1 percent of the programming went toward covering local public affairs, despite the fact that commitment to "localism" is considered a primary mechanism for broadcasters to serve the public interest. The survey concluded: "There is a near blackout of local public affairs."[73] When soliciting investors or doing business, on the other hand, even lip service about public service has ceased. "We're not in the business of providing news and information," Clear Channel CEO Lowry Mays told a business publication in 2003. "We're not in the business of providing well-researched music. We're simply in the business of selling our customers' products."[74]

The FCC has become the classic "captured" regulatory agency. The public, even Congress, is largely unaware of its activities, which receive little or no press attention except in the business pages as issues of interest to investors and managers. Most FCC members go on to lucrative careers with those they had been ostensibly regulating previously. As more than one skeptic has noted, when a commercial firm's executive comes before the FCC, the members do not know whether to regard him as someone to be regulated or as a possible future employer. Much of the data used by the FCC to make its policies have been spoon-fed to them by the broadcasting industry—data that is often "of

very questionable verisimilitude," according to a public interest advocate.[75] While the rhetoric of regulation remains ensconced in public
interest terminology, the logic of regulation has turned to the reality of
making broadcasters profitable. In the minds of the broadcasters, this
has always been the proper role of regulation and government media
policy making. The "public interest" perspective has gravitated from
striving for what would be best for the public and creating a system
that best produces those results to what would be best for the public
after the dominant firms maximize their profits. Their happiness is
the starting point for all that follows, and it cannot be challenged. The
system was structured in such a way that the public is nowhere to be
found in the day-to-day functioning of the FCC.

But it would be misleading to dismiss the FCC as a meaningless
puppet of the NAB. It is also a referee, arbitrating fights between the
broadcasting, cable, and telecommunication sectors.[76] William Kennard recalled his education when he assumed the chair of the FCC in
President Clinton's second term: "I came to the job feeling very strongly that the agency had become captive of corporate interests and was
really not connecting to its core mission." Kennard asked several former FCC chairs to join him for lunch and explain to him how he could
best do his new job. One pulled him aside and confided, "Bill, you have
to realize that when you are chairman of the FCC, you're basically a
referee of big money fights and they are fights between the rich on the
one hand, and the very wealthy on the other. The key to being a successful chairman is to keep the power in equilibrium. So if you give
something to one powerful lobby one week, you better balance it out
by giving their opponents something the next week." Kennard
remarked that "after having lunch with him" he felt almost unspeak-
ably "depressed." But his years at the FCC only reinforced the accuracy
of that previous chair's assessment.[77] His successor, Michael Powell,
acknowledged the same situation: "A day in the life of the FCC is listen-
ing to company after company argue for policy changes in their self-
interest." Powell, though, seemed untroubled by this job description.[78]

It should be noted that even in the warped world of broadcast regulation, advocates of the public interest—that is, those not representing

self-interested commercial organizations—have had some influence with the FCC and on Capitol Hill. But to be taken seriously—the ante for admission on Capitol Hill and at the FCC—these groups had to accept the commercial basis of the broadcasting system. The reformers could then only tweak the system to generate marginally better results. As a consequence, their range of legitimate options was often quite small, and their proposals were hardly dramatic enough to capture the public's imagination and support. It also did not help matters that press coverage was almost nonexistent. To have any hope for success, reformers have had to ally themselves with one corporate sector against another corporate sector. So it is that public interest groups tend to work with small TV and radio station owners to combat the networks and large station-owning groups.

Perhaps the most prominent public interest initiatives have been brought by civil rights and feminist groups to protest the lack of people of color or women in important media positions, the homogeneity of media owners, and the portrayal of race and gender issues in commercial journalism and entertainment programming. In particular, in the wake of the massive political movements of the 1960s and 1970s, groups pushed the FCC to become more aggressive in the review of licenses because all had been doled out between the 1920s and 1940s when anyone other than white men were essentially excluded from owning them.[79] Because these initiatives did not coincide with a critical juncture for the media, structural change and core media policies remained off-limits. Boycotting and otherwise pressuring the commercial interests were the only options for change.[80]

To most people and in most moments of history, the media system appears natural and immutable. Policy debates focus on marginal and tangential issues because core structures and policies are off-limits to criticism. In this environment, policy debates tend to gravitate to the elite level and public participation virtually disappears. After all, for most people, minor media policy issues are far down on the list of important topics. Sweeping media reform is unthinkable—and politically impossible. The public's elimination from the process is encouraged by the corruption of the U.S. political system, in which politicians tend to be comfortable with the status quo and not inclined to upset powerful commercial media owners and potential campaign contributors. The dominant media firms enjoy the power to control news coverage of debates over media policies; this is a power they have used shamelessly to trivialize, marginalize, and distort opposition to the status quo.

In the second half of the twentieth century, media policy making came to resemble the scene from *The Godfather II* in which Michael Corleone, Hyman Roth, and the heads of the U.S. gangster families meet on a patio in Havana to "divide" up pre-Communist Cuba. Roth ceremonially gives each gangster a piece of Cuba as he slices his birthday cake, which has the outline of Cuba on it. As Roth doles out the slices he applauds the Batista government for favoring private enterprise—that is, letting the gangsters plunder the country. The gangsters fight among themselves to get the biggest slice of Cuba—indeed, the film revolves around this theme—but they agree that they alone should own Cuba. So it is with media policy making in the United States. Massive corporate lobbies duke it out with each other for the largest share of the cake, but it is their cake.

THE NEOLIBERAL PERIOD

Antidemocratic tendencies in media policy making have grown more powerful over the past quarter century. The period has signaled upheaval in U.S. media regulation, far more so than in any period since the critical juncture of the 1920s and 1930s. But the main story of the final two decades of the twentieth century has been the decisive increase in the business domination of media policy making. The rather extensive coterie of public interest activist groups that formed in the late 1960s and early 1970s to get public interest media regulation enhanced in Congress and at the FCC drifted for the most part into obscurity when it became clear that the possibility of achieving anything more than the smallest victory was close to zero. These groups were soon overshadowed by another wave of policy activists, often very well funded by comparison, who began working to see that public interest regulation was reduced and ultimately discontinued.[81]

This rigorous drive for so-called deregulation is based upon the "neoliberal" view that markets and profit making should be allowed to regulate every aspect of social life possible. By the late 1970s, broadcasting's traditional regulatory regime had begun to unravel. On the one hand, the existing public interest regulation was clearly ineffectual, and even political liberals were becoming disillusioned with the status quo. They did not like the commercial broadcasting system, but they were increasingly willing to accept that the regulatory process was as much the problem as any sort of solution. The case of airline deregulation was similar, and liberal Ted Kennedy of Massachusetts and President Jimmy Carter were instrumental in putting that in place. On the other hand, commercial media interests pushed ahead with their campaign to dismantle public interest regulation, arguing that markets could do a better job of regulation than government bureaucrats could. This campaign emphasized that new technologies—then cable and satellite broadcasting, later the Internet—eliminated the scarcity rationale for public interest regulation. The market could accomplish seamlessly and without coercion what the government could do only clumsily and inefficiently. The campaign was in part a well-financed public relations operation to promote and widely disseminate pro-deregulation arguments and to discredit and marginalize opposing views as akin to the flat-earth society worldview or totalitarianism. But it also was a big-ticket political juggernaut, working the court system, Congress, the White House, and the FCC simultaneously to reduce or eliminate the legal basis for public interest regulation of commercial media.

In theory, this impasse and the emergence of new digital communication technologies could have led to a critical juncture. The new technologies certainly offered the promise of a media world with far less dependence upon advertising, for example, and a much wider range of economically viable media producers. In a different political climate, change might have been possible. But with the 1980 election of Ronald Reagan, the neoliberal moment had commenced. Neoliberal ideology became hegemonic not only among Republicans but also in the Democratic Party of Bill Clinton, Al Gore, and Joseph Lieberman. Differences remained on timing and specifics, but on the core issues both parties agreed that business was the rightful ruler over society.[82] It was a return to the 1920s, if not the Gilded Age of the late nineteenth century.

Few industries seized the neoliberal high ground as quickly or as firmly as the media and communication industries. A new generation of economists, with scholarly tomes published by the leading presses, trumpeted the value of applying market principles to all communication policy matters; as one of them put it, the *ancien régime* was "often dominated by ad hoc prescriptions premised on shaky economics applied to dubious histories."[83] These tended to be circular arguments—if you start from the presupposition that the market is infallible and appropriate to regulate media, it is awfully hard to justify anything that interferes with the market. Proper appreciation for free market competition and new technologies eliminated the need for public interest regulation, the industry argued, and such regulation certainly violated the free press and free speech clauses of the First Amendment. On these grounds the FCC eliminated the Fairness Doctrine in the 1980s, invoking the most eloquent phrases from the opinions of Supreme Court Justice William O. Douglas to do so. (Ironically, Douglas himself was a strong proponent of broadcast regulation in the public interest.)[84] Everyone from broadcasters to cable companies to advertisers claimed that any regulation of their affairs violated their First Amendment rights.[85]

Behind the mighty rhetoric, the stakes were clear. These corporations knew that if they were granted absolutist First Amendment protection, their existence and operations "would be placed beyond the reach of majorities," as Justice Robert Jackson once described the purpose of the Bill of Rights. Putting their legitimacy in question, even regulating them, would become vastly more difficult.[86] Or, as Herbert I. Schiller put it, the commercial "expansion" of the First Amendment protections to giant, monopolistic corporations led directly to the shrinking of democracy.[87]

Listen to the rhetoric and read the proclamations of the commercial broadcasters since the 1980s and one might think that as soon as onerous regulations like the Fairness Doctrine were eliminated companies could proceed unencumbered on their free market way. The truth of neoliberalism, however, is that while the rhetoric extols small government, free markets, competition, and entrepreneurial risk-taking, the reality is that a large government is doling out crucial contracts, monopoly licenses, and subsidies to huge firms in highly concentrated industries. Indeed, in the neoliberal environment, the only thing that changes aside from the market-worship rhetoric is that Washington is even *more* of an open trough filled with billions of dollars worth of goodies. Neoliberalism simply reduces or eliminates the *idea* that government should represent the public interest vis-à-vis the corporate interest. There is no longer a meaningful conflict between the public and the corporate sector—public service is bunk—so politicians and regulators can serve corporations with impunity.

The corruption in media policy making culminated in the passage of the 1996 Telcommunications Act, arguably one of the most important pieces of U.S. legislation. The law rewrote the regulatory regime for radio, television, telephony, cable television, and satellite communication—indeed, all of electronic communication including the Internet. It laid down the core values for the FCC to implement for generations. The operating premise of the law was that new communication technologies combined with an increased appreciation for the genius of the market rendered the traditional regulatory model moot. The solution therefore was to lift regulations and ownership restrictions from commercial media and communication companies, allow competition in the marketplace to develop, and reduce the government's role to that of protecting private property. There was virtually no dissent whatsoever to this legislation from either political party; the law sailed through both houses of Congress and was signed by a jubilant President Clinton in February 1996. Corporate CEOs regarded the bill as their "Magna Carta," and humanity was soon to enter an era of permanent and unprecedented economic growth and human happiness. The rhetoric of neoliberalism was at its most optimistic and flowery; as Thomas Frank remarked, thanks to the competition, deregulation, entrepreneurial genius, and the Internet, we were indeed becoming "One Market under God."[88] In actuality, however, the law merely amended the 1934 Communications Act; the statutory commitment to regulation in the public interest remained.

The details of how this law was drafted and passed have been chronicled elsewhere; herein the following points are worth noting.[89] The emergence of new communication technologies *did* require Congress to revisit the issue of regulation; the ability to use cable broadcasting wires and telephone wires to provide one another's services, to cite one example, would eventually undermine the technological rationale for having different regulatory systems for each system.[90] This was a critical juncture for media requiring a fundamental rethinking of communication regulation. According to democratic theory, it deserved the widespread and informed participation of as much of the political culture as possible. Ideally, it would have been the subject of contentious debate between political parties. Behind the lofty neoliberal platitudes, however, the drafting of the law was as corrupt and as antidemocratic as one could imagine. The world's most powerful lobbies squared off secretly to get the best concessions; free-market rhetoric notwithstanding, this was a mad dash to get government support for business, and the stakes were in the tens of billions of dollars. In a dramatic instance of collusion between media sectors, there was almost no press coverage—except in the business and trade press. Not surprisingly, Americans were uninformed on the law's consequences. One survey has found, for example, that only three Americans in ten understand that the public owns the airwaves, and only one American in ten knows that commercial broadcasters use the airwaves at no charge from the government.[91] The general public contributed to the legislation not at all; even the Washington-based public interest lobbying groups were kept out. This was high-stakes corruption, and penny-ante players were not invited.

When conflicts between the massive lobbies over which firms and sectors would get the best perks threatened to derail the bill in early 1996, the sides agreed to unite to pass the bill and then let the FCC work out the "deregulation" details. Their concern was that a gadfly like Ross Perot might make a political issue of the matter if it remained in Congress during the 1996 election. Once the law was in the safe hands of the FCC, the debates could be hidden from public view. Congress held no floor debate on the bill's core; most members had little or no idea of the law's contents when they voted for it. The notion that the Telecommunications Act was about promoting genuine competition was dubious from the outset—why would these powerful lobbies ram through a bill if it threatened their profitability?—although this point eluded members of Congress, not to mention the minuscule number of reporters who covered it. In truth, the bill promised the worst of both worlds: more concentrated ownership over communications with less possibility for regulation in the public interest. Accordingly, both the cable and the telecommunication industries have become significantly more concentrated since 1996, and customer complaints about lousy service have hit all-time highs. Cable industry rates for consumers have also shot up, increasing some 50 percent between 1996 and 2003.[92]

One of the more contentious areas during the backroom slugfests over the Telecommunications Act was media ownership. This was not exactly a neoliberal coming-out party. Large media owners despise these restrictions for self-evident reasons. As they get larger they enjoy economies of scale, face less competition, and increase profits. For years they have lobbied incessantly to get these ownership restrictions relaxed, if not eliminated. They faced significant opposition from small broadcast and independent media owners, who understood that they would be unable to compete if the caps were lifted. To the extent the public weighed in, there was no support for concentrated media ownership. In the 1980s and 1990s, under neoliberalism, ownership caps were gradually relaxed. With the 1996 Telecommunications Act, the big media companies went in for the kill, arguing that the caps were an outdated relic from a bygone era. In the age of the Internet and multichannel television, they claimed, the market could regulate media more efficiently and fairly than ownership policies could. In the world of converging media, it was unfair for the government to tie the hands of broadcast and cable-owning companies with ownership regulations while their competitors faced no similar handicaps.

The corporate campaign for eliminating media ownership rules flopped. Smaller media and members of Congress who did not like the idea of media concentration offered too much opposition. Indeed, going against the neoliberal flow, Senator Byron Dorgan nearly got majority support for an amendment to *tighten* TV station ownership regulations. The one media sector that had its media ownership caps significantly relaxed in the Telecom Act was radio. Big media companies had convinced enough small station owners that they would be better off with ownership "deregulation" and thereby minimized their opposition. The Telecom Act otherwise turned the matter over to the FCC, requiring it to reevaluate all of its media ownership rules every two years and change them if conditions had changed sufficiently to warrant such action. The crucial remaining rules were limits on the number of TV stations a single firm could hold in a single market or nationally, the limit on the number of cable TV systems a firm could own nationally, and bans on cross-ownership of cable TV systems and broadcast outlets in the same community or newspaper and broadcast outlets in the same community.[93]

The range of legitimate debate in the FCC after the passage of the 1996 Telecommunications Act remained locked in a neoliberal paradigm through the Clinton years. The Democratic FCC head William Kennard endorsed the notion that new technologies and competition eliminated the need for public interest regulation; he differed from hardcore neoliberals mostly on the question of timing. Kennard thought that ownership deregulation needed to be brought along slowly, to make sure that it actually led to some semblance of competition and not to monopolies.[94] During these years, crucial areas of concern for public interest advocates—areas that had widespread popular support to the extent that people knew about them, like increasing educational TV programs to children—continued to flounder. A 1999 University of Pennsylvania study concluded that one-fifth of all programs billed as educational for children had "little or no educational value." Hence, many broadcasters thereby failed to meet the FCC's requirement of three hours of children's educational programming per week, yet nothing was done.[95] A longtime public interest advocate

who had worked for years on policy matters with the FCC characterized the Kennard years as "a real failure."[96] It was no particular surprise that after leaving the FCC Kennard accepted a high-paying job
brokering wireless deals for the Carlyle Group. In view of the generous treatment Kennard had given Carlyle client SBC Communications
before the FCC, the hire reeked of corruption and cronyism, or, in
other words, business as usual at the FCC.[97]

In fairness to Kennard, he did try to enact positive change during
his tenure as FCC chair. He was deeply concerned about the drop in
minority radio station owners following the 1996 Telecommunications Act and developed low-power FM radio as a means to address this
problem. He also attempted to push through free TV airtime for political candidates to offset the obvious problems with access to paid commercial time. But here Kennard faced the historic problem any FCC
reformer faces: the relevant committees in Congress remained under
the thumb of corporate lobbies. The NAB was resolutely opposed to
free airtime, and many members of Congress informed Kennard in no
uncertain terms to back off. As Kennard explains: "When I first started
talking to people about free airtime for political candidates, some of
my oldest and closest friends in Washington took me to breakfast, and
they said, 'Bill, don't do this, it's political suicide, you know. You're
just going to kill yourself.'" Eventually Kennard abandoned his campaign for free airtime. He learned an important lesson, one that no
FCC member ever acted on before 2003: "In order to do things that are
in the public interest, where you have no powerful lobby behind you,
the only way that you can garner support for it is to reach outside
Washington, get outside the Beltway and build coalitions with people
who will speak to their legislatures at the grass roots."[98]

Kennard's run-in with Congress could have been predicted. Congressional committee members are well lubricated in cash and goodies from the media lobbies. A 2000 study by Charles Lewis and the
Center for Public Integrity revealed that the fifty largest media firms
and the four media trade organizations spent $111 million on lobby-
ing between 1996 and 2000, and the number of media-related lobbyists increased from 234 to 284. In the same time span, media firms

paid for 118 members of Congress and their senior staff to take 315 junkets, with a total value of $455,000. Rep. Billy Tauzin, chair of the House Commerce Committee that oversees the FCC, was the champion recipient of corporate largesse. He and his staff accounted for fully 42 of the junkets, and, in 1999, Tauzin and his wife enjoyed a six-day $18,910 junket to Paris courtesy of Time Warner and Instinet. Tauzin's daughter Kimberly worked as a lobbyist for the NAB in the late 1990s as well. This might have been purely coincidental, but Tauzin became the number-one promoter of corporate media interests in Washington during these years, with a slavish devotion to their cause. And he was not alone. Between 1993 and 2000 the same corporations gave $75 million in campaign contributions to candidates for federal office and spread the money to politicians on both sides of the aisle.[99] Sure, there were fights between the various corporate media sectors over who got the largest slice of cake, but on core issues, corporate media interests owned the policy debate in Washington. In 2000, large media firms were major contributors to both Bush and Gore, and Time Warner donated large sums to both sides.[100] As one media CEO euphorically remarked in 2000 when asked which candidate would best serve the interest of corporate media owners, "Bush? Gore? It doesn't matter!"[101]

The trajectory of this chapter is admittedly bleak. The consequences of corrupt policy making are apparent all around us and are much of what this book addresses. But as the unprecedented protest over media concentration in 2003 demonstrates, the future of media policy making is not necessarily doomed to be a repetition of its ignominious past. When the public is informed about how policy is created and what options for change are actually available—rather than the limited few the profit-driven media typically herald—a critical juncture may open again that will allow for revelation, debate, and democracy.

2

UNDERSTANDING U.S. JOURNALISM I: CORPORATE CONTROL AND PROFESSIONALISM

Democratic theory posits that society needs journalism to perform three main duties: to act as a rigorous watchdog of the powerful and those who wish to be powerful; to ferret out truth from lies; and to present a wide range of informed positions on key issues. Each medium need not do all these things, but the media system as a whole should make this caliber of journalism readily available to the citizenry. How a society can construct a media system that will generate something approximating democratic journalism is a fundamental problem confronting a free people. Citizens learn about the social world and politics from the entirety of the media, but journalism alone is expressly committed to this mission. That is why I devote two chapters to an evaluation of it.

In these two chapters I will explain why contemporary U.S. journalism fails in all three of its duties. The problem stems directly from the system of profit-driven journalism in largely noncompetitive markets that began to emerge over a century ago. This system was not "natural," but the consequence of a series of policies, most notably policies favoring monopoly and/or oligopoly in telegraphy and broadcasting, and commercialism in media. Concentrated private control over the press, with the aim of profit maximization, has been the rudder directing U.S. journalism for more than a century. I will first look at the rise of professional journalism roughly one hundred years ago and some inherent problems it presented for U.S. democracy. Grasping the origins and nature of professional journalism is necessary for any worthy critique of contemporary journalism.

I will then discuss the commercial media's attack on professional journalism, always lurking, but in recent years on the offensive. These discussions will be augmented by a focus on the attack on the so-called liberal media by conservatives, a point I discuss in the next chapter. A commitment to anything remotely resembling bona fide democracy requires a vastly superior journalism, and we can only realistically expect such journalism if sweeping changes in media policies and structures make it a rational expectation.

JOURNALISM'S GREAT CRISIS

The concept of journalism as politically neutral, nonpartisan, professional, even "objective," did not emerge until the twentieth century. During the first two or three generations of the republic such notions for the press would have been nonsensical, even unthinkable. Journalism's purpose was to persuade as well as to inform and the press tended to be highly partisan. A partisan press system has much to offer a democratic society—as long as there are numerous well-subsidized media providing a broad range of perspectives.[1] During the nineteenth century, newspapers became primarily commercial. The press system remained explicitly partisan, but it increasingly became an engine of great profits as costs plummeted, population increased, and advertising—which emerged as a key source of revenues—mushroomed. During the Civil War, President Lincoln faced press criticism—from some Northern newspapers—that would make the treatment of Lyndon Johnson during Vietnam, Richard Nixon during Watergate, or Bill Clinton during his impeachment seem like a day at the beach.[2] "As late as the 1890s," Michael Schudson notes, "a standard Republican paper that covered a presidential election not only would deplore and deride Democratic presidential candidates, very often it would simply neglect to mention them."[3] For much of the middle and latter nineteenth century this partisanship coexisted with a relatively competitive market. A major city such as St. Louis, for example, had as many as ten daily newspapers. Each tended to represent the politics of the owner, and if someone was dissatisfied with the existing choices, it was not impossible to launch a new newspaper.

It was only a matter of time before the commercial economics of the press would conflict with its explicitly partisan politics. During the Gilded Age, the commercial press system became less competitive and ever more clearly the domain of wealthy individuals, who usually held the political views associated with their class. It became a big business. In 1887 the trade association for the newspaper industry, the American Newspaper Publishers Association (ANPA), was formed to address "the business problems of daily newspapers." This was the first great media trade organization, and it went to work immediately to amend copyright law in favor of publishers. Commercialism also fostered corruption, as newspapers turned to sensationalism and outright lying to generate sales. Bribery of reporters was not uncommon.[4] Throughout this era, socialists, feminists, abolitionists, trade unionists, and radicals came to regard the mainstream commercial press as the mouthpiece of their enemies and established their own media to advance their interests. In his classic 1887 utopian novel *Looking Backward* the journalist Edward Bellamy wrote longingly of a time when newspapers would write the truth and not serve as pawns of the wealthy.[5] By the 1890s, over 1,000 populist journals, organized into the National Reform Press Association, dedicated themselves to countering the hostility and deceit of the business-run commercial press and the ANPA.[6] A widespread immigrant and foreign-language press pushed radical political perspectives.[7] In the early 1900s, members and supporters of the Socialist Party of Eugene V. Debs published some 325 English and foreign-language daily, weekly, and monthly newspapers and magazines. Most were privately owned or published by one of the 5,000 Socialist Party locals.[8]

From the Gilded Age through the Progressive Era, an institutional sea change transpired in U.S. media not unlike the one taking place in the broader political economy. Power became concentrated in fewer chains and the majority of communities had only one or two dailies. The economics of advertising-supported newspapers erected barriers to entry that made it virtually impossible for small, independent newspapers to succeed, despite the constitutional protection of a "free press." Most of the populist and socialist press was wiped out, but not because of declining subscriptions. These newspapers were unwilling or unable to compete for the advertising dollars that were necessary to keep the publications affordable. Even press magnate E. W. Scripps was foiled in his efforts to build a pro–working-class newspaper chain that did not require dependence upon advertising.[9] To survive and prosper, Scripps was forced to accept advertising. Indeed, despite spectacular rates of return—to this day newspapers operate on margins well above the norms for the rest of U.S. industry[10]—and enormous population increases, not one newspaper has been successfully launched in an existing local market in the United States since the 1910s.[11] Such was and is the power of newspapers' local market monopolies. (How much the collapse of the independent press contributed to the demise of popular politics is a matter of no small importance in media studies.) The handful of newspapers launched in the twentieth century without commercial advertising quickly discovered it was not a viable option.[12] This dependence upon advertising put an implicit pressure on the type of journalism that would be encouraged, which was why Scripps and so many other scrupulous editors attempted to avoid it.

At the beginning of the twentieth century these developments led to a crisis for U.S. journalism. It is one thing to posit that a commercial media system works for democracy when multiple newspapers are published in a community, when barriers to entry are relatively low and when immigrant and dissident media proliferate widely, as was the case for much of the nineteenth century. For newspapers to be partisan at that time was no big problem because alternative viewpoints were present. It is quite another thing to make such a claim when many communities have only one or two newspapers, usually owned by chains or very wealthy and powerful individuals. By the early twentieth century newspaper concentration was on the rise, but almost nowhere were new dailies being launched successfully in existing markets. For journalism to remain partisan in this context, for it to advocate openly the interests of the owners and advertisers who subsidized it, would cast severe doubt on its credibility.

Concurrently sensationalism, or "yellow journalism," blossomed. Concocting outrageous stories for their entertainment value developed logically from the profit-driven journalism of the 1830s.[13] But it exploded by the beginning of the twentieth century. Owners found it a relatively inexpensive means to generate profits, and the profits outweighed the effect of social disapproval. Sensationalism was the hallmark of the low-price metro dailies. Then as now, disaster, crime, sex, scandal, and celebrity sold well. Higher circulation meant higher ad rates and higher profits. More and more papers joined the tabloid game, and it became a race to the bottom as each tried to outdo the other to grab more readers. Fabrication was commonplace. The exclusion of serious news stories to make room for scandal became routine. Not all newspapers were explicitly partisan or sensationalist, however. A respectable press pitched to the upper classes lurked in large metropolitan areas, but it offered minor consolation to press critics, especially those on the Left who regarded these papers as equally anti-labor as the balance of the press, albeit with more genteel language.

This was the first great crisis of commercial journalism.[14] Critics on the Left, ranging from socialist labor advocates to progressive senators, saw through this facade of democratic journalism and blasted it unrelentingly. The political culture was radical enough and the dissident media still vibrant enough to support these efforts on a massive scale. These decades, characterized by the historian Richard Hofstadter as an "age of broad social speculation," featured oppositional politics in government at a level difficult to imagine today.[15] The Socialist Party presidential candidate Eugene V. Debs polled well in each of the first three elections of the new century, peaking at 6 percent of the electorate in 1912. In that year, two million Americans subscribed to socialist newspapers. The *Appeal to Reason*, a socialist newspaper printed in Kansas and distributed nationally, had a circulation of over a million and featured articles by well-known public figures such as Debs and Upton Sinclair.[16] The systemic challenge to the political and economic order carried out by the labor movement and crusading social reformers quite naturally extended to a savage critique of the press. Reformers saw clearly that no issue could mobilize the public if the power of the press was turned against it. Will Irwin commented in 1911 that "the American press has more influence than it ever had in any other time, in any other country. No other extrajudicial form, except religion, is half so powerful."[17]

It was not just the socialists. Across the political spectrum, writers spoke of a "crisis in journalism." Conservatives shunned what they considered the immorality propagated by tabloids and the dilution of proper social norms through exposure to indecent publications. Progressives writing in the magazine founded by Senator Robert La Follette of Wisconsin exposed the economic connections between the business community, publishers, and corrupt politicians. Journalists such as Will Irwin excoriated the dominance of the profit motive and conservative politics over editorial integrity. Academics such as Edward Ross, a sociologist, pointed to the deep contradictions between commercialism and democracy in the press. In his classic 1920 book of press criticism *The Brass Check*, Sinclair called for a total transformation of the commercial system. Sinclair's book teemed with examples of lying and distortion by the mainstream press in covering the labor movement and socialist politics. It is worth noting that he challenged those he criticized to find any error in his book, and he had no successful takers. The AP even established a committee to evaluate the book and denounce Sinclair's charges, but the committee quietly abandoned the project without comment.[18] Sinclair commented, "One could take a map of America and a paintbrush, and make large smudges of color, representing journalistic ownership of whole districts, sometimes of whole states, by special interests."[19] Public trust in the free press receded, as many perceived journalism to be corrupt and pro-business propaganda, and exhibited skepticism toward much that was written in the newspapers.

Press criticism extended widely; in the 1912 presidential race all three challengers to President William Howard Taft—Debs, Theodore Roosevelt, and Woodrow Wilson—criticized the press's capitalist bias.[20] By 1910 even pro-business President Taft was railing against the mailing permit granted to newspapers as an undeserved subsidy to publishers. After all, the subsidy was premised on the press being a political agency, not a commercial interest. In 1912, in the midst of this turmoil, Congress passed the Newspaper Publicity Act, which required newspapers to list their owners and editors and clearly demarcate paid advertising from news if they were to receive the postal subsidy. The ANPA argued that any regulation (though not any subsidy) violated the media's First Amendment rights, but the Supreme Court upheld the law as constitutional.[21]

The actual threat to the status quo of commercial newspaper publishing during this period appears, in retrospect, to be small. The roar of the critique was deafening, but the proffered solutions and movements to bring about structural press reform were inchoate. Yet the threat arguably was greater than that of any subsequent period, and the political turbulence—progressives and socialists would never again be so influential—encouraged the ANPA to act. Moreover, the commercial prospects of the industry were being undermined by sensationalism and disreputable journalism. The major publishers adopted three responses to thwart government policies that might interfere with their commercial prospects. First, they made sure coverage of these debates was either nonexistent or distorted to suit the interest of the press owners. This made it considerably more difficult for the public to participate in media policy debates, as they often had little information about what was going on. (In the dissident press, on the other hand, this was a golden age for press criticism.)[22] Second, the First Amendment was used as a bludgeon to prevent adoption of government policies that might interfere with their commercial prerogatives. Third, industry self-regulation, as opposed to government regulation or reorganization, was offered as the appropriate solution to concentrated private control of communication. That the market was not truly competitive in an economic sense was not a concern because the publishers took it upon themselves to act responsibly. They would not abuse their power. How much of the self-regulation was an effective solution to the problem and how much of it was a public relations move to undermine and disarm opposition is a subject for analysis and debate. At any rate, *these three planks would reappear in virtually every major media industry policy debate thereafter.*

RISE OF PROFESSIONAL JOURNALISM

In the case of newspapers, industry self-regulation assumed the form of professional journalism. Savvy publishers understood that they needed to have their journalism appear neutral and unbiased—notions entirely foreign to the journalism of the republic's first century—or their businesses would be far less profitable. They would sacrifice their explicit political power to lock in their economic position. Publishers pushed for the establishment of formal schools of journalism to train a cadre of professional editors and reporters. None of these schools existed in 1900; by 1920, all the major schools such as Columbia, Northwestern, Missouri, and Indiana were in full swing. The revolutionary and unprecedented notion of a separation of the editorial operations from commercial affairs—the "separation of church and state"—became the professed model. The argument went that trained editors and reporters were granted autonomy by the owners to make editorial decisions, and these decisions were based on their professional judgment, not the politics of the owners and the advertisers or their commercial interests. As trained professionals, journalists would learn to sublimate their own values as well. Readers could trust what they read and not worry about who owned or worked on the newspaper.[23]

By the logic of professionalism, if everyone followed its standards, press concentration would become a moot issue. Who needed more than one or two newspapers if every paper ran basically the same professionally driven content? Whether the newspaper was owned by a Democrat, a socialist (okay, this is hypothetical), or a Republican, and whether it received a great deal of advertising or none at all, the news coverage of the newspaper would be straight and unbiased because trained professionals were in charge of the process. Owners could sell their neutral monopoly newspapers to everyone in the community and rake in the profits. In 1923 the American Society of Newspaper Editors (ASNE) was formed to cement this separation of church and state and protect the purity of the editorial work from the business considerations of the ANPA. The ASNE issued professional codes of ethics for journalists to follow.[24] Of course, this was never a formal contract; journalistic autonomy existed purely at the whim of publishers, who still held all the legal and economic power.

In a political sense the ANPA's response to the crisis was a rousing success. In relatively short order, the notions that the ownership and support of a newspaper were crucial for understanding a newspaper's conduct and content—until then the starting point for all press analysis—diminished in importance. Criticism of owners and advertisers for not respecting the autonomy of editors and reporters was acceptable—some deadbeats had to be jawboned into submission— but criticism of the capitalist basis of the newspaper (and later, media) industry was now inviolable. Very quietly, with almost no media coverage, the newspaper industry continued to receive subsidies and favorable policies in Washington, but was seen as largely irrelevant to news content.[25] That was the province of professional journalists. Thereafter discussions of journalism and the press centered not on institutional control and government policies; instead the attention went mostly to evaluating journalists' conduct. To the extent that institutions mattered, concern lay with government efforts at explicit "prior restraint" censorship. The balance of a political economic critique fell from public view.[26]

During professional journalism's embryonic phase in the 1930s, prominent journalists such as George Seldes and Heywood Broun struggled for a vision of professional journalism that was ruthlessly independent of corporate and commercial influence. Their assessment of mainstream journalism was identical to that of Sinclair and the Progressive Era critics. In leading the fight for the establishment of the Newspaper Guild, the union for journalists, Seldes advocated a journalism that would aggressively ferret out the truth on behalf of democratic values and the dispossessed: "The difference between the Guild and the publishers is this: the former displays a social conscience while the latter still live in the golden but dying age of the socially irresponsible profit motive." The media system could not be democratic if journalists aligned their interests with the publishers, advertisers, and powerful government and business leaders and not the readers. If publishers could not be relied upon to put commercial and partisan biases aside to complete the work constitutionally guaranteed to the public, journalists would have to be entrusted with that right and protected in their employment by union contracts.

The most militant wing of the Newspaper Guild, represented by Seldes, demanded that journalists run the newspapers—that owners should have no control over the content. "In no other industry is the employee as capable of directing the whole works as in newspaper making," he argued. When owners lose power and the journalists come "into control, then the day of the free press would be at hand."[27] The Guild never adopted this radical position, and as the broader radical moment faded, the Guild came to see itself as a traditional union working to improve its members' wages and benefits. But for a brief moment a different vision of a professional code was on display; it appeared just long enough to demonstrate that there was nothing inevitable or natural about journalism's professional code. It resulted from a political struggle in which one side won and the other side lost.

It took decades for the professional system to be adopted by the major journalistic media. The first half of the twentieth century is replete with owners such as the *Chicago Tribune*'s Robert R. McCormick, who used their newspapers to advocate their fiercely partisan, often far-right, views.[28] (When the Nazis came to power, the *Tribune*'s European correspondent, a McCormick favorite, defected to Germany so that he could make pro-Nazi shortwave radio broadcasts aimed at the United States.[29]) But by midcentury even laggards like the *Tribune* had been brought into line. Urban legend has it that in the famed Tribune Building in Chicago, editorial workers and those on the business side of the paper were instructed to use separate elevators so that the editorial integrity of the newspaper would not be sullied. What is important to remember is that professional journalism looked awfully good compared to what it had replaced. The emphasis on nonpartisanship and factual accuracy, the discrediting of sensationalism—who could oppose that? It is still roundly hailed as the solution to the problem of journalism.

LIMITATIONS OF PROFESSIONAL JOURNALISM

Perhaps because of this context, what was lost in much of the debate over journalism was the elitist and antidemocratic bias built right into the notion of professional regulation. Professionalism became the preferred solution to the question of governance during the Progressive Era. As Woodrow Wilson put it in 1909, "We want one class of persons to have a liberal education, and we want another class of persons, a very much larger class, of necessity, in every society, to forgo the privileges of a liberal education and fit themselves to perform specific difficult manual tasks."[30] Walter Lippmann argued that this model should be applied to journalism as well, and professional experts should dole out the scientifically determined appropriate information to the unwashed masses. George Bernard Shaw once remarked that all professions are conspiracies against the common folk. He meant that those who belong to elite trades—physicians, lawyers, professors, and scientists—protect their special status by creating vocabularies that are incomprehensible to the general public.

Scholarship on professionalism suggests that one of its functions is to provide "ideological discipline," so practitioners will not question the presuppositions upon which their work is based.[31] And one of the features of professionalism in journalism has been to discourage journalists from taking public criticism seriously because public criticism is necessarily uninformed.[32] Trenchant critics such as Christopher Lasch understood that the turn to a professional model for journalism meant a reduction of what was most necessary for self-government and community, the fostering of informed public debate.[33] As James Carey eloquently notes, "It is a journalism of fact without regard to understanding through which the public is immobilized and demobilized and merely ratifies the judgments of experts delivered from on high. It is, above all, a journalism that justifies itself in the public's name but in which the public plays no role, except as an audience; it is a receptacle to be informed by experts and an excuse for the practice of publicity."[34]

Professionalism never really applied to journalism in the same way that it applied to law or medicine. Journalists were not partners who ran their own businesses; they were employees. So the term *professionalism* was misleading about how power operated in a newsroom and how news was generated. Moreover, the practice of journalism did not really lend itself to a unified scientific code. The claim that it was possible to provide neutral and objective news was suspect. Decision making is an inescapable part of the journalism process, and some values have to be promoted when deciding why one story rates front-page treatment while another is ignored.[35] This does not mean that some journalism cannot be more nonpartisan or more accurate than others; nor does it mean that nonpartisan and accurate journalism should not have a prominent role to play in a democratic society. It only means that journalism cannot actually be neutral or objective—and unless one acknowledges that, it is impossible to detect the actual values at play that determine what becomes news and what does not.

In the United States journalism evolved to incorporate certain key values in the professional code; there was nothing naturally objective or professional about those values. In core respects these values were formed in response to the commercial and political needs of the owners, although they were never framed in such a manner. To the extent that journalists believe that by following professional codes they are neutral and fair—or, at least, need not entertain the question of bias—they are incapable of recognizing and addressing this inherent limitation of the craft. Scholars have identified three deep-seated biases that are built into the professional codes that journalists follow and that have decidedly political and ideological implications.[36] These biases remain in place to this day; indeed, they may be stronger than ever.

First, to remove the controversy connected with story selection, professional journalism regards anything done by official sources—for example, government officials and prominent public figures—as the basis for legitimate news. In the partisan era of journalism, newspaper editors would claim that story selection represented their values and indicated what they thought was important. Because such an attitude was anathema in professional times, relying on official sources helped give stories legitimacy. Then, if chastised by readers for covering a particular story, an editor could say, "Hey, don't blame us, the governor (or any other official source) said it and we merely reported it." This has the added benefit of making the news fairly easy and inexpensive to cover—merely put reporters where official sources congregate and let them report what they say. This is a crucial factor in explaining why coverage of the U.S. presidency has grown dramatically during the twentieth century: there are reporters assigned to the White House and they file stories regularly, regardless of what is taking place. In the late nineteenth century, coverage of the president occupied a minuscule percentage of the "news hole" in U.S. newspapers. By the mid- to late twentieth century, the president dominated 10 to 25 percent of the news, depending upon the scope of the survey.

The limitations of this reliance on official sources are self-evident. Those in political office (and, to a lesser extent, business) wield considerable power to set the news agenda by what they speak about and, just as important, what they keep quiet about. Journalists who raise issues no official source is talking about are accused of unprofessional conduct and of attempting to introduce bias into the news. This deep-seated problem is widely recognized in the journalism scholarship. "If something important is being ignored," a writer for the *Columbia Journalism Review* asked in 2003, "doesn't the press have an obligation to force our elected officials to address it?" [37] While editors would love to proclaim "yes," the track record indicates that this does not happen unless powerful official sources are pushing the issue. Shrewd politicians and powerful figures learn how to use journalistic conventions to their advantage.[38] Journalists discover that they cannot antagonize their sources or they might get cut off from all information. For this reason the legendary I. F. Stone refused to have any relationships with people in power; he knew that once he did his ability to pursue controversial stories would be undermined.[39] Political journalism has largely degenerated into simply chronicling what one party leader says and then documenting the dissenting reply from a leader on the other side of the aisle. This reliance on official sources may give the news a conventional and mainstream feel, but it does not necessarily lead to a rigorous examination of major issues.

As the saying goes, the media do not necessarily tell you what to think, but they tell you what to think about and how to think about it. To find out why a story is getting covered and why it is getting covered the way it is, look at the sources. Because legitimate sources tend to be political and economic elites, journalists can appear as stenographers to those in power—exactly what one would expect in an authoritarian society with little or no formal press freedom. In 2003, the *New York Times* acknowledged that it should rescind the Pulitzer Prize its reporter Walter Duranty received for his coverage of the Soviet Union in the 1930s because a scholar's review of Duranty's journalism concluded that it was a "dull and largely uncritical recitation of Soviet sources." As more than one commentator noted, if U.S. news media were condemned today for "dull and largely uncritical recitation of official sources," few would escape censure.[40]

Some working journalists will recoil at this critique. For them reliance on official sources is justifiable as "democratic" because those official sources are elected or accountable to people who are elected by the citizenry. This is not a dictatorship. The reporter's job is to report what people in power say and let the reader/viewer decide who is telling the truth. The problem with this rationale is that it forgets a critical assumption of free press theory: even elected leaders need rigorous monitoring, the range of which cannot be determined solely by their elected opposition. Without outside surveillance the citizenry has no escape from the status quo, no capacity to criticize the political culture as a whole. If this watchdog function grows lax, corruption invariably grows and the electoral system decays.

In addition to this reliance on official sources, experts are also crucial to explaining and debating policy, especially in complex stories. As with sources, experts are drawn almost entirely from the establishment. Studies on the use of news sources and experts invariably point to the strong mainstream bias built into the news. An analysis of the nightly newscasts of ABC, CBS, and NBC for 2001, for example, found that the sources and experts used were overwhelmingly white, male, wealthy and Republican. (The emphasis upon Republicans can be explained mostly by the fact of a Republican administration.) The news also apparently accepts business domination of the political economy as legitimate. Only 31 representatives of labor appeared on newscasts as opposed to 955 representatives of corporations.[41]

A second flaw of journalism is its avoidance of contextualization. Contextualization was a strength of partisan journalism: it attempted to place every important issue in a larger political ideology, to make sense of it. Under professional standards, providing meaningful context and proper background tends to commit the journalist to a definite position and thereby generates the controversy professionalism is determined to avoid. Coverage instead barrages with facts and official statements. What little contextualization professional journalism does provide usually conforms to official-source consensus. To assure that news selection does not appear ideologically driven, reporters and editors grab a news hook to justify a news story. If something happens, it is news. This means that social issues such as racism and environmental degradation vanish from the headlines unless an event, such as a protest demonstration or the release of an official report, can justify coverage—or unless official sources choose to make it a story. For those outside power, generating a news hook is extraordinarily difficult and usually requires extraordinary action. The 1968 report of the Kerner Commission on Civil Disorders, for example, specifically cited the poor coverage and lack of contextualization by journalism of racial injustice issues as strongly contributing to the climate that led to the riots of the 1960s.[42]

Both of these biases of professional journalism—official sourcing and the need for news hooks—helped stimulate the birth and rapid rise of the public relations industry. By providing slick press releases, paid-for "experts," ostensibly neutral but actually bogus citizen groups, and canned news events, crafty PR agents can shape the news to suit their mostly corporate clientele. Powerful corporate interests, wary of government regulation, spend a fortune to ensure that their version of science gets a wide play in the news as objective truth.[43] Media owners welcome PR because it provides, in effect, a subsidy for them by offering filler at no cost. Surveys show that PR accounts for anywhere from 40 to 70 percent of what appears as news. Because PR is most successful if it is surreptitious, the identity of the major players and knowledge of their most successful campaigns is usually hidden from the general public. During the 1990s the PR industry underwent a major consolidation, and today the three largest advertising agencies, which now offer full service corporate communication to their clients, own eight of the ten largest U.S. public relations firms.[44]

The combined effect of these two biases and the prominence of spin produces a grand yet distressing paradox: journalism, which in theory should inspire political involvement, strips politics of meaning and promotes a broad depoliticization. Journalism is arguably better at generating apathy than informed and engaged citizens. Politics becomes antiseptic and drained of passion, of connection to the lives people lead. At its worst, journalism feeds a cynicism about the value and integrity of public life.[45] As a result, for some stories that receive massive coverage, such as unrest in the Middle East or the Clinton health care proposal in the early 1990s, Americans are almost as ignorant as they are on subjects that receive limited coverage.[46] Today's journalism is more likely to produce confusion than understanding and informed action. This creates a major dilemma for journalism. Democracy needs journalism; viable self-government in our times is unthinkable without it. But journalism also requires democracy. Unless the citizenry depends upon journalism and takes it seriously, reporters can lose incentive for completing the hard work that generates excellent journalism. The political system then becomes less responsive and corruption grows.

Thus we can restate the paradox of professional journalism as follows: Journalism in any meaningful sense cannot survive without a viable democracy. This implies that journalism must be aggressively and explicitly critical of the antidemocratic status quo and must embrace once again the old adage of "afflicting the comfortable and comforting the afflicted." In short, to remain democratic, to continue to exist, journalism must become . . . unprofessional.

The third bias of professional journalism is more subtle but arguably the most important: far from being politically neutral, journalism smuggles in values conducive to the commercial aims of owners and advertisers and to the political aims of big business. Ben Bagdikian refers to this as the "dig here, not there" phenomenon.[47] So it is that crime stories and stories about royal families and celebrities become legitimate news. (These stories are inexpensive to cover and rarely antagonize people in power.) The affairs of government are therefore subjected to much closer scrutiny than are the affairs of big business. And of government activities, those that serve the poor (such as welfare) get much more critical attention than those that serve primarily the interests of the wealthy (such as tax dodges or the role of the CIA and other institutions of national security), which are more or less off-limits. This focus on government malfeasance and this neglect of corporate misdeeds plays directly into the hands of those who wish to give more power and privileges to corporations and undermines the ability of government to regulate in the public interest. As Ed Baker observes, professional practices, along with libel laws, "favor exposing governmental rather than private (corporate) wrongdoing."[48] This, too, plays into the promotion of cynicism about public life. The corporate scandals of 2002 finally forced corporate excesses into the light, but also revealed just how much criminal or criminal-like activity had taken place for years without a shred of news media interest. The genius of professionalism in journalism is that it tends to make journalists oblivious to the compromises with authority they routinely make.

Although studies demonstrate that corporate power remains virtually unmentioned in U.S. political journalism, it is highly controversial to accuse journalism of a pro-corporate bias.[49] In the 1990s what amounts to a controlled experiment illuminated this bias. Charles Lewis, an award-winning journalist, left network television to form the Center for Public Integrity (CPI) in 1990. Receiving funding from foundations, Lewis assembled a large team of investigative journalists and researchers and had them work on several detailed investigative reports each year. The purpose was to release the reports to the news media and hope for coverage and follow-up investigative work. Lewis notes that when his group released exposés of government malfeasance, they typically received extensive coverage and follow-up. The CPI broke the story, for example, about President Clinton's "leasing" the Lincoln Bedroom in the White House to major campaign contributors. When the CPI issued reports on corporate malfeasance, however, Lewis found that press conferences were virtually empty and the stories generated almost no coverage or follow-up. What makes this striking is that the exact same research team issued both kinds of reports.[50] Were Lewis unprincipled, he would logically discontinue corporate exposés.[51]

Imagine if the president or the director of the FBI ordered news media to desist from examining corporate power in the United States. That would be considered a grotesque violation of democratic freedoms and a direct challenge to the republic's viability. It would constitute a much greater threat to democracy than Watergate. Yet when journalism—through professional practices—generates virtually the same outcome, it goes unmentioned and unrecognized in the political culture. It is a nonissue.

Arguably the weakest feature of U.S. professional journalism has been its coverage of the nation's role in the world, especially when military action is involved. Again, relying on official sources is the main culprit. Journalists who question agreed-upon assumptions by the political elite stigmatize themselves as unprofessional and political. Most major U.S. wars over the past century have been sold to the public on dubious claims if not outright lies, yet professional journalism has generally failed to warn the public. Compare the press coverage leading up to the Spanish-American War, which is a notorious example of yellow journalism—before the advent of professional journalism—to the coverage leading up to the 2003 Iraq war and it is difficult to avoid the conclusion that the quality of the reporting has not changed much.

When criticism gains prominence in the news media regarding a U.S. war, the change in coverage almost always reflects a split among the elite, as was the case with Vietnam and, more recently, Iraq during the occupation. Moreover, journalists have internalized the elite assumption that the United States is invariably a force for good in the world, determined to bring freedom and democracy to the planet. Even dissenting coverage in mainstream journalism tends to accept this assumption.[52] Similarly, journalism believes in the inherent right of the United States, and the United States alone, to invade almost any nation it chooses. Debate over whether a specific invasion is appropriate on strategic or tactical grounds might result, but the fundamental right to invade is usually off-limits to critical analysis. After all, it is a view shared across the spectrum of U.S. policy elites.

Woeful press coverage of the U.S. role in the world has grave consequences for everyone. Perhaps the most important issue for any society to decide is whether to go to war, to put people to death. The Supreme Court recognizes the special responsibility of the media in this regard. As Justice Potter Stewart wrote in his opinion on the Pentagon Papers case, "In the absence of governmental checks and balances present in other areas of our national life, the only effective restraint upon executive policy and power in the areas of national defense and international affairs may lie in an enlightened citizenry—in an informed and critical public opinion which alone can here protect the values of democratic government."[53] The press is granted privileges in exchange for providing this democratic service, although it is not apparently accountable to anyone to deliver on its end of the bargain.

Although the professional code incorporates these three general biases, professional journalism is also malleable. Over the years it has been influenced by factors such as the rise of new communication technologies.[54] Mass movements can also shape journalism. In moments of surging social movements, professional journalism can improve the quantity and quality of coverage. Certainly coverage of issues vital to African Americans and women shifted from the 1950s to the 1970s, reflecting the emergence of the civil rights and feminist movements. It works in the other direction, too. In the 1940s, for example, when the U.S. labor movement was at its zenith, full-time labor editors and reporters abounded on U.S. daily newspapers. Even ferociously anti-labor newspapers such as the *Chicago Tribune* covered the labor beat. The 1937 Flint sit-down strike that launched the United Auto Workers and the trade union movement became a major national news story. By the 1980s, however, no more than a couple of dozen labor beat reporters worked for U.S. dailies. (The number is well below ten and fast approaching zero today.) Hence, the 1989 Pittstown sit-down strike—the largest since Flint—went virtually unreported in the U.S. media. As the labor movement declined, coverage of labor was dropped. People still work, poverty among workers is growing, workplace conflicts are as important as ever, but labor issues are no longer considered newsworthy because organized labor is no longer powerful.[55]

The high-water mark for professional journalism spanned from the 1950s to the 1970s when U.S. journalists had relative autonomy to pursue their stories and considerable resources to hone their craft. Factual accuracy was emphasized. The best journalism came (and still comes) when official sources disagreed. In these cases, professional journalism could be sparkling. During this era, especially beginning in the 1960s, official sources were considerably more liberal than they would become by the 1980s. Along with the increase in social activism overall, this liberalism offered journalists the freedom to take risks and cover stories that would be much more difficult to cover in the 1980s, when nearly all the political class had become enthralled with "the market." Someone like Ralph Nader routinely received extensive press coverage for his consumer campaigns during the 1960s and early 1970s. The consumer and environmental legislation he is responsible for pushing into law during this period is little short of astounding by contemporary standards. By the conservative and corporate-oriented 1990s, however, he had been scripted out of the political culture and journalism, leading him to enter electoral politics to express his frustration with the status quo.

But the quality of journalism or the amount of autonomy should not be exaggerated, even during this "golden age." The 1950s were little short of a "dark age" for journalists who rejected the Cold War consensus. An underground press predicated upon the problems in contemporary journalism developed by the 1960s, and hard-edged criticism of journalism's flaws abounded. The mainstream media in every community maintained a code of silence about the area's wealthiest and most powerful individuals and corporations. Media owners still wanted their friends and business pals to receive kid-glove treatment in their media, and so they did, except after the most egregious maneuvers. Similarly, newspapers, even prestigious ones like the *Los Angeles Times*, used their power to aid the economic projects of the newspaper's owners.[56] Pressure to shape editorial coverage to serve the needs of major advertisers recurred.

Still, even with deep-seated biases built into journalism's code, some great journalists have done brilliant work for mainstream outlets. Decade after decade, newsrooms have produced outstanding journalists whose contributions to building a democratic and just society have been immeasurable.[57] In recent times, one thinks of the *Philadelphia Inquirer*'s Donald Bartlett and James Steele.[58] Some of the most impressive reporting has come in books, ranging from those by Rachel Carson and Robert Caro to those by Studs Terkel and Betty Friedan. The list is really quite long. To some extent this reflects a book's ability to convey detailed and complex material, but it also highlights how many great journalists have had to work outside the routine of standard newsroom journalism to cover the stories they deemed important. Their books point toward what can be done but generally isn't being done. Along these lines, it is worth noting that many of the twentieth-century's finest journalists—Ben Bagdikian, George Seldes, A. J. Liebling, I. F. Stone, Jessica Mitford, David Halberstam, Bill Moyers, and William Greider—have been among its foremost media critics. In short, this great work has often been completed not because of the system so much as in spite of it.

THE COMMERCIALIZATION OF JOURNALISM

Professional journalism, as we have seen, did not initially encounter opposition from most major media owners—indeed, professionalism was encouraged. Owners and progressive journalists struggled to demarcate professional journalism's contours, but by the middle of the twentieth century the discipline had settled into its current form. It made sense for media owners to grant some autonomy to journalists because it gave their product more credibility and worked to enhance their commercial prospects. The autonomy granted journalists was always relative, however, and the manner in which the professional code evolved put significant limitations on the capacity of professional journalism to serve as a democratic force.

Yet the professional journalism "deal" was never formalized, and newsworkers' unions could never garner enough power to wrest control of journalism (and budgets) from media owners. By the 1980s the "deal" made less and less sense for media owners. Relaxation of media ownership regulations, along with general market pressures, led to wave after wave of media deal making and mega-corporations. These gigantic firms, often media conglomerates that paid vast sums to purchase news media, wanted and needed to generate significant returns to pay down debt and satisfy investors. For these firms, autonomy for news divisions became nonsensical. After all, media conglomerates expected their other workers to directly enhance the bottom line.

In this context, journalism has increasingly become explicitly commercial; professionalism can no longer offer as much protection from commercial pressure. Although this is the primary and overarching factor explaining recent developments in journalism, it is not the sole factor. New commercial news media enabled by new technologies—in particular, round-the-clock TV news channels and the Internet—have intensified the need for fresh and attention-getting stories.[59] Libel court rulings and government secrecy laws and regulations have made it much more difficult and cost prohibitive to investigate corporations and governments.[60] One irony of neoliberalism—as manifested in the Bush-Cheney variant—is that its contempt for government (and its much professed love of citizens' wisdom) requires it to discourage the citizenry from knowing what the government is doing in its name. Similarly, as journalism becomes more explicitly directed by market concerns, the overall depoliticization of society generated by the media will discourage political coverage by journalists. And, as I will discuss in the next chapter, the conservative campaign against the "liberal media" has produced a chilling effect on journalism's willingness to ask tough questions of those in power. In combination, these factors have led to a crisis in professional journalism.

The widely chronicled commercial attack on autonomy assumes many forms.[61] News budgets have been subject to significant cuts. By the 1990s, commercial news media were "forced to embrace the financial discipline required by parent companies that no longer looked at news as a golden child and free-spending spirit even when it refused to be bound by life's practicalities."[62] A 2002 Project for Excellence in Journalism survey of U.S. journalists found them "a grumpy lot," due largely to budget cuts, lower salaries, no raises, and job insecurity.[63] There was a virtual newsroom uprising at the *Wall Street Journal* in December 2002, for example, when parent company Dow Jones announced sweeping cuts in the number of senior journalists while the firm's executive ranks remained untouched.[64] The media firms argue that such cutbacks are necessary to remain competitive, but many journalists claim that giant firms use their market power to cut resources for news in order to make a short-term profit grab. In 2001 the publisher of the *San Jose Mercury-News*, Jay Harris, resigned his position in protest of unnecessary editorial cutbacks mandated by the paper's parent company, Knight-Ridder. As Harris put it, cutbacks were unjustifiable because his newspaper, like most others, was raking in enormous profits.[65]

Lowballing editorial budgets has proven extremely profitable, at least in the short term. The great commercial success story of U.S. journalism has been the Fox News Channel, which has cut costs to the bone by replacing expensive conventional journalism with celebrity pontificators.[66] Using this formula, Fox News was able to generate roughly equivalent profits to CNN by 1999–2000 and spent far less than CNN to do so.[67] The operating profit at News Corporation's U.S. cable channels, which includes the Fox News Channel, more than tripled from the third quarter of 2001 to the third quarter of 2002.[68] The rise of media conglomerates has made it far easier for a firm to spread its editorial budgets across several different media, so that the same journalist can report for a media firm's newspaper, website, broadcast TV station, cable TV channel, and radio station.[69] The Internet only accelerates this process. It provides much of the incentive for firms to become large conglomerates because it offers tremendous cost savings compared to firms with a smaller arsenal of media properties.[70] Indeed, even separate firms are partnering (especially where regulations prohibit them from merging) to spread editorial budgets across several media.[71] When ABC News and CNN were negotiating a merger in 2002, one observer deemed it "an unholy alliance that could only make sense to cost-cutters."[72] One Wall Street analyst thought the merger would lead to cost savings (including labor costs) of $100 million to $200 million.[73] As Av Westin, the Emmy Award–winning ABC journalist and news executive, put it in 2001, "To expect that any corporate manager will reinvest savings in better news programming is, I fear, a delusion."[74]

The effects of this budget-cutting mania in journalism have been almost entirely negative. A relaxation or alteration, sometimes severe, of professional news standards has resulted, although professional standards have not collapsed entirely. Journalists still must not invent sources or consciously lie, and those caught will usually be fired and banned from the profession.[75] The scandal over Jayson Blair, the *New York Times* reporter who doctored stories and was fired in 2003, is instructive. Blair made the cover of *Newsweek* and received enormous media attention week after week and the *Times*'s two top editors were forced out.[76] (His lies and deceit were relatively trivial; far more egregious omissions and errors built into the professional code sail by without comment, a point I return to in chapter 3.) But what gets covered and how it gets covered—the meat and potatoes of journalism—have changed for the worse. Factual accuracy and honesty are all well and good, but they are fairly trivial in a story about a celebrity's trial or a donkey getting a shampoo. The broader question is how the decline in resources and the pressure to generate profits pushes factually accurate journalism to concentrate upon some stories over others. To quote Trudy Lieberman, "You can't report what you don't pursue."[77]

It is here that the attack on professional standards is striking. Fewer reporters means that PR operatives can more easily get their clients' unadulterated messages into the news. Two executives for Edelman Public Relations exulted in 2000 that media consolidation and conglomeration had created fewer reporters and resources and, therefore, "an increased likelihood that press releases will be used word-for-word, in part if not in whole."[78] International coverage has been a victim of corporate cost cuts, and it has plummeted over the past two decades. This decline only worsens the quality of news coverage of the U.S. role in the world.[79] The United States is the dominant global military power acting in the name of its people, and the large majority of the population has difficulty answering elementary questions about global geography, history, or politics.

Investigative reporting—that is, original research into public issues, once considered the hallmark of feisty "fourth estate" journalism in a free society—is on the endangered species list. Hard investigations cost more than official source stenography, and they require skilled, experienced journalists. For media companies, it is considerably more lucrative to have inexperienced journalists fill the news hole with easy stories regurgitating proclamations of the powerful. Investigative journalism has also become suspect in this corporate-driven society because media firms have little incentive to produce journalism that might anger powerful business or governmental institutions. A five-year study of investigative journalism on TV news completed in 2002 determined that investigative journalism has all but disappeared from the nation's commercial airwaves. Much of what was passed off as original investigative work—only 1 percent of TV news programming—included stories such as "women illegally injecting silicone at parties."[80] As Charles Lewis points out, much of what masquerades as investigative work on network TV news is actually spoon-fed leaks from government sources.[81] Even in these cases, as investigative reporter Greg Palast observes, little actual journalistic inquiry into the truth occurs.[82]

This combination of an increasing need to rely on PR and a declining commitment to investigative journalism plays directly into the hands of powerful commercial interests, especially on environmental and public health stories when scientific expertise is required to explain the issues. It is in such contexts, as authors Sheldon Rampton and John Stauber have documented, that corporations have been generous in providing the media with self-interested versions of science.[83]

In the current commercially stripped-down climate, professional reliance upon official sources as the basis for news—always a problem—has become debilitating. It is increasingly rare that reporters bother to determine who is telling the truth when official sources disagree on the facts. Investigating factual disputes takes time and could cast the pall of bias over the journalist, depending upon whom the findings favored. When, for example, in 2002 Democrats criticized Halliburton for not paying taxes under Dick Cheney's leadership, the press ran the charges and Halliburton's denial. Few journalists, in the professional mainstream press at least, appeared to determine who was telling the truth.[84] This environment becomes a scoundrel's paradise in which officials can lie with virtual impunity; and officials' opponents, not journalists, must establish the truth, and such opponents can always be dismissed as partisan. "Bound by professional strictures, news reporters can wind up giving a lie the same weight as the truth," David Greenberg warns. In such an environment "raising questions of truthfulness can seem awfully close to taking sides in a partisan debate." Frustrated journalists hungry for the muckraking mantle merely zero in on politicians' lies about personal matters because "here, the press can strut its skepticism without positioning itself ideologically." As Greenburg concludes, the "current rules end up encouraging media hysteria about personal lies of scant importance and deterring inquiry into topics that matter incalculably more."[85] "The nation's media," a *Washington Post* reporter acknowledged in 2003, "have yet to find a clear and effective way to report incorrect impressions and untruthful statements, particularly those that emanate from the White House. . . . Journalists are notoriously reluctant to use the word 'lie' when describing the statements of public officials."[86]

Today journalists are far more comfortable casting political debate in terms of strategies and spin than locating facts. As a result, much of the press coverage of the political response to the 2002 corporate scandals—to which I return below—dwelled upon how the parties hoped to spin the issue to their advantage.[87] (Of course this obsession with how politicians spin—indeed, journalists sometimes chastise politicians who fail to spin effectively—rather than with getting at the truth breeds a certain contempt for public life.[88]) Av Westin detailed the implications of professional journalism's deterioration in his Freedom Forum handbook for TV journalists: "As a result, the audience has become accustomed to shoddy reporting to the point that the average viewer does not necessarily expect quality journalism and probably could not discern the difference between a well-produced story and a below-average one. The sad truth is that because the mass audience cannot perceive the difference, management is reluctant to spend more money to improve the product."[89]

Corporate cutbacks also have allowed commercialism to penetrate journalism. Pressure to shape stories to suit advertisers and owners is not new, and much of the professional code has attempted to minimize it. But corporate management has been grinding away at news divisions to play commercial ball. Over time journalists have been worn down, and those who have survived have internalized the necessary corporate values. One survey conducted by the trade publication *Electronic Media* in 2001 found that the vast majority of TV station executives found their news departments "cooperative" in shaping the news to assist in "nontraditional revenue development," in which the news department co-promotes events that use advertisers as experts.[90] The Pew Research Center survey of three hundred journalists released in 2000 found that nearly half of them acknowledged sometimes consciously engaging in self-censorship to serve the commercial interests of their employer or advertisers, and only one-quarter of them stated that this never happened to their knowledge.[91]

This commercial penetration of professional journalism, insofar as it is direct, assumes two forms. First, commercial interests produce or directly penetrate the news itself, corrupting integrity. This process has been well chronicled.[92] To some extent it entails savvy corporate marketers who produce slick video features to be played on TV newscasts as news stories but include a plug for the firm's product.[93] When the traditional "news hole" is open for commercial messages, obituaries can be sold, ads might run on the front page, or commercials can overlay editorial content.[94] The practice of permitting advertisers to influence the news and how it is covered has become more common, especially in health care and medicine, where commercial corruption of reporting has become, pun intended, epidemic.[95] In 2002 an editor of the *New York Post* went so far as to inform publicists that buying an ad might buy coverage.[96] By 2003, some local TV stations were "selling" editorial segments to advertisers.[97] The *Des Moines Register* was engaged in "custom publishing," whereby its reporters would produce special editorial sections on behalf of major advertisers. "You could make the argument that we have already crossed the (ethical) line with advertorials," the president of the American Society of Newspaper Editors noted. "Once the barn door is open, people get together and rationalize how it can be done for anything," the president of the Society of Professional Journalists observed.[98]

Commercialism also extends to individual journalists, and the traditional prohibition against accepting compensation for particular content has been weakened. Journalists figure they might as well profit, and some have stooped to hawking products.[99] Charlie Rose, a correspondent for both PBS and CBS, for example, was the master of ceremonies for Coca-Cola's annual shareholders meeting in 2002.[100] Further, marketing newscasters as "celebrities" and "brands" offers a relatively inexpensive way for media firms to increase ratings, sales, and profits from their news assets.[101] In 2002, for instance, a New York TV weatherman agreed to go out on televised dates, which would be critiqued on-air by his colleagues the next day.[102] And the punishment for being explicitly commercial is not as dire as it once was—indeed, some reporters are being rewarded for their behavior. When an ABC medical journalist was suspended for a week for endorsing Tylenol in a radio commercial in 2002, she left ABC to accept a lucrative position at Johnson & Johnson, Tylenol's parent company.[103] In another case, a health reporter who had been fired by a Baltimore TV station because of her "blundering efforts to make money from the medical institutions she had been covering" parlayed her ties into a weekly TV health news program that was described by one Baltimore journalist as "an alarming parade of commercial tie-ins."[104] Accepting direct commercial bribes remains taboo, but the wealth of indirect commercial influences makes the prohibition practically moot.

The second form that commercial penetration of journalism assumes is another traditional problem that professionalism was intended to eliminate: journalists using their privileges to report favorably on their owner's commercial ventures or investments. The major TV networks have used their news programs to promote their other media fare, such as when ABC News promoted Disney's 2001 film *Pearl Harbor* or played up the fictitious town of Push, Nevada, which was the name of a short-lived prime-time series.[105] *NBC Nightly News* featured more than twice the amount of news coverage of the 2002 Winter Olympics than did *ABC World News Tonight*, and nearly seven times more coverage than did *CBS Evening News*. Is it any surprise that NBC was the broadcaster of the Winter Olympics?[106] CBS was not to be outdone. In 2000 it broadcast frequent "reports" on its "reality" program *Survivor* and loaned out a journalist to conduct a weekly interview program on another "reality" show, *Big Brother*.[107] Researcher Matt McAllister has demonstrated that the CBS morning program *The Early Show* was particularly weighted with "news reports" hyping *Survivor*.[108] An industry analysis of the content of morning news shows on network TV found them laden with promotional material for the network's programs masquerading as news, concluding, "The morning shows are shameless promotional vehicles."[109] In 2001 AOL Time Warner's *CNN Headline News* acknowledged that it was plugging other AOL Time Warner products and channels in its news headlines; the practice was in fact a logical outcome of the corporate commitment to synergy.[110] "The drive to achieve synergy," journalist Ken Auletta remarked in 2002, "is often journalism's poison."[111]

Corporate and commercial pressures exerted indirectly are less likely to be recognized as such by journalists or the public. The flip side of the reluctance to spend money on investigative or international coverage, and the equal reluctance to antagonize powerful sources, is an increased emphasis on trivial stories that give the appearance of controversy and conflict but rarely have anything to do with significant issues. Study after study reveal a general decline in the amount of hard news relative to fluff.[112] Some critics argued that in the aftermath of the 9/11 terrorist attacks, U.S. news media would return to their "historic mission," but such fantasies were short-lived.[113] A 2003 study published by the Council for Excellence in Government indicated that over the preceding twenty years news coverage of the federal government dropped by 31 percent on TV news shows, 12 percent in national newspapers, and 39 percent in regional newspapers. "Television and newspapers are the modern civics teachers for most of us," the council's president noted glumly.[114]

A central preoccupation of the news has become the activities and personal lives of celebrities.[115] Stories about Winona Ryder's shoplifting trial, Robert Blake's murder arrest, and Gary Condit's sexual affairs dominated 2001 and 2002 news.[116] By 2003–04 Kobe Bryant and Michael Jackson's legal travails were the flavors of the month.[117] Politicians stand a far greater chance of becoming the object of news media scrutiny if they are rumored to have ten outstanding parking tickets or to have skipped out on a bar bill at a topless club than if they quietly use their power to funnel billions of public dollars to powerful special interests. The justification for this caliber of journalism is that these stories are popular and therefore profitable, and commercial news needs to "give the people what they want." Even leaving aside the question of whether journalism should be determined by marketing polls, this is circular logic.[118] The motive behind this journalism is as much supply as demand, pressure from the powerful as much as pressure from the powerless. Fluff is cheaper and easier to cover than hard news and rarely angers those in power, while it provides an illusion of controversy to the public. Over time whatever taste the public has for this type of fare is encouraged through extensive exposure. Had a similar commitment to exposés of government and corporate corruption been made, a public taste might well have developed for those stories as well. But that is not an option that the people are given.

Celebrities and trivial personal indiscretions are not all that commercial journalism favors. Crime and violence meet commercial criteria as well. As with sensationalism, crime stories have existed as long as profit-driven mass circulation newspapers; in the current environment, however, crime and disaster news have become the centerpiece of journalism, especially local TV news. Television news is awash in stories about traffic and airplane accidents, fires and murders.[119] The Washington serial sniper story of October 2002 was a textbook example of this phenomenon. It generated high ratings and took no great skill or expense to cover. It received round-the-clock coverage, yet the news media had little to report, so much of the "news" was hashing over rumors, bland repetition, and idle speculation that turned out to be mostly incorrect. As Ted Koppel put it, the media were "going nuts" over what he termed a "dreadful but relatively minor threat" in the bigger scheme of things.[120] Outside of the affected region, it was largely a waste of time, but a commercially lucrative waste of time. The implications of all this crime coverage have been demonstrated by scholars: the plethora of crime stories has led heavy TV watchers to think crime is far worse in their communities than it actually is. The coverage has also overemphasized African Americans as criminals and whites as victims, with negative repercussions for racial attitudes and race relations.[121] Moreover, it has had the perverse effect of encouraging popular support for draconian measures to stem the bogus "crime wave," which has proven disastrous for African American communities.[122]

Commercialism also pushes journalists to make content directed at demographics considered desirable by media owners and big ticket advertisers.[123] The notion of journalism as a public service institution aimed at the entire population has vanished, except rhetorically. Today much of journalism is directed at the middle and upper classes while the working class and the poor have been ignored.[124] "I can't say we're going to sell more soap [than the competition]," a CNN executive exulted in 2003, "but we're damn well going to sell more financial services."[125] Coverage of labor issues has plummeted in the past generation.[126] African Americans and Latinos are invisible or misrepresented in the news partly because they are not considered economically attractive to advertisers.[127] This perception fuels the racially biased portrayals of crime, in part because whites are disproportionately the target audience. Ben Bagdikian captured this class bias well in a 2001 essay: "If the Dow Jones Industrial Average dropped steadily for twenty years it would be front page and leading broadcast news day after day until the government took action. That 32 million of our population have their housing, food, and clothing 'index' drop steadily for more than 30 years is worth only an occasional feature story about an individual or statistical fragments in the back pages of our most influential news organizations."[128] A survey released by the Catholic Campaign for Human Development in 2003 confirmed that most Americans had no idea that nearly 33 million citizens lived in poverty in this country; most thought the total was between 1 and 5 million.[129]

The flip side to the marginalization of the poor and working class in the news has been the elevation of business to center stage. If labor reporting went from being a standard position at daily newspapers two or three generations ago to being nearly extinct by 2004, business reporting skyrocketed to the point where business news and general news seemingly converged. Although the majority of Americans have little direct interest in the stock market—and it is far from the most pressing immediate economic issue in their lives—news media seemingly assume most Americans are stock traders with a passionate concern about equity and bond markets. Hence, even local TV broadcasts comment on daily New York Stock Exchange trading, cable news channels feature a constant stock market ticker, and even newspapers with relatively small circulations include a business section. Schools of journalism have responded to this development, and chairs in business journalism have mushroomed across college campuses. "Business journalism is hot," a Columbia University Journalism School official noted. "Journalists see it as a career track."[130]

Regrettably, however, the turn to business journalism has not encouraged critical scrutiny of corporations and their affect on public life. Even close examination of business behavior to protect investors and consumers has not increased.[131] To the contrary, business journalism is, as one observer put it, "teeming with reverence for the accumulation of wealth."[132] To some extent this is due to the rah-rah capitalist ethos that marinates corporate media, and is hardwired into business journalism, with its active promotion of wealth accumulation and barely concealed contempt for obstacles put in front of the pursuit of profit. But it is also due to the reliance upon corporate sources for business news, the marginalization of critical sources, the use of corporate PR as the basis for news, and the fear of antagonizing corporate advertisers.[133]

The corruption of business reporting had become so egregious that in 2002 the New York Stock Exchange was pressing for regulations that would require journalists to disclose the financial interests of the stock market analysts they used in their news stories.[134] By 2002 media critics at mainstream outlets concurred that business journalism, rather than monitoring the excesses of the business expansion of the 1990s, actually played a strong part in magnifying them and "inflating the bubble."[135] As columnist Norman Solomon observed, "The bubble was filled with hot air from hyperventilating journalists."[136] Yet few journalists questioned the turn away from labor coverage and toward lavish business reporting because it conforms to the norms of the professional code. It is not seen as "self-censorship" to shape news content in such a manner. That is the genius of professionalism as a form of regulation.

COVERING THE CORPORATE SCANDAL

These core problems for contemporary journalism came together in the 2001–02 corporate scandals. The result was one of the darkest and most depressing episodes in the recent history of U.S. journalism and its nearly complete abrogation of its watchdog role. The news coverage played a large, perhaps even decisive, role in the collapse of anything remotely close to a democratic resolution to this crisis.

Enron filed for bankruptcy in 2001; WorldCom's $107 billion free fall and bankruptcy followed in 2002.[137] Arthur Andersen, Global Crossing, and a host of other firms collapsed shortly afterward.[138] These historically unprecedented corporate collapses were fraught with fraud and corruption and bilked workers, taxpayers, pensioners and investors out of billions of dollars. But this might be considered capitalism as usual, if you can get away with it, and many did and do. What was striking about these scandals, as two journalists put it, was that "the fraud occurred in the most heavily regulated and monitored area of corporate activity."[139] Enron was described by Charles Lewis, the journalist responsible for much of the investigation into its activities, as "a company inordinately dependent on government favors."[140] Much of the fraud perpetrated by Enron, WorldCom, Global Crossing, and the others resulted from politicians pushing through highly dubious "deregulation" schemes.[141] Enron and Arthur Andersen were among the largest political contributors to political candidates in the nation, with most of the money going to Republicans.[142] Global Crossing "tossed more money around town than Enron," observed *Business Week*, and, if anything, spread its largesse more toward Democrats than Republicans as it sought government support for its activities.[143] In short, this was not a business scandal. This was a political scandal of the highest magnitude. It demonstrated the built-in corruption in governance and the broader political economy that occurs at the highest levels.

Yet despite the vast resources devoted to business journalism in the 1990s, the media missed the developing story entirely. It failed utterly in its role as an early alarm system for social problems.[144] By the mid-1990s the alternative press was already reporting evidence of Enron's chicanery, and Ralph Nader and his cohorts were aggressively condemning the highly dubious nature of Enron's and WorldCom's activities, among others. These reports were resolutely ignored by the mainstream.[145] Indeed, as the *New York Times* later conceded, when WorldCom CEO Bernard Ebbers spoke to the National Press Club in 2000, even as the Ponzi scheme WorldCom had been using to grow was unraveling, the assembled journalists gave him a loud round of applause and the mood was "celebratory."[146] Enron was named by *Fortune* magazine as "America's Most Innovative Company" every single year from 1995 to 2000.[147] A data search of mainstream news (and business news) coverage for "Enron" prior to 2001 finds "little but praise for its market innovations."[148] Only later did the public learn that these firms had courted the media with the same vigilance and skill that they usually reserved for politicians. Both the *New York Times* and Viacom had major business ventures with Enron, for example, and Enron paid several prominent journalists amounts ranging from

$50,000 to $100,000 to "consult" for them.[149] Enron played all the angles; it was an original underwriter for a PBS six-part series on globalization. While it eventually aired in 2002, Enron's name was quietly removed from the list of funders.[150]

The financial collapse of these firms by 2001 and 2002, along with the transparent use of fraudulent and illegal techniques to bilk people out of billions, finally made this a very big news story. Moreover, there were grounds to believe that it would become a political scandal of the highest magnitude, arguably on a par with Watergate. For starters, George W. Bush, Cheney, and others in the administration had extremely close relations with Enron and its executives.[151] Enron CEO Kenneth Lay and his fellow executives had been major contributors to Bush's political career.[152] At a 1997 party for Enron executive Rich Kinder—at which company executives joked about using bogus accounting tricks to make "a kazillion dollars," that was attended by then-governor George W. Bush—former president George H. W. Bush told Kinder, "You have been fantastic to the Bush family. I don't think anybody did more than you did to support [my son] George."[153] The payoff for Enron of having George W. Bush enter the White House was immediate: Enron executives played a prominent role in helping Cheney develop an energy policy in 2001, and the Bush administration helped reduce Enron's culpability (and that of many other corporations) for the California energy scandal in the newly deregulated market in 2001.[154]

Democrats should have had a field day with this issue. After all, the comparatively trivial Whitewater scandal generated a special prosecutor who was given more than five years and a large staff and budget to investigate Clinton's conduct, though no crimes concerning Whitewater were ever established. And had the Democrats gone to war on this issue, journalists would have had ample support from "official sources" to warrant massive coverage. But Democrats didn't pursue an investigation primarily because they, too, were culpable. They had presided over the deregulation fiascos as well and they had corporate blood money filling their campaign coffers.[155] In the 2002 election cycle, corporations convicted of crimes since 1990 contributed over $9 million to the two major parties, and this does not include corporate PAC donations or individual donations by corporate executives.[156] While the Republicans received the vast majority, the Democrats got their share. If this story had been pursued, no one could predict where it would stop. Consequently, the Democrats, led by longtime deregulation proponent Senator Joseph Lieberman of Connecticut, shared the Republicans' desire to downplay the political aspects of the crisis and convert it into a business scandal in which a few rogue CEOs had stepped out of line.[157] Accordingly, without high-level official sources pushing it as a political scandal, journalists easily focused on it as a business story. Some business and trade press reporting was first-rate, but the crucial link between corporate crime and political corruption all but disappeared. Because of its focus, the story was primarily relegated to the business pages, where it could become a story of inappropriate accounting methods and private malfeasance. On the front pages, meanwhile, it was replaced by whatever the official sources wished to talk about, like the prospective war in Iraq.

But the dwindling press coverage of these corporate scandals went beyond the traditional limitations of professional journalism. It also reflected the core problem of entrusting the news to large profit-motivated and self-interested business organizations. The CEO of the New York Times Company stated it well in 2002:

> Historically, the press's ability to act as a check on the actions of government has been helped by the fact that the two institutions are constitutionally separated, organizationally and financially. The press does not depend on government officials either for its standing or its resources.

> But it has a much more intricate relationship with big business. Today's news media are themselves frequently a part of large, often global corporations dependent on advertising revenue that, increasingly, comes from other large corporations. As public companies themselves, the news media are under the same kind of pressure to create "shareholder value," by reducing costs and increasing earnings,

as are other public companies. And they face numerous conflicts of interest as they grow larger and more diversified.[158]

In short, the corporate news media have a vested interest in the corporate system. The largest media firms are members in good standing in the corporate community and are closely linked to it through business relations, shared investors, interlocking directors, and common political values. This status pushes the news media, as Tom Shales put it, to "paint as rosy a picture of the economy as possible."[159] It encouraged the press coverage of the corporate political scandals of 2001 and 2002 to revert to a "crisis management mode" in which the structural and institutional determinants of the corruption remained unexamined and unexposed.[160] By golly, the system works.

One more layer to this story is necessary for a full understanding of the news coverage of the corporate scandals, and it concerns the media corporations' conduct. These firms were hardly innocent bystanders perched on the moral high ground as they reported upon the Enrons and Global Crossings of the world. Their CEOs, like the executives at Enron, had watched their salaries shoot off the charts while earnings for ordinary workers stagnated and layoffs abounded.[161] Their CEOs, too, made killings selling off vastly overpriced stock when they knew their firms were clunkers but the media were still reporting on them as if they were up-and-comers.[162] Media firms, too, like WorldCom and Enron, employed questionable accounting practices that inflated profit expectations and fleeced workers.[163] Moreover, a stunning number of major media corporations and executives were under investigation for criminal activities by 2002, including Disney CEO Michael Eisner, Rupert Murdoch's News Corporation, Charter Communications, and Vivendi Universal.[164]

In keeping with the notion that the closer an industry is to being explicitly regulated, the higher the likelihood of extreme corruption, media firms are a natural hotspot for flimflam. In 2002 five former executives at the bankrupt Adelphia Communications (a regulated cable TV company) were arrested and charged with "orchestrating one of the largest frauds to take place at a U.S. public company."[165] The media company atop the corporate crime blotter was none other than Time Warner, which faced a series of lawsuits and criminal investigations from the Securities and Exchange Commission and the Department of Justice. It was charged with heavily distorting its books, including inflating one-time advertising revenues by nearly $200 million.[166] Under investigation were complex transactions Time Warner made with the discredited Qwest Communications and WorldCom.[167] And of course some media giants, such as Viacom, had links to Enron and its fraudulent activities.[168] Media firms historically have been understandably reluctant to cover their own misdeeds in their news media, and they could hardly be enthusiastic about a no-holds-barred journalism that would uncover the entire corporate crime story.[169]

Press coverage of the scandal calmed a potential hurricane of a story to a mild rain shower. In the summer of 2003, Enron's court-appointed examiner acknowledged that several leading Wall Street banks had participated in Enron's deception; a *Fortune* magazine investigation concluded that the banks had been in on the fraud for years.[170] But, as *Fortune* concluded, "the banks got off easy."[171] World-Com, which had committed the biggest known fraud in U.S. history, renamed itself MCI and, in 2003, was awarded a $30 million contract by the federal government to build a wireless network in Iraq.[172] "Looking back on 2002," a public interest group observed, "it is hard to avoid the conclusion that the big corporations won. Confronted with a crisis of epic proportions, they emerged with bloodied noses and sullied reputations, but little more."[173] In the summer of 2002, when the crisis was at its peak, both Bush and Cheney gave speeches railing against corporate misconduct even as they aggressively pursued corporations and wealthy individuals for campaign contributions.[174] But even before then, in the spring, the business press acknowledged that the storm had passed and that corporate reform would be modest.[175]

It was left to syndicated columnist Molly Ivins to put the matter in perspective. In a piece outlining the chummy connection between the relevant members of Congress responsible for overseeing the investigation of corporate fraud with the very industries most likely to be engaged in crime, Ivins concluded, "They've already called off the reform effort; it's over. Corporate muscle showed up and shut it down. ...Bottom line: It's all going to happen again. We learned zip from our entire financial collapse. Our political system is too bought-off to respond intelligently."[176] The economist Mark Weisbrot captured the irony of the situation: "Our Congress and the executive branch have become so corrupted by our system of legalized bribery—political campaign contributions—that they cannot even enact positive reforms that are desired by most of the business class."[177]

Direct and indirect commercial pressures upon journalism, have had an almost entirely negative impact on reporting. Yet a broader political economic pressure is perhaps more insidious. In a largely depoliticized society, as ours has become with the rise of corporate culture, there may be little effective demand for political journalism. Depoliticization is built into the broader political culture of the United States; the media encourage the process but are not primarily responsible for it. Without a strong political culture excellent journalism will flounder; the public will not demand it. And if the political system is corrupt and removed from popular influence, journalists will have less incentive to produce hard-hitting exposés because no tangible political reform will result. So in the United States outstanding investigative reports are still delivered, but other journalists do not push these stories along, especially if no one in power takes an interest. The stories fall like stones to the bottom of the ocean without a ripple.

This culture brings media outlets to a fork in the road. Do they battle the trend and provide powerful political journalism even if it costs more and may not have a great deal of immediate market demand in the hope of generating a strong market for hard news down the road?[178] Or do they acknowledge depoliticization, especially among the commercially crucial 18–34 age group, and tailor the news to make it more entertaining and engaging to that target audience—and therefore profitable for their company? [179] Do they, in other words, opt for what Susan Douglas calls the "narcissism bias," meaning news that accepts and therefore encourages political withdrawal by emphasizing trivia and "lifestyle" reporting?[180] The news media have opted for this latter route since it makes far more commercial sense in the short term and because it costs less. But it undermines journalism's *raison d'être*.[181] Major daily newspapers have recently launched free weeklies to attract young readers; these papers have little of what is traditionally regarded as quality journalism.[182]

People who want light entertainment and unchallenging tidbits that pass for journalism should watch a comedy program rather than the news, and many Americans do exactly that. One 2000 study showed that more than one-third of Americans under thirty regard comedy shows like Jay Leno's *Tonight Show* as their primary source for news.[183] After watering down and dumbing down TV news until it is a joke while making a killing with inexpensive and inane fare, stations eventually found that their shrinking audience made news programs untenable. Accordingly, some local commercial television stations have discontinued their news programming.[184]

One measure of the deep crisis afflicting U.S. journalism is the morale of working editors and journalists. For decades journalists were highly sensitive to outside criticism of their profession and proud of their role in society. Bookstores teemed with volumes penned by journalists telling of their impressive accomplishments. No more. Journalists' morale has gone into a tailspin. Prominent journalists and media figures such as John Hockenberry, David Halberstam, PBS president Pat Mitchell, and Walter Cronkite decry the state of journalism, with Cronkite going so far as to question whether democracy can "even survive."[185] Rank-and-file reporters compile volumes on the decline of journalism, replete with case studies.[186] Even Leonard Downie Jr. and Robert G. Kaiser, the current national and associate editors of the *Washington Post*, in their 2002 *The News about the News: American Journalism in Peril,* make a devastating critique of the bankruptcy of U.S. journalism brought on by commercial pressures.[187]

Harvard's Howard Gardner and two other scholars published a long-term study of journalists in 2001 that revealed how "overwhelmed" journalists feel by commercial pressures and the "nightmare" atmosphere of their craft. They despair because they are not "allowed to pursue the mission that inspired them to enter the field."[188] The *Columbia Journalism Review* published the results of a survey of TV news directors who admitted that, due overwhelmingly to commercial factors, "pessimism rules in TV newsrooms."[189] Linda Foley, president of the Newspaper Guild, reported that the number one concern of her members, far more than wages and job security, is the decline in the quality of the profession.[190] A 2001 survey of working journalists by the *Columbia Journalism Review* showed 84 percent found newsroom morale low, due significantly to profits taking priority over good reporting.[191] (A 2003 Indiana University survey, however, found journalists more satisfied than they had been ten years earlier and optimistically posited that this might mean journalistic culture is improving.[192] It seems more likely that those who remain in newsrooms had simply lowered their expectations.)

Contemporary U.S. journalism still has its defenders though they are fewer in number and appear to be more prevalent the higher one goes in the media pecking order. [193] The United States may have as many outstanding journalists today as ever (though they typically are among those criticizing the status quo). Often, the defense of U.S. journalism today falls back upon the less-than-inspiring position that this is the media system we have, it is the best possible system for our society, so that anything it generates has got to be good.

But measuring the U.S. news media solely by the caliber of their journalism may be unfair. The system is not set up to create good journalism; it is set up to generate maximum profits for news media companies. It has been far more successful at doing that. Criticizing media owners for their conduct in the hope of improving journalism is misguided; owners are simply trying to maximize returns for their investors. The solution to the problem of the media is to change the nature of the system so that it is no longer rational to produce what passes for journalism today.

3

UNDERSTANDING U.S. JOURNALISM II:
RIGHT-WING CRITICISM AND
POLITICAL COVERAGE

Along with commercial influences, political pressure from powerful self-interested parties—and to a lesser extent, the general public—has also shaped contemporary journalism. Pressure from elites remains constant, and a main purpose of professionalism, in theory at least, is to acknowledge this reality while preventing it from having undue influence. Broader, non-elite pressure exerts less influence because the professional code regards the general public as not sufficiently knowledgeable to participate in journalism discussions.

A particular form of elite criticism of journalism has become more prevalent over the past quarter century than perhaps at any time in U.S. history. This critique generated by well-funded political conservatives calls journalism excessively sympathetic to causes favored by liberals and the Left and prejudiced against the concerns of business, the military, social conservatives, and religious-minded people. This campaign has become especially effective because it has been linked to the populist strain in conservative politics and aligns the "liberal" media elites against the interests of regular Americans. Between 2001 and 2003 several books purporting to demonstrate the media's leftward tilt rested atop bestseller lists.[1] Such charges have already pushed journalists to be less critical of right-wing politics. The result has been a reinforcement of the corporate and conservative bias built into the media system. Indeed, the critique of the "left-wing media" meshes perfectly with the corporate interests that own the media and with the commercial pressures that are altering U.S. journalism for the worse.

I begin this chapter by reviewing the conservative critique and evaluating its effects on the media culture. Somewhat like the "commercial media give the people what they want" thesis, which I will address in chapter 5, the strength of the "liberal media" argument is that it contains an element of truth. The problem with it is that this truth is distorted, decontextualized, and used opportunistically to push a distinct political agenda. But it has had considerable effect politically. Among other things, the right-wing campaign has led to a double standard in covering politicians. After reviewing this critique, I will bring together the elements of chapters 2 and 3 and assess the manner in which the news media encourage or discourage a viable electoral system in the United States and, with that, effective self-governance. It is in the caliber of our political culture, as reflected in our electoral system, that the true measure of our journalism may be found.

CONSERVATIVE CRITIQUE OF THE "LIBERAL MEDIA"

Mainstream analysis over the past half century has been mostly concerned with documenting commercial and government encroachment on journalistic autonomy and professional training. The conservative critique is a variant of this analysis and contends that establishment journalists, who are seen as primarily left of center, abuse their power by distorting the news to serve their own political agendas—in a violation of the professional code. Such criticism would have been nonsensical prior to the professional era, when journalists explicitly represented the values of newspaper owners, who tended to have the politics of the business class and thus were conservative. Indeed, the idea of journalism, especially that generated by the largest and most prestigious newspapers, having a "left-wing" or anti-business bias in the Gilded Age or Progressive Era would have been about as plausible as the argument that *Pravda* had an anti-Communist bias in the old Soviet Union.

The conservative critique is based on four propositions: 1) the decisive power over the news lies with journalists—owners and advertisers are irrelevant or relatively powerless; 2) journalists are political liberals; 3) journalists abuse their power to advance liberal politics—thus breaking the professional code; and 4) objective journalists would almost certainly present the world exactly as seen by contemporary U.S. conservatives. Upon review, the conservative argument goes zero for four, although it does make contact with the ball on occasion.

The first proposition is intellectually indefensible and is enough to call the entire conservative critique into question. No credible scholarly analysis of journalism posits that journalists have the decisive power to determine what is news, what is not news, and how news should be covered. That is the fight that George Seldes and progressives in the Newspaper Guild lost in the 1930s. In commercial media, owners hire, fire, set budgets, and determine the overarching aims of the enterprise. Journalists, editors and media professionals who rise to the top of the hierarchy tend to internalize the values, both commercial and political, of media owners.[2] As one critic put it, at leading news outlets like the *Washington Post* and *New York Times*, "the batting average in elevating safe figures is one hundred percent. The chances of an eccentric editor reaching the upper branches of the tree are zero, and near zero for reporters."[3] Editors who toe the party line can be given autonomy because those in power know it will not be abused.

In terms of organizational sociology, the commercial newsroom is not unlike the media setup in the old Soviet Union. The top editors at *Tass* and *Pravda* did not have armed KGB agents hovering over them to enforce the party line; by the time they hit the big office in Moscow, they had internalized the necessary values and could be trusted to police the system themselves. And, of course, they were rewarded for their compliance. "The notion that largely conservative media owners hire left-wingers to run their news outlets is no more credible," argues media critic Jeff Cohen, "than owners of restaurant chains hiring militant vegetarians to run their steakhouses."[4] In the United States, sophisticated scholarly analysis examines how commercial pressures shape what have become the professional values that guide journalists.[5] Indeed, the genius of professionalism in journalism is that it allows journalists to adopt many of the values of media owners, yet because they are following a professional code, they are largely oblivious to their compromises with the status quo.

Even with these limitations, the rise of professionalism did grant journalists a degree of autonomy from the immediate dictates of owners, and the socially volatile period of the 1960s and early 1970s allowed reporters the freedom to follow risky stories. Journalists do have less autonomy today than they did twenty-five years ago, thanks in part to media owners' efforts. In fact, conservatives tacitly acknowledge the transparently ideological basis of the claim that journalists have all the power over the news. The real problem for conservatives isn't that journalists have all the power or even most of the power; the problem is that they have *any* power to be autonomous from owners and advertisers, whom conservatives seem to regard as having both the proper political worldview and the unique right as owners to determine media content. Conservative critics thus depict individual journalists as covert operators attacking conservative values from within what by all property rights should be conservative corporate media.

Former Speaker of the House Newt Gingrich, with typical candor, has laid bare the logic behind the conservative critique—eliminate journalistic autonomy and return the politics of journalism to the politics of media owners. "The business side of the broadcast industry ought to educate the editorial-writing side of the broadcast industry," Gingrich told a trade magazine. "I went into a major cable company that owns a daily newspaper, and the newspaper's editorial page is attacking the very position of the cable company.... And then they come to lobby me and say, 'Please ignore the editorials [in the paper] that we own because they don't know what they're talking about.' I think, wait a second, that is a totally irresponsible statement."[6] At a private meeting with media CEOs in 1995, when Gingrich was asked by Time Warner's chair how they could make coverage of Gingrich "fair," Gingrich reportedly told the CEOs that they were responsible for keeping journalists in line: "It was like, 'Get your children to behave,'" confided a staffer present at the meeting.[7] This helps explain why U.S. rightists, exemplified by Gingrich, also obsess about pushing public broadcasting to operate by commercial principles; they know that the market will effectively push the content in a more politically palatable direction.[8]

The second proposition of the conservative critique—that journalists are liberals—has the most evidence to support it. Surveys show that journalists tend to vote Democratic at a greater proportion than does the general population. In one famous (though highly criticized as methodologically flawed) survey of how Washington correspondents voted in the 1992 presidential election, something like 90 percent voted for Bill Clinton.[9] To some conservative critics, that settles the matter. But the weakness of the first proposition undermines the importance of how journalists vote and their political beliefs. What if owners and managers have most of the power, both directly and through the internalization of their political and commercial values through professional norms? Surveys show that media owners and editorial executives vote overwhelmingly Republican. An *Editor & Publisher* survey found that in 2000 newspaper publishers favored George W. Bush over Al Gore by a 3-to-1 margin, while newspaper editors and publishers together favored Bush by a 2-to-1 margin.[10] And why should a vote for Al Gore or Bill Clinton be perceived as a reflection of leftist politics? On many policies, especially economic, these are moderate to conservative Democrats—very comfortable with the status quo.

A problem with the argument is already apparent: the terms *liberal* and *left-wing* are used interchangeably. In the conservative argument, the great divide in U.S. politics fall between conservatives and "the Left," a group that runs seamlessly from Al Gore and Bill Clinton to Ralph Nader, Nelson Mandela, Noam Chomsky, Subcommandante Marcos, and Fidel Castro. In the right-wing worldview, there are no centrists—or, if one insists, those on the right are the centrists. According to the shock troops for the current conservative assault on the journalistic profession, support for Gore or Clinton is virtually indistinguishable from anarchy or socialism. Bernard Goldberg, author of the recent bestseller *Bias*, which purports to demonstrate left-wing media bias, links, albeit flippantly, political strategists for Clinton with Marx in their contempt for the rich.[11]

Blurring distinctions comes naturally to conservatives who see any concession to social welfare needs as evidence of creeping socialism. Clinton Democrats and radical leftists become interchangeable because conservatives categorize leftism so broadly. This lumping process is based almost exclusively upon support for what are called social issues, such as gay and lesbian rights, women's rights, abortion rights, civil liberties, gun control, and affirmative action. And indeed, on these issues a notable percentage of journalists tend to have positions similar to many of those on the Left. For Goldberg, "the real menace, as the Left sees it, is that America has always been too willing to step on its most vulnerable—gays, women, blacks. Because the Left controls America's newsrooms, we get a view of America that reflects that sensibility." These positions are not exclusively left ones; many corporate executives, even some conservative ones, would be comfortable supporting these "liberal" stances.

This framing of liberalism as leftism is misleading and ignores a more fundamental divide in U.S. society between elite opinion—formed by those high atop our leading institutions—and those outside it. On most issues, and certainly on the economy and militarism, there is more common ground between Clinton and the Republicans—between the liberal and conservative branches of elite opinion—than there is between Clinton and the Left. The U.S. news media, including the media most often characterized as liberal by the Right, pays little direct attention to the political Left. The Left—not only genuine radicals but also mild social democrats by international standards—lies outside the spectrum of legitimate debate. What attention the Left actually gets tends to be unsympathetic, if not explicitly negative. Foreign journalists marvel at how U.S. left-wing social critics like Noam Chomsky, who are prominent and respected public figures abroad, are virtually invisible in the U.S. news media.[12] Because the Right has no apparent principled concern about media coverage of diverse political views, that the Left is ignored and marginalized concerns it not a whit. And since the term *leftist* is pejorative in mainstream U.S. political culture, the term offers a useful tool to tar moderate liberals.

But the notion that journalists are more liberal than most Americans on social issues is the strongest card in the right-wing media critic's hand, and it is the card played most often. Journalists supposedly use their power to push their urbane liberal lifestyle on red-blooded

Americans who are less tolerant of gays and lesbians, less committed to civil liberties, less supportive of feminism, less supportive of affirmative action, more interested in owning guns, and more religious. In holding these views, journalists are like most educated professionals. Some recent research, however, indicates that far more Americans may be "liberals" on these issues than the Right would have us believe. A 2003 *Chicago Tribune* state-wide poll of Illinois residents found them overwhelmingly supportive of women's rights, gay rights, and gun control.[13] Unquestionably, however, journalists are far less likely to be fundamentalist or evangelical Christians than is the balance of the population.[14] Fundamentalist Christianity, however, cannot necessarily be equated with conservative politics, especially on issues concerning the economy, social spending, and regulation. It also is misleading to think that fewer evangelical journalists creates a hostility in journalism toward organized religion. Christianity and Judaism, if anything, are either sacred cows or third rails—one would have to look for a very long time to find mainstream news reports challenging the existence of God or the sanity of people who put their faith in a metaphysical entity.

This takes us directly to the Achilles' heel of the conservative critique of journalistic liberalism, which is conveniently absent from their pronouncements. Journalists tend to be more pro-business and conservative than the bulk of the population on the economy, militarism, and regulation of business in the public interest.[15] Commercial journalism has generated a stridently pro-capitalist viewpoint to the point where business news arguably exceeds traditional political journalism in prominence. No one claims that this mother lode of business reporting has anything remotely close to a liberal bias or holds any skepticism toward the role of business in the U.S. political economy. Moreover, all the economic pressures in journalism are pushing the news to accommodate the interests of affluent consumers, those targeted by big ticket advertisers. When Bernard Goldberg looks for concrete examples of left-wing bias in the media on economic issues, he trips over his feet. He accuses CBS News and the liberal press of being unfair to millionaire and 1996 long-shot presidential candidate Steve

Forbes for his flat tax proposal, even though that scheme was roundly criticized by a large segment of the mainstream economics and business community.[16] Goldberg does not even quibble with the manner in which Ralph Nader's ideas on the economy were ignored or trivialized in campaign coverage in 2000.

Most striking, Goldberg accuses journalists of a liberal-elitist contempt for the poor, which is of course not difficult to prove. Goldberg notes: "Edward R. Murrow's 'Harvest of Shame,' the great CBS News documentary about poor migrant families traveling America, trying to survive by picking fruits and vegetables, would never be done today. Too many poor people. Not our audience. We want the people who buy cars and computers. Poor migrants won't bring our kind of Americans—the ones with money to spend—into the tent. This is how the media's 'Liberals of Convenience' operate."[17] This criticism, although correct, is employed in a sleight-of-hand fashion to conclude that the media are too left-wing. A more perceptive critic might draw the opposite conclusion.

Indeed, any serious look at questions surrounding class and economic matters would quickly free the journalistic profession from any charges of liberal or left-wing bias. Over the past two generations, journalism, especially at the larger and more prominent news media, has evolved from a blue-collar job into a desirable occupation for the well-educated upper middle class. Urban legend has it that when news of the stock market crash came over the ticker to the *Boston Globe* newsroom in 1929, the journalists all arose to give Black Monday a standing ovation. The rich were finally getting their comeuppance. In contrast, when the news of the stock market crash reached the *Globe* newsroom in 1987, journalists frantically phoned their brokers. As recently as 1971 just over one-half of U.S. newspaper journalists had college degrees; by 2002 nearly 90 percent did. The median salary for a journalist at one of the forty largest circulation newspapers in the United States in 2002 was nearly double the median income for all U.S. workers.[18]

To become a top-tier journalist today increasingly requires paying high tuition to attend a journalism school and then working for free or next to nothing at an internship to build experience. This strongly weights the profession toward the children of the affluent.[19] Journalists at the dominant media are unlikely to have any idea what it means to go without health insurance, to be unable to locate affordable housing, to have their children in underfunded and dilapidated schools, to have relatives in prison or on the front lines of the military, to face the threat of severe poverty. For a U.S. journalist, that nearly 100,000 Americans die annually due to inadequate health care is about as relevant as the standings in the Pakistani cricket league; the coverage—or lack thereof—of health care policy and other urgent issues for the working class and the poor cannot help but be influenced by this disconnect.[20] Russell Baker, legendary columnist for the *New York Times*, put the matter well in December 2003: "Today's top-drawer Washington news people are part of a highly educated, upper-middle class elite; they belong to the culture for which the American system works extremely well. Which is to say, they are, in the pure sense of the word, extremely conservative."[21]

This provides context for Professor David Croteau's fascinating survey of journalists in the Washington press corps, which demonstrates that they are to the right of the U.S. population on core economic issues.[22] While journalists' private political attitudes do not dictate their journalism, they certainly complement and reinforce the structural pressures when economics are covered. Consider one of the most pressing economic issues currently affecting working-class Americans (and probably all of us): global trade deals. Blue-collar workers, including many evangelical and fundamentalist Christians, are concerned about job losses and lowered living standards because of the increased threat of super-cheap labor; environmentalists worry that U.S. protective standards can't be enforced; many citizens dislike the secretive nature of trade negotiations and the undermining of democratic governance. Polls place a significant percentage of Americans in opposition to these trade treaties, though Croteau reveals that mainstream journalists overwhelmingly support them.

Media coverage has been heavily weighted to present global trade deals as enlightened policy and opposition to trade deals as Cro-

Magnon thinking. The coverage has also distorted the issues, most notably referring to "free trade," when that is an often inaccurate description of complex agreements involving corporate-negotiated protectionism and subsidies. The distortion stems from an interconnection between politicians, business leaders, media companies, and journalists. The political elite in both parties has aggressively pushed these deals, and their campaign coffers have been greased accordingly. The corporate community has applied a political full-court press to put NAFTA and the WTO in place.[23] Major media owners strongly support global trade deals that make it easier to buy media abroad, get cheaper labor for their consumer goods, tighten up intellectual property laws, and sell their wares in new markets. The sources used for business journalism, where economic stories are largely covered, applaud global trade deals because they promise increased business and profit. The audience for business news is primarily the upper middle class, who see much to gain from the trade deals and little downside. Journalists fit squarely in this camp: they have little reason to fear they will lose their jobs to cheaper Haitian or Vietnamese laborers. Free trade deals seem A-OK to them, and all the institutional pressures are pushing in one direction. Hence, stories tend to herald "free trade" agreements and ignore the important democratic issues involved.[24]

Even if many mainstream journalists are often characterized as social "liberals," their positions on social issues should not be exaggerated. Right-wing critics regularly lambast journalists for being "soft" on race, meaning that journalists are unwilling to ask tough questions about affirmative action or African American leaders.[25] In view of this nation's history with racism and the considerable inequality between whites and people of color today, this is clearly a sensitive issue, and not just for liberals. Few African Americans think the news media are bending over backward to give them the benefit of the doubt, and for good reason. Research shows that African Americans rarely appear as sources in the news but regularly appear as criminals.[26] Martin Gilens's important book on why Americans hate welfare demonstrated that distorted coverage was to blame. News media erroneously covered welfare as a social service that went preponderantly to African Americans. When welfare was seen as helping people down on their luck, in great need, and white, the program soared in popularity. When Gilens investigated why the press coverage presented an erroneous and racially charged picture of welfare, he determined that the lack of minority journalists in newsrooms played a major factor.[27] Ethnic minorities are woefully underrepresented among journalists, typically around 5 percent of the total.[28] And, as even Bernard Goldberg has noted, ethnic minorities are not a significant part of the audience for news, which is aimed at middle- and upper-middle-class whites.[29]

As for the third proposition—that journalists use their autonomy to advance aggressively liberal politics—the evidence is scant. A core point of the professional code is to prevent journalists from pushing their own politics onto the news, and there is little indication that this is not taken seriously. If anything, the evidence points to a near obsession with reporting from the midpoint in the range of official sources. For a political figure to be dubbed a centrist or moderate is invariably a compliment in mainstream news. Many journalists are proud to note that though they are liberal, their coverage tends to be conservative so that they won't be accused of unprofessionalism. For example, conservative critics charged that Frank Bruni of the *New York Times*, because he was openly gay, could not fairly cover George W. Bush during his 2000 campaign due to Bush's lack of enthusiasm for gay rights. In fact, Bruni was quite sympathetic in his treatment of Bush and failed to pursue many issues a more aggressive reporter might.[30] This right-wing criticism of journalists has paid big dividends by chilling scrutiny of conservatives. As one news producer stated, "The main bias of journalists is the bias not to do anything that could be construed as liberal."[31] "One of the biggest career threats for journalists," a veteran Washington reporter confirmed in 2002, "is to be accused of 'liberal bias' for digging up stories that put conservatives in a bad light."[32]

In fact, research suggests that most journalists are far from political partisans; the profession does not attract people with strong ideological inclinations.[33] Many journalists are cynical and depoliticized, like much of the general public. If they are obsessed with advancing a progressive political agenda, they tend to become freelancers or leave the profession because the professional constraints on their work would be too great. Moreover, as Russell Baker argues, the increasingly comfortable background of elite journalists is unlikely "to produce angry reporters and aggressive editors ... because the capacity for outrage has been bred out of them."[34] If journalists wish to push a conservative political agenda, however, they find few barriers in the current media environment. Just ask John Stossel. After all, anytime a journalist pushes the conservative agenda they are justified because they are balancing the "liberal bias" of the dominant media.

The unwillingness of traditional professional journalists to commit to a partisan ideology has led to a striking bifurcation of stances. Mainstream journalism is cautious and attempts to do nothing that would suggest it favors Democrats over Republicans, and most research indicates that Republicans fare well in this climate. Conservative critics, and the increasing number of explicitly conservative media, argue that the mainstream is blatantly favoring Democrats. They then feel no obligation to be fair to Democrats since they are "balancing" the bias of the mainstream. A study released by the Shorenstein Center at Harvard University in 2003 concluded that so-called liberal newspapers are more open-minded and willing to criticize a like-minded U.S. president (that is, Bill Clinton) than their "conservative" counterparts would criticize George W. Bush. The study also found a "striking difference in tone between the two sides as well," with the conservative media using far "harsher" language to describe President Clinton and engaging in *ad hominem* attacks.[35] "We've created this cottage industry in which it pays to be un-objective," a senior writer at Rupert Murdoch's right-wing *Weekly Standard* admitted in 2003. "It's a great way to have your cake and eat it too. Criticize other people for not being objective. Be as subjective as you want. It's a great little racket."[36]

The final proposition—that truly objective journalism would invariably see the world exactly the way Rush Limbaugh sees it—points to the ideological nature of the exercise.[37] Indeed, no conservative has ever criticized journalism for being too soft on a right-wing politician or unfair to liberals or the Left. Favorable coverage of the Right is quality unbiased journalism. Unfavorable coverage of Democrats is equally unbiased. Unfavorable coverage of conservatives is, almost by definition, riddled with bias. It is a no-win proposition. For but one example, when Representative Cynthia McKinney, a Democrat, was accused erroneously by the *New York Times* and National Public Radio of claiming President Bush had prior knowledge of the 9/11 attacks and did nothing to stop them—a bogus charge that may have cost her her seat in the House—no conservative media critic rushed to her defense, even though conservatives are supposed to hate both "liberal" media outlets.[38]

In 1992, Rich Bond, then the chair of the Republican Party, acknowledged that bashing the "liberal media" was aimed at intimidation, to "work the refs" like a basketball coach does so that "maybe the ref will cut you a little slack" on the next play.[39] Some players on the Left probably hold a similarly unprincipled attitude toward media criticism, and everyone is prone to putting their thumb on the scale to some extent to weight the evidence in their direction, but that doesn't make such tactics acceptable. Honest scholarship attempts to provide a coherent and intellectually consistent explanation of journalism that can withstand critical interrogation. The conservative critique of "liberal" news media is an intellectual failure, riddled with contradictions and inaccuracy.

The intellectual bankruptcy of the conservative critique of the liberal media is demonstrated by its limited credibility in academic studies of journalism. Before one protests, "Of course not, professors are a bunch of leftists," recall that pro-market and conservative research thrives in business schools, economics departments, and to a lesser extent in law schools and political science departments. There is a lot of money to support media professors who want to wave the conservative banner. The withering of journalistic autonomy over the past two decades has also undercut the basis for this claim. Perhaps that is why Brent Bozell, arguably the best-known conservative media critic of recent times, seems to be switching his emphasis from the alleged left-wing bias of journalism to the prevalence of vulgarity in entertainment fare, especially on television. This is the new evidence of a liberal media, Bozell suggests. The irony is unintended, as the main purveyors of the most vulgar shows, News Corporation (owner of the Fox TV network) and Viacom (owner of MTV), are the same media conglomerates that deliver some of the most rabid right-wing journalism and punditry: the Fox News Channel, the *Weekly Standard*, and the Infinity radio network.

RIGHT-WING POLITICAL CAMPAIGN AGAINST THE MEDIA

So why does the conservative critique of the "liberal" news media remain such a significant force in U.S. political and media culture? It certainly isn't the quality of the arguments. It is kept alive by hard-core political organizing. Launched in earnest in the 1970s by financial backers with deep pockets, conservative critics blamed the liberal media for losing the Vietnam War and for fomenting dissent in the United States. Pro-business foundations were aghast at what they perceived as the anti-business sentiment prevalent among Americans, especially middle-class youth who had typically supplied a core constituency. Mainstream journalism—which, in reporting the activities of official sources, was giving people like Ralph Nader sympathetic exposure—was seen as turning Americans away from business. At that point the political Right, supported by its wealthy donors, began to devote enormous resources to criticizing and intimidating the news media.[40] This was a cornerstone of the broader campaign to make the political culture more pro-business and more conservative. Around half of all the expenditures of the twelve largest conservative foundations have been devoted to moving the news rightward. During the 1990s, right-wing think tanks, almost all of which were not established until the 1970s, were funded to the tune of *$1 billion*. By 2003, the Heritage Foundation had an annual budget of $30 million, 180 employees, and its own television studios in its eight-story Washington, D.C., headquarters.[41] Brent Bozell's Media Research Center has an annual budget in the $15 million range and some 60 employees. These conservative groups tend to coordinate their propaganda with that of the Republican Party.[42]

The campaign to alter the media has entailed funding the training of conservative and business journalists at universities and bankrolling right-wing student newspapers to breed a generation of pro-business Republican journalists.[43] It has meant starting right-wing print media such as the *Washington Times* and the *Weekly Standard* and supporting existing right-wing publications such as the *National Review*, not only to promote conservative politics but also so that young journalists have a farm system to develop their clips. It also includes conservative think tanks flooding journalism with pro-business official sources and incessantly jawboning coverage critical of conservative interests as reflective of "liberal" bias.[44] A comprehensive Nexis search for the twenty-five largest think tanks in U.S. news media for 2002 showed that explicitly conservative think tanks accounted for nearly half of the 25,000 think-tank citations in the news, whereas progressive think tanks accounted for only 12 percent. Centrist groups such as the Council on Foreign Relations and the Brookings Institution accounted for the rest.[45] The pro-business Right understood that changing media was a crucial part of bringing right-wing ideas into prominence and their politicians into power. "You get huge leverage for your dollars," a conservative philanthropist noted when he discussed the turn to ideological work.[46] A well-organized, well-financed, and active hardcore conservative crew is pushing the news media to the right. As a *Washington Post* White House correspondent put it, "The liberal equivalent of this conservative coterie does not exist."[47] As Senate minority leader Tom Daschle commented in 2003, "We don't come close to matching their firepower in the media."[48]

To the general public the conservative critique is not packaged as an effort by the wealthiest and most powerful elements of our society to extend their power, weaken labor and government regulation in the public interest, and dramatically lower their taxes while gutting the public sector, aside from the military. To the contrary, this conservative critique, much like the broader conservative political movement, is marketed as a populist movement. It is the heroic story of the conservative masses (Pat Buchanan's "peasants with pitchforks") battling the establishment liberal media elite. In this righteous war, as spun by right-wing pundits such as Ann Coulter, Rush Limbaugh, Newt Gingrich, Bill Bennett, and Sean Hannity, conservatives are the blue-collar workers (white, of course, though that is only implied) and self-made business leaders while the liberals are Ivy League snobs, intellectuals, hoity-toity limousine riders, and journalists who hold power. As one conservative activist put it, the contest over media is a "David and Goliath struggle."[49]

At its most effective, the conservative critique plays off the elitism inherent to professionalism and to liberalism. But it is hard to avoid the conclusion that the populist airs of the conservative criticism are strictly for show, as they tend to collapse as soon as class—the one unmentionable term in the conservative lexicon—is introduced. In fact, many right-wingers who swear allegiance to the working class hark from well-to-do families and oppose traditional policies to improve the conditions of the working class, even trade unions. The same conservative pundits and politicians who wrap themselves in the military and fire the starting gun at NASCAR races typically dodged the draft themselves, like most other upper-middle class and rich folk. And the same upper-class conservative pundits who galvanize working-class Christians to support right-wing politics with thunderous moral pronouncements sometimes turn out to be liars, philanderers, drug users, and chronic gamblers.[50]

The success of this right-wing campaign has been predicated to some extent on constant repetition unquestioned by a countervailing position. Crucial to the promotion of the idea that the news media are liberal have been, ironically enough, the so-called liberal media. Promoted by talk TV and talk radio, books bashing the media from right-wingers become instant bestsellers; media criticism from the Left (such as Noam Chomsky's work) is typically ignored by talking heads and unreviewed in the mainstream press. One study of press coverage between 1992 and 2002 finds that references to the liberal bias of the news media outnumber references to a conservative bias by a factor of more than 17 to 1.[51] It is trumpeted far and wide by the media, such that the conservative complaint is well known to millions of Americans, who view it as the *only* dissident criticism of the media. It should occasion no surprise, then, that a 2003 Gallup Poll found that 45 percent of Americans thought the news media were "too liberal," while only 15 percent found them "too conservative."

In fact, it is hardly surprising that the conservative critique of the media is so prominent—given that this myth is cultivated to some extent by the so-called liberal media themselves. The conservative critique is in some respects the "official opposition" cultivated by professional journalism itself, because in a sense journalists *have* to be viewed as "liberals," fiercely independent and out of step with their corporate owners, for the system to have credibility. Were journalists seen as cravenly bowing before wealth and privilege, journalism would lose credibility as an autonomous democratic force. After all, the quest for autonomy played a significant role in the development of professional journalism in the first place. The conservative criticism is also rather flattering to journalists; it says to them: you have all the power but you use that power to advance the interests of the poor and minorities and environmentalists (or government bureaucrats and liberal elitists) rather than the interests of corporations and the military (or Middle America). A political economic critique, which suggests that journalists have much less power and are too often the pawns of forces that make them agents of the status quo, is much less flattering and almost invisible. (When the "left" critique is on rare occasion presented in mainstream media, one suspects it is included so journalists can claim they are being attacked from both sides and therefore must be neutral, nonpartisan, and straight down the middle. The problem with that rationale is that nearly all news media get attacked from differing sides. Some purport that the Nazi lunatic fringe at times considered some of Hitler's media to be insufficiently anti-Communist or anti-Semitic.)

The campaign to move journalism to the right has been aided by three other factors. First, the right wing of the Republican Party, typified by Reagan and now George W. Bush, has gained considerable political power while the Democratic Party leadership has become steadily more pro-corporate in its outlook. This means that editors and journalists who simply follow the professional code have much greater exposure through official sources to neoliberal and conservative political positions. The body of relatively progressive official sources used more frequently in the 1960s and 1970s is viewed today as irrelevant. The hallowed political center of officialdom has moved sharply to the right.

Second, as I discussed above, the real target of the conservative critique of "liberal" media—the supposed autonomy of journalists—has diminished over the past twenty years. There is less protection for journalists and less independence from media owners' politics or interests.

Third, and most important, conservatives move easily in the corridors of corporate media. This conservative campaign has meshed comfortably with the commercial and political aspirations of media corporations. This is precisely what one would expect. Many prominent media moguls are hardcore, rock-ribbed conservatives such as Rupert Murdoch, John Malone, former GE CEO Jack Welch, and Clear Channel CEO Lowry Mays. Although some media executives and owners donate money to Democrats, none of the major news media owners is anything close to a left-winger. Journalists who praise corporations and commercialism will obviously be held in higher regard (and given more slack) by owners and advertisers than journalists who are routinely critical of them. Media owners don't want their own economic interests or policies criticized. Murdoch's Fox News Channel, which operates as an adjunct of the Republican Party, is an obvious example of blatant corporate shilling, but the point holds at other outlets, too.[52] Punditry and commentary provided by corporate-owned news media almost unfailingly ranges from center to right. According to *Editor & Publisher*, the four most widely syndicated political columnists in the United States speak from the Right. TV news runs from pro-business centrist to rabidly pro-business right, and most newspaper journalism is only a bit broader. Perhaps most important, the explicitly right-wing media are now strong enough and incessant enough to push stories until they are covered by more centrist mainstream media.[53]

The upshot is that by the early years of the twenty-first century the conservatives had won the media battle. The *Washington Post*'s E. J.

Dionne termed this a "genuine triumph for conservatives. . . .The drumbeat of conservative press criticism has been so steady, the establishment press has internalized it."[54] By 2001, CNN's chief Walter Isaacson was polling conservatives to see how he could make the network more palatable to them. In their quieter moments conservatives acknowledge the victory, though they will insist that their triumph is justified.[55] "There's been a massive change in media in this country over the last fifteen years," Rush Limbaugh exulted. "Now it's 2002 and the traditional liberal media monopoly doesn't even exist anymore."[56] But such celebratory comments are usually confined to more private back-slapping sessions. The dominating conservative pundits still sing the incessant refrain that the media are dominated by. . . liberals. It is the one, loud, mandatory, unifying call in conservatives' public orations, and it is an article of faith delivered without evidence. But the truth is the opposite: the news media diet of the average American is drawn from a menu tilted heavily to the Right.

A staple entrée in this diet is political talk radio. Partisan radio went national in the late 1980s following the rise of satellite technology, toll-free 800 numbers, and the elimination of the Fairness Doctrine, which called on broadcast news to provide balanced viewpoints on social and political issues.[57] Talk radio has not only stormed into prominence on the AM dial but it also "tends to run the gamut from conservative to . . . very conservative," as one reporter characterized it.[58] "There are 1,500 conservative radio talk show hosts," the conservative activist Paul M. Weyrich boasts. "The ability to reach people with our point of view is like nothing we have ever seen before."[59] The right-wing dominance of broadcasting is demonstrated by the shift of groups such as Reed Irvine's Accuracy in Media and Phyllis Schlafley's Eagle Forum. Back in the 1970s and 1980s they crusaded for the Fairness Doctrine—which required broadcasters to present contrasting perspectives on politics—as a way to battle liberal bias on the airwaves; since the ascendance of Rush Limbaugh et al. these groups now oppose the Fairness Doctrine.[60]

By 2003, a Gallup Poll showed that 22 percent of Americans considered talk radio their primary source for news, double the figure of 1998.[61] Every city has its own local Limbaughs trying to outdo the master on the pro-Republican political Richter scale. The Republican National Committee has a Radio Services Department whose sole function is to provide daily talking points to feed "the voracious appetite of conservative talk show hosts."[62] Even in the liberal college town of Eugene, Oregon, for example, a 2002 study determined that 4,000 hours per year of conservative Republican talk shows and zero hours of liberal Democratic talk shows were broadcast on the local radio dial.[63] Were foreigners never to visit the United States but only listen to a steady diet of its radio fare, they might imagine that Americans were overwhelmingly on the right wing of the political spectrum, that George W. Bush won the 2000 election by a near unanimous vote, and that the average IQ of those opposing President Bush was around 40. But this obviously is not the case, so how can talk radio be so rabidly and so overwhelmingly right-wing?

To some extent right-wing talk radio reflects media owners' and advertisers' politics. Since they can be counted on to denounce group after group except big business, conservatives are often granted a long leash if their ratings are marginal in the hope that controversy will spur listener support. Progressive radio hosts, in contrast, have had their programs canceled although they had satisfactory ratings and commercial success because their shows' content did not sit well with the station owners and managers.[64] Oftentimes, too, what passes for a liberal pundit in mainstream media culture is such a Milquetoast that the result is lame radio. Instead of populists like Jim Hightower or Michael Moore feistily impaling corporate power, Alan Combes plays dead in the face of Sean Hannity's antics. Further, as radio ownership concentrated due to the 1996 Telecommunications Act, editorial power concentrated in the hands of companies like Clear Channel, which have long histories of supporting right-wing politicians. As talk radio became right-wing talk radio, non-right-wingers turned their dials off. In this climate it is not especially rational or profitable to hire non-right-wing hosts because cultivating an audience will take too long. Only liberals with political agendas, not capitalists in pursuit of profit, would be willing to invest in developing that audience. Not many liberals of that type own big radio chains or are that cavalier with their capital.

Some defend the dominance of right-wing media and dispute its influence by pointing to the Internet. While acknowledging that cable TV news and talk radio tilt to the right, they say that the Internet now offers a voice for all. No one can be stopped from putting up a website, so people wanting dissenting or alternative views can find them there. This would be a comforting thought were it accurate. The Internet does indeed positively affect our journalism and our political culture in many ways, but it cannot eliminate or even seriously undermine concerns about journalism. Although the Internet does host the full gamut of political views, it is hardly a level playing field or a suitable alternative to mainstream quality journalism. It takes money and labor to turn out good journalism, so putting up a website or blog can't compare with a report in the *New York Times* or on CBS. The market treats the Internet the same as it does other media; large commercially oriented firms have a decided advantage in marketing their websites. Nearly all of the popular news websites are connected to media giants, and quality independent journalism gets marginal attention. The right-wing gadfly Matt Drudge became the first commercially viable journalist spawned by the Web. Why? In large part because Drudge's sensational reports could be fed into the pipeline of the commercial and conservative news media.

PARTISAN COVERAGE IN PEACE AND WAR

The average American cannot help but be exposed to the noticeable double standard in the treatment of politicians and issues in the media, depending upon party and ideology. The fate of Bill Clinton and George W. Bush reveals the scope of the conservative victory. A Nexis search, for example, reveals that 13,641 stories focused on Clinton avoiding the military draft but a mere 49 stories featured Bush having his powerful father use influence to get him into the Texas Air National Guard instead of the draft.[65] Clinton's comment about smoking marijuana but not inhaling made headlines and monologues for weeks. His small-time Whitewater affair justified a massive seven-year, $70 million, open-ended special investigation of his business and personal life that never established any criminal business activity but eventually did produce the Lewinsky allegations. Rick Kaplan, former head of CNN, acknowledged that he instructed his employees to provide the Lewinsky story with massive attention despite his belief that it was overblown; he knew he would face withering criticism from the Right for a liberal bias if he did not pummel it.[66] "I think if you look at the way Clinton's been treated," former Christian Coalition director Ralph Reed said, "you'd be hard-pressed to say that the personal liberal ideological views of most reporters ... have somehow led to a free ride for Bill Clinton."[67]

Bush, in contrast, had a remarkably dubious business career in which he made a fortune flouting security laws, tapping public funds, and using his father's connections to protect his backside, but the news media barely sniffed at the story. His questionable connections to Enron during his presidency—even at the height of the corporate scandal in 2001 and 2002—produced no special prosecutor and no media drumbeat for one to be appointed.[68] His conviction for driving under the influence of alcohol barely attracted notice. Clinton-bashing then extended to Al Gore. Studies demonstrate that Bush tended to get more favorable coverage in the mainstream press than Al Gore did during the 2000 presidential campaign.[69] Even the conservative Republican Joe Scarborough argued, when he appeared on MSNBC in 2002, that the news media "were fairly brutal to Al Gore.... If they had done that to a Republican candidate I'd be going on your show and say you were being biased."[70] Indeed, the kid-glove treatment of Bush only got gentler following 9/11.

The crucial change toward this double standard was not an increased marginalization of the Left—the Left was already in media purgatory—but, rather, an increase in recent years in favorable coverage for the conservative branch of elite opinion. For much of the 1980s and 1990s, it was primarily critics on the Left, such as Fairness & Accuracy In Reporting and Edward S. Herman and Noam Chomsky, who directly rebutted the charge that the media were left-wing. (Herman and Chomsky emphasized the similarities between Democrats and Republicans on core issues surrounding foreign policy, trade, and corporations.) Liberals and Democrats responded slowly to the conservative critique during this period in part because their views were still getting airplay. But with the ascendance of the conservative domination of the news media in recent years, liberals such as Joe Conason, Al Franken, Eric Alterman, and Paul Krugman have responded with a vengeance.[71] Subjected to close scrutiny, the works of Ann Coulter and Bill O'Reilly are revealed to be filled with errors and outright lies and liberals are calling them on it. Suddenly a veritable cottage industry has emerged to chronicle the double standard in media treatment. By 2003, when some liberals were finally returning fire against the Right, suddenly some conservatives, with no sense of irony or history, began bemoaning the lack of civility in public discourse.[72]

This conservative campaign against the press has also contributed to a collapse in reporting standards. The 2003 invasion and occupation of Iraq clearly showed the breakdown of even rudimentary standards for journalism in the United States, with consequences we are only beginning to grasp. With regard to international affairs, the range of mainstream debate in U.S. journalism is the range of debate among the elite, which tends to have a different set of priorities and concerns than the general population. For journalists to question the elite consensus on their own would leave them open to charges of being ideological and unprofessional, so it is rarely done. The caliber of international coverage in U.S. news media suffered further with the sharp cutbacks in foreign coverage beginning in the 1980s. The conservative badgering of the news media made the press, if anything, even more reluctant to question President Bush as he made his case for war in the fall of 2002 and the spring of 2003.

The appropriateness of the U.S. invasion of Iraq hinged on the alleged link between Saddam Hussein and terrorists and Saddam Hussein's possession of usable stockpiles of weapons of mass destruction. Even though evidence for these claims bordered at best on the nonexistent, the charges were repeated ad nauseam in the news with little effort to examine their veracity. In-house weapons experts, presented on an hourly basis on cable news channels, provided little or no skepticism about the allegations and some even trumpeted their import.

The news media roundly praised the February 5 speech to the United Nations by Secretary of State Colin Powell in which he laid out the Bush administration's case for war. As *Editor & Publisher* put it, "The media's unquestioning endorsement of Powell's assertions made invasion inevitable."[73] Only in August did a mainstream U.S. journalist dissect Powell's contentions, and when Associated Press correspondent Charles J. Hanley completed his work, he "utterly demolished" Powell's presentation, according to *Editor & Publisher* editor Greg Mitchell.

Precisely as the news media trumpeted reports of the successful invasion of Iraq, the Jayson Blair scandal hit at the *New York Times,* and media attention turned in that direction. How fitting that the "sin that led the list of his trespasses," according to a retired *Times* reporter, "was a fictitious description of the farm where Pfc. Jessica Lynch lived."[74] The Blair scandal centered on transgressions around a trivial point. The much more important point that Jessica Lynch's capture and rescue had been greatly exaggerated by the military for the folks at home received only passing mention and never came close to scandal status. Lynch, to her credit, complained repeatedly that the military and the Bush administration were lying about her experience and turning her into a hero to generate popular support for the war, but no journalistic heads had to roll for letting that whopper spread far and wide.[75] Even more striking was that another *Times* correspondent, Judith Miller, had relentlessly hyped the notion that Iraq possessed weapons of mass destruction—based on flimsy allegations and ignoring all evidence and logic to the contrary—in the months leading up to the invasion (and after). Yet her mistakes were not considered nearly as serious as Blair's crimes against journalism.[76] No editors, nor Miller herself, feared losing their jobs over her dubious and overhyped reporting. The episode calls to mind C. Wright Mills's famous dictum about "crackpot realism." Small and trivial matters are ruthlessly and publicly monitored while high crimes built into the logic of the system are ignored.

During the summer of 2003 when even some supporters began to agree that the Bush administration's case for war had been built on deception, the conservatives who had almost universally demanded that Clinton resign or be removed from office for lying under oath were startlingly quiet.[77] Predictably, even before the invasion, conservative media critics were hunting vocal war critics. In March, the Media Research Center released a report chastising the "liberal bias" of the U.S. news media, especially ABC News, with regard to covering Iraq. The media were "channeling Iraqi propaganda," "sanitizing radical protests" in the United States, and "championing France and the U.N. over the U.S."[78] When CNN's Christiane Amanpour conceded that media coverage of the war had been "self-muzzled" because journalists were intimidated by the Bush administration and "its foot soldiers at Fox News," a Fox spokesperson called Amanpour a "spokeswoman for al-Qaeda."[79] When the news media persisted in suggesting that the Iraqi campaign was not going swimmingly for the Bush administration, the White House criticized the news media, with no sense of irony, for being biased against it.[80]

As early as the fall of 2003 it was obvious that news coverage of the Iraq war buildup, invasion, and occupation rank among the very darkest moments in U.S. journalism history. In November BBC Director General Greg Dyke denounced the U.S. news media coverage as "banging the drum" for war, in a manner that was intolerable for credible journalism.[81] In September the *Washington Post* released a poll showing that 69 percent of Americans still believed that Saddam Hussein was connected to the 9/11 attacks. The administration had been linking Hussein to al-Qaeda and 9/11 in its efforts to generate support for the war, and the media had done a miserable job of correcting the record.[82] One can only imagine what people would have thought about the news media and the government if, two years after Pearl Harbor, a majority of the American people believed that the Chinese had attacked the United States in December 1941. In what was not necessarily unusual, MSNBC contributed to the confusion. When airing a live news conference by Tom Ridge, the head of the Department of Homeland Security, about new al-Qaeda threats to the United States, a banner across the bottom of the screen read "Showdown with Saddam."[83] In September, when the president finally admitted that there was no known link between Saddam Hussein and 9/11, only three of the nation's twelve largest newspapers made the confession a front-page story, and two of them (the *Wall Street Journal* and Rupert Murdoch's *New York Post*) did not cover it at all.[84]

In October 2003 the University of Maryland's Program on International Policy Attitudes (PIPA) released its study of Americans' attitudes toward the war in Iraq, their knowledge of the issues, and what media they consumed. It revealed that the more that Americans consumed commercial TV news coverage of the war, the less they knew about the subject and the more likely they were to support the Bush administration's position. This was especially true of viewers of Murdoch's Fox News Channel, but it applied across the board to commercial TV viewers.[85] One can quibble with the accuracy of such a survey, but it was conducted by a reputable and mainstream organization. Even allowing for a significant margin of error, a more damning comment on the U.S. news media would be difficult to imagine, as it goes directly against what a free press is supposed to do in a democratic society. Instead, it seems to follow the dictum Josef Goebbels had for the Nazi media: the more people consume, the less capable they are of being critical, and the more they will support the Nazi Party.

JOURNALISM'S LITMUS TEST: ELECTION COVERAGE

The decision to go to war may well be the most important one a government can make; the failure of the U.S. news media to encourage citizens to participate fully in that decision and to monitor their elected leaders' actions creates an obviously serious problem. But an even more fundamental measure of the news media's efficacy is their campaign and election coverage, since this offers citizens their main route for exercising power over their leaders. If the news media can spur the electoral system, all of journalism's other problems will seem less foreboding. If the news media fail in this vital task, however, not much else matters.

The performance of the election system (and, with that, accountable governance) can be judged not just by the caliber of journalism but also by the level and nature of popular political involvement. While no nation can ever be a perfect democracy, it is worth analyzing where on the continuum the United States lies. And there is little dispute that by almost any criteria of voter participation and civic awareness, our country is only formally democratic. As neoliberal policies have grown in importance, the democratic foundations of governance in the United States have deteriorated. In core respects, our nation is less democratic today than it was two or three generations ago, and it was by no means a golden age then. As author William Greider pegged it: If by democracy one means "the idea of people being able to participate in deciding things that affect their lives," then the U.S. polity "is in deep decay."[86] This assessment is neither particularly controversial nor particularly partisan. Even the conservative Richard Posner acknowledges the severe weaknesses of U.S. citizens' political involvement by democratic standards, though he is not especially troubled by the situation.[87]

Consider the criteria of social and economic inequality. As I discussed in chapter 1, inequality is a cancer for a viable democracy. The more inequality present, the more difficult it is to ensure a strong democracy. After reductions in inequality in the middle of the twentieth century, the United States has returned to the standards of the Gilded Age; inequality has bloomed over the past two decades. Between 1979 and 1997 the share of the national income going to the top 20 percent of households grew from 45.9 percent to 53.2 percent; over the same time span the bottom 60 percent of households saw their share of income fall from 32.2 percent to 26.9 percent, and the bottom 20 percent watched their share drop from 5.3 percent to 4.0 percent.[88] And the higher one goes up the economic order, the greater the increase in wealth and income relative to the balance of the population. As Paul Krugman noted in 2002:

> In 1970 the top 0.01 percent of taxpayers had 0.7 percent of total income—that is, they earned "only" 70 times as much as the average.... But in 1998, the top 0.01 percent received more than 3 percent of all income. That meant the richest 13,000 families in America had almost as much income as the 20 million poorest households; those 13,000 families had incomes 300 times that of average families.[89]

In 2001, the International Labor Organization confirmed another distressing long-term trend: workers in the United States were working more hours than they had for generations, and more than workers in any other industrialized nation, save the Czech Republic and South Korea. German workers, to give some sense of comparison, work on average 500 hours *less* per year—some three months' worth of 40-hour weeks!—than their American counterparts.[90] All of this is hardly conducive to civic participation. As Kevin Phillips has noted, this is inimical to any notion of democratic politics, and, if it is not reversed, will lead inexorably to plutocracy.[91]

The political culture has shriveled as inequality has mushroomed. Some three-quarters of the U.S. House wins reelection by landslides, and no more than a fraction of the seats are seriously contested. One of seven members of the House runs for reelection without any challenger from a major political party. State and local elections are even worse. Nearly half of all state legislature candidates run without serious opposition. But elections are only part of the story. Political ignorance and uninvolvement have reached epidemic levels. Survey after survey shows an astounding—and growing—degree of public ignorance and apathy about the political system. A 1998 survey found that two in five Americans could not identify the vice president of the United States, while two-thirds could not identify their representatives in Congress. [92]

Voter turnout rates in presidential years have plummeted over the past forty years—from nearly 70 percent of eligible voters in 1960 to just over 50 percent in 2000—and the figures fall precipitously in non-presidential election years and among poor people and young people. It is not unusual today to have elections decided by fewer than 20 percent of the adult population.[93] Whether one votes is best determined by one's income level; the richer one is, the more likely one is to vote. As Thomas Patterson puts it, "When you compare the low turnout rates in the United States and Europe, most of the explanation for the difference comes in looking at how it works across class lines."[94] Young people, too, barely evince any interest in electoral politics; in 1998 and 2002 only around 12 percent of those 18–24 voted.[95] These disturbing numbers require little statistical elaboration, though plenty exists.

The depoliticization of the population is stunning. Pundits and analysts aggressively debate the reasons or whether this is even an area for concern but its truth remains unquestioned. This political languor is incompatible with any known theory of democracy.[96] It also leads inevitably to political corruption.

In such a politically devoid culture the questions concerning the media are simple. How much are the media responsible for society's depoliticization? Or, perhaps to put it in a more manageable light, do the news media reinforce the pressures that produce this climate or does the media system, on balance, counteract those forces and act as an agency for enriching informed self-government? I will not keep you in suspense, but you can probably answer these questions now. The media system acts in many ways as an antidemocratic force.

For starters, for reasons discussed in chapter 2, press coverage strongly emphasizes the "spin" politicians deploy, endless analyses of polls, and predictions of winners rather than issues. This inexpensive journalism is easy to fashion into both serious and entertaining reports.[97] A 2000 study by the Project for Excellence in Journalism of forty-nine major television news stations concluded that 93 percent of the presidential campaign stories "were about the horse race or tactics of the campaign, as opposed to what the candidates stood for [or] how their proposals might affect people locally."[98] Television news, fed by sound bites and video clips, is not the sole culprit. The venerable *New York Times*, for example, in a lengthy profile of Senator John Edwards following the announcement of his presidential bid, focused on how Edwards packaged himself, not on his platform.[99] Aside from ignoring the issues, the emphasis on spin and tactics also encourages a certain cynicism about politicians and politics.[100]

Every bit as damaging to the body politic has been the paucity of electoral coverage. In our depoliticized culture, journalism simply devotes far fewer resources to campaigns and elections than it has historically. A 2002 study of television news in the fifty largest media markets found that only 37 percent of the stations studied carried any electoral coverage. Nearly half the stories dealt with governors' races, while only 5 percent focused on races for the House.[101] In the week before the 2002 election there was scarcely a word about it on the local TV news in Columbus, Ohio; instead, viewers were regaled with news stories on "a topless car wash, shopping bargains, and senior citizens who don't understand safe sex."[102] Even formal candidate debates are not routinely televised. A study of the 2000 election by Curtis Gans found that 60 percent of candidate debates were not televised at all, and almost one-half of those that were televised appeared on public broadcasting stations.[103] Accordingly, candidates tend to obsess on fundraising for paid ads. As "the ability to attract so-called free media has pretty much disappeared," one scholar observed in 2002, "candidates spend next to no time doing public events. They don't go talking to people. They don't do the kinds of visits to public fora that they used to, because they know it's a total waste of time."[104]

This is what one would expect when the broader operations of government get less coverage as well. "In my thirty-five years in politics," Representative Barney Frank commented in 2003, "one of the things that makes me saddest is that I've seen a deterioration of the coverage of government in the media."[105] "What we have now is an increasingly uneducated public—especially in what used to be called civics—dealing with ever more complex issues with which they are unequipped to knowledgeably deal," scholar Gary Brechin warned. "We have a population ripe for manipulation by powerful public relations firms and political consultants who are expert in sound bites and seductive imagery."[106]

It is in this context that paid TV political advertising has become the lingua franca of the electoral culture, and a massive industry in its own right. Funds spent on TV political advertising increased from around $210 million in 1982 to $410 million in 1994 and to more than $1 billion in 2002.[107] Adjusting for inflation, the amount spent on TV political spots increased 600 percent from 1972 to 2000.[108] Over the past decade the rate of increase in TV political ad spending every four years has been on the order of 40 or 50 percent. It more than doubled from 1998 to 2002.[109] The amount spent on political advertising has grown so much as to become a significant factor in the advertising industry's assessment of its overall health.[110] Wall

Street investment analysts study this new industry, and forecast a staggering $1.6 billion in political campaign advertising for local TV stations alone in 2004.[111]

These numbers reflect the sheer blizzard of TV political ads that occupy the airwaves in the weeks and months leading up to an election. In 2002, for example, 1.5 million TV political ads aired in the nation's hundred largest markets. To see them all would take forty hours per week for six years. And, as campaign watchdog Paul Taylor commented, after viewing them all, "you'd surely have gone bonkers."[112] In the 2003 California gubernatorial recall election, the three leading candidates aimed at having every voter with a TV set see their ads at least fifteen times in the final five days of the campaign. "You know the answer to overkill?" one candidate's strategist asked rhetorically. "More. People will do about as well as they advertise."[113] The amount of TV advertising by presidential candidates through November 2003 in Des Moines, in anticipation of the 2004 Iowa caucuses, was *five times greater* than four years earlier. "This is the most [political] advertising on TV I've ever seen," one Iowan stated. "Already, you just don't feel like turning on the TV."[114]

This juggernaut of TV political advertising has significantly molded U.S. electoral politics. For starters, political advertising has replaced press coverage as the main vehicle by which candidates are exposed to the citizenry. In 2002, for example, a viewer was four times more likely to see a political ad during a TV newscast than to see an election-related story, and this does not even factor in the torrent of political ads during all other programs.[115] "The picture of politics has become all ads, all the time," Paul Taylor observed in 2000.[116] TV political advertising has become a cash cow for commercial broadcasters; an election can be the difference between making a profit or going into the red.[117] The average commercial television station earned 3.8 percent of its ad revenues from political ads in 1992; by 2002 that figure approached 10 percent.[118] Cable system operators (e.g. Comcast, Time Warner and Cox) want to get in on the gravy train, too. They aimed to have political advertising account for 12 percent of their advertising revenues in 2004.[119] This means that commercial broadcasters and

cable companies have little incentive to provide free coverage of candidates during their newscasts or debates; they certainly don't offer free
publicity to beer or soft drink manufacturers.

In short, money explains the decline in TV news election coverage.
A survey of late-night local TV news coverage in Los Angeles in the
fifteen days prior to the 1997 mayoral election found almost no time
devoted to the election (although there was time for coverage of skate-
boarding dogs and Easter egg–hunting chimpanzees). The NBC and
CBS stations devoted a combined 5 minutes to the election, while campaign ads during their newscasts totaled 23 minutes—four times as
much advertising as reporting.[120] A study of the candidate coverage on
122 TV stations for the seven weeks prior to the 2002 election found
that just about half of them "contained no campaign coverage at all."
Half of the coverage that did exist came in the last two weeks and
"focused on strategy and polls."[121] Money also explains why commercial broadcasters are the most important lobby that opposes campaign
finance reform. Moreover, in TV news coverage of campaign finance
issues, the corporate media lobby's role in torpedoing campaign
finance reform is rarely, if ever, mentioned.[122] That this cash windfall
comes to networks over the publicly owned airwaves for which they
pay the public not one penny is another matter rarely mentioned.

Even the print media, which do not benefit directly from political
advertising all that much, find their coverage hinged to what candidates are proclaiming in their TV ads.[123] As considerable research
(and almost any sober anecdotal observation) concludes, the veracity
of the information in these political ads tends to be low.[124] Many candidate ads would not be permissible by law if the candidates were
instead hawking commercial products. So misleading are the ads
that a considerable disconnect has emerged between what candidates proclaim in their ads and what policies they pursue once in
office. As one frustrated political columnist put it in 2002, "I am
impressed by how many Republicans around the country come off as
flaming liberals in their commercials. If all I knew about George
Pataki were his political ads, I would think he was a Green social
democrat."[125] Nor is this perception an accident. Precisely as the Bush

administration was gutting environmental regulations, GOP strategists were coaching Republican politicians on how to talk "green."[126] Even representatives of the advertising industry expressed dismay over how misleading or offensive TV political ads had become by 2002.[127] The public response to the barrage of TV political ads ranges from weariness and disgust to apathy. Few praise them for having much value.[128] Although political advertising does not in itself create depoliticization and cynicism about the electoral process, it certainly does nothing to discourage them.

The turn to TV advertising also dramatically raises the cost of political campaigns. The average cost of a successful campaign for the U.S. House of Representatives increased from $87,000 in 1976 to $840,000 in 2000, a dramatic increase even after accounting for inflation.[129] The better-funded candidate won the House race in 2000 95 percent of the time.[130] Were it not for the widespread increase in gerrymandering over the same period—such that only 39 of the 435 races in 2002 were won with less than 55 percent of the vote, and three-quarters were effectively uncontested—the cost of the average House campaign would be radically higher.[131] (As the British *Economist* noted, "In a normal democracy, voters choose their representatives. In America, it is rapidly becoming the other way around."[132])

Statewide races cannot be gerrymandered, but the effects of having big money pour into TV political ads can produce similar results. In 2000, TV political advertising accounted for 52 percent of all the money spent on Senate campaigns, and if the largely uncontested races are removed—for example, Edward Kennedy spent a measly 3.6 percent of his campaign budget on TV ads in his reelection landslide victory—the figure would shoot up closer to 60 or 65 percent.[133] According to the *New York Times*, the cost of gubernatorial campaigns in the nation's largest states doubled or even tripled between 1998 and 2002, and, again, most of the money went toward TV ads. As the top aide for former California governor Gray Davis put it, since local TV stations provide almost no news coverage of the race, "commercials have to fill a void."[134] Some argue that the radical increase in political advertising—in terms of cost as well as number—has actually reduced the ads' effectiveness; candidates will therefore search out different uses for their money. That may well happen, but nothing indicates that the quantity or quality of election news coverage will change as a result.[135] Indeed, much serious political reporting on candidates is already centered on how successful candidates are at raising money.

This massive increase in campaign costs has only magnified the degree of corruption in U.S. governance. Politicians are now obsessed with fund-raising, and it serves as the main prerequisite for success. Indeed, much of a candidate's time, sometimes more than meeting with the general public or boning up on the issues, is spent courting potential contributors.[136] It helps if the candidate is rich, and that seems to be increasingly the pattern. In 2003 numerous millionaires in Illinois were already flooding the airwaves with ads in hope of winning the open Senate seat in 2004. Jim Durkin, the Republican who lost a Senate bid in 2002, acknowledged, "It's extremely difficult for a candidate who is not a multimillionaire to run on TV in Chicago."[137] Those politicians who can attract money stand a far better chance of having a successful career. And who provides the funds for these campaigns? Overwhelmingly the money comes from corporations, special interest groups, and, in particular, wealthy individuals.

In the election cycle ending in 2002, a mere *one-tenth of one percent* of Americans provided 83 percent of all itemized campaign contributions, and the vast majority of these individuals came from the very wealthiest sliver of Americans.[138] These individual contributions account for some 80 percent of all campaign contributions. In the key first quarter of 2003, each of the top four Democratic candidates for president had raised more than 60 percent of their contributions from individuals giving the $2,000 maximum.[139] The emphasis put on money makes sense: since 1976 the candidate who has raised the most money by the end of the year preceding the election has gone on to win his party's nomination. George W. Bush planned to raise more than $200 million in individual donations for his 2004 reelection campaign.[140] In this "wealth" primary, the 96 percent of Americans who never give a campaign contribution count for nothing at all.[141]

To be accurate, campaign spending is not all that counts for corruption in U.S. governance; expenses for lobbying by corporations far exceeds corporate campaign donations, and it is this lobbying armada that contributes greatly to government policies shaped to serve private interests.[142] And this means lobbying, too, is largely the preserve of extraordinarily wealthy individuals and organizations.

The resulting corruption is palpable. Piles of studies highlight how powerful interests manipulate elected officials as the legitimate concerns of working-class and middle-class Americans get lost in the shuffle.[143] So inequality, aided and abetted by public policies, has prospered.[144] Consider federal taxation: In the 1950s, corporations paid 25 percent of federal tax dollars; by 2001 the figure was down to 7 percent. Similarly, the marginal tax rate on the wealthiest Americans has fallen from 91 percent in the Eisenhower years to 38 percent by 2002.[145] In 1998, according to one study, the difference between what corporations reported to shareholders as profits and what they reported to the government as profits (and therefore taxable income) was a whopping $154 billion, yet few in Washington demanded justice and fewer still in the mainstream media broke the news.[146] Even so, with little fanfare the budget for the Internal Revenue Service to investigate tax cheats—who are found predominantly among the wealthy and corporate community, where there are huge incomes to protect—is conceded by the agency itself to be woefully inadequate. As one corporate tax lawyer observed, "The government needs to devote ten times as many resources as it does now if it wants to tax capital effectively."[147] By contrast, government budgets to lock up poor people and blue-collar criminals have bloated. From this perspective, poor people are apparently victims of making dismal campaign contributions and poor lobbying efforts.

MISSING THE STORY—FROM D.C. TO FLORIDA

Much of this corruption escapes the news media's attention, especially since both parties are often in on the fix and there aren't official sources calling journalists' attention to these machinations. Although the Republicans have justifiably earned a reputation as eager to serve their corporate patrons, the Democrats frequently play the same game, albeit with less success.[148] It is now commonplace for major campaign contributors and lobbyists to be "ambidextrous," that is, to work both political parties with equal aplomb.[149] "There's no longer any countervailing power in Washington," former Secretary of Labor Robert Reich wrote in 2001. "Business is in complete control of the machinery of government."[150] Bill Moyers concurs: "In no small part because they coveted the same corporate money, Democrats practically walked away from the politics of struggle, leaving millions of working people with no one to fight for them."[151] If anything, the situation is far worse at the state level, where lobbying, conflict-of-interest, and campaign contribution regulations often are even more lax, and press coverage has generally declined to virtual nonexistence.[152] Corrupt government available to the highest bidder is in some respects more prevalent today than at any time since the Gilded Age.[153] It is effectively institutionalized and beyond critical review by the news media.

One way the news media might provide a corrective to this bipartisan corruption would be to emphasize the activities of "third parties" during electoral campaigns—outsiders, if you will—to broaden and enrich the political culture. Why not have a policy of providing substantial coverage to all candidates who qualify for ballot access and are running serious campaigns? During primaries for the Republican and Democratic parties, why not give substantial coverage to all organized campaigns, and not just the media-designated "frontrunners"? Such a democratic approach would provide attention to the poorest candidates so that they would not be penalized for failing to appeal to the 1 or 2 percent of Americans who bankroll most campaigns. Such a prospect, of course, goes directly against journalism's professional imperative to rely upon official sources as well as the commercial imperative to generate as much revenue as possible. Indeed, apparently the main criterion for serious consideration of a candidate by the news media is having the purchasing power for TV advertising. Serious journalists are well aware of all these problems with electoral coverage, but there is little sense that the situation can or will change under present circumstances.[154]

A key factor is that the news media are part of commercial organizations who hold a distinct stake in the existing order. As they benefit from the political status quo, news media have no desire to publicize candidates that rock the boat. The treatment of Green Party presidential candidate Ralph Nader by the news media in the 2000 election is instructive in this regard. Despite decades of public service and a command of the issues that was arguably unrivaled, Nader was mostly ignored or trivialized in the press. True, U.S. election laws make the prospect of a third-party candidate winning a national election highly remote, but that does not justify his ostracism.[155] In October 2003, the *New York Times* ran a front-page story lamenting that even longshot candidates for the Democratic nomination for president had to be covered since all were entitled to participate in candidate debates. The tenor of the piece suggested that *Times* reporters would not protest if someday they could totally ignore "stragglers in the polls" and, not surprisingly, stragglers in raising money.[156] In this case, journalists were blatantly reinforcing the limits on legitimate debate determined by money-driven politics instead of challenging them on behalf of democracy.

The 2000 presidential election coverage is instructive on this topic because many of the problems of the news media converged. The media did not just fail to protect the public interest but was complicit in a travesty of electoral politics. This topic has received extensive attention elsewhere, so permit me to make a few pertinent points about coverage.[157] The issue is simple: if our news media cannot guarantee—or at least contribute to—an environment in which the candidate who gets the most votes wins the election, then our democratic claims ring hollow.

There are two components to assessing the press coverage of Florida and the 2000 election. The first came during the fateful days between the election and the Supreme Court decision, when the eyes of the nation were focused on Florida and journalists were clamoring for information. Most striking is that despite the plethora of journalists, many potential stories of voting irregularities went unexamined or were covered superficially. As usual, journalism was in most cases reduced to reporting what the two sides, the "official sources," were saying and rarely investigated the "spin." The two sides thus set the range of debate. For reasons that go beyond the point I want to make, the Republicans were much more aggressive in their claims than were the Democrats, and their voices set the tone. A dominant line was that the Republicans had won the election, albeit narrowly, and that the Democrats were trying to use legal manipulation—a voting technicality—to undo it. Because the Democrats failed to forcefully counter Republican claims, such as the charge that the ballots had already been counted and recounted when in fact 175,000 ballots were never counted at all and another million were never recounted, journalists failed to pursue those stories.[158] No one was pushing them to do so. Indeed, Democratic vice presidential candidate Joseph Lieberman even accepted the Republicans' claim that military absentee ballots should be included in the vote tally even if there was doubt about their legitimacy, whereas the Republicans refused to countenance any of the numerous reports of voting irregularities among African American and other largely Democratic constituencies.[159]

Because journalists relied upon official sources and mostly regurgitated inside spin, the most aggressive side handily controlled the emphasis. Lonely souls who believed that the most important thing was to determine who got the most votes, and that whoever got the most votes should win, had too few outlets representing their interests. This shoddy coverage was encouraged by the right-wing media machine, which worked in overdrive to dismiss as "liberal bias" any report that might undermine Bush's claim to victory.

The second component came after the Supreme Court decision in December that handed the election to Bush. This was an extraordinary decision and mostly incomprehensible by constitutional standards.[160] Yet many news media greeted the Supreme Court decision with open arms as settling the matter once and for all. The joy of having established a victor was palpable, and the dubious nature of the victory was virtually ignored. The system worked! Then, over the next several months, investigative reports revealed how Republicans had monkeyed with the Florida electoral system both before and after

election day to take the election away from Gore and from the voters.[161] Most of these stories could have been written in November or
December 2000 had journalists been inclined to dig. The moment of
truth came late in 2001 when the consortium of news media revealed
the findings of their comprehensive recount of the Florida ballots.
According to virtually every headline, the result was clear: Bush won
the election after all.[162] As one newspaper editorial put it, "Bush's status is no longer the subject of serious debate. . . . Can we please move
on to something else?"[163]

In fact, the consortium's recount showed that Bush would only win
a recount of the ballots in the few counties in which Gore had request-
ed such a recount and which looked only at undervotes. By any method
a recount of the entire state or a tally of the intent of voters on over-
votes—as called for under Florida law—showed that Gore would have
won.[164] (Moreover, when one factored in all the chicanery that prevented thousands of people from voting and votes from being counted at
all, Gore won by a decent margin.) In other words, the obvious lead—
that Gore had more votes in Florida—was buried deep in the story.
Mainstream news media had a distinct and obvious interest in
confirming Bush as the legitimate ruler. If they acknowledged that he
had not won the 2000 election, citizens would rightly wonder what the
heck these media were doing during those fateful weeks in November
and December 2000 when the election hung in the balance.

The problems highlighted in the last two chapters associated with
coverage of our political system and elections (including in 2000) and
with coverage of the war in Iraq—the problems with our journalism in
general—are becoming more and more clear. In academia and elsewhere, sober voices are beginning to ask (and write and speak) the forbidden: is the corporate, commercial regulation of journalism
compatible with a democratic society? Jay Harris, the former publisher of the San Jose Mercury-News, argues that the media are "so essential
to our national democracy" that they should not "be managed
primarily according to the demands of the market or the dictates of a
handful of large shareholders."[165] James Carey of the Columbia Journalism School, arguably the most influential U.S. journalism scholar

of the past generation, concluded a 2002 essay on the state of the news media with the somber assessment that "the reform of journalism will only occur when news organizations are disengaged from the global entertainment and information industries that increasingly contain them." As Carey added, "Alas, the press may have to rely upon a democratic state to create the conditions necessary for a democratic press to flourish and for journalists to be restored to their proper role as orchestrators of the conversation of a democratic culture."[166] The problem of the media is again before us.

4

THE AGE OF HYPER-COMMERCIALISM

The major historical development in U.S. media has been the corporate domination of the media system, which was created and protected primarily by corrupt policy making. An important aspect of corporate domination, in addition to media ownership, has been the increasing role of advertising as a source of revenues for media firms. In the first century of the republic, advertising played an insignificant role in both media and society. Democratic theory, free press theory, barely paused to consider it. Advertising emerged in response to the needs of corporate capitalism. It quickly and necessarily came to colonize much of the press, radically transforming its logic and content, and making most media part of the broader commercial marketing system. As a driving force in our media system, advertising has brought commercial values into our journalism and culture in a manner unforeseeable in classical democratic theory and incompatible with traditional notions of a free press. Advertising has become such a dominant source of revenue for media industries that outlets unattractive to advertisers find themselves at a decided disadvantage in the marketplace.

Today we stand on the threshold of a qualitative breakthrough in the commercialization of our media: the traditional distinction between editorial or creative work and advertising—the separation of church and state—is being toppled by commercial pressures. Advertising is anything but a benign process of communicating information about product prices and attributes. And there is nothing "natural" about its existence. Any effort to address the problem of the media has to deal directly with advertising and commercialism.

RISE OF ADVERTISING

Although advertising is nearly synonymous with contemporary media, it developed as a particular response to a specific economic problem: how to allocate goods and services effectively in a profit-driven economy typified by oligopolistic markets. For much of U.S. history advertising remained a minor enterprise. The more competitive economic markets are—as they were before the late nineteenth century—the less likely advertising will play a significant role. In pure competition, meaning markets with innumerable buyers and sellers in which producers can easily enter or leave the market as profit conditions dictate, advertising makes little sense. Producers can sell all they want of what they produce at the market price, a price over which no individual producer has control. Therefore, all emphasis goes to producing as much as possible at the lowest possible cost. Imagine a wheat farmer in the middle of Iowa in 1890. Or, for a contemporary example, imagine someone holding ten shares of GM stock. Why would she advertise the shares if she wanted to sell them? No matter how great her advertising—"My GM shares make you feel better than anyone else's GM shares"—she would not be able to find anyone to pay more than the market price for them. She could also lower her price below the market rate, but that would make no sense because she could sell them at the market price.

Although advertising is not rational for firms in competitive markets, it becomes mandatory for firms in less competitive, especially oligopolistic, markets. In these markets, barriers to entry are high, meaning that even if profits are very high, outside firms or entrepreneurs find it cost prohibitive to attempt to enter the industry. Firms in oligopolistic markets have more control over their fate: they are price makers, not price takers. This is a much more desirable market structure for a firm than is a competitive market; it can lock in profits, through maintaining higher prices, because new firms probably won't enter the market. The handful of firms that dominate oligopolistic industries find explicit price competition to increase market share a dangerous proposition; done improperly or clumsily it could lead to a price war that would shrink the size of the revenue pie of which they are all trying to get the largest slice. (Instead, such markets are typified by inflation. This means that prices in general only go one way—up.) But the firms are still in direct competition. So how does one expand their market share vis-à-vis the competition without engaging in aggressive price warfare that will hurt all the participants? The answer is what economists call monopolistic competition. Its main form in marketing and advertising is the nuclear weapon in the marketing arsenal. While advertising serves many functions, in the end it allows corporations to compete for new customers without engaging in price cutting that would hurt profits.

Leaving aside the notion of advertising as a competitive weapon, it can be put this way: in modern industry, firms have the capacity to produce far more than they can sell unless they lower their prices significantly and therefore cut into their profits. Advertising to generate demand for products increases sales without reducing prices. That is why advertising played only a minor role in pre-twentieth-century capitalism, in which markets tended to be localized and competitive, and a firm could sell all it produced at the market price, over which it had little or no control. The emergence of national markets dominated by giant corporations changed all of that.

The emergence of advertising thus parallels the rise of corporate capitalism. In 1865 advertising accounted for well below 1 percent of the GDP. It was small potatoes. By 1920, following the massive merger wave at the beginning of the century and the rise of big business, advertising accounted for 2.9 percent of GDP. It was during this period that the U.S. political economy made its transition from a largely agrarian economy typified by regional and relatively competitive markets to a much more industrialized economy with national markets. Since 1920 advertising has hovered between 2 and 3 percent of the GDP, making it one of the biggest sectors in the economy.[1] The institutional apparatus of advertising—advertising agencies, trade associations, professional training—only began in earnest in the twentieth century. Advertising as we know it, then, is not a function of capitalism; it is a function of a certain type of capitalism. In 2004 more than $260 billion is expected to be spent on advertising in the

United States.[2] The largest firms in the least competitive markets tend to do the most advertising.[3]

A wave of consolidation in the 1980s and 1990s produced a situation in which a handful of advertising agency supergroups have come to dominate advertising worldwide.[4] The five largest agency groups in the world do more than three-quarters of the industry's business.[5] To give some sense of proportion, the twenty-fifth largest ad agency group in the world had revenues in 2002 of $101.2 million, while Omnicom Group, the largest, had revenues of $7.5 billion.[6] To some extent this consolidation was encouraged by concentration in the media industries. In the United States, eight companies receive 97 percent of television advertising; worldwide, twenty media companies receive 75 percent of advertising spending.[7] With advertising supergroups, advertisers can negotiate eyeball-to-eyeball with media giants. As a result, a flurry of enormous "cross-platform" deals were cemented between 2000 and 2002 by the likes of Pepsi, McDonald's, Procter & Gamble, Philip Morris, and Toyota with media titans Disney, Time Warner, and Viacom.[8]

But what, exactly, is the appeal of advertising for a large corporation? For starters, advertising is crucial to building brand identity. The more a firm can convince its customers that a product is truly distinct from its direct competition (e.g., Coke vs. Pepsi), the less likely its customers will switch to a competitive brand, even if the competitor's price is a bit lower. At the same time the firm hopes that the brand identity being built will attract new customers. Some will come over from competitors, and some will newly enter the market. Advertising is also indispensable for launching new products. The bottom line, so to speak, is that advertising is not an optional business expense. Those few firms that have curtailed it have eventually paid dearly in lost market share. This sometimes is maddening to capitalists, who find it hard to believe that advertising can be so effective. A corporate CEO once supposedly muttered, "I know half of my advertising doesn't work. I just don't know which half."

Built into the structure of oligopolistic markets are problems for advertising content that render it controversial. In the more open markets of the nineteenth century, the advertising content tended to be dry and informational, much like that of a classified ad, or explicitly fraudulent for products of questionable content, such as patent medicines. All in all, advertising was not held in especially high regard as an industry and was ignored for the most part by economists. Dry and informational advertising is not especially effective in an oligopolistic market, however. Advertising must establish a brand's distinctiveness, such that people would prefer it over a competitor. For some brands tangible differences can be elevated into advantages by a talented advertising agency. Even in these cases the suspicion persists among consumers that advertising stretches the truth until it is almost unrecognizable. Advertising in more competitive markets tends also to have a greater emphasis on price and product quality—think of retail advertising in the local newspaper.

But for many brands in oligopolistic markets the differences between them are minimal or irrelevant; they are called parity products. Advertising that simply told the truth—"There is little difference between our brand and the competition and they all cost around the same"—would be counterproductive and absurd. Increased sales offer considerable incentive to fudge the truth; truth is coincidental to the undertaking, if not an obstacle to success. Advertising in such a context must resort to what is called "image" advertising in an attempt to create an illusory difference between brands. (Some sense of the disconnect between advertising and products came with the formation of Thought Equity in 2003. Thought Equity takes TV ads, strips away references to the product, and then resells them to other companies so they can use the same ads to sell different products.)[9] The paradox of advertising is that those products that are most alike require the most advertising to convince people that they are different. So it is that advertising for products like soft drinks and beer rarely contain legitimate product information.

In other words, advertising sells the idea that purchasing a product or service can solve a problem, sometimes one only loosely related to the actual product. Advertising amounts to propaganda.[10] The advertising industry understood its own work along these lines well into the

1930s, when global developments saddled that term with negative connotations. Even if one does not consider whether advertising has any influence on surrounding media content, advertising in and of itself acts as a significant ideological and cultural force in our society. A critique of advertising segues to a critique of "consumer society." Oliver James, among others, has written a devastating critique of consumer society—driven to no small extent by advertising and commercialism—on both mental health and environmental grounds.[11] As numerous critics, especially feminists, have pointed out, advertising often relies on convincing people that there is something wrong with them and that purchasing a product or service will solve their problem. Advertising encourages the intense dissatisfaction so many people today have with their physical appearance, increasingly men as well as women.[12] After all, advertising that said to people, "Hey, you are okay just the way you are," would not get the job done. When negative messages are pounded into people's heads incessantly, they have an effect.

One irony of advertising in our times is that as commercialism increases, advertisers find it harder to succeed and are pushed to even greater efforts: commercialism on steroids. Many in the advertising field are not necessarily excited by increased commercialism—sometimes they are downright critical of the effect on culture—but feel powerless to fight it.[13] "It's the ultimate challenge," one ad executive stated in 2000. "The greater the number of ads, the less people pay attention to them. One ad is the same as another now. People simply don't believe them anymore."[14] The declining effectiveness of individual ads, as overexposed consumers develop immunities, has become a source of real concern for marketing firms, which find themselves forced to run faster and faster just to stand still. One consequence is that television advertising has turned to racier ads to attract attention.[15] In the words of David Lubars, a senior ad executive in the Omnicom Group, consumers "are like roaches—you spray them and spray them and they get immune after a while."[16] The only answer is to spray them some more.

For a democracy, the relationship between advertising and media is of paramount concern. To a significant part of the media, satisfying the needs of advertisers is the most important job. This can change media content dramatically, since the needs of the audience have to be filtered through the much more important needs of the advertiser. For example, advertisers as a rule do not wish to be associated with controversial social or political topics. Even slight opposition by an audience is enough to keep most advertisers away from such content—witness the many advertisers who pulled spots when *NYPD Blue* first featured nudity or when *Murphy Brown* discussed abortion.[17] Advertisers tend to prefer shows that reach their desired audience and do nothing to undermine their sales pitch. Advertisers often pressure networks to have their particular message incorporated into the editorial content as much as possible, as this greatly enhances the likelihood that their commercials will succeed. To the extent this happens, the integrity of the media content, from the perspective of the public and the artist, is inevitably compromised. And, perhaps most important, advertising accentuates the class bias in media. Advertising, on balance, tends to be interested in affluent consumers with disposable income. Hence media firms find it far more rewarding to develop media fare for the upper middle class than for the poor or working class. One look at a typical newsstand provides a clear example of this bias.

The rise of advertising has also affected the structure of media industries. When advertising emerged as the primary means of financing newspapers, professional journalism's development was practically ensured.[18] Advertising accelerated consolidation of newspaper markets and the disappearance of competing dailies, making partisan journalism more suspect. Professional journalism was viewed as a barrier to corruption. Revenues in these newly consolidated markets were more narrowly dependent on advertising. If advertisers could not influence story selection and the tenor of coverage, news maintained integrity.[19] Likewise, national advertising's eruption in the late nineteenth and early twentieth centuries transformed the magazine industry.[20] The role of advertising in influencing content was self-evident at the outset of U.S. commercial broadcasting, because advertising agencies produced the programs that went on the air as well as the advertisements. Even after ad agencies discontinued this practice, broadcasting remained, for all intents and purposes, a branch of the advertising industry.[21]

Ironically, the lesson from commercial broadcasting is that rather than posing the issue as how advertising affects the media, it might be more fruitful to see the issue as how the media are incorporated into the nation's broader advertising and marketing system. As has been widely stated, the product created by commercial media is not so much the broadcast program or print story as it is the audience, which is then sold to advertisers. In the case of entertainment and artistic fare, a boundary has traditionally divided advertising and non-advertising fare. A crucial concern for citizens, artists, and regulators has been to restrict advertising to its clearly defined section of the media. Its job was to sell a product or service and provide the revenues necessary to produce quality programming, over which it should have no direct control. Of course, advertising had all kinds of indirect control over media content—after all, he who pays the piper calls the tune—but practices were established to keep the areas distinct.

Understanding advertising as the motor force in the media helps explain why this barrier between church and state is under such severe attack. It also helps explain why media sectors traditionally not reliant upon advertising and commercialism—motion pictures, books, and recorded music—are being brought into the marketing system. In combination, these developments suggest that the commercialization of the culture is becoming so powerful that the distinction between media and pure commercialism is ceasing to exist. The traditional concern that advertising has a negative effect upon editorial content appears quaint in the age of hyper-commercialism.

HYPER-COMMERCIALISM AND MEDIA

Institutional pressures are combining to generate a commercial tidal wave that is engulfing the culture. It means that traditional commercial media are increasing the amount of advertising. On radio advertising has climbed to nearly 17 or 18 minutes per hour, well above the level only a decade earlier. Television has been subjected to a similar commercial flooding. Until 1982, commercial TV broadcasters operated under a nonbinding self-regulatory standard of no more than 9.5 minutes per hour of advertising during prime-time and children's programming.[22] Even with that standard, commercial broadcasters were lambasted for carpet-bombing the population with ads. Today, however, that looks like a veritable noncommercial Garden of Eden. By 2002, advertising accounted for between 14 and 17 minutes per hour of prime-time programming on the major TV networks.[23] The amount of time devoted to advertising on television during prime time grew by more than 20 percent between 1991 and 2000.[24] Popular programs such as *The Drew Carey Show* had over 9 minutes of advertising in just a half hour.[25] And there is less advertising during prime time than during any other period.[26] In addition, the shorter 15-second spot, which barely existed in the 1980s, has come to account for nearly a third of the commercial time on TV, so the total number of ads has increased even more dramatically.[27] Broadcasters took advantage of new digital compression technologies to "squeeze" programs down in length to allow even more time for advertising.[28] The quest to commercialize the airwaves was pushing to new frontiers, as the UPN Network even considered running onscreen advertisements *during* its programs.[29]

All this advertising reduced the effectiveness of any particular commercial. An advertising industry study completed in 2003 concluded that viewers' attentiveness to TV programs and advertising had fallen sharply. With so many commercial breaks, viewers were "multitasking."[30] Combined with the plethora of channels, it meant that by 2003 it took 97 TV spots to reach 80 percent of the women in the nation. In 1995, one study showed it took only 3.[31] New technologies, such as digitalized personal video recorders, make it easier to avoid advertising, much to the dismay of media executives.[32] "You're getting to the stage where television advertising in certain product sectors and to certain target groups simply becomes wallpaper," one ad executive stated in 2002, "and even if you did spend more on it, it wouldn't work."[33]

Advertisers and commercial media have responded to viewers' inattention. To keep viewers tuned in, NBC experimented in 2003 with interspersing minute-long movie vignettes in the middle of its commercial breaks.[34] Advertisers search for new media, and profit-hungry owners are eager to oblige. Movie theaters, where advertising before films barely existed a generation ago, are being transformed into significant commercial vehicles.[35] "When people are watching TV at home, they might get up and go to the refrigerator during the ads," a Wall Street media analyst said. "But in the movie theater, nobody's going anywhere." Theater advertising increased by 30 percent in 2003 alone.[36] By 2004, Regal CineMedia, the largest movie theater company with six thousand screens, had introduced Digital Content Network, a twenty-minute advertising package to show before all its films, with content tailored to the demographics of the specific theater.[37]

But guaranteeing a captive audience is difficult. The immediate solution to this problem has been a massive increase in "product placement," in which the product is woven directly into the story so it is unavoidable and its message can be smuggled in when the viewer's guard is down. "Traditional advertising will not go away," an ad executive confirmed in 2002, but it "requires an entirely new set of creative tools."[38] Traditionally product placement simply meant using a commercial brand in a movie or TV show when the story called for it. The classic example is when Steven Spielberg used Reese's Pieces in *E.T.* in the early 1980s. The media company could pocket some money, and the advertiser got some attention. Nor was this product placement inconsequential; the candy's sales shot up 65 percent following the film's release.[39]

New technologies make product placement easy. ESPN, with the help of the digital ad firm Princeton Video Image, has been inserting what seem to be product billboards on the walls behind home plate in its Major League Baseball broadcasts. Fans at the games, however, can't see them because the billboards are not there. Other broadcasters have followed suit.[40] During the coverage of the arrival of celebrities at the 2001 Grammy Awards, TV viewers saw a virtual street banner and logos on an entry canopy and sidewalks. The arriving celebrities, however, saw none of these advertisements, because they had been inserted digitally for television viewers.[41] Time Warner has developed "virtual" advertising, in which products are placed retroactively in reruns of popular shows like *Law & Order*.[42]

Product placement has limits, however; at some point the screen will get cluttered and the content that attracts viewers in the first place will get lost in the shuffle. So product placement is undergoing another transformation, one that will alter our media culture—and further weaken the separation between advertising and media content. Now marketers play a direct role in creating entertainment fare, what is called *branded entertainment*. "With product placement, the product is there but doesn't necessarily have a meaningful integration with the story," a Hollywood agent says. "Branded entertainment goes beyond set-dressing and moves into the realm of narrative and character."[43] In November 2003 a major watershed was reached when Coca-Cola announced that it was diverting a significant share of its marketing budget from traditional advertising to new approaches including branded entertainment.[44]

As advertising has grown, so has advertisers' clout; approximately 80 percent of U.S. ad spending is funneled through eight firms, which gives them considerable muscle to push corporate media firms in new ways to present commercial messages. "The tables have turned," Wendy's marketing chief stated in 2002. If media firms do not accommodate their wishes, "marketers will take their ad dollars to other places. There are too many ways to reach consumers." Accordingly, Wendy's was able to have Rosie O'Donnell tout its salads during an episode of her talk show and eat one of them on air.[45] In 2000 cable television's USA Network held top-level "off-the-record" meetings with advertisers in which it allowed advertisers to dictate programming content in exchange for advertising.[46] "The networks didn't use to want us," the J. Walter Thompson executive in charge of Ford's TV account stated in 2002. "I sense a sea change. . . . I've been amazed by people's willingness to write [Ford] into scripts. I've had to remind them to keep it entertaining."[47] AOL Time Warner's TNT cable channel sent out an open call to advertisers in 2000 in an effort to secure product placement wherever possible.[48] Comcast's G4 game-show channel offered advertisers an opportunity to have their commercial appear as part of the programs. As a G4 executive quipped to advertisers, "If you have an idea, we'll play."[49]

Indeed, it is a sea change. "In the old days of product placement, it was all about, 'Can you work it in somewhere?'" a media executive noted. "Now it gets built in instead of forced in." Another media executive observed in 2003, "More and more, the two words 'product placement' are spoken very early in the development process. It's just on the edge right now in basic cable. It's just getting to the point where the networks are completely overhauling how they think about it."[50] In December 2003 Disney and Mindshare, a unit of advertising conglomerate WPP Group, reached an agreement to jointly produce numerous shows for Disney's ABC network, "a deal that would allow advertisers to weigh in early on the programs they sponsor." As ABC president Alex Wallau put it, "This could be an important portion of our prime time programming."[51] ABC also launched an "Advertisers Beyond Commercials" division to "offer advertisers a vast array of opportunities to interact with our programming."[52]

Evidence of product placement's explosion abounds. An episode of the ABC series *Alias* in 2003 featured an extended car chase with a Ford Focus SVT—with a close-up of the car's logo. To make sure the point was driven home two characters on the program mentioned how much they wanted to buy a Ford Focus SVT.[53] Coca-Cola paid $25 million to AOL Time Warner so that, among other things, characters in the WB Network's *Young American* series would "down Cokes in each episode."[54] Much of the impetus for inexpensive "reality" programs has been their affinity for product placement.[55] Coca-Cola had such success as the "almost ubiquitous" product displayed on Fox's 2002 *American Idol* program that the fee for "joint sponsors" for its second season was set at $25 million apiece.[56] "In so-called reality shows," one industry observer noted, "branded products have become as prominent in the plot as in the commercials."[57] ABC's *Extreme Makeover: Home Edition* reality show, launched in December 2003, was sponsored by and starred Sears products.[58]

Mark Burnett, the producer of *Survivor*, claimed that he "looked on *Survivor* as much as a marketing vehicle as a television show."[59] NBC's

2003 reality show *The Restaurant*, also Burnett's creation, was produced by Interpublic, the advertising agency giant, so it could give their "top clients access to product integration deals."[60] This partnership was lucrative, as viewers were treated to obvious hawking of products intended to be part of the story line of this "reality" show. Home Depot effectively underwrote the 2003 reality series *Merge*, which concerned how newlyweds combined their belongings into one household. Home Depot contributed traditional 30-second spots as well as having "product integration on the set."[61]

Television product placement has mushroomed to such an extent that by 2003 it generated a formal independent rating service, iTVX. The iTVX service evaluates product placements on the basis of how long the product is on screen, how prominently it is displayed, and whether it is incorporated into the story line. Product placements are assigned to ten levels depending upon their quality, ranging from a clear product logo in the background of a scene to a level 10, "the ultimate in product placement," when "a show's entire episode is written around the product." One classic example of a level 10 placement was the *Seinfeld* episode in which the characters ate branded candy, Junior Mints, throughout the show.[62] According to one industry observer, the value of a level 10 placement is "off the charts" because it is more likely to be watched and remembered than is a traditional commercial.[63] Not to be outdone, by September 2003 Nielsen Media Research had more than one hundred people working full-time to rate the product placements on prime-time network TV programs.[64] Absolut Spirits "hit the product placement mother lode" when its vodka advertisement for a nude hunk was the center of the story line in an episode of Time Warner's HBO series *Sex and the City*. "This is product placement taken to new heights," an Omnicom executive exulted.[65]

In a sense this is a return to broadcasting's early days, when advertisers actually produced the programs that went on the air. And, fittingly enough, soap operas have embraced the explicit commercialization of content. In 2002 Revlon was given a prominent role in ABC's *All My Children* in exchange for millions of dollars in advertising.[66] There may seem to be nothing new in this. But what is happening now goes far beyond what was done from the 1930s to the 1950s in radio and television, in both scope and intensity. Media firms are now piloting content and pushing the commercial envelope. "As the competition for ad dollars intensifies," one Disney-owned ESPN executive stated, "we are exploring alternative ways to give advertisers added value for their time. We have to think outside the box." Sports programming has proven to be ideal for this new type of product placement. ESPN has begun work on "long-form" commercials in which products are integrated into entertaining segments on sport.[67] ESPN co-sponsored an editorial segment with Wendy's in which famous athletes traveled across the country to ESPN's headquarters, stopping for Wendy's burgers along the way.[68] In 2002 ABC's *Monday Night Football* featured ads with announcer John Madden that were virtually indistinguishable from the program itself.[69] News Corporation's cable television sports show, *The Best Damn Sports Show Period,* assumed by 2003 the "leading role in blurring the boundaries between advertising and programming" when it made the mascot for its largest advertiser, Labatt's beer, a recurring character.[70] "What we are doing is really immersing products into program," a Fox Sports executive acknowledged, "so that they really feel like it is part of the show."[71]

Nor is product placement limited to television. On commercial radio, broadcasters increasingly promote products during regular programming. In 2003 an ad deal between Time Warner and Viacom's Infinity Broadcasting called for radio announcers to plug the America Online service during their on-air banter, as if their testimonials were coming from the heart.[72] Product placement in motion pictures has become standard practice and is thriving, even when the most respected directors are at the helm. In addition to explicit payments, advertisers make deals to promote a film in their other advertising in exchange for having the product appear in a film.[73] *Advertising Age* praised Steven Spielberg's 2002 *Minority Report* that "starred" Lexus and Nokia, while numerous other products, including Pepsi's Aquafina and Reebok, had supporting roles.[74] Even Disney's Miramax

Films, the vaunted "independent studio" of Hollywood lauded for its edgy work, made a deal with Coors in 2002. Coors will be the only beer to appear in Miramax movies, and Coors will be, in effect, the official beer of the studio, sponsoring Miramax movie premieres and promoting Miramax films. Whenever the name Miramax is seen, the name Coors will not be far behind.[75]

Not much can top Agent 007 in the product placement department. Back in the 1960s, directors of the first few James Bond films refused product placement because they considered it "unseemly." "In today's very competitive movie environment," an executive working on the 2002 Bond film, *Die Another Day*, acknowledged, "these additional marketing monies have become a necessity."[76] *Die Another Day* was so laden with product placements that *Variety* called it an "ad-venture," and the *Financial Times* noted that James Bond has now been "licensed to sell." The film featured twenty-four major "promotional partners" that ponied up more than $120 million in promotions and advertising to support the film.[77] James Bond has become a "walking, talking, living and killing billboard."[78] All of this has self-evident implications for what types of films will attract product placement and what types of films will therefore be more likely to get made. David Mamet's 2000 *State and Main* had as a running gag the effort of a Hollywood producer to place a computer product in a nineteenth-century period film.

More profound change is on Hollywood's horizon. All the studios now have top-level executives in charge of departments dedicated to giving "corporate America" what it wants, as one trade publication described it.[79] In 2003 Time Warner's New Line Cinema launched a marketing group to promote "integrated marketing," as this latest genre of product placement is also termed. "The team's goal is to bring in partners earlier in the process, beginning in film pre-production, and potentially fit them into marketing and promotion plans," a New Line executive explained. "It's a cradle-to-grave scenario that we can offer marketers."[80] At around the same time Universal Pictures (then being acquired by General Electric) created a department to "co-create" films with corporations wishing to brand their products.

The purpose was to get the largest marketers to think very big, like "sponsoring a season or slate of movies."[81]

THE CRUMBLING WALL

Product placement and commercialism now permeate the media and culture. Once people become accustomed (or resigned) to rampant commercialism, standards fall. Liquor advertising, mostly banished for decades on commercial television as an example of industry self-regulation, came to cable TV and hundreds of local TV stations by 2003.[82] "Our internal guidelines are more stringent than the [television] industry's," the chief marketing officer for Jack Daniels whiskey said. "A minimum of 75 percent of the audience of a show has to be of legal drinking age before we'll advertise on it."[83] Video games are beginning aggressively to incorporate products into their content. "This is the next frontier of product placement," an Intel executive confirmed. "You're not just watching products, you're actually using them."[84] With the unique ability of video games to reach highly desirable and elusive youth markets, ad industry experts expect this area to flourish.[85] The British author Fay Weldon was paid a handsome fee to place Bulgari jewelry prominently in her 2001 novel, aptly named *The Bulgari Connection*. The book was not especially successful and the practice was greeted with criticism, but the direction is clear.[86]

A whole new paradigm for media and commercialism is being formulated in which traditional borders are dissolving and conventional standards are being replaced. This is more than a power shift from media firms to advertisers; it is about the marriage of content and commercialism to such an extent that they are becoming indistinguishable. Newhouse's Condé Nast publishing house launched *Lucky*, a magazine pitched to women in which advertising motifs appear in the design of every editorial page and all editorial copy is linked to specific products. "Articles in the traditional sense are nowhere to be found."[87] *Lucky* was such a success that plans were quickly drawn up for a similar magazine for men.[88] The largest advertising agencies have begun working aggressively to co-produce programming in conjunction with the largest media firms.[89] In 2003, Time Warner's

WB network worked with advertisers to plan the first program without commercial interruptions but with advertising messages incorporated into the show.[90] Produced by Michael Davies, who developed the
reality show *Who Wants to Be a Millionaire*, the idea is to create "a contemporary, hip Ed Sullivan show" in which singers and other entertainers will perform on a set completely dominated by a product logo,
such as Pepsi, and comedy routines will be designed around particular products being sold.[91]

Infomercials, which once were Madison Avenue's tackiest contribution to commercial culture and which generated $14 billion via TV
sales in 2001, increasingly resemble standard commercial entertainment programming.[92] Apple Computer and Philips Electronic ran
lavish "infomercial" films in paid TV spots that were the first commercials designed not to sell a product but instead to simply draw
viewers to the companies. General Motors followed suit with its 30-
minute infomercial "Monster Garage" in 2003.[93] Budweiser produced
a 7-minute "movie-mercial" that ran on several cable TV networks.[94]
In 2003 Daimler Chrysler brought twenty-five young filmmakers to
the trendy Sundance Film Festival and commissioned each to make a
5-minute entertaining short about Chrysler automobiles, with the
winner earning the right to make a feature-length film on the subject.[95] Daimler Chrysler and Microsoft have already produced film
shorts (and paid for them) to be shown in theaters before feature pre-
sentations; these were meant to be regarded as entertainment with
low-key sales pitches.[96] "Eventually there will be entire channels
devoted to commercials," one advertising executive predicted. "It's all
just content."[97] Indeed, the pioneer in this regard is BMW, which
launched its own 24-7 channel on DirecTV in 2002. The channel
features entertainment programming based around BMW automobiles. "I'm hoping it's the tip of the iceberg," an enthusiastic DirecTV
executive stated.[98]

Similarly, advertising agencies and corporate marketing departments are now producing their own glossy magazines, which are
often indistinguishable from traditional commercial media. This
"custom publishing market" was valued at $1.5 billion in 2001 and

has been growing at 10 percent per year; traditional magazine pub-lishing revenues, in contrast, dropped 11.7 percent in 2001. "These magazines are direct marketing vehicles, but they're more than that," one publishing executive observed in 2002. "They are also intended to have a look and a feel of a real magazine."[99] In 2003 Bloomingdales, for example, began publishing its own magazine to be sold in its stores and to appear like other lifestyle magazines with distinct ads; all the articles about clothing, however, will feature Bloomingdales' products.[100]

The crucial development here stems from the logic implicit in cor-porate advertising. It is to give brands personality, to "brand" that personality on our brains, and all of this has precious little to do with the attributes of the product or service being sold. As Coca-Cola's chief marketing officer put it in 2002, when people buy a can of Coke "they are not buying a product. They are buying the idea of the branding imagery, the emotional connection—and that is all about entertainment."[101] An executive working with Anheuser-Busch remarked, "The idea is not about promoting a product specifically, but connecting with consumers on an emotional level."[102]

Another key area in which the merger of commercialism and con-tent has become more prevalent is in recorded music, and here again the consequences are troubling. "We've decided to work with strong brands where we're targeting a similar market," a top music industry executive noted in 2003, stressing the importance of linking advertis-ers to the music industry. "We've gotten very good at the youth-cul-ture, lifestyle-marketing thing. Together, we can really penetrate the consumer and make things happen."[103] Late in 2002 Pepsi and Sony Music signed a groundbreaking deal, whereby Sony artists will be promoted and distributed in many places Pepsi is sold, while Pepsi will get exclusive rights to use Sony music in its global marketing campaigns. "Music is part of our DNA," a Pepsi executive stated. "Working with Sony lets us bring it to life in the marketplace. The umbrella idea is that Pepsi is bringing you music first. It reinforces Pepsi's connection and leadership in music as a marketer at the same time it allows Sony to get airplay for artists early and often."[104] Time

Warner struck a deal with Toyota in 2002 that, among other things, called for a single from Phil Collins's new CD to be used during Toyota TV commercials for its Avalon sedan. "We are looking for new and innovative ways to get music out to the public," a Time Warner executive explained. "Toyota is the most collaborative partner we ever had. This is real co-marketing."[105]

Toyota, Chrysler, and Honda all sponsor "alternative" music tours, "hoping to slip in some brand messages to a jaded demographic."[106] In 2002 Chevrolet sponsored the "Come Together and Worship Tour" of evangelical Christian artists at the same time it was the exclusive sponsor of Rolling Stone's 28-page 2003 calendar insert in an issue with Eminem on the cover.[107] "Now every record label," one Disney executive stated, "is searching for a strategic marketing person to reach out to corporate America as a way to extend marketing budgets." All these corporate connections fly in the face of popular music's long-standing role as a rebellious and anti-authoritarian medium. Yet it is that anti-authoritarianism that makes music so attractive to corporations as a sales vehicle.[108] One can only wonder how rebellious the music sponsored by marketers and advertising agencies can be. "You don't want it to appear like you are selling out," the president of a teen marketing firm explains. "There's a fine line."[109]

Nowhere in popular music is this tension more dramatic than in hip-hop. After taking a while to warm up, corporate America has fallen in love with the genre. "It influences fashion trends and it is how corporate America builds credible relationships," one advertising executive noted.[110] Because of the music's nature—lyrics are central—and its access to younger audiences, this has become a hot area for marketers. "Once our audience takes to a product," the editor of the hip-hop magazine The Source stated, "their influence is tremendous on the rest of the population."[111] Bragging about products in rap music has been a staple since its inception; in 1979 the Sugarhill Gang rapped about their "Lincoln Continental and sun-roof Cadillac." When Run DMC rapped about Adidas sneakers in 1986, the group's promoter was able to win a breakthrough $1.5 million endorsement contract from Adidas. That appears quaint by today's standards. As one reporter put it, "On any given week, *Billboard*'s Hot Rap Tracks chart is filled with songs that serve as lyrical consumer reports for what are, or will be, the trendiest alcohol, automobile, and fashion brands."

By the end of 2002 the hip-hop label Def Jam was negotiating a deal with Hewlett-Packard to have the computer maker's products featured in the songs of Def Jam artists in exchange for extensive play in the company's advertising campaigns.[112] Sean "P. Diddy" Combs has converted his music career into a marketing empire; his Blue Flame company works with corporations to "build brands that are targeted to trend-setting consumers." This is "the future of advertising and marketing in America," one observer predicted, "a really good example of the avant-garde of the advanced entertainment-hype complex. They have managed to take what started out as a single product—which was music—and turn it into a lifestyle."[113] The commercial cart is pulling the hip-hop horse.[114] "We sang 'My Adidas' because we liked them," said Darryl McDaniel of Run DMC. "That's the difference. Now a lot of guys are just hoping to get that phone call."[115] As one critic wrote, "Is Eminem still a rebel if his videos are tailored by the Gap and furnished by IKEA?"[116]

But to break commercialism down by media category, like music or film, is somewhat misleading in the era of the media conglomerate. Marketers commonly link with larger conglomerates and work massive product placement/advertising/promotional deals across the media firm's entire arsenal of media assets. So it was in 2002 that MasterCard negotiated a deal with Universal Studios worth over $100 million to make MasterCard an integral part of Universal theme parks, movies, home videos, and, possibly, music. This is where the commercial value (and competitive advantage) of having a media conglomerate comes into play.[117]

Although the trend toward hyper-commercialism in media is apparent, the precise outcome of the process remains undetermined. On the one hand, it will take time and experience for marketers to make the new system work. The editor of *Advertising Age*, Scott Donaton, characterized NBC's flagship "brand-integration" program *The*

Restaurant "nearly unwatchable" due to "product placements that are aggressive, intrusive and clunky—anything but the seamless blend necessary to make them bearable, never mind bringing them near to the (perhaps unattainable) standard of enhancing the programming." Donaton pointed to the hit *Queer Eye for the Straight Guy* as the way to go: "It mixes in products without ever stomping on the story."[118]

On the other hand, the public needs time to become acclimated to the new world of commercially marinated entertainment. Marketers express outward confidence that consumers are unperturbed by the increase in stealth advertising. "Maybe it is a subliminal commercial message," one executive remarked about film product placement in 2002, "but there are so many much more overt commercial messages, especially in America, that I don't think anybody worries about it."[119] At their most bombastic, some media firms assert that all this commercial involvement has no influence over actual media content, but this claim is so preposterous that it fails to pass even the most basic giggle test. "Who are they kidding?" the *Los Angeles Times* TV columnist Brian Lowry exclaimed in 2002. "Why would companies pony up cash without expecting some input over how it is spent?"[120] The same critic framed the dilemma a year later: "The ultimate goal after all, is to pull a fast one—to squeeze ads into shows in a manner that makes them both subtle and unavoidable."[121]

When Sony and Liberty Media began selling 15-second "live billboards" for products on their cable TV channel, the Game Show Network, they attempted to address consumers' unease by allowing the host to "poke fun at the product, and be a little sarcastic and funny." The catch is that the quips were preapproved by the sponsor.[122]

HYPER-COMMERCIALISM'S NEW FRONTIERS

Much of the media have been commercial institutions in the United States for generations, so their hyper-commercialism is simply a massive and qualitative leap in a familiar direction. But commercialization is also moving into new frontiers, areas formerly or largely exempt from explicitly commercial values.[123] Public broadcasting and the arts are now overlapping with advertising.[124] Museums, such as the publicly owned and funded Smithsonian, are increasingly turning to commercial sponsors, like Bud Light.[125] Consider colleges and universities. At one time, not too long ago, these were largely noncommercial zones for students, for faculty, and for researchers. Today the college campus looks like a shopping mall. Former Harvard president Derek Bok has written a measured tome on the commercialization of higher education, concluding, "Something of irreplaceable value may get lost in the relentless growth of commercialization."[126] Much of academic research is now driven by the needs of corporations. As the leading scholar of this process observes, what has been lost as a result is "the social role played by universities in American life" and "the integrity of America's research institutions."[127]

Even "anti-establishment" institutions such as independent filmmaking have begun turning to explicit corporate sponsorship.[128] As Thomas Frank and Matt Weiland put it, we are in an age when people are channeled to "commodify your dissent," with all that suggests about the range of opinions that will be encouraged.[129] Fittingly, "cause-related marketing," in which advertisers link their product to some worthy social cause in an attempt to enhance their bottom line, has boomed over the past decade.[130]

Another consequence of hyper-commercialism is that advertising and public relations are converging.[131] PR had once been all about surreptitiously infiltrating the editorial side of the media to plant stories of service to the client, but in the new hyper-commercial order it is effectively merging with what advertisers are doing. Accordingly major marketers like Altria's Miller Brewing Company are shiftng more of their branding budget into PR.[132] The four largest advertising organizations now conduct only one-half of their business through traditional advertising; the balance is in PR, direct marketing, sales promotion, and the like.[133] In this sense the commercial tidal wave is interchangeable with a broader information torrent that overwhelms our senses.[134] The culture it generates, many argue, is more depoliticized, garish, and vulgar than what it has replaced.[135]

The spread of commercialism is so vast as to be almost immeasurable. In 2002 Nike and Microsoft pasted advertising decals on the

streets and subway stations of Manhattan, while the Broadway show
La Boheme featured commercial props in its set.[136] Everything now
seems fair game: buildings use digital technologies to sport "urban
wall displays" that are to old-fashioned billboards what rocket ships
are to the horse-and-buggy;[137] public garages, subway entrances, the
walls above urinals, bathroom stall doors, even baby buggies are
being festooned with advertising.[138] Advertising-packed TVs have
been placed on city buses, in elevators, and in checkout lines.[139] The
new Toyota Center basketball arena in Houston is covered top to bottom with information promoting Toyota products; this is part of the
process of commercializing all places where people gather in public.[140] NBC even established a Patient Channel to bombard people
with advertising during hospital stays. A correspondent for *Electronic
Media* quipped, "If you're sick of TV advertising, a hospital bed might
not be the best place for you."[141] In 2001 the California Horse Racing
Board voted to drop bans on advertising on jockeys and horses.[142]

Even traditional commercial venues are ratcheting up the commercialism. Retail outlets ranging from Wal-Mart stores to shops in New
York's trendy SoHo neighborhood feature ubiquitous TV sets blaring
commercial messages to shoppers.[143] It is a booming ad market. The
Premier Retail Networks operates in-store TV networks that beam ads
in 5,700 stores, including 2,500 Wal-Marts and other chains like Circuit City and Ralph's supermarkets. According to Nielsen Media
Research, the average Wal-Mart shopper stays "glued to Wal-Mart TV
for an average of five minutes per visit, and there's no TiVo ad-zapping
option." "I get a chance to have the last say before he [the consumer]
pulls his wallet out," a marketing executive says about Wal-Mart TV.
"There's no chance of Wal-Mart having bad ratings."[144]

Taking it one step further, D-list celebrities such as Tonya Harding
and Danny Bonaduce were among the twenty or so public figures that
began sporting temporary tattoos for advertisers.[145] Meanwhile,
actress Melissa Joan Hart allowed Sears Craftsman to sponsor and provide products for her groom's bachelor party and then have the event
taped for an edited broadcast of the entire wedding week. The happy
couple stopped off at McDonald's for a quick bite as they went about

some last-minute shopping.[146] Nor are celebrities the only ones who can cash in on their bodies or personal lives. Reebok hired five hundred college students to put bright red tattoos on their foreheads—"head advertising"—during the 2003 Boston Marathon.[147]

The fiscal crisis confronting state and local governments has pushed many to accept commercialization of their activities and operations. Termed the "city-for-sale phenomenon," corporations were sponsoring public spaces from New York's Bronx Zoo to the Beverly Hills City Hall.[148] Illinois' governor loudly announced his plan to "find corporate sponsors for a wide range of state assets to help underwrite the costs of government" in 2003.[149] In 2002 a firm called Government Acquisitions LLC began selling advertising space on police cars in scores of communities.[150] Nextel Communications announced in November 2003 that it would be one of the primary sponsors of the new Las Vegas monorail system, with all the perks sponsors get.[151] Using a special steamroller-like machine, Dori's Beach N' Billboards, Inc., in New Jersey has imprinted the state's beaches with more than 650,000 square feet of Snapple iced tea and Skippy peanut butter ads.[152] Some of these efforts might seem laughable, but they point to some serious issues about democratic governance and accountability.

This is more than just the commercial colonization of new turf. Marketers have had to become much more sophisticated in their techniques to command the attention of their desired target audience. The extent of the research deployed by marketers and advertising agencies to brand their imprint on consumers' brains is staggering. Focus groups, psychologists, and cultural anthropologists are *de rigueur* in market research.[153] Modern marketing is clearly the greatest concerted attempt at psychological manipulation in all of human history. A crucial development in the early twenty-first century has been the rise of "guerilla" marketing; that is, smuggling sales messages into particular "target audiences" by aggressively spreading "buzz" about a hip new product or using other unorthodox and surreptitious methods.[154] Alissa Quart's 2003 book *Branded* chronicles these techniques for marketing to teenagers and their implications in chilling detail.[155] "One of the tenets of teen advertising is that they don't smell the sell," a top ad executive confirmed in 2000. "You can do amazing things if you live where [teens] live and learn to speak to them in a voice they find appealing."[156] The ideal is to have "potential buyers" learn "about a brand from their coolest friends."[157] Or as another marketer put it, "Buzz doesn't happen by accident. This is just real-life product placement."[158]

One striking attempt at guerilla marketing tactics is called "urban marketing," in which a firm such as Coca-Cola sends teams of cool young African Americans with vans full of soda and hip-hop music "to the sweltering streets to engage in a block-by-block battle to win over the hearts and wallets of lower-income, mostly African-American consumers." Maze Jackson, the director of "urban marketing" for one advertising agency, claims this approach is "more authentic" than traditional advertising and allows the firm to zero in on "urban trendsetters." Jackson adds, "We incorporate ourselves into the urban landscape."[159] In short, even personal relationships are now deployed to sell.

Such tactics appear most ominous, and most suspect, when directed at children. Research shows that children respond more favorably to commercials than do any other age group, so they offer the most fertile soil for marketers.[160] In 2001, children's programming accounted for over 20 percent of all U.S. television watching.[161] (This statistic is somewhat misleading, as it refers to children under 12. Another large chunk of television programming is so-called grown-up fare watched by 12–16-year-olds, and created with that market in mind.) Because of these big numbers and the captive audience, entertainment aimed at children has pioneered product placement techniques. In an April 2001 news release, Threshold Digital Research Labs declared that its new animated film *FOODFIGHT!* "incorporates thousands of products and character icons from the familiar packages of products in a grocery store." The story line of this movie involves internationally branded characters who battle the evil Brand X for control of the grocery store. Corporations holding brand names that star in the film include Procter & Gamble (Mr. Clean, Mr. Pringle), Interstate Food Brands (Dolly Madison, Twinkie the Kid, Wonderbread), Pepsi/Frito Lay (Chester Cheetah), Coca-Cola Company

(Coke), Starkist/Heinz (Charlie the Tuna), M&M Mars (M&M's, Skittles), and Uncle Ben's (Uncle Ben).[162]

Essentially the same tactics have been used in children's books, which are full of branded objects and licensed characters. Today millions of books are being sold that have snack foods as protagonists. Parents can currently choose between books starring Cheerios, Froot Loops, M&M's, Pepperidge Farm Goldfish, Skittles, Reese's Pieces, Sun-Maid raisins, Oreo Cookies, and others. In most cases publishers and authors pay licensing fees to food companies who are thus enabled to market products to toddlers sitting on their parents' laps. More than 1.2 million copies of Simon and Schuster's *The Cheerios Play Book* were sold in just two years. One of Simon and Schuster's newest entries is *The Oreo Cookie Counting book*. "It teaches children to count down from 10 cookies to 'one little Oreo . . . too tasty to resist.'"[163]

Children represent a vital market; in 2004 children under 12 in the United States will spend $35 billion of their own money and influence another $200 billion in family spending.[164] But it also must be noted that marketers are increasingly recognizing children as the necessary point for building brand awareness, even for adult products. The key is to reach them before their brand decisions have been made and before their defenses to advertising have been developed. Mike Searles, president of Kids "R" Us, a chain of specialty children's stores, explains that where commercial marketing to children is concerned, "All these people understand something that is very basic and very logical, that if you own this child at an early age, you can own this child for years to come." In effect, "companies are saying, 'Hey, I want to own the kid younger and younger and younger.'"[165] As the editor of *Parents* magazine put it in December 2003, "The idea is these children are active consumers at very young ages, so let's get them now before somebody else does."[166] This is why tobacco and alcohol companies, among others, have been criticized for aiming their advertising at people who are not old enough to use their products legally. Although the PR fallout can be brutal, it makes rational economic sense.[167]

The hunger for new consumers also explains why the hotel chain Embassy Suites, for example, signed a $20 million deal with Viacom's

children's channel Nickelodeon. "We found in research that 95 percent of kids could name at least one hotel chain," a Nickelodeon executive enthused.[168] Ford Motor Company signed up with Nickelodeon
for the same reason.[169] Traditionally noncommercial venues such as
public television, public schools, and school textbooks are now
loaded with commercial messages.[170] The funding crisis facing public
education has opened the door for marketers. According to Joel Bab-
bit, the former president of Channel One—a news program with ads
that is seen daily in schools across the nation: "The biggest selling
point to advertisers" of this type of compulsory education via commercial TV is the lack of freedom it imposes in "forcing kids to watch
two minutes of commercials." The virtue from an advertiser's stand-
point, he explains, is that "the advertiser gets a group of kids who
cannot go to the bathroom, who cannot change the station, who cannot listen to their mother yell in the background, who cannot be
playing Nintendo, who cannot have their headsets on."[171] In 2003
marketers led a successful campaign to get commercial messages into
some 25,000 of the nation's 75,000 preschools.[172]

For a society whose politicians and citizens love to speak of their
great love for children, we certainly have a lot of suffering children.
The Centers for Disease Control is now calling attention to the epidemic of childhood obesity spurred to some extent by nonstop TV
advertising for sugary products and junk food.[173] Two-thirds of the
commercials aimed at children during Saturday morning TV shows
feature high-calorie, high-sugar foods.[174] Here the problem includes
the booming practice of licensing popular children TV and film characters to junk food manufacturers. Nearly half of the $700 million
market for dry fruit snack products have such licensing agreements
in 2004; in 1996 only ten percent of them did. Betty Crocker affiliates
its products with PBS's Dragon Tails characters, Scooby-Doo, Winnie
the Pooh, and Buzz Lightyear. The target audience is often children
under the age of six.[175]

Childhood in our country is becoming largely about commercial
indoctrination designed to enhance marketers' profitability.[176] In the
words of Nancy Shalek, the president of Shalek Advertising, which

handles advertising campaigns for children's clothing, "Advertising at its best is making people feel that without their product, you're a loser. . . . Kids are very sensitive to that. If you tell them to buy something they are resistant. But if you tell them they'll be a dork if they don't, you've got their attention. You open up emotional vulnerabilities and it's very easy to do it with kids, because they're the most emotionally vulnerable."[177] As one market researcher said at the Seventh Annual Consumer Kids Conference in Arizona in May 1995, "Imagine a child sitting in the middle of a large circle of train tracks. Tracks, like the tentacles of an octopus, radiate to the child from the outside circle of tracks. The child can be reached from every angle. This is how the [corporate] marketing world is connected to the child's world."[178] Gary Ruskin, the head of Commercial Alert, a group founded by Ralph Nader, observes: "In our business culture, children are viewed as economic resources to be exploited, just like bauxite or timber."[179]

As marketers intrude deeper into our children's lives, many roundly detest their efforts. Yet hyper-commercialization goes mostly unmentioned in the media or political culture. If we had a media system that truly "gave the people what they want," commercialism would likely be radically reduced. An advertising industry survey conducted in December 2002 found that a "whopping 75% of U.S. consumers believe advertising intrusion into content has increased over the past year," and most of them found the development negative. The only good news for marketers was that younger people tended to be somewhat less critical of hyper-commercialism than their elders, although their antipathy was still pronounced, with 44 percent of people under thirty-five expressing concern about the encroachment of advertising into editorial content.[180] Indeed, this slightly more welcoming attitude among the young appears to be the hope of marketers. One ad agency executive claimed that he did not think young people cared about commercial encroachment at all: "For them, the ads and editorial are all part of the same experience."[181]

But any way one spins it, hyper-commercialism does not "give the people what they want." To the contrary, people are given a "choice" from within the range of what content/advertising bombardment generates the most money for large corporations. As a *Los Angeles Times* TV critic noted in 2003, people may grow "indifferent to such excesses or, more likely" be "bludgeoned into submission by them."[182] In due time, as people select from this commercially saturated menu, they can expect to be informed by academics and pundits that they are getting exactly what they want.

Hyper-commercialization and its effects on consumers lead to deeply troubling implications for the exercise of democracy in the classical sense of the term. The democratic philosopher Alexander Meiklejohn said it well when he noted that if commercialism provides the logic for all speech, the commitment to public communication disintegrates under the obsession with material self-interest. Truth is far less important than what one can convince people to believe in order to get them to serve your commercial needs.[183] What was written by Paul Baran and Paul Sweezy over forty years ago holds true for today:

> It is sometimes argued that advertising really does little harm because no one believes it anymore anyway. We consider this view to be erroneous. The *greatest* damage done by advertising is precisely that it incessantly demonstrates the prostitution of men and women who lend their intellects, their voices, their artistic skills to purposes in which they themselves do not believe, and that it teaches [in the words of Leo Marx] "the essential meaninglessness of all creations of the mind: words, images, and ideas." The real danger from advertising is that it helps to shatter and ultimately destroy our most precious nonmaterial possessions: the confidence in the existence of meaningful purposes of human activity and respect for the integrity of man.[184]

What such a commercial culture tends to produce—and what the avalanche of commercialism encourages—is a profound cynicism and materialism, both cancerous for public life. The message is constant: all our most treasured values—democracy, freedom, individuality, equality, education, community, love, and health—are reduced in one way or another to commodities provided by the market. Social problems either cannot be solved or can be solved only through individual material consumption. Likewise, human happiness derives from material consumption.

Rafts of academic books have been published in the past decade—and more are certain to come—explaining that this commercialization of life is actually complex and nuanced and cannot be criticized in such a categorical manner. James Twitchell has spent much of his time arguing that this commercialization is, in fact, a populist phenomenon that bodes well for the species.[185] Some assert that commercial cultures hold the potential for popular sovereignty, albeit in a form we may not yet understand. But in the classical sense of the term *democracy*—the notion of informed self-government—there is no plausible democratic destination to the path upon which we currently travel. As James Rorty wrote some seventy years ago, advertising represents "Our Master's Voice," the voice of the wealthy, and the culture it dominates will always ultimately be biased to serve the interest of the privileged few.[186]

In hyper-commercialism, corporate power is woven so deeply into the culture that it becomes invisible, unquestionable. The type of "democracy" that grows out of our current commercially drenched culture—at its best—is one with little room for participatory governance. In it people have the "freedom" to pick from commercial options provided to them by marketers. A 2002 newspaper advertisement extolling the status quo by the advertising industry PR group, the Advertising Council, stated it clearly:

> By deciding to continue reading, you've just demonstrated a key American freedom—choice. And, should you choose to turn the page, take a nap or go dye your hair blue, that's cool too.
>
> Because while rights like freedom of speech, freedom of religion and freedom of the press get all the attention in the Constitution, the smaller liberties you can enjoy every day in America are no less important or worthy of celebration.
>
> Your right to backyard barbecues, sleeping in on Sundays and listening to any darned music you please can be just as fulfilling as your

right to vote for the president. Maybe even more so because you can enjoy these freedoms personally and often.[187]

The Ad Council's view of freedom could serve as the Magna Carta for Madison Avenue's new world order.

ADVERTISING AND POLICY

Advertising and commercialism tend to be regarded by Americans and mainstream political culture as inevitable, the price of living in a free society. Such was not public opinion prior to the twentieth century. When advertising crystallized into its modern system in the first decades of the twentieth century it was hardly embraced by the populace. In fact, advertising exists today not because people want it but because crucial policy decisions made it viable. In a broad sense, advertising as it developed was dependent upon policies that not just made profit making sacred, but more crucially, made the giant corporation the dominant economic unit. In a narrow sense, advertising required several distinct policy measures specific to its needs to survive and prosper. It needed a commercial media system, so there would be places for advertising to be displayed. It needed to be considered a business expense, so the money spent on it would not be taxed; otherwise businesses would be less likely to advertise. It needed to have the right to make irrelevant or misleading claims or inferences about products; it certainly could not prosper were it required to emphasize price and product information, and accurately represent that material. In more recent times, other key policy issues emerged: for example, should advertising be permitted in public schools; should billboards be permitted and, if so, where; should advertising by political candidates be limited; and, quite fundamentally, should advertising have absolute protection under the First Amendment? All told, there is nothing natural about advertising at all. Its contours are the result of numerous public policies.

Even when the corporate political economy became entrenched and advertising began to blossom, the first narrow policy issues were far from settled. Public concern with fraudulent and misleading advertising became widespread during the Progressive Era. Several newly formed trade organizations, including the Association of American Advertising Agencies and the Association of National Advertisers, worked the corridors in Washington to ensure friendly treatment for the industry. Because advertising was primarily conducted by big businesses, these lobbies generally supported the business agenda regarding trade, taxes, and regulation. Most important to the advertising industry in the 1930s was how advertising would be regulated. Since advertising was a recent development, few laws on the books addressed its regulation. The only federal regulation permitted by law was when fraudulent advertising adversely affected competitors; adverse effects on the general public went unregulated. These practices combined with the political tumult of the Depression years to create a critical juncture for advertising as an institution in the United States.

A feisty consumer movement, led by the group that became the Consumers Union, emerged in the late 1920s and 1930s, and it made the regulation of advertising the centerpiece of its organizing campaign. Advertising was lambasted in numerous bestselling books as an unethical enterprise that disempowered consumers with corporate propaganda, rather than informing them so that they could become wise and efficient consumers. As Inger Stole has documented in her pioneering research, the consumer movement argued that advertising should serve the public rather than business because in an oligopolistic consumer economy people *needed* reliable product information. For those in the consumer movement, advertising was an irrational and corrupt solution to the serious problem of informing people about consumer products. Throughout the 1930s the consumer movement lobbied for the federal regulation of advertising, which would require advertising to be truthful and place the burden of proof upon the advertiser to establish that truth. Half-truths, a staple of advertising, would not be acceptable. Moreover, advertising would not be permitted to make grandiose and irrelevant claims, what is called puffery. In short, the consumer movement wanted to outlaw advertising as we know it, transforming it into an honest source of information for consumers. In addition, there was a parallel critique of the negative influence of advertising upon media, culture, and other social institutions—what it called "ballyhoo." The consumer movement wanted to wrestle commercialism to the ground.[188]

The advertising industry responded to the consumer movement with an avalanche of public relations and lobbying activity, all designed to prevent regulation in the public interest. As Stole chronicles, public pressure finally led Congress to authorize the regulation of advertising on behalf of the public by the Federal Trade Commission (FTC) in 1938, but after years of world-class lobbying the resulting law was business-friendly and did not threaten anything except explicit cases of fraudulent advertising. Newspapers, magazines, and commercial broadcasters—which did not want to see the amount of advertising threatened—were crucial to undermining popular awareness of and support for the consumer movement's demands. The practice of advertising as a whole remained unchanged by the new law.

Even with this relatively weak law, the door was open for the government periodically to pursue fraud aggressively. Much depended upon the political temper of the times. To reduce the possibility of serious FTC regulation, the advertising industry, through its Advertising Council and other mechanisms, conducted heavily promoted public relations activities to establish its ability to regulate itself and to suggest minimal government regulation.[189] The consumer movement backed down—the nature of the industry was now off-limits to critical discussion—and turned its attention to other issues, such as product and workplace safety. To the extent advertising remained in its purview, the movement concentrated on explicit examples of fraudulent advertising or advertising of dangerous or fraudulent products. This approach concentrated on restricting crude nineteenth-century-style "snake oil" advertising, while allowing more sophisticated and less directly poisonous advertising to fly underneath the regulatory radar.

Crucial regulatory issues remain. Of foremost concern to the advertising industry has been maintaining the right of businesses to deduct advertising expenses from their taxable incomes. To lose this

privilege—a subsidy if you will—would make advertising considerably less attractive to businesses.[190] Similarly, whenever governments suggest that they might tax advertising to generate revenues,
the industry goes into full wartime mode, invariably arguing that a
tax would violate their free speech rights.[191] At regulators' most
aggressive point, during the halcyon days of the 1960s, TV advertising for cigarettes was required to be followed by advertising chronicling the health hazards of smoking. In such an environment,
tobacco advertisers elected not to advertise at all on television.[192]
This was the caliber of regulation sought and abandoned by the
1930s consumer movement.

Since the 1970s, as the political climate has become more business-
friendly, the FTC has come to accept "tougher self-regulation" as "the
best response" to criticism of advertising.[193] Advertising remains a bitter pill for many Americans to swallow, and it continues to prompt
activists of various types to demand active regulation. In recent times
the commercial blizzard aimed at children has prompted many to call
for tougher regulation of marketing to kids. In parts of Europe, advertising to children is strictly regulated, even forbidden—but in the United States, the advertising industry characterizes that as imposing
"government censorship."[194] Along these lines, the spread of commercialism to public education has attracted activist attention. As political ads have become a major source of revenue for both commercial
media and the advertising industry, battles for campaign finance
reform have erupted. In 2003 Commercial Alert launched a proposal
to require TV networks to disclose when they engage in product placement, thereby putting a damper on hyper-commercialism.[195]

The system of advertising as a whole, however, has never been
more powerful or privileged. Indeed, the U.S., state, and local governments have become major advertisers in their own right—including
on the public airwaves. (Those ubiquitous lottery ads come to mind.)
In this manner the public provides another important subsidy to
both the advertising industry and the commercial media system.

The advertising industry has also been working the court system
to ensure that the First Amendment be extended to advertising, or

what is termed commercial speech. The Supreme Court had ruled in a unanimous decision in the 1940s that the regulation of advertising—a purely commercial undertaking—did not violate advertisers' First Amendment rights. This position had been commonly accepted at that point and continued to be prevalent for decades thereafter. By the 1970s, however, the advertising industry began lobbying incessantly to see that the First Amendment was extended to advertising; such protection would virtually eliminate the prospect of government regulation. In the new hyper-commercial environment proponents of such a view argue that commercial speech is every bit as important as political speech and therefore deserves the same treatment.[196]

Some conservatives suggest that commercial speech, since it is related to the market and since the market is the foundation of a free society, is arguably *more* deserving of First Amendment protection than political speech.[197] With no sense of irony, the industry's main contention for extending the First Amendment to advertising—and thereby precluding public interest regulation—was that consumers had a right to reliable commercial information.[198] The broader problem of hyper-commercialism made the extension of the First Amendment to advertising logical: If everything in the media culture is becoming commercial, if editorial content is chock-full of commercial messages, then either everything is protected by the First Amendment or nothing is. It appeals to our sensibilities to see the ground covered by the First Amendment expanded, although in truth what that means is that a huge area of public life will be effectively removed from popular accountability. In that sense, as the First Amendment "expands," the space for democratic discourse and policy making shrinks. Corporate power is written into the Constitution. This issue is not yet settled, though it may be within a few years.[199]

Under hyper-commercialism, every new significant communication technology is heralded for its ability to empower citizens and undermine the hold of advertisers over the media and the audience. Remote controls made switching away from commercials a couch potato's delight. Cable television was going to bring channels for

every possible interest and reduce the power of the Big Three networks to pummel us with lowest-common-denominator programming and advertising. The Internet was going to render advertising
and commercialism moot; after all, who would put up with advertising when a noncommercial nirvana was a mouse click away? Then
along came TiVo, with its magical ability to make commercials disappear seamlessly. Technology, it would seem, was constantly hammer-
ing nails into advertising's coffin.

The irony, of course, is that the rise of these advertising-slaying
technologies has also been a period in which commercialism has car-
pet-bombed every corner of the nation. In chapter 6, I return to this
subject and review the role of the Internet and TiVo on the media system. For present purposes the point to be made is that new technologies can assist advertisers as much as those who do not wish to be the
recipients of advertising. Some developing technologies assist marketers in linking their messages to what consumers actually purchase and track consumers across their use of different media.[200]
They will also provide research useful in helping advertisers locate
new advertising-ready realms.[201] In short, they give advertisers new
power to corner people and pummel them.

Despite advertising's ubiquitousness, the industry remains the
Achilles' heel of the commercial media system because it is so dubious and unpopular. The massive public support for banning telemar-
keting phone calls—to the point that no politician dared support the
telemarketers—is a clear indication of this sentiment.[202] What is striking about the resurgence of interest in media policy issues at the
dawn of the twenty-first century is that the issue of hyper-commercialism is beginning to register as a significant political concern. Most
people do not like it, and when they understand that there is something they can do to lessen it, they tend to be open-minded, if not
enthusiastic. Hyper-commercialism's detractors cover the political
spectrum; indeed, some directives to keeping advertising out of
schools and off children's TV programs come from the political Right.

In the United States the question of advertising and commercialism is at the very heart of the problem of the media; if there is going

to be a democratic resolution to that problem, advertising must be confronted. As media critic Janine Jackson concluded, after chronicling the many ways in which advertising corrupts media, at some point it becomes logical, if not imperative, to "reconsider the whole idea of commercial sponsorship as a way to fund media."[203] Such an encounter will mean, in addition to taking on media giants, butting heads with the largest and most powerful corporations in the nation, indeed the capitalist political economy as it exists in the United States today.

5

THE MARKET *ÜBER ALLES*

Even though many Americans agree that our media system fails to promote an informed participating citizenry and instead bombards us with unwanted hyper-commercialism, that is not enough to generate action. One crucial barrier keeps citizens from opposing the current structure: the notion that the U.S. media system is based upon the competitive market, and the competitive market, despite its limitations, is the best possible system because it "gives the people what they want." As one communication professor presented this conventional wisdom in 2003: "In the marketplace of entertainment, the public determines what's successful, not the producer."[1]

In this chapter I address the notion of the market as a democratic institution in the realm of media in the United States. Because the claim is made most strongly for entertainment media, they will receive the brunt of my attention. I will first look closely at just how competitive media markets actually are. To the extent that media markets veer from the competitive ideal, their value as accountable or democratic institutions becomes dubious in conventional market theory. At the same time, the problem with market regulation is not merely a matter of economic concentration—even competitive markets are problematic. Perhaps we should not even expect the market to be the appropriate regulator for the media system, or many components of it, because media present many unique attributes that undermine the suitability of market regulation.

I then turn to a consideration of the strongest and arguably most powerful defense of the market, that it "gives the people what they want." Markets do compel media firms to please the people, though nowhere near as single-mindedly as market proponents would have us believe. It is also true that the market compels firms to give us plenty of what we don't want, whether we like it or not, and gives us no recourse to address these flaws within the market. I conclude the chapter by reviewing what remains of the arguments in praise of the commercial media marketplace, as provided by its leading academic advocates.

IS THE MEDIA SYSTEM A COMPETITIVE MARKET?

The case for markets, at its simplest, is elegant. Markets are voluntarist mechanisms in which people interact freely, and they invariably lead to the most efficient deployment of resources and maximum human happiness. Applied to media, the model works as follows: if people desire a particular media content, competition will force media corporations (or entrepreneurs, for a sexier, swashbuckling designation) to provide such content. Media firms will be forced to give people what they demand or go out of business. If none of the existing firms has a sufficient grasp of public sentiment, new firms will enter the fray, capture the business, and force the existing firms to get with the program or face ruin.

If one regards the content of media as deficient, the problem is not with media firms, who are forced by economic pressure to provide the audience with what it demands, but with the people themselves, who demand such fare. The system works, as long as the government does not try to interfere with its operations. Government regulatory intervention to alter media content, no matter how well intended, will only interfere with the ability of the market to regulate media, and therefore interfere with the people's will. Similarly, some theorists emphasize how labor unions interfere with market mechanisms and thereby distort the ability of the market to represent perfectly the will of the people with the utmost efficiency.

One factor, though, above all others, can undermine this model's theoretical basis immediately. If a market is imperfect, meaning not competitive in an economic sense, a market cannot work its magic—and the system cannot be entirely responsive to the audience or offer the most efficient use of resources. Although this point is often lost in discussions, contemporary media markets are not even remotely comparable to competitive markets in the microeconomic sense of the term. Media markets are in many respects textbook examples of corporate-dominated oligopolistic markets ruled by a small number of firms. And these firms, as we shall see later in this chapter, are typically vast conglomerates that function as oligopolies in not just one media market but in many.

In media, as elsewhere, these monopolistic/oligopolistic markets are predicated upon high barriers to entry that severely limit the ability of small start-up media firms to enter the market successfully. Indeed, one major development in media markets over the past century has been the manner in which they work to the advantage of the largest players, making the possibility of becoming a commercially viable media producer difficult. To the extent that the dominant firms in these oligopolistic markets use their market power to limit the range of offerings, notions of a free press are severely compromised.[2] There are thousands of media firms in United States, but only a minute fraction of that total reach significant audiences.

This type of economic concentration, in which a firm attempts to have as large a percentage of the industry's output as possible, is called horizontal integration. A monopoly like Rockefeller's Standard Oil is the ultimate form of horizontal integration. Media markets stop short of monopoly and settle into oligopoly. The economic incentives for media corporations to be in such a market are obvious. Economic concentration tends to reduce risk because barriers to entry shut out newcomers and therefore raise profits for those inside. It does this by giving the large firms that dominate these oligopolistic markets considerable control over pricing. Unlike competitive markets, oligopolistic markets tend to force prices up.[3] Firms in oligopolistic markets have much greater leverage over their suppliers (and labor) to negotiate better prices. As a result of its acquisition of AT&T's cable systems, for example, Comcast expected to cut its costs for carrying cable channels by $270 million.[4] Media firms also have the leverage to extract high rates from advertisers. The more concentrated the ownership, the higher ad rates tend to be.[5]

Horizontal integration also opens new profit-making opportunities. Wal-Mart, for example, accounts for 30 percent of all U.S. DVD and video sales, as well as 20 percent of all U.S. music sales.[6] In addition to giving Wal-Mart strong influence over what will be produced—because it can choose what to promote and sell—this integration also allows Wal-Mart to leverage its market power to strike deals with entertainment firms and move into entertainment-related merchandising.[7] Similarly, Barnes & Noble used its domination of retail book selling to launch its imprint of books reprinting works in the public domain. "Since they don't pay a 50 percent markup" to a publisher, a Disney executive explained, "they can apply that advantage to price and still make more money than publishers selling the same Charles Dickens title."[8]

Major media markets—television networks, cable TV systems and channels, music, motion pictures, newspapers, book publishing, magazines, and retail sales—are almost all classic oligopolies with only a handful of significant players in each market. In the U.S. music industry, for example, following the 2003 announced merger of Sony's and Bertelsmann's music subsidiaries, four firms sell almost 90 percent of the music.[9] In motion pictures, no more than six firms rule the roost, accounting for over 90 percent of the industry's revenues. Moreover, the number of significant firms is stagnant or shrinking in almost every case. The three largest publishers of college textbooks accounted for 35 percent of the U.S. market in 1990; by 2002 they had almost doubled their share.[10] Magazine and book publishing overall has undergone considerable consolidation over the past decade.[11] In radio broadcasting, the two largest firms, Clear Channel and Viacom's Infinity, do more business than the firms ranked 3–25 combined.[12] Concentrated ownership tends radically to improve the profit picture for successful media firms: newspaper publishing—long based on local market monopolies and chain ownership—has been one of the most lucrative industries in the United States throughout the twentieth century; local television stations—always an oligopoly—routinely generate returns on sales in the 50 to 60 percent range.[13]

The cable TV systems industry (e.g. Comcast, Time Warner, and Cox) has undergone perhaps the most striking consolidation over the past fifteen to twenty years. It has gone from a "ma and pa" industry of the 1970s to an enterprise in which six giant firms control over 80 percent of the market.[14] The power of such consolidation is immense: since 1996 (when the Telecommunications Act was passed) cable TV rates have increased at three times the inflation rate.[15] Comcast claims over 30 percent of the market, and by all accounts further consolidation is inevitable, as smaller firms cannot compete with such a Goliath.[16] "Size has always mattered in this business," a Comcast executive noted in 2003.[17] For one thing, large cable systems have negotiating leverage with the stations that need to be carried on their systems; independent cable TV channels cannot survive, because they have no negotiating power, unless a large media company, more often than not a cable TV systems operator, owns them.[18] Comcast had so much leverage over cable TV channels by the fall of 2003 that even the other media giants were forced to make concessions unthinkable in earlier times to remain on Comcast systems.[19] "There are three companies" that will own cable TV channels, "Viacom, AOL Time Warner, and News Corporation," mogul Haim Saban predicted in 2003. "The rest are going to get gobbled up."[20] As the trade publication *Variety* puts it, "Congloms are stalking the media jungle like Armani-clad velociraptors, ready to swoop down on low-flying cable nets, increasingly vulnerable in the new age of accelerating takeovers."[21]

By 2003, the standing joke was that it was easier for an independent cable entrepreneur to "touch the moon" than to get a new cable TV channel carried by the giant cable TV systems operators.[22] It was left to CNN founder Ted Turner to offer perspective: "The days of starting up a cable-television network or trying to do it from outside the media business are over. It's almost impossible."[23]

This result points to one great feature of media consolidation: it begets further consolidation. Firms need to grow to be able to survive high-stakes competition.[24] As Nicholas Garnham asserts, media "concentration is, in different forms, the essence of survival in the media sector, since it alone ensures the necessary economies of either scale

or scope."[25] It is on these grounds that media concentration is defended as necessary and economically justified.[26] If, in fact, concentration
is unavoidable to a certain extent in commercial media markets, it
places a premium upon media policies that account for and compen-
sate for it. But much of this concentration is not necessitated by markets but results instead from policy making that encourages it. That is
transparently the case in radio and television broadcasting and in
cable television. There is no evidence that the mega-firms in these
industries would become economically unviable if they were banned
from owning so many stations or channels.

Media concentration is also promoted through vertical integration, which denotes owning both the content and the conduits to distribute that content. It has manifested itself in U.S. media over the
past fifteen years, and the recent merger of General Electric's NBC
and Vivendi means that all commercial TV networks are owned by a
media corporation that also owns a major Hollywood film studio.
Each firm also owns TV show production studios as well as cable TV
channels. Vertical integration makes particular sense for media
because it helps lessen the risk associated with an industry like
motion pictures, in which films can be blockbusters or complete box
office duds.[27] Vertical integration is a powerful stimulant to concentration; once a few firms in an industry move in this direction, others
must follow suit or they can find themselves at an insurmountable
competitive disadvantage—possibly blocked at all turns by opposing
gatekeepers. This, too, raises the barrier to entry for prospective newcomers because they must be able to generate vertically integrated
operations in order to compete.

This is why regulators have previously prohibited vertical integration in media. The most striking examples historically are the prohibition of the film studios from owning their own movie theaters and
the prohibition of TV networks from producing their own prime-
time entertainment programs. Large commercial lobbies have done
everything in their power to get these ownership restrictions eliminated. Vertical integration lowers costs, lowers risk, and increases
profit. It is almost always good for the vertically integrated company;

whether benefits are shared with the public is another matter. The effect of lifting the prohibition on TV networks producing and owning their own prime-time programs in the early 1990s has been to throw the independent TV production industry in Hollywood into turmoil. "Consolidation has killed my business as an independent producer," one executive remarked. "I think anytime you have a business where it's in the hands of five companies, then it's bad for everyone."[28] Well, not quite everyone.

Vertical integration also combines with horizontal integration to sound the death knell for major "independent" film studios. "Being a producer that isn't under the same umbrella ownership as major network, cable or satellite channels," a writer in the trade publication *Television Week* observed, "can be a deadly experience."[29] The independent studio DreamWorks, for example, has produced hit after hit, but without a more vertically integrated structure, its hopes for profitability are remote.[30] "Wall Streeters are adamant that both MGM and DreamWorks will have to find a way of sizing up their operations," according to the trade publication *Variety*. "Not having the vertical integration and ownership of cable networks hurts MGM's ability to sell deeply into their film library," an industry analyst maintains. "Pure-play is a difficult environment when every one of their competitors is vertically integrated."[31] In November 2003 DreamWorks sold its music division to the giant Vivendi Universal, and signed a deal to let General Electric's Universal Studios continue to distribute DreamWorks films until 2010.[32]

By 2000 these pressures fomented such frenzied deal making that *Variety* noted, "U.S. media and entertainment companies are pairing off faster than New York yuppies at happy hour."[33] When AOL and Time Warner merged in 2000 the value of the deal at the time was nearly 500 times greater than the value of the largest U.S. media deal just twenty years earlier. The recession of 2001–02 cooled deal making a bit, but the trend toward increased consolidation remains strong.[34] Even in hard times, media firms revealed a desire to merge and acquire. "We need new revenue streams because the name of the game is growth," Time Warner's executive in charge of the magazine division, the world's largest magazine company, announced in 2003.[35] The GE–Vivendi deal was valued at $42 billion in 2003, making it the second-largest media merger in history.[36]

As the dust begins to clear from the mergers of the past decade, the contours of the U.S. media system come into focus. There tend to be three main tiers of media firms. The first tier, composed of Time Warner, Viacom, News Corporation, Sony, General Electric, Bertelsmann, and Disney, are vertically integrated powerhouses—indeed vast conglomerates—with various combinations of film studios, TV networks, cable TV channels, book publishing, newspapers, radio stations, music companies, TV channels, and the like. Their annual revenues tend to run in the $15–$40 billion range, placing them squarely among the few hundred largest firms in the world. Cable giant Comcast certainly is large enough to be a first-tier firm, though it is not especially vertically integrated. Expect that to change, if Comcast has its way.[37] To get some sense of the scope of a first-tier firm, consider just some of the holdings of Viacom: Paramount Pictures; Blockbuster video rental chain; Simon and Schuster book publishing; 183 U.S. radio stations; cable channels MTV, Nickelodeon, VH1, and Showtime; billboards; CBS television network; and 39 U.S. TV stations.[38]

Most of these first-tier firms, including Viacom, have been put together in the past fifteen years. A *New York Times* examination of nine major media sectors—encompassing film, radio, TV, cable, music, theme parks, and publishing—revealed that the five largest first-tier firms, on average, were each major players in more than seven of them.[39]

This produces an irony of the contemporary U.S. media system. Americans now receive hundreds of cable and satellite TV channels, such that observers often note that the dominance of the old "Big 3" TV networks—ABC, CBS, and NBC—has been broken. No longer can these three networks command 90 to 95 percent of TV watchers, as they routinely did from the 1950s through the 1970s. But what is lost in the blizzard of channels is that twenty of the twenty-five largest cable TV channels are now owned by the five first-tier media firms, the same firms that own the networks and many of the TV stations in the largest markets.[40] These five companies, between their cable and broadcast properties, still reach around 90 percent of the total television audience.[41] As a Viacom executive states, the same five companies "are controlling music and films."[42] One trade publication assessed the state of commercial television in December 2003: "For the big fish, the water's fine."[43]

The second tier is composed of another twenty firms—such as Cox, New York Times, Gannett, Clear Channel—that tend to be major players in a single area or two related areas. These firms have annual media sales in the $3–$10 billion range and rank among the six or seven hundred largest firms in the United States.[44] The lion's share of the U.S. media system is dominated by the firms in the first two tiers: they provide or control the vast majority of TV and cable programs, stations, networks, motion pictures, recorded music, magazines, books, newspapers, radio stations, and so on. The third tier is made up of the thousands of much smaller media firms that fill the nooks and crannies of the media system, though they can sometimes have influence in certain markets. They tend to be dependent in some ways on first- and second-tier firms and are often the targets of mergers and acquisitions. Many survive because their markets—and profits—are too small to interest the giants.

CONGLOMERATION AND SYNERGY

A significant form of media concentration in the past decade has been conglomeration. While conglomeration—a company owning and managing several unrelated operations—occurs across the economy, it has come to have special potency in media. The largest media firms have built empires (through mergers and acquisitions) with major players in several media sectors that have traditionally been regarded as unrelated. This goes beyond traditional vertical integration with its emphasis on production and distribution of similar content. A media company like Time Warner, for example, is a global leader in movies, cable television systems and channels, magazines, books, and music, among other things. Media conglomeration offers such a company tangible benefits: programs can be extensively promoted across all the company's platforms; media "brands" can be used to create new programming in different sectors; spin-off properties like sound-tracks, books, video games that are generated by movies can be kept in-house; firms have increased leverage with advertisers; they have increased negotiating leverage with labor and suppliers; and, in a hit-or-miss business like media, the increase in scope reduces overall risk. In short, the theory behind media conglomeration is that the profit whole is greater than the sum of the profit parts. The word used to describe this is *synergy*.

Synergy drives much media activity today. Time Warner uses open advertising space in its media to promote its products.[45] TV programs on Time Warner's WB network constantly feature songs by Warner Music artists.[46] Time Warner's *Entertainment Weekly* magazine carried two cover stories in a single month on Time Warner's 2003 film *The Matrix Reloaded*. Along with the balance of Time Warner's promotional efforts, this meant that 95 percent of the public were aware of the movie upon its release. At the exact same time, observed columnist Frank Rich, "two-thirds of the population could not name any of the nine Democratic candidates for president."[47] Viacom uses its "hip" MTV and VH-1 networks to push younger viewers to its CBS television network.[48] For the 2004 Super Bowl which aired on CBS, Viacom inte-grated related programming, promotional campaigns, and advertis-ing packages with its numerous cable channels, including MTV, BET, and Nickelodeon. "Super Sunday" was expected to generate $170 mil-lion in ad revenues for the Viacom empire.[49] When Disney purchased the right to make a TV movie for its ABC network about the Pennsylva-nia miners who were trapped underground in 2002, it could also make plans to have its Hyperion book subsidiary publish a related book.[50] By 2002 Disney had turned synergy into an art form, linking, for exam-ple, its ABC prime-time shows to promotional events at its amusement parks and hyping them incessantly on its other media properties.[51]

Some of the most important synergy comes from developing mer-chandising opportunities. By 2002 entertainment licensing revenues totaled $42 billion, with Disney-affiliated products alone generating $13 billion.[52] Much of the appeal of *Harry Potter* or *The Company Bears* for film subjects, to mention but two, is that they offer tremendous possibilities for sequels, spin-offs, and merchandising.[53] The first *Harry Potter* film licensed eighty-five associated products, and the entire campaign for the film was coordinated with promotions for Coca-Cola.[54] The idea for *The Company Bears* came from a Disneyland ride. The same was true of the successful 2003 *Pirates of the Caribbean,* and more Disney films are expected to be adapted from other rides.[55] Viacom's *Rugrats* TV program on Nickelodeon has evolved into a maze of products all cross-promoted by the Viacom empire. The *Rugrats* "franchise" generated $3.5 billion in retail sales between 1997 and 2003.[56] The 2001 Sony film *Final Fantasy* was so devoid of plot that one reviewer determined that the film's main point was to sell Sony's PlayStation 2 games.[57] In 2003 Viacom's Nickelodeon co-developed a video game with plans to eventually turn the game into a TV program.[58] As these examples suggest, conglomeration can significantly affect media content and push companies away from directly addressing the audience's needs and desires.[59]

Conglomeration spurs further media concentration. To compete successfully in many media sectors, a firm must be a conglomerate. Consider animation, which is basically the province of DreamWorks and three or four first-tier media conglomerates.[60] Pixar, the pioneer in computer animation, prospers through its partnership with Disney, so it can "take advantage of [Disney's] clout in theaters, theme parks, and retail stores." In short, it has to give Disney a piece of the action to ensure its survival in the conglomerate jungle.[61] To a certain extent, media conglomerates seek cradle-to-grave operations in which they can produce much of the content used over their distribution channels. When Vivendi put together its conglomerate in 2000 one executive enthused that the firm had become "a totally integrated communications group, controlling 100 percent of its content production, 100 percent of its Internet integration, and 100 percent of its subscriber base."[62] But media conglomerates often find it more productive to buy and sell material to and from the other giants—knowing they always have a fallback position if negotiations break down with a supplier or distributor. Either way, the role for small independent media companies, never enormous to begin with, has been reduced.[63] As with oligopolistic markets in the broader economy, small independents exist to do the stuff the big guys find too risky or unprofitable. If successful, they tend to get bought out or enter into a formal dependent relationship with a giant.[64]

First-tier media conglomerates tend to have very close relationships with one another. Although they compete ferociously in some markets, they are also one another's best customers. Perhaps their sheer size causes them to be wary of too much competition. As Viacom's Mel Karmazin puts it, "You find it very difficult to go to war with one piece of Viacom without going to war with all of Viacom."[65] Indeed, media giants would rather make love than war. Each of the eight largest U.S. media firms have equity joint ventures—in which they share ownership of a property—with, on average, five of the other seven first-tier firms. And they often have more than one such venture.[66] They also maintain common shareholders, like John Malone, who owns big chunks of Time Warner, News Corporation, Viacom, and Liberty Media.[67] Gordon Crawford's Capital Research & Management Company is one of the five largest shareholders for Viacom, Time Warner, News Corporation, Clear Channel, and USA Interactive.[68] Crawford can broker major deals and get CEOs fired.[69] The knot between the largest firms is further tightened when one looks at their boards of directors. Although sharing a director is prohibited among firms in the same industry, corporate media boards are filled with directors who serve on other corporate boards, and in that capacity these board members rub shoulders with directors for other media firms. The media world is a small one.[70]

Consolidation only increases the pressures on media groups to cooperate. As former FCC chairman William Kennard notes, "As the industry consolidates, you have fewer and fewer owners, and each of the owners have more reason to do business with each other."[71] The top media moguls stay in constant touch, meeting annually in Idaho to discuss mutual interests and map future deals.[72] By 2003 the leading media CEOs were in the midst of what one reporter termed a "love-in." At a Chicago cable TV convention Viacom's Mel Karmazin stated, "I can't imagine being a competitor with any of these guys."[73] Time Warner CEO Richard Parsons chimed in, "If you get out of the '70s and '80s paradigm about competition, yes, we compete on more fronts now, but we can cooperate more effectively to expand the pie for consumers."[74] In many respects the media market is the polar opposite of the competitive market advocated by the likes of Milton Friedman. In his vision innumerable firms compete to produce as much as possible as efficiently as possible for the market, with all that that suggests about consumer sovereignty. The media market, on the other hand, is more like a cartel.

In areas of the economy other than media, conglomeration has rarely proven effective; management expertise in one area does not translate well to unrelated fields. In media, conglomeration has been a success, but not without a few missteps. In 2001–2 two leading media conglomerates—Time Warner and Vivendi Universal—experienced severe crises as high debt, overvaluation of assets, and the recession sent their stock prices reeling. To address their financial trouble, both firms were forced to sell off some assets, negotiating from a position of weakness. Time Warner sold its music division for $2.6 billion to a group headed by Seagram heir Edgar Bronfman in 2003.[75] Vivendi merged its media assets (except for its music division) with General Electric's NBC in 2003, on not especially favorable terms. To some observers, this offered sufficient evidence to prove that media conglomeration, or synergy, was fool's gold, and that all the giants would eventually have to be broken up into smaller and more efficient units.[76] In fact, it proved no such thing. Neither firm had been consolidated long enough to tell how well its parts might mesh; indeed, the underlying assets for both firms were profitable.[77] The problem was that severe debt and crumbling earnings resulted when the firms vastly overpaid for the assets initially.[78]

Other leading conglomerates, such as Viacom, Sony, and News Corporation, were exemplars of synergy and came roaring through the recession.[79] Viacom enjoyed tremendous profit growth in 2003, and much of it was ascribed to the firm's ability to cross-promote and cross-pollinate its content, while drawing in advertisers in big cross-platform packages.[80] Viacom's cash cow, Nickelodeon, "has leveraged its cable success into everything from magazines to live shows to toys."[81] Similarly, by 2003 News Corporation's "communications empire [was] thriving as never before" thanks to the "strong cohesion of its operations."[82] Even Disney, which struggled by comparison, was hardly stagnating. What was arguably its most profitable operation in 2002–3 surrounded the TV program *Lizzie McGuire*, which was synergistically spun off into a major film, CDs, toys, clothes, and books.[83] NBC CEO Robert Wright estimated that the immediate synergistic value of its merger with Vivendi's film and TV properties would be a combination of savings and new revenues totaling $500 million.[84] Even second-tier media firms enjoy the benefits of synergy. Clear Channel uses its 1,200-plus radio stations to promote the shows at one hundred thirty concert venues it controls in the United States. That helps Clear Channel produce 70 percent of the live concerts in the United States.[85] As one trade publication asked, after reviewing the evidence, "Who says synergy is a bad word?"[86]

Recent experience has taught two important lessons about media conglomeration and synergy. First, the initial efforts by media giants to expand into the Internet have been costly and ineffectual.[87] They were a casualty of the economic bubble that burst in 2000. Second, synergy does not always develop with conglomeration.[88] Disney has several hundred Disney Stores that specialize in selling merchandise drawn from Disney products.[89] By 2003 the company realized that it was better off reducing its number of stores and instead working with other retailers.[90] Similarly, many media conglomerates sold off their professional sports franchises in 2002–3, as the promise of synergy between the teams and the media properties failed to materialize.[91] Viacom considered unloading its market-dominant Blockbuster video-rental chain in late 2003.[92] The moral of the story: synergy takes time and is risky. It is also helped by astute management. All in all, the smart money is betting on further concentration.[93] "If history is anything to go by," as a writer for *The Economist* observed in 2002, the largest media firms will prosper "by swallowing the creative independents, growing bigger still—and not by breaking themselves up."[94]

The bottom line is clear: a competitive market structure does not exist for media in the United States and probably cannot exist in the real world of corporate capitalism. This does not mean there is not some competition between media giants. But cartel-like arrangements are frequently evident. Like all oligopolists, these firms rarely compete in the area of price. They use their economic and political power to advance their interests and to dominate consumers. Although policies can encourage markets to be much more competitive than they otherwise would be, corrupt policy making has crafted regulations to suit the less competitive markets desired by dominant commercial interests.

IS THE MARKET APPROPRIATE TO REGULATE MEDIA?

Conventional thinking assumes that if media markets were more competitive and more responsive to the public, they would provide the best possible way to regulate the media system. This assumption merits examination. Media industries do enjoy certain characteristics that are unique to them or that are shared only by a minority of major markets in the economy. These unique attributes call into question just how appropriate the market is as a tool to regulate media in the public interest. The most glaring difference between media markets and other markets that we have already examined is the role of advertising as a significant source of revenues. This changes the logic of media markets radically, since the interests of consumers must be filtered through the demands of advertisers. The implications for content can be striking, and are not necessarily positive from the consumer's perspective. But several other important differences separate the media market from conventional markets.

First and foremost, the *nature* of media content is different from that of other commodities. Subjecting ideas, culture, and journalism to the market is problematic. Concerns about commercializing education, or the sheer revulsion at the idea of commodifying religion, point to the problems attendant to commercializing culture. At first glance, using markets to regulate the production and distribution of ideas and culture is troubling. If one follows the logic of the "marketplace of ideas" metaphor closely, it may well be that the rational thing for media firms to do is to produce exactly what the market shows a preference for, what everyone else is producing. Diversity may then be squashed. This may not cause a problem in the production of washing machines or chocolate bars, but in the realm of ideas it poses deep problems for traditional liberal democratic notions. The market can prove to be a quiet, but ruthless, commissar.[95]

In addition, ownership of idea production is a unique power. If there are a small number of soft drink manufacturers, for example, one owner insisting that the bottle labels be green instead of purple would not cause concern for citizens. While society holds general reservations about oligopoly in terms of pricing and product quality, that sort of management prerogative is probably well down the list. Not so with media. Having concentrated control in media is precisely a problem because such ownership power is extremely important and attractive to owners. Control over public information, over the news, over the culture offers tremendous benefits for media owners, and it is a privilege owners have historically enjoyed, sometimes to democracy's detriment.

Media markets are distinctive in other ways. Most media are by nature *non-rivalrous* public goods, and this undermines the traditional justification for market regulation. In typical markets, if one person consumes the product or service, another person, a rival for the product or service, cannot. Imagine a fast-food hamburger or dry cleaning service or a suit or an automobile. Consumers vie for use of the resource, and the market price rations the good or service to those who are willing to cover the marginal cost of production. Everyone willing to pay the marginal cost gets the product or service. Not so for most media products. If I watch a movie, that does not prevent anyone else from watching the same movie. This is also true in the consumption of a television program or an Internet website, and for the most part with a book, newspaper, magazine, or CD. Because the difference in cost between showing a film to one person or to five people or to five hundred people is virtually nothing—compared with what it costs to make one candy bar versus the cost for five hundred—

the traditional economic justification for rationing by price seems, well, unjustified. So when a media producer charges a price for a product above marginal costs, that producer limits the number of people who would otherwise enjoy the product in a standard market. It is this inherent incompatibility of media with market regulation that stimulated the rise of copyright, the entire point of which is to *prevent* competition that would drive prices down to marginal costs and make media commercially impractical.[96]

Media markets, too, are shaped by the formation of *networks*. These include distribution networks for newspapers, books, music, and films; television networks; and computer networks like the Internet. A classic example is the telephone network or the postal system. Networks for production and distribution of media content violate the premises of the competitive market model because as collaborative mechanisms they act in many ways as "natural monopolies." The value of networks for all involved improves dramatically as the network gains more users. Small networks with few users are virtually worthless and cannot survive. To get off the ground, networks require high fixed investment. The implications of network economics are clear: they tend to promote large and noncompetitive industries, far beyond what a traditional market would generate. It is one reason for the long tradition of government ownership and regulation of communication networks.

All these traits influence one striking feature of media economics: the importance of "first copy" costs. Most of the expense of a newspaper, a film, a book, a CD goes into making the first copy. All subsequent versions are quite inexpensive to produce. This means that media industries tend to incur more risk than do many other areas because a relatively large investment must be made before the size of the product's demand becomes clear. What this translates into is the "blockbuster" phenomenon, when media firms look for the super-successful film, CD, book, or TV show that will generate massive profits to more than cover losses on flops. MGM, for example, jacked up its profits by 50 percent and added $100 million to its bottom line in 2002 thanks to the James Bond film *Die Another Day*.[97]

Book publishing for years lived by the "80-20 rule," whereby "80 percent of the revenues are earned by 20 percent of the authors."[98] Jane Friedman heads News Corporation's HarperCollins book publishing unit; her greatest asset is her "instinct for bestsellers."[99] Such a precarious position offers firms a powerful motivation to get large, so they can better handle the risk, otherwise a string of flops could bankrupt them. Syndicated TV producers faced this type of crisis when none of them had had a hit show for years; they were looking to consolidate to survive.[100] This climate also means that media firms rarely if ever compete on the basis of price, since, as media scholar Nicholas Garnham points out, "there is no calculable relationship between costs of production and revenues received for any one product."[101]

Finally, media markets are different from most other capitalist markets with regard to labor relations. As in all other capitalist enterprises, media firms wish to pay their laborers as little as possible, and there is an important (and understudied) history of labor-management conflict here similar to other major industries.[102] But a crucial difference is in how creative talent produces content. Media corporations must employ people specifically hired for their artistic talents—no one wants to hear Rupert Murdoch's version of a guitar solo or see a movie written and directed by Viacom CEO Sumner Redstone. Because the amount of money generated in media industries by bestselling content can be so enormous, successful creative people can earn astronomical salaries. This occurs because there is a scarcity of people who can generate blockbusters by becoming marketable "brands." The "star system" of Hollywood's golden years—as well as its more recent and less codified incarnation—resulted largely from commercial media markets. Media firms, especially film studios, thought that by creating stars they could attract consumers to otherwise unknown films and thereby reduce their risk in undertaking production. To some extent, then, celebrity obsession is the product of commercial media.[103]

CREATIVITY VERSUS COMMERCE IN THE CONGLOMERATE ERA
The relationship of creative talent to media firms and the commercial media market tends to be ignored by proponents of commercial

media. Economist Tyler Cowen, for example, sees little conflict between commercialism and creativity and views the market as a spur to creativity.[104] But Cowen frames the matter largely in terms of how an individual artist fares in the market, which makes his analysis of limited value to understanding the creative process in complex media industries. It is similar to the tendency to conflate concerns about free speech with free press in such a way that protecting a media conglomerate from government regulation is the same as protecting the right of a dissident citizen to stand on a soapbox and speak her mind. Along similar lines, proponents of a commercial press system rarely distinguish between the interests of owners and the interests of editors and reporters, though their roles and interests in the media system are far from interchangeable.

Even if creative people are heavily motivated by fame and fortune, their interests are not necessarily identical to those of media corporations. Often artists have social, political, and creative impulses they value in addition to their desire to make money. Moreover, quality media content requires that creative talent be given a certain amount of autonomy; this goes directly against the corporate imperative to intervene and thereby reduce risk and maximize profit.

This tension between creative talent (and journalists) and corporate media structures is built into the system.[105] Entertainment programming has mostly gravitated toward a handful of commercially successful genres with formulaic characters and plots. In commercial radio and television, risk was reduced through developing ongoing series featuring the same characters. One great irony of commercial media is that the market, instead of generating experimental content, tends to be quite conservative. Smart media owners rarely want to try something the public is unfamiliar with; it is far wiser to do what has worked in the past. If someone else hits a gusher with a new drill, that's the moment to jump in—à la the game show glut after *Who Wants to Be a Millionaire* hit big or the many supernatural thrillers that nipped the heels of *The Sixth Sense*. Commercial media have 20-20 hindsight. As a columnist for the *Financial Times* put it, "The low-risk, bureaucratic way to run a media company is to focus on products similar to those that have already succeeded." The only "genuinely original works" to be found on the bestseller list were the offspring of small, independent publishers.[106] The media conglomerates "want guarantees in a business where there are no financial guarantees," the actor James Spader observed. They try to cover their "bets most efficiently, and that breeds awful filmmaking, because it doesn't call for originality but repetition of previous success—preferably as close to a replica as possible."[107]

Variety noted that, to "limit risk," prime-time television shows "run the gamut from generic themes to classic icons."[108] The *Wall Street Journal*'s TV critic termed the new 2003 network shows virtual clones of their existing programs.[109] *Variety* reported that Hollywood, "to minimize risk," tapped "into the tried-and-true."[110] In recent years, movie studios have turned to sequels, prequels, and remakes of successes as the safest route to profitability.[111] One-third of Sony's new releases were sequels, while the major studios cranked out sixteen in the summer of 2002.[112] As one reporter noted, "Hollywood has more money riding on big sequels in 2002 than any other year in movie history."[113] The total increased yet again to twenty-three sequels in 2003, although a string of disappointments suggested that the number of sequels would level off.[114] But the idea of building movie brands or "product lines" around a series of films based on known characters is hardwired into the media conglomerate's psyche. The Batman franchise, for example, has generated $2 billion for Time Warner since the first film was released in 1989. Some $400 million of that total came from licensing and merchandising.[115]

It is this conservatism built into the logic of media markets that has drawn ire from artists and critics. Often the criticism has taken aim at what is termed "lowest common denominator" programming, meaning programming with wide appeal across the population. (This term is usually used disparagingly, under the assumption that popular entertainment must sacrifice artistic originality and quality. But such need not be the case—commercial pressures rather than "popular tastes" may play the larger role in reducing the quality of mass fare.) In a commercial market, what media firms are pushed to do is provide content that will not be difficult for audiences to grasp, will not be too expensive to produce, yet will capture people's attention. This is especially difficult among multitudes of media options (albeit with fewer media owners). The tried-and-true mechanisms for commercial media are sex, vulgarity, and violence. These proven inexpensive attention-getters have, by most accounts, been on the rise in U.S. television.[116] In 2003 the TV critic Tom Shales complained "there are so many shows with amplified sex and violence that even pressure groups have given up."[117] A trade publication editor acknowledged, "You could argue that network television and *Maxim* magazine are the only places that still seem to attach illicit values to sexual activity. To the rest of us, it's just commerce."[118]

In recent years, television networks have turned more and more to inexpensive fare that succeeds most often through vulgarity and shock value.[119] Programs in this genre "race to the bottom" in an attempt to beat the competition.[120] The shock comedian Tom Green complained about the dilemma he faced when he launched a new talk show on MTV: "You can turn on 'Survivor' and watch anyone eat worms."[121] As a *New York Times* headline put it: "Fox TV Finds Another Way to Sink to Top of the Charts."[122] The point is not that the commercial media system generates a paucity of good material, but, rather, that the market has a strong economic bias toward the cheap and the imitative.[123] "If the good stuff is better than it has been in years, the crap is even crappier," Tom Shales remarked in 2003. "You despair for the state of the nation's mental health."[124]

In recent years, the corporate pressures on content—or, to put it another way, the effects of media concentration, conglomeration, and commercialism—have made it more difficult for creative artists attempting to do original and interesting work. And the more commercial domination of the creative process there is, the more likely the work produced will be lousy. Viacom's Mel Karmazin termed the low-cost, high-profit gross-out movie *Jackass* his "quintessential movie."[125] Larry Gelbart, the legendary TV writer whose credits include the TV show *M*A*S*H*, terms the programming desired by the networks "hamburger helper," because "they are more or less doing it by the numbers."[126] "Movie studios finally found the formula for a perfect summer," a writer for *Fortune* magazine observed in 2001. "Unfortunately, every element of it contributed to horrible filmmaking."[127]

"Do people who work in the film business actually see what the industry puts out?" a *Variety* columnist asked, while calling the films execrable. "Have the studios entirely given up even pretending to make pictures of respectable quality for the mass audience?"[128] Peter Bart, a *Variety* editor and former studio head, railed against the media conglomerates in 2002, summing up much of the criticism: the film studios have "succumbed to certain ineluctable economic forces. Their vertically integrated corporate parents demand 'numbers,' and the most risk-averse way to produce those numbers is to focus on sequels and effects-laden tentpole pictures, not on edgy 'people pictures.'" Bart concluded that this climate has left creative talent severely frustrated. "Actors want meaty parts. Directors post-9/11 yearn for more meaningful scripts."[129] In 2003, Bart observed, "No matter where you turn, corporate sameness is pervasive."[130] Noting the lack of original comedy on television for years, Bart asked, "Is there such a thing as corporate comedy?"[131]

Media corporations are not deaf to this criticism; some conglomerates have spawned faux-independent "art" film studios to produce "edgy" fare that commercial pressures in their main studios would not permit.[132] While artists need latitude to develop their work, the structural pressures of conglomerates tend to reduce their freedom. The good stuff usually gets made not because of the system but because of what creative people can do when they work against the logic of the system.

Consider the music industry. For artists music is the most accessible of the popular arts because the capital required for good music is minimal compared with the outlay typically necessary to produce a good movie. Three people in a garage can record the greatest rock and roll CD of all time. Yet the corporate system does a dreadful job of exploiting this characteristic to the public's benefit. The irony is that the four firms that dominate popular music production and distribution worldwide now seem unable to generate original and compelling popular music. Most of the great movements in popular music have risen outside the corporate music system, in inner-city neighbor-hoods, garages, small towns, and campuses. But the music giants cannot leave well enough alone: competitive pressures demand that they attempt to engineer the creative process as much as possible to ensure commercial success.

The resulting stale, derivative music has little of the originals' spark.[133] So, the better the music conglomerates do their job, the lousier the music.[134] One *Variety* writer terms the present era of corporate music, the "epoch of the Rolling Clones" and observes, "Marketing-driven acts drown out fresh voices at music congloms."[135] The problem has been magnified in recent years by the incessant push by music companies to have artists link their activities with commercial sponsors.[136] "Just think of bands as brands," Jay Coleman, the "father of music marketing" proclaims. "Reinforcing that can help sell merchandise, records, tickets and content."[137] Even the industry trade press is appalled by the shallowness of contemporary popular music. A *Variety* writer noted about a Christina Aguilera concert: "This slick production reeked of commercialism."[138] The *New York Times* critic concluded that the best place to hear "daring pop music these days" was to "listen to the background music in TV commercials."[139]

The tension between owners, advertisers, and creative talent also manifests itself in the media's political content. Many Americans learn more about the political and social world from entertainment fare than from journalism or the educational system. Moreover, entertainment does not have as many professional filters to restrict explicit social criticism, as does journalism. Owners want to make money and need to give creative people some autonomy to do so. Entertainment producers therefore can be more open to dissident perspectives than journalists are. Popular commercial entertainment has an intermittent history of artists bringing left and populist themes into entertainment fare.[140] The implicit commercial codes of owners and advertisers, however, do not encourage these political themes; artists need to navigate a difficult course to incorporate such perspectives into their work.[141]

Moreover, the stakes are understood by those in power; control over entertainment is no trivial matter. In times of crisis, such as the Red Scare of the 1940s and 1950s, the powers-that-be will punish entertainers who dare to step outside the mainstream. The track record in these instances is clear: media corporations and advertisers will be the government's willing accomplices.[142] An artist's dissident politics are tolerated only to the extent that the artist is commercially useful to the firm. Mainstream politics, of course, are welcome and celebrated at all turns.

I do not wish to romanticize the role of creative artists in the entertainment industry. Some are selfish and unprincipled; some have internalized the crassest of commercial values. Unfortunately, some artists have been willing to go along with the production of racist, sexist, or homophobic fare.[143] On balance, however, the case is clear: the more influence creative talent has over media content vis-à-vis media corporations, the better the content.

SO *DO* COMMERCIAL MEDIA GIVE PEOPLE WHAT THEY WANT?

Even if one acknowledges that markets are deeply flawed as democratic mechanisms, one fundamental challenge to media policy making in the public interest remains: commercial media, due to the pressure to maximize profit, will invariably strive to "give the people what they want." The corollary to this argument is that any other means of organizing media will by definition interfere with popular control over media; by definition it will be paternalistic or downright authoritarian, depending upon the political system's nature.[144]

This argument's strength is that it contains an element of truth, and a self-evident one at that. Media firms obviously attempt to produce music and films and TV shows that people will want to consume. Much that is good and bad about media can be attributed to the audience. The trend toward multiethnic fare, for example, can be attributed to an increased recognition by media producers of the audience's changing nature and tastes.[145] My argument is not that the current media system does not sometimes produce outstanding content; it certainly does, but structural constraints make it produce far less than it could or should. Moreover, the notion of "giving the people what they want" respects a crucial liberal freedom, the right to choose one's own media to consume. Any effort to tamper with this through censorship rings alarm bells, quite rightly, among all freedom-loving people. It is this point that media giants take out of context, overstate, and wield to obliterate criticism. As Rupert Murdoch puts it, those who criticize the media status quo are "snobs" who "want to be imposing their taste on everybody else."[146] It is a powerful and effective public relations gambit because it taps into a fundamental liberal freedom.

The "we give the people what they want" argument is a half-truth at best, and taken out of context it serves as an ideological fig leaf to protect naked commercial interests. Concentration and conglomeration, as I've demonstrated, raise significant barriers to an effectively operating free market. To the extent that the market is oligopolistic and vertically integrated, power shifts from consumers to producers. This is, of course, exactly what producers want because they will garner more power to produce content that will be more profitable for them. It means that media markets may "give the people what they want," but will do so strictly within the limited range of fare that can generate the greatest profits. The more competitive the market, in economic theory, the more control consumers have over expanding that range. The argument in oligopolistic markets becomes circular: people consume from a relatively narrow range of what media firms find most lucrative to produce; then when consumers select from these options, the firms say, "See, we must be giving you what you want." Media culture's overwhelming and growing commercialism—disliked by a large percentage of Americans—is ample evidence of how much power consumers actually have today. The people want 18 minutes of ads per hour on radio? Right.

The problem with this argument extends beyond concentrated markets to flaws inherent in markets in general. For starters, and it can barely be overemphasized, markets are hardly democratic regulatory mechanisms. They are predicated upon one dollar, one vote, rather than one person, one vote. Affluent people therefore have considerably more "votes" in determining the course of the media system, while the poorest people are effectively disenfranchised.[147] For the production and distribution of some products this may not be an especially pressing concern; in the realm of journalism and culture it conflicts with the core informational requirements of a self-governing and egalitarian society. A market-driven media system in a society with pronounced inequality will have structural pressures to reinforce rather than to challenge such inequality; those on top will tend to drive the media to benefit those on top.

Further, the "we give the people what they want" argument provides only the most superficial understanding of the "audience," how it generates its demands, and how it votes. So far I have emphasized the supply side of media as being decisive, but this does not mean that the audience can be neglected. Nicholas Garnham has done trailblazing work in conceptualizing the role of the audience, and he emphasizes the need to place audiences in a social context and count their disposable income as a crucial factor in determining the media options they consider.[148] Other researchers claim that audiences are "active" and have the capacity to "decode" commercial media messages critically far beyond what its producers intend. According to this argument, concerns about media structures and content are overstated or even irrelevant because the power of interpretation rests with the audience. Whether the commercial system gives the people what they want is not especially central because people will take what they need. Garnham rightly observes that this so-called trade-off between an active audience and a powerful media is bogus. The important thing—what we can study and influence—is that institutions and structures limit what audiences are permitted actively to interpret.

To some extent the "we give the people what they want" argument is circular. People are exposed to the media fare that the giants can profit from, they develop a taste for it, they consume it, and then the media giants claim they must make more of it to satisfy demand. What is demanded depends to a very large extent on what is produced rather than the other way around, what John Kenneth Galbraith called the "dependence effect" in *The Affluent Society*.[149] To paraphrase Say's Law, supply creates demand. In the immortal words of Walton Hale Hamilton, "Business succeeds rather better than the state in imposing restraints upon individuals, because its imperatives are disguised as choices."[150] Indeed, the massive amounts that media firms spend on marketing their products—the five largest first-tier media firms spent $4.5 billion on TV advertising in 2002, making the media industry one of the largest advertisers overall[151]—combined with the nevertheless high rate of failure suggest that these firms (and the market in general) are not particularly good at determining what people want.[152]

For examples of supply creating demand, consider the following. In the 1970s foreign-language films accounted for nearly 10 percent of the U.S. theater box office; by 2003 the figure was under 1 percent.[153] Evidence suggests this was not triggered by a drop-off in audience demand but instead to the sharp decline in foreign film distribution once the theater industry switched over to multiplex theaters.[154] To be commercially viable, movies must open on 1,500 screens and be supported by sizable advertising, "a cost that requires the active participation of a wealthy studio parent."[155] "If you don't hit it within 24 to 72 hours," a Universal executive commented on the importance of a film's opening, "you're out of the game."[156] While there is the occasional exception, this logic basically priced most foreign film producers out of the U.S. market. Similarly, classical music accounted for nearly one-quarter of U.S. recorded music sales in 1960; that figure plummeted to 3.2 percent by 2001.[157] Whereas once classical music sometimes could be found on several commercial radio stations in a large city, today listeners are fortunate to find it on a single public station.[158] A key part of any explanation: classical music was discontinued or downgraded in the curricula of a significant percentage of U.S. schools in the intervening years.

In both cases, media giants would claim, accurately, that foreign-language films and classical music evoke little demand in the United States today. But the lack of exposure—the low supply— eliminated the basis for demand. The same thing could be said for several other media, such as documentary film.[159] This is no surprise because there is no incentive over the long term for commercial media to cultivate tastes or develop interests in new material. Having a commitment to generating new cultural genres and ideas may be good for society, it may be something people value, but it is bad business. People can't reasonably express their desire for an alternative in the marketplace if the choice does not exist and they have not had enough exposure to it to evaluate it.

Furthermore, the marketplace is incapable of addressing preferences that require avoiding the market. How does a consumer use the market to register discontent with advertising-saturated broadcasting, when all the channels reek of advertising? How does one express a desire for noncommercial presentation of political candidates on television—say through a series of multi-party debates—when one gets only endless TV paid political advertising? There is no way to use the market to express nonmarket values—aside from withdrawing from media altogether—which is hardly an option, nor should it be.

Along these lines, using people's personal preferences as a measure of where they wish to see funds allocated in media may not be an accurate gauge of their desires. People can be citizens as well as consumers, and as citizens they may well have a broader purview than they do as media consumers. People may wish to see more documentaries on television, even as they watch *The Jerry Springer Show*, just as citizens may wish to have large and effective national parks, even if they do not plan to personally visit any of them, or they may wish to have excellent public schools even if they do not have school-age children. Acting only as consumers, citizens cannot address their social concerns effectively. Markets cannot address all sorts of important values people may wish to see upheld in their media. As Ed Baker notes, all of this points to the crucial importance of public participation in media policy making; how else can the people voice their needs?[160]

But if the media system does not necessarily give us exactly what we want, it does certainly give us plenty of what we do not want. The most striking limitation of a market-driven media system, competitive or otherwise, is the generation of externalities. *Externalities* refer to the economic and social costs of a market transaction that do not factor into the decision making of the product's buyer or seller. Industrial pollution is the classic case of an externality: neither the producer nor the consumer has to factor this into the market price, but society as a whole suffers and has a huge price to pay to clean it up. In media the externalities are numerous. Advertising, for example, is a market activity that has significant negative externalities in the type of materialistic values it incessantly promotes. Another classic example of a media externality is violent programming. As media scholar James Hamilton has demonstrated brilliantly, media producers find this lucrative to make, and consumers provide a market for it. But if widespread exposure to exceptionally violent content produces a more violent society, which leads to more crime, the need for larger police forces, and a much less enjoyable society, this cost of violent media fare is not borne by the media producer. It is paid for by society, whether it likes it or not.[161] Indeed some, perhaps much, of the profit media producers generate comes from passing on part of the true costs to the broader public.[162] Similarly, to the extent that media glorify the use of tobacco products or alcohol, the costs associated with smoking-related diseases and alcoholism constitute an externality.[163] Addressing (and anticipating) media externalities is one task of media policy making.

While media externalities are widespread, two in particular lie at the very center of media policy making and concerns—two of the issues that dominated chapters 2, 3, and 4 of this book. First are those affecting children.[164] By the late 1990s the U.S. children's market for commercial media had grown to astronomical proportions. In 1983 about $100 million in TV advertising was aimed at children. By 1997 that figure had climbed to $1 billion, and the total amount of advertising and marketing aimed at children reached $12.7 billion.[165] The total U.S. market for children's products was valued at $166 billion in 2000, and another study estimated that children influence up to $500 billion per year in purchases.[166] The media markets have responded with a barrage of media aimed at children, from toddlers to young teens.[167] Attracting children to commercial media and commercial messages is a major industry.[168] A 2003 study sponsored by the Kaiser Family Foundation determined that America's youngest children were "immersed" in commercial television, and to an extent that was "astounding" even to longtime researchers in the field.[169]

The social implications of this carpet-bombing of children by commercial media have been the subject of considerable research.[170] The range of debate extends from "this is probably not a good thing we are doing to children" to "this is a massive crisis for our society."[171] Britain's Archbishop of Canterbury, Rowan Williams, falls into the latter camp. In 2002 he blasted the "intrusion of consumerism into childhood," specifically attacking Disney for the "corruption and premature sexualization of children."[172] No one without a material interest in the status quo is arguing that this process could possibly be beneficial to children or our society over the long haul. But because it is an externality, this process concerns the media producers only to the extent that unfavorable publicity might undermine their profits. Otherwise it is utterly irrelevant, and pressure to generate profit assures that it remains that way.

Second are the externalities regarding journalism. In a commercial media system, the quality and social implications of journalism remain externalities because they exist in a profit-driven enterprise. There is no small amount of irony in this, as the enlightenment of citizens was the major force behind the creation of media policies at the founding of the republic, including the First Amendment. Rational capitalists will produce the journalism that generates the greatest profit, that is, what costs the least to produce and generates the greatest market. Whether this type of journalism best serves a free society is not, cannot be, part of their calculations. It is coincidental. Low-budget regurgitation of official sources plus an emphasis on celebrities and crime are the rational outcome of the commercial media market. What is rational for media owners to generate as they pursue maximum return for their shareholders creates a disaster for informed self-government. The cost to society in the form of ignorant, lousy governance, and less fulfilled individuals arguably is immensely high, economically, culturally, and politically. Everyone in our society suffers the consequences, not merely those who partake directly in the commercial news market.

Externalities need not always be negative, however. If a society generates a high-quality journalism or a provocative entertainment culture it will have the positive externality of producing a well-informed and enlightened citizenry that will make wise public policy decisions. The entire society will benefit, not just those producing or purchasing the journalism or entertainment. But just as media firms can slough off the true social and economic costs of their negative externalities, they cannot capture the social and economic value of their positive externalities. Therefore, the marketplace cannot offer much incentive for a rational media firm to devote resources to generating positive externalities. The lessons are clear: public regulation of commercial media markets must address negative externalities. Even more important, a significant nonprofit and noncommercial media sector must help generate positive externalities.

THE CASE FOR THE STATUS QUO

There is considerable debate in the academy over specific points I raise in this chapter. Two scholars who have done much research on these topics, and who have come to articulate positions contrary to mine, are the economist Tyler Cowen and the media scholar Benjamin M. Compaine. Between 2001 and 2003 each wrote short essays to defend the status quo from criticism. Cowen focuses primarily on the production of art and culture in the market system.[173] Compaine has also coauthored a book that elaborates on his main points.[174] It is worth reviewing their core arguments in light of my evidence.

Cowen makes a few distinct points.[175] First, he maintains that conglomerates do not control the culture, but that consumers do. Cowen cites as evidence how often heavily promoted commercial media fare flops while unexpected material rises to the top. Interestingly enough, he does not defend corporate power. "Large media corporations are often too removed from their customers, too risk-averse, and they are too focused on their past successes rather than on the future." But not to worry, says Cowen. The conglomerates do not have much power. Movies, for example, are individual projects that compete in a dynamic marketplace. Unfortunately, the material Cowen provides as support—

that offbeat material sometimes succeeds while expected blockbusters fail—is somewhat beside the point. And there is little evidence that Hollywood movie making is the province of *auteurs*, rather than a corporate undertaking,

Cowen's second and third arguments are closely related. He states that most conglomerates earn poor returns because their structure does not make economic sense and that conglomerates are breaking up because synergy has failed. Cowen's evidence for these claims are the failed deals for Vivendi–Universal and AOL Time Warner. But as I have demonstrated, those outcomes are exceptions to the rule and may be attributed to issues beyond the failure of synergy or conglomeration. Many mergers have failed in business history, but this has not altered the general trend toward increased concentration. If Cowen wants to make a credible case, he needs to address the firms that have their heads above water or are swimming like fish: Viacom, News Corporation, Sony, Clear Channel, and General Electric. Because he ignores these companies, his second and third arguments are of limited value.

Compaine makes several points based on one bit of empirical data he compiled.[176] He states that an analysis of the list of the fifty largest U.S. media corporations from 1986 to 1997 shows that the degree of ownership concentration in the media has not changed significantly. Therefore, all the headline-grabbing media mergers are countered by firms breaking up and new firms bursting onto the scene. The media system is far more competitive than critics allow. Compaine acknowledges that ownership patterns tend toward concentration in specific media sectors but implies that since his one statistical review shows little change in media concentration overall between 1986 and 1997, concentration in any one sector will have to be matched by an increase in competition somewhere else. So it is essentially a wash. He touts the rise of cable TV channels as undermining the TV networks and providing "scores of programming choice from dozens of owners" without acknowledging that most of the cable TV channels are owned by the five media conglomerates that own the TV networks and also own many of the cable TV systems.

C. Edwin Baker has made a systematic critique of Compaine's argument and his empirical data.[177] According to Baker, Compaine errs by treating the "media as a whole" as the lens through which to examine media concentration. Compaine's assumption is that all media firms can be thrown into one massive media market. It would be like throwing all the automobile, airline, concrete, car rental, auto repair, trucking, bus, tire, glass, taxicab, steel, and oil companies into a single list to study market concentration in the motor transportation industry. By that measure it would be an exceptionally competitive industry—even if automobile production and oil refining were full-blown monopolies. On the basis of this dubious formulation, Compaine states that the claim that fewer and fewer companies own more and more of the media "is wrong." Baker, however, closely reviewed Compaine's data and discovered that over the years studied, the four largest media firms had in fact increased their market share fairly dramatically, from 18.79 percent to 24.13 percent.[178]

Compaine has one set of empirical data to hang his arguments on, and it does not establish his case. He argues that concerns about commercial control over journalism are unfounded: "News or information of real value has a way of getting picked up by the mainstream media." His evidence: Matt Drudge was able to break the Monica Lewinsky story. He argues that "ownership of the media, especially in the United States, is extremely democratic." His evidence: pension funds representing workers own shares in these companies. He argues that communication policy making is not corrupt but, to the contrary, "democracy at work." His evidence: competing lobbies try to influence policy. In the end Compaine throws up his hands and acknowledges that the system may not be perfect, but it is the best we can do. Criticizing concentrated media ownership or the workings of our economic and political systems is a waste of time because this is the best possible media system in the best of all possible worlds.

Compaine and Cowen do touch on one crucial point: the idea that the Internet is going to introduce significant levels of new competition. Media giants face an uncertain future at best and demise at worst according to this view. Traditionally powerful broadcasters, film producers, and music companies are about to be overwhelmed by online media that will use cyberspace's easy access to attack existing profit centers. "We should feel sorry for them rather than vilifying them," Cowen advises. This is a powerful argument, and it is made widely by corporate media and their champions in Washington to back up their claim that citizens should not be concerned by relaxing the existing media ownership rules. After all, with a blizzard of new media online, who cares if a company owns some more radio or TV stations? Compaine points to the thousands of Internet radio broadcasters, suggesting that conventional radio broadcasters are soon to get their comeuppance.

Yet the evidence is far from conclusive. After a decade of the commercialized Internet, few major commercially viable online media content providers have emerged to challenge an existing media giant. There are many reasons for this, but the Internet is chiefly part of the commercial media system and therefore looks toward complementing, not challenging, the work of existing media giants. If the Internet really held out this threat to the commercial media status quo, one would logically expect that the value of traditional media would begin to plummet. Isn't that how markets work? Market power in traditional media industries is being parlayed into market power over the Internet to the extent it is drawn into the commercial media system.[179] The Internet and digital communication are beginning to affect greatly our media system in general and some sectors, like music, more than others. But that does not mean that the Internet is eliminating concerns about concentrated media ownership.[180]

Cowen and Compaine are right about two things: media ownership doesn't explain everything, and concentrated media ownership does not cause all the problems with the media. In some cases concentration may be unavoidable. But if these are the best arguments that can be mustered on behalf of the status quo, one can better understand why the media giants have been so insistent about keeping debates on media policy removed from public attention.

The evidence is clear: strong biases within media markets steer away from competition, and this direction undermines the case for

markets as best serving the public interest. It means, especially insofar as the media system is the result of public policies, there should be
a strong policy bias toward encouraging more competitive markets.
Where concentrated markets are unavoidable, policies must be developed to address negative externalities. And even somewhat more competitive media markets still exhibit significant flaws. This means that
strong policy measures and subsidies are needed to encourage a
vibrant nonprofit and noncommercial media sector.

6

MEDIA POLICIES AND MEDIA REFORM

It may appear that the profit-driven nature of the U.S. media system generates an inexorable logic that requires businesses to act as they do, for better or for worse. There is an element of truth to such a position, but taken in isolation it is also misleading. The larger truth is that the current media market's nature is set by explicit government policies, regulations, and subsidies. For the cable TV industry or the commercial broadcasting industry, this linkage between policies and market structure and logic are transparent. The government creates these markets and sets the terms for the firms to operate; only after policies are set does market logic become inexorable. But this same relationship defines all media industries: behind every media system is a government policy or set of policies, and behind every policy is a policy-making process.

A myriad of policies establish and regulate the U.S. media system, and they control areas such as advertising, libel, and access to information. On the website for the media reform group Free Press, over forty distinct media policy issues are listed.[1] Most policies are national in scope and developed in Washington, D.C., but more than a few are the province of state and local governments. Moreover, broader policies such as tax, trade, and labor laws also affect the nature of the media system, sometimes dramatically.

Boiled down, however, these policies can be placed in at least one of three broad areas that define how a nation addresses the problem of the media. First are policies—ranging from subsidies to the setting of technical standards—surrounding the development and deployment of communication technologies. These policy decisions often set the course for the long-term development of media, even though to the casual observer technologies appear like natural forces that come hurtling to Earth. Second are laws and regulations for media ownership in commercial markets. On the one hand, this encompasses the broad issue of codifying all private ownership and market privileges in a society, not just those for the media, including discussions of antitrust. On the other hand, media ownership itself generates specific rules to encourage particular values, such as competition, creativity, and localism. This includes broadcast ownership rules or prohibitions against media cross-ownership. Copyright is indirectly a media ownership policy because in granting and protecting monopoly rights to media content, copyright law discourages competition. Although the third broad policy area is really a subset of media ownership policies, it is so important that it deserves its own category. This is the use of regulations and public subsidies to generate nonprofit media that would not exist without them but that society deems worthwhile—what I term public media. The most prominent nonprofit media subsidy goes to public broadcasting.

In this chapter, I present a general overview of how policy in these areas has developed historically. In the first area, I will address the claim that the new technologies undermine the legitimacy of public policy making. In the areas of media ownership and public media, I make a series of specific arguments about how each of these traditions can be invigorated to better serve the needs of a self-governing people.

TECHNOLOGY AND THE INTERNET

Media and technology are so closely wed that media sectors are defined by the differing technologies they employ. It is clear, too, that differing media technologies have distinct effects. The printing press, for example, was a force for radical social change. Harold Innis and Marshall McLuhan pioneered much of the work emphasizing the singular importance of dominant media technologies in determining society's overall nature.[2] Neil Postman argued that the replacement of print culture with a culture dominated by television has led to a general dumbing down of society because television produces lazy minds (and shallow institutions) less capable of rigorous and sustained thought compared to those weaned in a society immersed in reading.[3] Likewise, Jerry Mander left a successful career in the advertising industry to write a seminal critique of television along similar lines.[4]

These arguments can veer toward technological determinism, seeing media technology as a super-powerful social force while reducing the importance of other factors, including economics and public policy. Writers who focus on the influence the Internet and digital technologies are having upon our society sometimes adopt a similarly myopic view. Because of their often startling effects upon society, it is assumed these technologies are larger than life. But in fact they result from explicit policies, and policies and commercial pressures significantly determine how they develop. Critics that emphasize media technology are worth taking seriously nonetheless, because they remind us that media technologies have distinct characteristics that require special attention, going beyond the manner in which they are socially controlled.

The great communication technological revolutions of the past century stemmed from significant public sector involvement, often in the form of direct subsidy, more often than not through the military. Radio broadcasting, satellite communication, the Internet, to name but three, were spawned under the auspices of the U.S. government. This is not to deny the role of the private sector; its influence was crucial, especially once a clear market had been established. Built into the corporate market structure, in fact, are significant incentives for firms to develop new technologies.[5] Typically, however, government intervention creates a new market for a major new communication technology, and only after a lucrative market becomes viable is the technology turned over to commercial interests. The most striking example is broadcasting's development in the 1920s and 1930s. The government also shapes how communication technologies are to be deployed—for example, by setting technical standards.[6] These areas are vital for government policy making in media, but the process tends to be dominated by self-interested commercial parties: recall the mobsters in *Godfather II* dividing up Cuba on the Havana patio.[7]

Digital broadcasting exemplifies bad policy making in action. Digital technology radically departs from traditional analog broadcasting and opens the door to innumerable new policy options for television broadcasting. For example, on the same amount of spectrum that provided five analog stations to a community, digital broadcasting could offer considerably more channels, well over twenty. Alternatively, society might elect to utilize the spectrum to provide higher-quality transmissions, using more spectrum per station, what is called high-definition television. (Or a combination of the two approaches could be chosen.) The emergence of digital broadcasting technology in the 1990s offered an ideal opportunity to discuss the future of television, electronic media, and fundamental communication policies. Policies could have been crafted and implemented to establish numerous new digital TV stations in every community to complement the existing broadcasters. It would not have been inconceivable, for example, to establish enough over-the-air channels that many citizens would no longer need to subscribe to a cable or satellite service to receive the channels they desire. The possibilities opened up by the technology were enormous.

The corrupt drafting of the 1996 Telecommunications Act, however, denied citizens their right to choose what television would become. The last thing the existing commercial broadcasters wanted was for the public to get the crazy idea that they could reconstruct the TV system to make it superior. So the NAB lobbied successfully to get a clause added to the Telecommunications Act that required the FCC to allocate to each existing broadcaster double their amount of spectrum so that they could simultaneously transmit their signals digitally. This massive amount of scarce spectrum would be given at no charge; other commercial users of the spectrum, like cellular telephone companies, would still have to pay the government. That commercial broadcasters were gobbling up the spectrum and therefore hijacking any possibility for public debate over digital television barely raised an eyebrow in Washington.

What did raise eyebrows was that broadcasters were getting an enormous commercial gift—then valued at $70 billion. It struck many observers as an extreme case of corporate welfare. Senator John McCain called the digital TV giveaway "one of the great rip-offs in American history. They used to rob trains in the Old West, now we rob spectrum."[8] And the NAB antagonized a powerful (though not quite powerful enough) lobby by taking this spectrum from the wireless companies hankering to develop it.[9] For a few years after the law's passage some politicians and regulators occasionally bellyached about how criminal the spectrum giveaway was and made some threats, but, in the end, the NAB got exactly what it wanted. As *Business Week* concluded, commercial broadcasting is an industry "accustomed to getting its way in Washington."[10]

Beyond the sheer corruption of the digital TV spectrum giveaway, what should be clear is that the rhetoric about "letting the market determine the course" for digital television was just that—rhetoric. In addition to the wireless firms that wanted the spectrum for their own use, the relevant industries central to the transition to digital television—large network broadcasters, smaller broadcasters, cable companies, TV program producers, consumer electronics manufacturers, satellite broadcasters, software firms—are all highly concentrated oligopolies and lobbying powerhouses. Digital television was always going to be settled through backroom politicking. Each industry maintains a distinct interest in pursuing a certain type (or types) of technology for digital TV because that approach will be most advantageous to its commercial prospects. These technologies are incompatible, so, as often as not, the "competition" of these semimonopolistic firms produces an impasse rather than innovation. Until everyone agrees on one technology that everyone will use, firms have little incentive to spend money and effort on digital technology. The firms themselves have demanded that the government intervene to set technical standards (or encourage the establishment of a cartel-like body of relevant firms to do so) and mandate that everyone comply. Such has been the dilemma facing the FCC and Congress in 2002–3; the digital spectrum—still considered a hot property—has lain fallow since 1996.[11] Indeed, by 2001, one Wall Street analyst estimated the spectrum that had been given to the commercial broadcasters as having grown in value to $365 billion.[12] The industries are exerting significant pressure on the government to settle the issues and get this spectrum generating profit.[13]

But one should not confuse this brokering of a compromise for digital TV by the FCC as policy making in the public interest. The FCC will merely set terms so that these industries in combination can generate as much profit as possible from public property.[14] This is regulation in the private interest taken to extremes. Once the digital TV system is in place, years from now, policy makers and industry CEOs alike will almost certainly characterize it as a natural development of free market competition. And any future effort to exact public service from the huge firms granted all these privileges will be dismissed as a callous attempt by the government to interfere with the free market.

If anything, the shift from analog to digital in radio has been even more corrupt than the backroom wheeling and dealing with digital TV. The process was as privatized and as secretive as any imaginable. IBiquity, a private firm whose major shareholders include the fifteen largest radio broadcasters such as Clear Channel, Viacom, and Cox Communications, put the plan together and the FCC approved it in 2002. Under it, the transition from analog to digital radio broadcasting occurs gradually and without change in the radio dial.[15] Because the dial will remain the same, listeners will come to think of digital radio as merely a technical enhancement of the signal, not as a new technology that could have reformed the industry. An opportunity to easily add numerous stations in every community has been squandered because existing radio owners want no new competition for "their" listeners.[16] In addition, because the digital plan calls for broadcasters to transmit identical analog and digital signals simultaneously adjacent to each other, it leaves less room for low-power stations. Arguably .001 percent of the American people, aside from those in the radio industry, have any knowledge of the digital radio plan—there was virtually no press coverage, and even members of Congress are ignorant of it. Yet the plan may well lock radio into an unnecessary system for generations.[17]

Once a specific communication technology such as digital TV or digital radio "takes off," it can become a powerful force. Dominant media technologies often exhibit what are called "bandwagon effects." Such a technology will grow in value as more people use it until it monopolizes the field over even superior rivals. The classic case is the VHS videocassette system, which defeated the Beta system in the 1970s simply because more people bought VHS recorders.[18] Once a technology becomes dominant, it creates a "path dependency," which makes the technology extraordinarily difficult to challenge. As with the VHS-Beta battle, research reveals that the dominant technology is not necessarily the best one or the most rational one. Consider the standard "qwerty" keyboard setup, an inefficient and archaic design developed to keep commonly used letters on a manual typewriter from colliding. It is now impossible to replace because its path dependency is more like an eight-lane highway. Markets tend to be poor at determining appropriate technological standards; self-interested commercial parties, of course, are taking care of themselves, not considering what is good for society as a whole.

Another difficulty for policy making is that the power of technologies can be mesmerizing. Who cannot be astounded by the scope of the Internet or by tiny cellular telephones that are turning into virtual supercomputers?[19] The media and communication system is being transformed in ways we can barely predict, almost like science fiction.[20] How can we create policies to control a radically different future? The Internet already has transmogrified media and political culture, and its influence is likely to intensify. For those outside the mainstream of political debate, the Internet has proven to be a remedy to their isolation, offering access to alternative and dissident media worldwide. For a significant percentage of politically active people in the United States—though a distinct minority of the population—the Internet serves as the primary means of gathering news and information.

The $64 thousand question is if the Internet will simply make existing fare easier to distribute or if it will provide the platform for quality journalism where none exists. Activists can download critical articles from the foreign press on global politics, but they cannot download quality articles on politics in their own community if nobody is uploading it. The Internet also allows immediate and virtually cost-free distribution of material worldwide to seemingly limitless numbers of people. This has permitted political activists to engage in organizing that would have been impossible in years past. The 2003 campaign against the relaxation of media ownership rules probably would have been a shadow of what it became without the Internet. But while it is easy to be impressed by the Internet's power as an organizing tool, it is unclear how much independence in the long run the Internet will provide citizens from the commercial media system. It is also unclear to what extent the emergence of the Internet as an alternative will have an appreciable effect upon mainstream journalism or entertainment.

POLICY MAKING IN THE INTERNET ERA

While the Internet's future is difficult to predict, its emergence has reinforced the claim that new technologies render moot the traditional concerns of media policy makers, or even the need for public policy making. The rise of the Internet, for example, is often touted as the rise of limitless media. After all, the cost of launching a website is minimal, there are millions and millions of websites, and people have access to a range of information and ideas that was simply unfathomable as recently as ten or fifteen years ago. So who needs to worry about concentrated media ownership? Who needs public media? The Internet will set us free.

In one sense, this is a blatant ideological ploy by powerful media firms to distract attention as they gobble up more media so they may be better poised to crush competition generated by new technologies. If media firms are allowed to become vastly larger they will in effect be handed tremendous power to shape how new media technologies are developed, and to reduce the possibility of alternative development paths, not to mention the possibility of new competition. And as they get larger, their political muscle in Washington gets the equivalent of a steroid injection. It is not that these firms do not want explicit policies governing the Internet and new technologies—rhetoric about keeping the Internet "unregulated" is just that—it is just that they want to make these policies themselves without public "interference."

What are these policies? Crucial issues concern copyright, the role and nature of advertising, and privacy.[21] Regulation of spam and pop-ups gather the most immediate attention, not only because consumers despise these practices but also because certain business interests see spam and pop-ups as undermining their efforts to do business online.[22] The more obscure matter of how copyright applies to the Internet—obscure because commercial interests have no desire to make it a public issue—however, will ultimately be more important, even fundamental, toward determining how content evolves online.[23] The right of computer users to go online expecting a right to privacy comes into conflict with the desire of corporate interests to monitor people's behavior to enhance their commercial prospects.

The allocation of electromagnetic spectrum will also determine the course of the Internet. New technologies permit much more efficient use of spectrum, like wireless Internet or "wi-fi," and hold the promise of blasting open access to the Internet.[24] The barrier is that powerful corporate interests that possess monopoly licenses to the spectrum continue to use their political influence to set the terms on which such technologies are implemented. In November 2002, the FCC's Spectrum Policy Task Force, in a bow to this lobby, recommended that incumbent licensees be granted permanent, private-property-like rights in the frequencies they currently borrow. The theory is that these firms will then have incentive to lease their spectrum for more productive uses. As policy analysts Norman Ornstein and Michael Calabrese argue, this is a "bribe," which "confers a massive and undeserved financial windfall—up to $500 billion—on a few lucky industries."[25] *Welcome to Havana, Mr. Corleone.*

An entire raft of other telecommunication policies float into the picture as the Internet converges with the interpersonal electronic communication system. Setting technical standards on digital communication services can strongly influence how the Internet develops. A crucial regulatory struggle surrounds how the regulation of cable systems, telephone companies, satellite companies and other Internet Service Providers will be reconciled—they are presently subject to differing regulations—as they increasingly compete directly for Internet (or broadband) access and telephone services.

Along these lines, the open nature of the Internet heretofore has not been natural to the technology but, rather, has been premised on the long-standing "common carrier" telecommunication policy requiring telephone companies to permit all who wish to use their services, including Internet access services, the right do so on a favorable, nondiscriminatory, basis. This has been the main barrier preventing firms from erecting lucrative commercial toll booths for websites and users. Cable successfully won a Bush FCC policy in 2002 that eliminated the rights of Internet Service Providers to have any access to their broadband networks. Soon after, the FCC also awarded telephone companies similar control on their all-fiber networks. "At the behest of powerful interests, the FCC is buying onto a warped vision that open networks should be replaced by closed networks and that the FCC should excuse broadband providers from long-standing non-discrimination requirements," FCC Commissioner Michael Copps cautioned in December 2003. "If we continue down this path, the basic end-to-end openness that made the Internet great will be gone."[26] With cable the leading residential broadband provider, and given its new architectural control as a result of lobbying, the Net will take on more of the characteristics of the U.S. entertainment media marketplace.[27] But it is still up for grabs. The outcome of this policy battle will go a long way toward determining how open access to the Internet will remain in coming years.[28]

When attention turns beyond the borders of the United States, the central role of government policies in regulating the Internet becomes even more striking. A 2003 survey by the International Telecommunications Union—the global regulatory body—discovered that "virtually every government" in the world directly manages important aspects of the Internet, including the United States.[29] The dominant role of the United States over Internet policy making is being challenged by other nations, and is now an issue before the

United Nations.[30] Linked closely with the tempestuous negotiations surrounding global and regional trade deals and economic agreements, the future of the Internet is anything but certain.

In sum, the course of the Internet has everything to do with a range of crucial policy issues, most of which are unknown to the general public, unreported in the news media, and undebated in the mainstream political culture. What is clear is that if people assume the technologies come prewired with how they are to be deployed, it is more likely that the public will remain blissfully unaware of the crucial policy deliberations taking place.

This argument that the Internet frees us from media policy concerns also appeals to some critics of the commercial media system. Hallelujah, they exult, we can go online and avoid corporate media altogether. Those who believe that all they need is a website and protection from government censorship to leapfrog the commercial media are dreaming. Good journalism—and good media generally— requires money and institutional support. The ability to launch websites is well and good, but that access does not guarantee the ability to launch well-funded economically viable news or entertainment sites. And that is the crucial issue here: journalism and entertainment typically require substantial resources and institutional support to be effective. Consider the emergence of Independent Media Centers, an exciting new use of the Internet and digital technologies. Despite all the energy these multimedia centers have attracted and generated, as community public access centers of sorts, they remain woefully impoverished and dependent upon volunteer labor. Their poverty distinctly limits the role they can play in our media and political culture. If support isn't coming from advertising, the historical record shows that it is unlikely to come from direct sales either, especially if the product is outside the mainstream. Devising a means to subsidize a tier of media, online or otherwise, becomes imperative for the public interest.

The moral of the digital radio and TV rip-off is clear: we need to develop policies that encourage the best that technologies can offer. Economist Dean Baker proposes to let any American divert $100 from her federal income taxes to any nonprofit media outlet.[31] This subsidy would avoid government bureaucracy and allow conservatives, liberals, radicals, and apoliticals alike to choose their beneficiaries. It is content-neutral (no restrictions on what types of media to choose) and viewpoint-neutral (no restrictions on what political outlooks are acceptable). This effective public subsidy of billions to independent media, without government control, is an idea thought up by one economist in his spare time. Imagine what our society could generate if we devoted anywhere near as much energy to devising and debating viable media reform proposals as we did to trying to get rich off the Internet. The more people understand that the media system is the result of policies, and that those policies are subject to change, the closer we get to the floodgates of policy options opening.

It remains to be seen exactly how the Internet will reshape the media system or, as appears more likely at present, how the Internet will be incorporated into the existing media system. In the current "whoever makes the most money, wins" environment, profits will plow the path, and commercial lobbies will hammer out the necessary policies. Most large media companies have already lost fortunes attempting to get the inside track online.[32] So while the Internet has certainly dramatically changed our culture, one must be careful in assessing exactly what has changed. The Internet has not spawned a new group of commercially viable media companies to compete with existing firms. The power of the oligopolistic market trumps the subversive potential of the technology.[33] According to the *Columbia Journalism Review,* the leading media content websites are primarily associated with media giants, and advertising litters the Internet.[34] From spam e-mail to advertising-supported, and sometimes advertising-driven, search engines, the Internet is going hyper-commercial.[35] The most successful Internet media mogul is Barry Diller, and his USA Interactive online empire is almost exclusively centered on e-commerce without a trace of traditional media content in sight.[36] The once accepted argument that the Internet would radically transform our media culture for the better is more difficult to support today.

This doesn't mean that technology can't subvert existing media industries. Today new technologies are undermining established commercial media practices, especially for music, films, and books. The ease of copying and sharing digital music files has proven nightmarish for music industry executives. It is difficult to isolate and calculate how much of music industry's financial troubles are due to the Internet, since the industry has proven so dreadful at generating compelling new artists and since radio variety has been flattened by corporate consolidation. The music industry is in a desperate jam, because one of the main factors that explained their domination of the global market was that it required massive networks to distribute music. With digital distribution, much of the industry's *raison d'être* is gone. In a free market economy, these firms might follow horse-and-buggy makers into history's dumpster—or, in a genuine democracy, policies would be crafted to structure a music industry that better served the public in light of the new technologies. But in the United States music firms can use their immense political and economic power to get technical standards changed, PR campaigns launched, and copyright laws altered so they can maintain control over the industry.[37] The outcome is far from clear, but the music industry arguably has already lived longer than the technology necessitates. They are working every possible angle to see that the Internet can be turned into a vending machine for their wares.[38]

The film industry is also in the process of being digitized—so it, too, may be facing difficulties similar to the music industry. Already the video rental business is counting its remaining hours as cable and satellite video-on-demand, not to mention Internet distribution, makes jaunts to the video store far less attractive.[39] The film industry, however, carries certain advantages over the music industry, in particular that the downloading of films is more complicated than downloading music. Also, much of its revenue comes from theatrical distribution, which provides a social and esthetic experience difficult to reproduce in one's home.[40] Seeing a new movie still requires consumers to pay money for a ticket. The industry has already adopted a cartel-like united front to address the impending problems, like the music industry.[41] The conventional wisdom is that the film industry will not be damaged as badly by the Internet as the music industry has been.[42] It helped matters that the FCC approved industry-desired technical standards to make the ability to copy digital material much more difficult, despite the objections of public interest and consumer groups who warned that this would unnecessarily limit individual rights on the Internet.[43]

The picture is brighter for books despite broad speculation that e-books, digitally transmitted books, would effectively eliminate traditional books because they would lower the cost radically. In this case an old technology has proven difficult to replace—partly because innovators have failed to produce an effective gadget for displaying lengthy electronic material. By 2004 the traditional book business had won, at least for the foreseeable future. "Most people are very happy with that technology," one analyst observed when Barnes & Noble halted its e-book sales in September 2003.[44]

The incompatibility of some digital technologies with media industries' corporate desires remains a problem. As a writer for *The Economist* notes, media powerhouse Sony stands at the forefront of developing consumer electronic goods that bring easily shared games and media into handheld consoles. Sony "must find a way to keep those brilliant devices from wreaking havoc on the media business by encouraging piracy."[45] One example of dangerous technology for business as usual is the digital video recorder, often referred to as TiVo after one brand that pioneered the technology. DVRs present TV viewers with a novel and easy way to record programs and skip commercials. Research shows DVR users skip commercials 60 percent of the time.[46] Although only 3 percent of U.S. homes had DVRs in 2003, the figure is expected to climb dramatically. They are popular with viewers, for self-evident reasons, and cable and satellite companies are rushing to add DVR capacity to their systems to attract customers. DVRs, of course, greatly undermine the effectiveness of TV commercials, which is problematic for media conglomerates, all of which maintain a large stake in advertising-supported television. In response, media giants have been working to make it more difficult to skip commercials and meld commercialism more directly into programs so it cannot be avoided. Moreover, DVR companies are hardly a bulwark against TV commercialism; they are beginning to cultivate relationships with advertisers themselves.[47] It looks like the initial noncommercial nirvana promised by TiVo is going to be compromised by powerful commercial interests.[48]

Because of their power, corporate interests disproportionately win struggles against new technologies' innovations. The public gets to vote with its feet in the market, but only for a range of options that is constantly manipulated to serve business interests. Self-interested commercial parties end up better off, but society as a whole is diminished. The results of these battles clearly demonstrate that media policies heavily determine how the Internet and media technologies develop and what role they play in the media system and our culture. To the extent that the Internet is incorporated into the overall media system, traditional media policies governing that system will go a long way toward shaping the Internet as well. Which is another way of saying that policies surrounding media ownership and support for public media will be central to determining the future of the Internet.

MEDIA OWNERSHIP POLICIES

Any discussion of media ownership raises questions about heavily concentrated private control over media. It is a worldwide phenomenon and a worldwide problem. Around the globe media systems are primarily controlled by a small number of wealthy firms or individuals, who use their power to advance their political agenda. In extreme cases private control over media can be a direct threat to democratic rule. In Weimar Germany, for example, a handful of mighty press barons fostered Hitler's advance to power. After the war, the U.S.-led occupying forces implemented strict media ownership rules to prevent concentrated ownership because of its role in the rise of fascism.[49] For a more recent example, Venezuela's private media system is the province of a few wealthy families who despise the elected government of Hugo Chavez for its purported antagonism to their class interests. The privately controlled media have explicitly lied and distorted the news to encourage the removal of Chavez from office. "The private media have gone on attack," a Canadian journalist writes about Venezuela, "in ways that make the U.S. feeding frenzy on the Bill Clinton thong-gate look like a Victorian ladies' tea."[50] In Italy, Prime Minister Silvio Berlusconi owes no small part of his political success to ownership of much of his country's media; his holdings dominate commercial television broadcasting.[51]

But launching a discussion of media ownership policies by assessing existing market concentration skips over several layers of policy making. First is the notion of turning control of the media over to private interests seeking to maximize profits. An immediate problem with private ownership is that it limits the relevant groups of people who can own and control the media to a very small number, those who possess enough capital to enter the industry: it limits media control to the rich. This implicit slant toward the wealthy was a main reason late-eighteenth-century Americans, especially progressive ones, fought to subsidize newspapers through printing and postal subsidies: without subsidies the press would have disproportionately represented the political interests of a tiny segment of the population, and that is obviously bad for democracy. Today's policies to encourage African American and minority ownership of media recognize the market tendency.[52] Ownership does matter, especially in media, where control over ideas, news, and culture rates as a unique power even among powerful corporations. Private ownership of media, in nonegalitarian societies, is not content-neutral or viewpoint-neutral; the best ideas do not automatically rise to the top. Add advertising's role, as well as the workings of the oligopolistic marketplace, and private ownership becomes a vise that directly and indirectly pressures content. The "market" can be a most effective censor. Hence, by definition, capitalist control over media poses a serious problem for democratic press theory.

This nation's commitment to a press independent of government control did not necessitate the current corporate-driven, advertising-supported media system. In First Amendment case law, an argument can be made, by a close reading of Supreme Court opinions on seminal cases like *Miami Herald v. Tornillo* (1974), that the freedom of the press privilege is intended primarily for editors and journalists; publishers win that privilege only because it is assumed that their interests are synonymous with those of editors and journalists. In complete accord with the First Amendment, the government could craft policies favoring different forms of media ownership, such as nonprofit cooperatives or journalist-owned companies. Similarly, as some critics have argued, certain crucial media, such as monopoly daily newspapers, could have been established as nonprofit, municipally owned entities controlled by publicly elected boards of directors. Even more obviously, radio and television broadcasting could have been established as nonprofit sectors, similar to higher education, and structured as anything from state-supported noncommercial networks to local community stations based on listener and viewer contributions, or a combination thereof.

The eventual model that won out in the United States, the corporate form, did so not as a result of broad public debate with an evaluation of alternatives, but, rather, because the powerful commercial interests were able to have their way with policy makers. This is a subject much larger than media. As U.S. history shows, the power of corporations was a central political issue throughout the late nineteenth and early twentieth centuries; it dominated the thoughts of the Populists and was a pressing concern to many people during the Progressive Era. The granting to corporations of personhood and constitutional protection remains one of the most controversial legal and economic developments in U.S. history.

Once a commercial media system is established, the issue of concentration moves to the fore. In much of economic theory, competitive markets are regarded as much better at serving the public interest than are concentrated markets; in these livelier environments, Adam Smith's invisible hand supposedly best works its magic. In addition, by virtually all known theories of democracy and according to world history, concentration in media ownership is highly correlated with authoritarianism and political corruption. The bias in free societies must therefore be toward diverse and decentralized media ownership whenever possible. Those in favor of concentrated ownership must establish that concentrated media ownership, on balance, will be a positive development for society. If significant doubt lingers or if the argument is merely that concentrated media ownership will not worsen matters, the prudent course is to steer toward too much diversity, too much competition. Once media industries become concentrated in the hands of a small number of enormous firms, the political and economic barriers to reforming the system are immense. It is like getting toothpaste back into the tube.

The thrust of commercial media markets is clear: private ownership reduces the number of people who can own the media to a handful, strongly promotes concentration, and eliminates smaller and commercially marginal media. The political problem is simple: oligopolistic markets and reliance on advertising revenue undermine efforts to launch new media. The bar was raised much higher for small media by the twentieth century; even with no drop-off in readership or audience, commercial survival had become much more difficult. The newspaper industry has been the most striking example of oligopolistic market economics. There were 689 U.S. cities with competing dailies in 1910; by 1990 the figure had fallen to 21.[53] Despite being enormously profitable throughout the twentieth century compared to other investment opportunities, newspapers have not generated a stampede toward fresh entrepreneurial activity, as Milton Friedman would predict. "The history of survival of start-up newspapers in markets that already have at least one daily is not a happy one," a newspaper analyst concluded in 2002. "In fact, there is no history. There has never been one survivor."[54] To some extent, the commercial media market is as effective a media commissar as an authoritarian government might hope for—and has the advantage of achieving its ends without resorting to explicit repression.

If newspapers, magazines, and books formed the core of the media through the end of the nineteenth century, that changed rapidly as the twentieth century began. By 1920 major new national media industries either existed or were visible on the horizon: recorded music, motion pictures, radio broadcasting, and advertising. Media offered a major new area for profit making and investment, and played an ever-larger role in people's lives. This new world was a radically different one from James Madison's or Abraham Lincoln's, and the establishment of these new media industries raised significant questions about how they could best be organized and regulated. Even traditional media, as we have seen with newspapers, were radically transformed in their wake. Magazine publishing, for example, was revolutionized with the rise of national advertising in the late nineteenth century. Magazines became our first truly national commercial medium, predating film and radio broadcasting by decades.[55] Its trade association, the Magazine Publishers of America, went to battle to hang onto its lucrative second-class mailing permit—a subsidy essential to the industry's growth and profitability—and to claim First Amendment protection from other regulations.[56] Each new media industry followed the pattern laid down by newspapers: it began as a competitive enterprise and evolved into a concentrated oligopoly. This movement away from diversity undermined the open access claimed as the primary defense for the market as a democratic press regulator.

Left unaddressed, such concentration can erupt into a political crisis, akin to what happened with journalism in the Progressive Era. Each new media industry also took the solution to this problem from the newspaper industry's playbook: aggressive PR and industry self-regulation. Large media firms would prove that they deserved the market privileges they enjoyed and that they would not abuse them. Self-regulation meant that firms would occasionally act against their short-term commercial interests to serve the broader public good, but, because it would eliminate the threat of regulation, it would actually serve the industry's long-term commercial objectives. In doing so, media industries hoped to eliminate for all time the notion that the government should implement policies to encourage a broader and more diverse press—a hallmark of the constitutional era's media policy making. Instead, the government should assist the dominant firms in becoming even more profitable—though this point was never prominent in the industry's PR manifestos.

Every major media industry developed a trade association and self-regulatory code of conduct for its members. These continue to be given considerable publicity—after all, why else have them?[57] In the case of film, for example, between 1900 and 1920 it was transformed from a small-scale competitive enterprise with a fairly broad range of political and esthetic genres to a tightly knit oligopoly built around a handful of Hollywood studios.[58] By the 1920s the industry was rigorously implementing a self-regulatory code that monitored Hollywood films' sexual and political content in the hope of keeping government regulation at bay.[59] At the same time the industry trade association was hard at work in Washington to get favorable regulations concerning issues like copyright or to get the government to push products onto overseas markets.[60]

At a PR level, self-regulation codes were successful; as for how much these codes enforced actions in favor of the public interest, the evidence is mixed at best. In the absence of public pressure, firms are generally driven by profit to violate the spirit and intent of self-regulatory codes, especially when there is good money to be made and competitors have no qualms about making it. As the editor of a 1998 review of media self-regulation codes concluded, his research "paints a rather gloomy picture of how well many of them work."[61] The following year another published report on the topic concluded that media "self-regulation rarely lives up to its claims." With regard to the Internet, the author added, "self-regulation is not likely to be successful."[62] In short, while self-regulation works well as a political strategy for media industries, it is by no means the best solution to concentrated media's problems for the public.

The United States has developed a range of media policies to address concentrated media ownership, but these policies tend to be made on the proverbial Havana patio; so whatever the stated public interest intent, it tends to get lost in the muck of special interest superpower lobbying and backroom deal making. Consider the Newspaper Preservation Act of 1970 (NPA), a law with the stated purpose of maintaining more than one daily newspaper in at least a handful of communities. The NPA allowed newspapers to operate together as a monopoly in their relationship with advertisers and divvy up the proceeds, thereby entering into what is called a joint operating agreement. It was a modest and largely ineffective policy solution. As one analyst concludes, "The NPA has not succeeded in preserving these trailing newspapers, but rather has hastened their decline."[63] The law, however, did reflect the "massive newspaper lobbying" effort that pushed it through, and a handful of existing publishers were able to rack up increased profits by taking advantage of these monopolies.[64] In short, the legitimate public desire to have multiple newspapers in a community was converted into a measure to serve the interest of a handful of large newspaper publishers.

Three major policy areas address media ownership, and each of these has been corrupted, much like the NPA was. The first of these is broadcast ownership. This is an obvious policy issue because the government assigns monopoly broadcast licenses to prospective broadcasters; the government can determine who owns what. The government also puts conditions upon licensees, limiting how many monopoly broadcast licenses a single firm can hold and what other media it can own. To promote competition and diversity, the FCC has prohibited broadcasters from owning newspapers or cable TV systems in the same community where they broadcast. It has also traditionally placed limits on how much of their own programming broadcasters can produce, with the aim of spawning an independent production industry.[65]

Broadcast ownership regulation arguably has been the only form of media control with teeth. Its strength came in part because media ownership rules were popular with the general public and, to a larger extent, because politically influential small media companies knew that without these limits they would not be able to survive in the marketplace. But large media companies chafed at these restrictions, knowing the massive profits awaiting them if they could grow larger, face less competition, and lower risk. For decades the big commercial broadcasters pounded on politicians and regulators to relax or eliminate the rules. In 1996 they triumphed when they inserted a section into the Clinton administration–backed Telecommunications Act eliminating the national caps on the number of radio stations a single company could own.

What has happened with U.S. radio broadcasting since 1996 has often been characterized as a case of market forces running wild; in fact, it is a case of corrupt policy making that allowed a handful of large companies to run wild. Almost overnight the radio industry's structure was turned upside down. Well over half the stations were sold until a few massive firms like Clear Channel (owner of more than 1,200 stations) and Viacom came to rule the roost.[66] With the maximum number of stations it was allowed to own in 1995, Clear Channel accounted for 1.3 percent of the radio industry's revenues; by 2001, the "deregulated" Clear Channel had garnered more than 20 percent of the pot. In addition, overall industry revenues shot up more than 55 percent over the same six years, thanks to large companies' greater leverage over advertisers.[67] The value of stations skyrocketed as well since they were far more valuable as part of massive empires than they had been as stand-alone operations. And of course the market values of these stations had nothing to do with the actual costs of production, which were quite low.

Radio broadcasting, which due to its low cost of transmission and reception was ideally suited for local control, decentralization, and creative risk-taking, quickly became a nationally directed enterprise run by a few massive firms in service to Wall Street and Madison Avenue. To top it off, the FCC has been lax in enforcing the admittedly weak new regulations. Although the 1996 rules limit a company to owning eight radio stations in a market, the FCC has permitted a company to exceed that number in thirty-four different markets.[68]

The implications for radio content have been striking. Local content is hardly a cost-effective method for a national chain—the whole idea is to lower production costs while jacking up advertising revenues—so local radio news has declined, as has much of locally originated programming. Clear Channel and Viacom have gained notoriety for developing a technique that permitted a corporate announcer to give the illusion that they were speaking locally to different stations around the nation simultaneously.[69] By 2000, advertising comprised around 18 minutes per hour on commercial stations, according to Variety, a sharp increase from a decade earlier.[70] And payola, the long outlawed practice of bribing stations to play certain recordings, has returned to radio as a source of over $100 million in revenues. Now, however, the money goes to the owners, not the disc jockeys, and therefore it is considered quasi-legal.[71]

Between payola and the conservatism built into large commercial organizations, the range of music getting extensive airplay in the United States has shrunk, and the notion of localism in music content has been nearly eliminated. And people are not happy. Journalists, music lovers, those in the music industry, and the public at large typically express dissatisfaction with what passes for U.S. commercial radio broadcasting today. Rocker Tom Petty devoted the lead track on an album to radio's decline in 2002. "Saying that things were better [before] is kind of tiring when it comes from old people," Petty remarked, "but they were."[72] In September 2003 Senator John McCain, the chair of the Senate Commerce Committee that oversees broadcast regulation, weighed in on the Senate floor: "I think there is one area of agreement. . . . There is too much concentration in radio. I know of no credible person who disagrees with that."[73]

Copyright is the second core media ownership policy. It is at the foundation of many commercial media industries; corrupt policy making is also readily apparent in this area. The concept, of course, is purely artificial. In theory, copyright protection was written into the Constitution to provide authors with limited monopoly control over their work; such protection would allow them to earn enough income to have incentive to produce new works. Once that income threshold is reached, however, the author's work should pass into the public domain, where anyone can publish or use it for free. Copyright is thus a government-created and government-enforced monopoly that directly prohibits one type of competitive market.

During the constitutional debates and later when Congress passed its first copyright laws, copyright was considered a necessary evil that had to be carefully held in check. Some called it a "tax on knowledge" because the much higher book prices brought by monopolistic control made books far less accessible to the population. In that spirit the Constitution prohibited Congress from making copyright permanent; after a certain period of time all books had to go into the public domain, where anyone could make use of them. It was widely understood that artistic and scholarly work—a society's cultural heritage—naturally belonged in the public domain, so copyright was the exception, not the rule. Some indication of the effect of copyright comes by looking at the work of Charles Dickens. In 1843, *A Christmas Carol* cost the equivalent of $2.50 in England, where Dickens's work was covered by copyright. In the United States, where Dickens was not covered by copyright because he was not an American—an exemption since changed—*A Christmas Carol* was produced by numerous publishers and sold for 6 cents. It was a bestseller, as were all of Dickens's books in the United States.[74]

Congress initially called for copyright terms of fourteen years. From the beginning prominent publishers such as Noah Webster worked to expand the length and terms of copyright. In the nineteenth century Mark Twain did the same. But the public benefited tremendously by having limited copyright—as the Dickens example demonstrates—and formed a strong bulwark against extending copyright. The balance between copyright and the public domain began to change dramatically in the twentieth century with the rise of the corporate media system.[75]

With virtually no press coverage whatsoever and zero public involvement beyond self-interested commercial parties, copyright law has been rewritten in recent decades to serve the interests of the largest media companies. Both corporations and individuals qualify for copyright, and the term for copyright has been extended to ninety-five years total for corporate-held copyrights and to the lifetime of the author *plus* seventy years for individual authors. Every twenty years or so, most recently in 1998, the length of copyright gets extended; today anything produced after 1923 will not be in the public domain unless it has no commercial value, which is difficult to assess. Law professor Peter Jaszi calls what Congress is doing the granting of permanent copyright on the installment plan. Extensions are applied retroactively to work produced under an earlier copyright limit.

It should be obvious that copyright rules no longer have any connection to the desire to balance the needs of authors with the needs of the public domain. "Is it really plausible that potential authors of enduring classics will be deterred by the knowledge that the stream of royalties will dry up fifty years after their death?" a *Financial Times* columnist asked. "The retrospective nature of the change in the law shows the object is not to stimulate new creative activities but to protect owners of the rights to old ones."[76] Indeed, few authors would decline to write books if copyright lasted for only twenty-eight years, as it was for much of American history. And once an author is dead, or all the people who have created a collective piece like a film are dead, extending the terms of the copyright for their work is nothing short of a gift to the current owners at the expense of the public. Copyright has become an inalienable property right for media corporations.[77]

In short, the changes in copyright law are all about using corporate lobbying muscle to protect valuable monopoly rights, the public be damned. Copyrights are now a tradable commodity, sold and transferred long after works' creators have died. Because there is no corporate accounting to determine the value of copyrights, we can only speculate how much revenue these monopoly privileges have generated for private interests. But we do know the amount is staggering. Consider a recent suit against Disney by the heirs to the U.S. investor who in 1930 bought the rights to *Winnie the Pooh* author A. A. Milne's estate. The suit claimed they were owed as much as a billion dollars in copyright payments. Although Disney was already paying the heirs $12 million per year, they claimed that Disney had shortchanged them.[78] In 1930 the characters were not worth much, but today Milne's creations of eighty years ago have become extremely lucrative, so the family wants to shop Winnie the Pooh and friends to other companies.[79] And the Winnie the Pooh characters are just a drop in the copyright bucket. Viewed in this light, when a government extends copyright terms on existing works it may well have created "value" into the tens and possibly the hundreds of billions of dollars. These copyright extensions are little more than corporate welfare, pure and simple.

The irony here, as law professor Lawrence Lessig points out, is that Disney's empire and others in commercial media have been built on material from the public domain—because past copyright laws were less restrictive. Today's media conglomerates are now ensuring that no one can use their material in a similar fashion.[80] In this way, copyright fiercely protects established concentrated corporate media power and fights competitive markets. The bottom line, going beyond corporate welfare, is not pretty, but it reflects where power lies in Washington: the public pays much more for many media products than it should because monopoly markets are protected; creative artists and the general public suffer because much less art is available in the public domain than it should be.[81] Our cultural heritage has been privatized.

MEDIA AND ANTITRUST LAW

After broadcast ownership regulation and copyright, the third core ownership policy in the United States takes the form of antitrust law. To many Americans antitrust regulation seems like the logical and obvious approach to dissolve large companies and thereby protect diverse media ownership. This has rarely happened, especially in recent decades. Rigorous enforcement of antitrust statutes has been done sparingly with media industries; generally only in the most severe cases of vertical or, especially, horizontal integration (that is, to stop classical monopolies). Typically the application of antitrust laws has been largely based upon explicitly commercial criteria—when companies have too much power over price or too much power to obtain monopoly profits. In 2003 the *New York Times* observed that the federal government "has generally stood by as media companies of all types have consolidated."[82] The constitutional law professor Lucas Powe, no fan of media regulation, terms media antitrust attempts "toothless."[83]

Today's lax antitrust regulation has its defenders: they sometimes characterize it as apolitical and concerned solely with the scientific evaluation of markets. To them, antitrust rules can balance concerns about excessive market power that harms consumers or other businesses with the need to permit businesses to operate efficiently, with as little restriction on market activities as possible. Their studied and serious world has no place for emotional concerns about media concentration or monopoly; this is the world of hard science that requires an unsentimental devotion to facts and statistics. If antitrust law appears weak and ineffectual, that is because uninformed people do not understand its nuances and complexities.[84]

Such characterizations, or rationalizations, for the media antitrust regulations are dubious at best. The current "scientific" approach of applying antitrust law to media rests upon the assumption that the market works to produce the optimum media system. This presupposition leads seamlessly to the belief that antitrust policies—and more generally, policies limiting ownership—should be used rarely and primarily to prevent especially egregious instances of horizontal integration or monopoly market power. Unless clear evidence demonstrates that a merger will allow a firm to restrict production and thereby obtain "monopoly profits," usually by raising prices, the merger must be approved.

This fairly recent interpretation of antitrust law shows no concern over concentrated and undemocratic power; instead it shows a virtually single-minded concern with "market efficiency." It is thus of quite dubious value. Antitrust law was spawned during the eras of the populist and progressive movements, which held distinctly political concerns about the effects of concentrated wealth as an impediment to equality and the exercise of self-government. In 1888, Senator John Sherman advocated the first great antitrust law, the Sherman Antitrust Act, not to lower prices for shoppers, but because the trusts' political power threatened to tear the nation apart and undermine the government's legitimacy.[85] This political element to antitrust law was reaffirmed in the 1935 Public Utilities Holding Company Act, in which Congress demonstrated anxiety about the political power that could be harnessed by utility-based conglomerates, so it prevented utilities from owning other enterprises.[86]

In the landmark 1945 *Associated Press v. U.S.* case, the Supreme Court ruled that antitrust regulations could be applied to the media with no violation of their First Amendment rights. Hugo Black's famous opinion—"The assumption that the widest possible dissemination of information from diverse and antagonistic sources is essential to the welfare of the public, that a free press is a condition of a free society"—opened the door for a proactive initiative against media concentration. Leaving little doubt about the court's opinion, Justice Felix Frankfurter wrote in his concurring statement: "Truth and understanding are not wares like peanuts or potatoes. And so, the incidence of restraints upon the promotion of truth . . . calls into play considerations very different from comparable restraints in a cooperative enterprise having merely a commercial aspect."[87] Immediately following the *Associated Press* decision, Morris Ernst, the legendary ACLU First Amendment lawyer, called for the government to break up the big media companies because they violated the spirit and intent of both antitrust law and the First Amendment.[88] There is no reason to believe that the Constitution prohibits media-specific antitrust or competition laws that would require greater restrictions on mergers. And there is good reason to follow Justice Black in thinking such a response would serve First Amendment values. In his opinion in the 1994 case *Turner Broadcasting System v. FCC*, Justice Anthony Kennedy concluded, "Assuring the public has access to a multiplicity of information sources is a governmental purpose of the highest order."[89] Indeed, the only barrier to aggressive antitrust policies in the realm of media comes from Congress and the White House, from lack of political will, and from corruption of the policy-making process. None of this changes the fact that strict application of antitrust law in the media realm has the constitutional seal of approval and can thus be seen as a basic responsibility of government—however much the executive and legislative branches refuse to shoulder that responsibility.

So the question then becomes, what would constitute a viable democratic media antitrust policy?

First, we need to remember that generating effective commercial media markets cannot be presumed to be the optimum outcome of a media system in a democracy. As demonstrated by our hyper-commercialized culture, this system generates a profitable media system for a handful of businesses who deliver woeful public service, and too often, terrible journalism. Such a system is typified by a degree of public ignorance and depoliticization that would make a tyrant envious. The guiding principle for antitrust in media, as well as in all communication policy making, cannot be merely the prevention of monopoly pricing and monopoly profits—although even this has not been prevented in the media realm. The goal in a democracy must always be the generation of a media system that best advances informed and active self-government. A commercial media system is legitimate in a democracy only to the extent that it helps achieve this goal; otherwise, it must be regulated and complemented with a noncommercial sector. There is no justification, empirical or historical, for the belief that what is good for General Electric is good for empowering the citizenry in a democracy.

Second, the major criterion used for antitrust intervention, in media as elsewhere, is centered on how companies use their market power to fix prices. In narrow economic terms, this makes sense. Firms seek market power (or monopoly power) so they can raise prices and drive up their profits. But there are deeper issues involved in the media area. As Ed Baker puts it, "Market power over price is only one possible concern in identifying and objecting to concentration in the media realm. . . . Even a market competitive from an antitrust perspective could still look extraordinarily concentrated" from a democratic perspective.[90] As legal scholar Donald Simon notes, "Non-economic factors, such as diminished quality, reduced consumer choice, and the potential for self-censorship must be taken into consideration by antitrust regulators."[91] One suspects a wide-ranging inquiry could locate other values as well.[92]

Third, arguments used to justify concentration in other industries cannot automatically be applied to the media sector. In particular, a core defense of concentration and oligopoly in heavy manufacturing industries is that the costs of production are so high that it is impossible to expect there to be, say, ten thousand viable automobile manufacturers. This idea may be true to a certain extent in some media sectors, say motion pictures, but it is absolutely untrue in areas like radio broadcasting, in which the physical cost of production is so low as to permit exceptionally competitive markets by contemporary media market standards.

Fourth, antitrust regulation in media needs to focus on the complex nature of media industries and how vertically integrated media conglomerates function in oligopolistic markets. To put it crudely, if a single company A produced all the movies, a single company B owned all the TV networks, a single company C produced all the music, a single company D owned all the cable systems, and a single company E owned all the cable channels, the current application of antitrust regulations would almost certainly require dissolution of these monopolies. Deals permitting the creation of these horizontally integrated monopolies would never have been approved. Yet if firms A, B, C, D, and E each were conglomerates accounting for roughly 20 percent of each of the five media genres, by current standards that would not arouse much interest from antitrust authorities. Whatever the merits of this line of reasoning for other sectors, in the realm of media it is half-baked. At the end of the day, we still only have five companies running everything across five markets. Antitrust enforcement, if it is serious in media, needs to pay more attention to vertical integration and cross-ownership.

This leads to the fifth and final point—and the policy recommendation that captures all of the above ideas. We need our government to generate a coherent policy for media ownership that encompasses the entirety of the media industries. It must result from detailed study and debate, and it must lay down a set of values and specific guidelines that will anticipate and shape future developments. It should be seen as a huge undertaking, similar in magnitude to the government's response to the energy crisis or the threat of terrorism. It should also eliminate the current piecemeal logic of current antitrust thinking, in which each merger is dealt with separately— which serves only to weaken any possibility of meaningful antitrust enforcement. Once a single large company is allowed to get bigger, then all its competitors have to be granted the same privilege or a power imbalance will result.

An effective antitrust policy would also have to undermine the "politicization"—i.e. corruption—of antitrust review. How a merger fares in Washington appears to be affected more by the relative political power of the parties involved than by the issue's importance to the public.[93] In 2002 Senator Ernest Hollings threatened to slash the Federal Trade Commission's budget, partly because evidence linked a Time Warner lawyer to a draft of antitrust guidelines that Hollings believed would make it less likely that proposed mergers would face a rigorous review.[94] At the very least, the policy must contain a presumption against media mergers. The democratic goal should be to have as many voices as possible.

Perhaps most important, such a policy-making process can formally address the two-ton gorilla that looms over media ownership—how the Internet and digital technologies will alter the media landscape. Rather than sitting back and letting powerful commercial interests make those decisions in the market and, through lobbying powers, dictate the policies that will enhance their commercial domination, a formal government policy can shape the Internet so that its extraordinary potential can be best deployed in the public interest. The public sector created the Internet; the public should call the shots.

PUBLIC BROADCASTING, YESTERDAY AND TODAY

The United States has never had a "free market" media system in which entrepreneurs competing for profits determined the system's nature. Throughout U.S. history extensive government subsidies have created and altered media systems in ways that the market never could have. By the end of the nineteenth century, however, the rich tradition of public debates over how to deploy large public subsidies to best enhance the breadth and diversity of the press in a democratic society gradually faded into oblivion as powerful commercial media industries began to emerge. Thereafter public subsidies remained— indeed, they were much larger than ever—but they were doled out quietly to the victors of contests between strong commercial media lobbies. The public had no role in this process, virtually no press coverage could draw people into the policy debates, and to the world at large the dominant media firms proclaimed that the United States had a "free market" media system that was the pure embodiment of a free press, as drawn up by Madison and Jefferson.

A radical new development in publicly subsidized media came with the invention of public service broadcasting in the early twentieth century. Unlike previous subsidies, this plan called for the use of public money explicitly to generate media content directly, not simply encourage commercial entities to do so. It stemmed from two other media evolutions. First, radio broadcasting presented an unprecedented problem for every nation: how to best utilize the scarce spectrum that could be devoted to this revolutionary communication technology. Second, the emerging commercial media system, even at its very best, had inherent flaws—*externalities*—that could be damaging to a self-governing or humane society. In combination, these factors prompted the belief that it was not just a right but also a duty of citizens in a democratic society to subsidize and promote a viable nonprofit and noncommercial broadcasting media sector. The result, public service broadcasting, has become a major institution in much of the world, though much less so in the United States. Still, this public service tradition has much to offer democratic media policy making in general.

Public service broadcasting refers to a nonprofit, noncommercial broadcasting service directed at the entire population and providing a full range of programming. At its best, it is accountable to the citizenry, has some distance from the dominant forces holding political power, and does not rely upon the market to determine its programming. Such a setup presents a difficult problem, although not an insurmountable one, for a free society, because it allows the state possibly to control media content far more than classical liberal theory would countenance. In authoritarian political systems, public broadcasting quickly becomes little more than state propaganda. Managing a viable public broadcasting service can be difficult in a democracy, but the international experience shows that it can be done, if there is a political commitment to make it happen. A democratic state can be enhanced by public broadcasting just as an authoritarian state can corrupt such broadcasting. To assume the latter is always the case is to give up the possibility of the former. To some extent, without intending to be overly dramatic, it is to abandon the idea that people can govern themselves.

Several other important variants of nonprofit and noncommercial broadcasting have arisen in the United States, and most stem from specific government policies. Religious institutions, schools, and universities conduct broadcasting as well. Cable TV systems are required to turn over channels (and subsidies) for "public access" broadcasting if communities demand them when local monopoly cable contracts are negotiated. These public access channels are legally content- and viewpoint-neutral—they have no editorial position, and, ideally, they teem with a vibrant range of political opinion. Public access channels tend to be most attractive to those who feel boxed out of the commercial system.[95] Similarly, community radio broadcasting—nonprofit and noncommercial stations dependent largely upon listener donations—exists in scores of U.S. cities. The model was pioneered by the innovative Pacifica system, which has "listener-sponsored" stations in five cities.[96] C-SPAN has provided an invaluable nonprofit and noncommercial service on cable television, though it is not the result of public policy so much as a PR gesture by the cable industry to fend off regulation in the public interest. In other words, the public pays a high price for C-SPAN—to the extent it succeeds as a PR maneuver to permit cable companies to jack up their rates—and the public has no control over its operations.[97]

By far the largest government expenditure to create nonprofit and noncommercial broadcasting has been for the Voice of America and various clandestine services like Radio Free Europe. But these programs are designed for overseas audiences—for diplomatic or propagandistic purposes, depending upon one's perspective—and are not meant to be consumed by the people who pay for them. Most Americans barely know they exist.

But it is public service broadcasting that has the broadest and richest tradition. In most democratic nations of the world, a significant section of the spectrum is devoted to nonprofit (and usually noncommercial) radio and television. The most notable example in the English-speaking world is the British Broadcasting Corporation (BBC). Maintaining public service broadcasting has been a difficult task in the United States for any number of reasons, but in particular because the dominant commercial interests have little interest in coexisting with a strong nonprofit sector that would peel away "their" audience. Today U.S. public service broadcasting is in crisis. Never lavishly funded or supported, the system struggles to survive in a fairly small niche of the media market. Its most vociferous critics charge that public broadcasting is a dubious institution in principle and now has become a bureaucratically ossified relic of a bygone era made irrelevant by the plethora of new cable channels and Internet websites. These critics argue that the market, combined with new technologies, can do a superior job of serving the public interest—and with no public broadcasting subsidy to boot. Because public broadcasting retains an element of political support, especially from the influential upper middle class, its existence is accepted by most of its critics, but only if it remains marginal and poorly subsidized.

To provide some sense of public broadcasting's dilemma, consider this: in 2003 public broadcasting received a federal subsidy of around $365 million, about what Disney's ESPN receives in subscriber fees from cable TV systems every two months.[98] If the United States subsidized a public broadcasting service at rates comparable to Britain's per capita rate for public broadcasting, for example, it would have an annual subsidy in the $15 billion range.[99] This would make it one of the three or four largest media operations in our country and provide an enormous spur to audiovisual production—conceivably large enough to change the industry's direction. In Europe, a huge and impressive variety of programming that would never pass commercial muster has been produced as a result of these subsidies.[100]

Why has public service broadcasting been a marginal phenomenon in the United States in comparison to elsewhere? The main reason is that proponents in other nations were able to get their systems established before commercial broadcasters had achieved dominance over the airwaves. The defeat of the broadcast reform movement in 1934 quashed the hope for this caliber of public broadcasting in the United States. At the time, commercial broadcasters argued that few would listen to their stations if people had access to advertising-free stations with quality entertainment—which they conceded that people wanted—so it was unfair to allow public broadcasting to exist and thereby undermine commercial broadcasting. The U.S. government did establish extremely well-funded noncommercial broadcasting services in the 1940s and beyond—but they were directed at those outside the United States. Indeed, the deal made with the commercial broadcasting industry was that those services—Voice of America, Armed Forces radio and television, Radio Free Europe— would not be accessible in the United States. The explanation was that explicit government propaganda should be restricted to foreigners, but a clear concern for the commercial broadcasters was that the American public not be exposed to well-funded noncommercial fare.

In the 1960s, the commercial broadcasting lobby finally relented, and a national public radio and television service started, but it was not a BBC type of operation, providing a full range of noncommercial programming to the entire population. The plan for what became the Public Broadcasting Service (PBS) and National Public Radio (NPR) did not call for such a system—the commercial dominance of the airwaves was a given—but rather for a broadcasting service that concentrated exclusively upon providing the public service programming that commercial stations were constantly lambasted for avoiding. The commercial broadcasters laid first claim to popular programming, and public broadcasters were left with programming that had less immediate audience appeal.

At its best, as envisioned in the Carnegie Commission reports that helped birth the system, U.S. public broadcasting was seen as producing cutting-edge political and creative programming that commercial broadcasting found unprofitable, and serving poor and marginalized audiences of little interest to commercial networks.[101] As Senator Hugh Scott of Pennsylvania said during the congressional debates on the matter in 1967, "I want to see things on public television that I hate— things that make me think!"[102] In the minds of the original Carnegie Commission, this was to be a well-funded service based on an excise tax on the sale of television sets that would eventually reach 5 percent; this money would be placed in a trust fund over which politicians would have no direct control.[103] When the Public Broadcasting Act of 1967 was passed, this key element of the Carnegie plan was dropped. Had it been fully implemented, public broadcasting would enjoy an annual subsidy in the $3 billion range in 2003 dollars.[104]

The Carnegie vision was doomed from the start because the independent funding mechanism had been sabotaged. When PBS broadcast muckraking programs such as 1970's *Banks and the Poor*, it sent some politicians into a tizzy. President Nixon vetoed the public broadcasting budget authorization in 1972 to express his displeasure.[105] The Democratic platform that year, arguably the most left-wing one since the New Deal, stated, "We should support long-range financing for public broadcasting, insulated from political pressures. We deplore the Nixon Administration's crude efforts to starve and muzzle public broadcasting, which has become a vital supplement to commercial television."[106] PBS eventually did get its funding, but with it public broadcasters got a clear message: be careful in the coverage of political and social issues and expect resistance if you proceed outside the political boundaries that exist in commercial broadcast journalism.

This pattern recurs. Conservatives use what little money Congress provides as leverage continually to badger public broadcasters to stay within the same ideological range found on commercial networks.[107] Conservatives are obsessed with public broadcasting because in it the traditional sources of control in commercial media—owners and advertisers are absent, so a greater possibility exists that the public system will produce critical work. Milton Friedman has called for subjecting public broadcasting to "market discipline."[108] Soon after the Republican takeover of Congress in the 1994 elections, Speaker Newt Gingrich announced his plan to "zero out" public broadcasting due to its alleged liberal bias. He abandoned the plan when Republicans were flooded with public opposition, much of it from well-to-do people who vote and make campaign contributions.[109]

Accordingly, NPR and PBS at a national level tend to provide a bland variant of mainstream and conventional journalism, comparable to what's on the commercial networks, especially on highly sensitive matters such as the economy and the U.S. role in the world.

Public broadcasting is so obsessed with conservative criticism, even more than commercial news media journalists are, that it bends over backwards to appease the Right and appear "balanced." When the conservative pundit Bill O'Reilly stormed off Terry Gross's NPR radio interview program in 2003 because he was upset with the tenor of her questions—by all accounts much milder than how O'Reilly routinely badgers his guests—the response by the NPR ombudsman sent a chilling message to all public broadcasters. "Listeners were not well served by this interview," he said. "Unfortunately, the interview only served to confirm the belief, held by some, in NPR's liberal bias."[110] The message is loud and clear: hands off the Right.

A traditional concern surrounding public broadcasting was that it would become a propaganda agency for the reigning political party and therefore would be insufficiently independent as a democratic force. In nations with poorly designed systems or too much corruption, such as France, this anxiety has had legitimacy. By 2003 irony abounded when U.S. commercial television companies stridently supported the war in Iraq, while some of the most unflattering and critical journalism of pro-war allies Britain and Australia came from their public broadcasters. If sufficiently insulated, public broadcasting can indeed be a critical force. In the United States, thanks to structural constraints, its capacity for being an independent and critical force is greatly compromised.

Entertainment and cultural fare has had a slightly different experience. U.S. public broadcasters were consigned to do programming for which there was little audience, so members of Congress concluded that an underutilized service (with little popular support) did not need a lavish budget. Public broadcasters rarely dared to schedule prime-time entertainment programs with mass appeal. Such shows would have helped develop the broad audiences and public support that European public broadcasters enjoyed, but U.S. public broadcasters understood that such an approach was political suicide; the muscular commercial broadcasting lobby would have complained to Congress that the government was subsidizing unfair competition, and thus interfering with the free market. Public broadcasters quickly realized they could count on the federal government for only a fraction of their budgets if they were to produce anything at all. They turned almost entirely away from their original commitment to experimental programming and to marginalized and poor audiences, and instead began cultivating an upper middle class sliver with business and high-culture programming. This tactic provided a solid base for periodic "pledge drives" as well as a political constituency that commanded respect in Washington. It also made public broadcasting increasingly attractive to advertisers—or "underwriters," as they were euphemistically termed.

The prospect of government subsidy continues to decline because as public broadcasting grows more and more commercial within the limits allowed to it, its justification for a subsidy decreases. Similarly, management of public stations increasingly adopts the mores and obsession with ratings and target demographics of commercial broadcasting, because the stations must rely on delivering a wealthy audience to stay afloat.[111] In this context public broadcasters have come to brag about their affluent audience, rather than bemoan their lack of a working-class following.[112] Public broadcasting becomes increasingly dependent upon corporate money, and that requires it to compete with commercial media for those funds, with all that that suggests.[113] By 2003 PBS formally authorized the airing of 30-second advertising spots.[114] As all of this happens, the government sees less and less justification for public subsidy. Between the government and the market, U.S. public broadcasting experiences the worst of both worlds.

This, too, has become the dilemma faced by more established public broadcasters outside the United States. As their media systems become increasingly regarded as commercial undertakings rather than public service institutions, these public broadcasters face difficulty in winning their subsidies and considerable pressure to turn to commercial revenues, thereby undermining their case for receiving public subsidies. What was once the U.S. exception is becoming the global rule. As the director-general of the BBC put it, "The accusation is that the BBC is too successful, too powerful and

too competitive. This is one of the few jobs where you get crap for losing and crap for doing well."[115]

In fairness to U.S public broadcasters, many are principled and dedicated public servants who have done wonders with often inadequate
resources. Local PBS and, especially, NPR stations have often been jew-
els in their local media environments. The children's programming
on PBS, at least until commercialism intruded, offered a welcome
respite to commercial fare.[116] But the overriding pressures have been
too great; libraries and bookstores are filled with tomes by former
public broadcasters and scholars chronicling the failure of the institution.[117] Although public broadcasting still has life in it because of its
public and corporate support and because it has built its own "brand
name," its long-term trajectory is toward oblivion. In the short term,
the challenge simply to maintain the status quo is daunting.[118] Public
radio has fared better than public television, if only because the costs
of production are dramatically lower, and commercial radio has gone
into a hyper-commercial free fall since 1996, making NPR's programming more attractive. A private bequest to NPR of $200 million in 2003
will help put NPR on a solid footing for the foreseeable future, but
there is little reason to think it will move beyond being a relatively
marginal medium in the lives of most Americans, or that it move
toward aggressive, independent journalism.[119]

INVIGORATING PUBLIC MEDIA

So where does this leave U.S. public broadcasting? What needs to be
done to turn it into a powerful force in our society? We first must recognize that we need a strong nonprofit and noncommercial media sector.
Such a sector is necessary for high-quality children's programming,
experimental entertainment, and high-quality material frowned upon
by the market. Most important, a nonprofit media sector is mandatory
for providing some, perhaps much, of the journalism and public
affairs material befitting a democracy. If such a sector is well funded
and well managed, it can have repercussions across the entire media
system, across the entire social culture, and across the entire political
culture. As economists would put it, public broadcasting can have a

"multiplier" effect. Recent developments in our media culture do not undermine the need for public broadcasting; they make it a more necessary institution than ever before.

Although the United States desperately needs a strong nonprofit and noncommercial media sector, today's public broadcasting is nowhere near satisfactory. Because it is severely limited by the manner in which it has developed, it is at best a marginal and semicommercial enterprise. The United States could easily generate a public broadcasting network that would dwarf what currently exists, but it will require an entirely new strategic approach and a much more sweeping vision of its mission. A crucial problem for U.S. public broadcasting, and for the nonprofit media sector in general, is that it has been relegated to the margins. The commercial system "gives the people what they want," while the nonprofit sector gives them what they need and they accept it only grudgingly. Public broadcasting needs to reject its marginal status and the structural constraints under which it has been forced to live; until then, it will be impossible to mobilize the popular support necessary to generate the resources the system needs to be truly effective.

This means rethinking the organizational structure of public broadcasting. It means abolishing commercialism. It means infusing public broadcasting with a localism that is largely absent in commercial broadcasting. And, more than anything, it means critiquing the limitations of the corporate media system—not merely its worst transgressions but also its inner logic. Advocates need to make a strong case that public broadcasting, rather than being a paternalistic enterprise that ignores popular wishes, is actually capable of generating a democratic relationship with the audience that is not mediated by advertisers or determined by the need for profit maximization. We need to develop concrete proposals for a revamped public system. Professor William Hoynes has drafted a new model for public broadcasting that directly addresses the matter of funding.[120] The point is not to tout Hoynes's proposal as the final word, but simply to make it clear that there are alternatives to the status quo. If there is a political will, there is a way that addresses all of these issues.

The movement for a supercharged public broadcasting may well have to come from without, because those within it may be too structurally bound to the *ancien régime*. Moreover, if people inside public broadcasting are too critical of the commercial media system, it would only enrage their enemies on Capitol Hill, making the budget fights in Washington that much more difficult. Hence, those within public broadcasting are prodded toward the easy road—to see the dreadful state of journalism and mainstream media as acceptable because it makes such a clear and overwhelming case for the need for PBS or NPR as an alternative. This is the public broadcasting of fools. It makes a virtue of a (let us hope short-term) necessity. The historical record and the international experience are clear: viable public broadcasting cannot survive if it is to remain an island of virtue in a sea of vulgarity and commercialism. Public broadcasting has been at its best in an environment where there is a healthy commercial sector that produces quality content. Conversely, commercial media are forced to better serve the public when there is a viable public system.

This new vision for public broadcasting will have to draw new communication technologies into its core. How ironic that opponents of public broadcasting use the emergence of new communication technologies as the basis for their argument against its necessity. There is nothing inherently commercial about digital communication. It can be deployed to further public service media just as much as commercial media. Why cannot the emergence of new digital channels lead to a plethora of diverse noncommercial media, rather than, or in addition to, an expansion in commercial channels? It all comes down to policy, to politics.

Indeed, in view of the new technologies, the very term public service *broadcasting* may be misleading; it is truly public service *media*. We need to conceive of public media as including a variety of institutions—for example, community and low-power radio and television stations, public access channels, and Independent Media Centers, along with a strengthened public broadcasting sector. When NPR sided with the commercial broadcasters in 2000 and worked against the creation of one thousand new noncommercial low-power FM radio stations, it was one of the darkest moments for democracy in recent U.S. media history. Let us hope it is never repeated. Public broadcasting must see itself in a cooperative, not a competitive, relationship with other nonprofit and noncommercial media. We need a broad and diverse nonprofit, noncommercial media sector. Some participants could receive direct state support, and some might receive none, but effective means of generating effective subsidies must become a central component of democratic media policy making.

What this all points to is that the traditional inside-the-Beltway lobbying for public broadcasting is a dead-end street or, at best, a dimly lit cul-de-sac. Polls show widespread support for public broadcasting, but this support must be nurtured and invigorated. To do so, the campaign for public broadcasting has to strike out boldly in a new direction at the grassroots level. It needs to generate a whole new tier of support from sectors of the population that have felt no connection to public broadcasting. A grassroots campaign for public broadcasting must see itself as an integral part of a broader movement for democratic media and media policy making. Indeed, only as part of a broader media reform movement does the campaign for renewed and recharged public broadcasting stand much chance of success. As Saul Alinsky famously noted, to defeat organized money, one needs organized people—and in the realm of media, corporate money is highly organized.

This point applies to all the various media policy issues that currently galvanize popular interest: media ownership limits, copyright, open Internet access, hyper-commercialism, low-power radio, vulgar media content, spectrum giveaways, global trade agreements weakening public interests, inadequate journalism, and the commercialization of education, to mention but a few. Only when those citizens and organizations come together to find common ground to work on each other's battles, and to reach out to untapped sectors of the citizenry, will they have much hope for success. The question to be answered is whether or not this will happen.

7

THE UPRISING OF 2003

There is no single solution to the problem of the media. It is not a matter of objective science. That is why informed public participation in media policy making is so crucial. The more debates over media policy see the light of day and the more proposals are introduced, evaluated, and considered, the more likely it is that resulting policies and systems will serve the public interest. Christopher Lasch's prescription for politics applies in spades to media policy making: "What democracy requires is vigorous public debate, not information. Of course, it needs information too, but the kind of information it needs can be generated only by debate. We do not know what we need to know until we ask the right questions, and we can identify the right questions only by subjecting our own ideas about the world to the test of public controversy."[1]

When policy is left to be fought over by powerful commercial interests behind closed doors with no public awareness or participation—by what self-interested commercial parties call "experts"—one gets what one would expect: a media system that serves powerful corporate interests first and foremost. As the axiom goes, if you are not at the table you are not part of the deal. The American people have not been at the media policy table for a long time, and never in the past have they been present to the extent necessary today.

For years media scholars like myself have felt like theoretical physicists working in obscurity to explain the universe as we laid out the importance of media to our society, the deep flaws in the existing commercial media system, and the role of corrupt policies in producing that system. The evidence is overwhelming, we thought, that meaningful self-government is simply unthinkable under the current media system. Isn't it obvious, we argued, that the solution to this problem is for people to change the media by popularizing and democratizing media policy making? We wrote essays and books not only detailing the media's importance but also explaining why it garnered so little popular interest or involvement. The issue is too abstract, we decided. The news media almost never cover possible media reform, so people have no way of learning about the significance of media policy making. The corporate media own most of the politicians and regulators, so it will be the toughest political fight imaginable, and not the first issue most people would want to take up. People are pummeled with misinformation about the media in the media, so they have no basis for understanding how the system really works. People seem all too content with the media system or too apathetic and depoliticized to care.

As we toured the lecture circuit, critical media scholars were seen as depressing figures—especially in a culture that has little patience for critics who offer no happy ending to the problem they describe, no magic button to push and make everything better. We did offer a happy ending, but in U.S. political culture it struck many people, including those who sympathized with us, as wildly utopian. People can organize to change the media? You must be kidding.

The case for popular participation in media policy making seemed especially preposterous during the 1980s and 1990s. This was the era of neoliberal ascendance, when government policy making in the public interest was regularly cast in a dubious light. Public involvement, we were told, would lead to bureaucratic interference with the marketplace, that realm of freedom in which competition invariably produced the best and most efficient outcome for society. This thinking held as true for media as it did for any other area. So it was that during these decades, policies and regulations for media were gradually stripped of concern for the public interest and became centered on better serving powerful commercial players' interests. In the realm of media, efforts toward corporate control shifted into even higher gear when the Internet and other digital communication technologies burst onto the scene. In combination with free market theory, these technologies, we were promised, would soon take us to the Promised

Land, so long as government bureaucrats stayed out of the way.

At the same time, however, this market mania only exacerbated some core problems with the media system. Beginning slowly, and on the margins, a concern with media began to grow, a concern focused on how media industry structures produced deplorable media content. Along the way, without much notice, media reform became a catchword, and activists began organizing on a variety of issues. Then, in 2003, media policy absolutely exploded into the public consciousness as millions of Americans registered their opposition to the relaxation of long-standing media ownership rules. Suddenly, everything had changed.

In this chapter, I chronicle the uprising of 2003. To do justice to this topic will eventually require the luxury of time and much more than a single chapter in a book. I will concentrate on the first half of 2003, when the popular movement moved from the margins to the mainstream and put media reform activism in the public eye for the first time in generations. In some ways this event also provides a textbook case of corrupt policy making, as the FCC majority, following standard operating procedure for that less-than-august body, acted reprehensibly in view of the public feedback it received. The Republican leadership in Congress was no better. I will emphasize the activities and arguments of FCC members Michael Powell and Michael Copps because they came to lead the respective sides and became the leading public faces of the media ownership debate. Important organizing work took place in previous years—centered around groups like Consumers Union, Media Access Project, and Center for Digital Democracy—and made what happened in 2003 possible. Once the struggle reached Congress in the summer of 2003, popular opposition to the relaxation of media ownership rules was already organized, and the outcome remained undetermined even into 2004.

As extraordinary as the events I describe in this chapter are, it is too early to say whether we might be on the road to what this nation so desperately needs—a new critical juncture for media policy making. All we know for certain is that we have taken a remarkable and mostly unanticipated first step.

MEDIA REFORM MOVEMENT COMES TO LIFE

Today we can see that hidden from public view in the 1990s had been a mounting concern over media. The changes wrought by neoliberal measures such as the 1996 Telecommunications Act only fanned the flames of this burgeoning movement. Magazines such as *The Nation*, *The Progressive*, and *In These Times* began to feature stories not only criticizing mainstream media but also chronicling nascent efforts to change media policies. The progressive media watch group Fairness & Accuracy In Reporting (FAIR) flourished, as did the Media Education Foundation, the premier producer of critical videos on media. Across the nation local media watch groups, reform organizations, and independent media outlets began to sprout. Critical books on media and journalism began selling better than they had in the past. National "media and democracy" conferences were held in San Francisco and New York in 1996 and 1997, respectively, drawing many hundreds of activists.

These events reflected a broader, albeit largely inchoate, public sensibility. A 2000 survey sponsored by the Ford Foundation determined that 50 percent of Americans were "highly concerned about media mergers," while 86 percent were at least "somewhat concerned."[2] The same study indicated that 70 percent of Americans thought media companies were getting too big and that 60 percent of Americans did not believe that media mergers led to "better content and services."[3]

Media activism was enjoying a distinct dynamism. The emergence of Independent Media Centers in the wake of the Seattle protests against the WTO in 1999 galvanized opposition to corporate media among a generation of young activists. Already media reform activism had reached a level not seen in many decades, but it still had not reached the levels of the Progressive Era and the 1930s. Despite all the activity and despite evidence that the American people were concerned about this issue, the media reform movement was almost entirely outside the mainstream political culture and invisible within the commercial news media.[4] It did not exist in the minds of the overwhelming majority of the American people.

At the dawn of the twenty-first century, the media reform movement had its first notable skirmish in the battle for low-power FM radio (LPFM). The technology began in the late 1980s when it became possible to transmit radio signals easily and inexpensively, and soon several people began conducting low-power broadcasting on the open FM dial slots in their communities. The pioneer was an African American activist, Mbanna Kantako, who began broadcasting to his neighborhood in Springfield, Illinois. By the 1990s scores of people were engaging in low-power broadcasting, and they were doing so without FCC licenses. Commercial broadcasters demanded that the FCC stop the "pirates," and the FCC obliged—taking legal action against several microbroadcasters. But it soon became apparent that the low cost and ease of use of the technology made it virtually impossible to police. That these broadcasters were able to easily locate open slots in the FM band—and therefore not interfere with existing stations—made LPFM seem benign, and it aroused no public concern.

FCC chairman William Kennard recognized the difficulty in policing LPFM and decided to implement a widespread but cautious program to legalize LPFM stations across the nation. He was especially concerned with how the lifting of the radio ownership caps in 1996 had led to a sharp decline in the number of African American station owners. Because most minority station owners generally held only a small number of stations, they found it impossible to compete with emerging giants like Clear Channel and were forced to sell out. Kennard wanted a plan that would get LPFM licenses into the hands of community groups representing people underserved by the commercial radio system.

After months of study the FCC released its plan—generally regarded by LPFM advocates as being more cautious than necessary—for the establishment of more than one thousand LPFM stations in 2000. These noncommercial stations would be licensed to locally based nonprofit organizations. On the surface this looked like a clear victory for the American people: more stations, more choice, no commercialism, and more local content. Only one very small group of individuals disliked the plan: owners and managers of commercial broadcasting companies. These broadcasters did not want more competition for "their" listeners, especially of a noncommercial and local variety. Such competition might require them to reduce advertising and increase local content to keep listeners from defecting, and those changes would come directly out of their profit margins.

The NAB put a full court press on Congress to overturn Kennard's LPFM plan. The lobby could not, for PR purposes, admit to greed as a motive; instead it argued that one thousand new LPFM stations would create interference with the signals transmitted by existing broadcasters. The problem with this claim, as Kennard futilely explained, was that the engineering plans for inserting the new stations into the FM band were drawn largely from recommendations made a few years earlier by engineers who represented commercial broadcasters—when they wanted to make their own changes to the radio dial. Those changes had been implemented without causing signal interference.

The House, led by the commercial broadcasters' chief advocate in that body, Representative Billy Tauzin, voted to overturn Kennard's plan and reduce the number of LPFM stations to around two or three hundred, mostly in small cities and rural areas. The Senate was less willing to oblige corporate broadcasters, significantly because the ranking Republican on the relevant Senate Commerce Committee, Arizona's John McCain, refused to comply with the NAB's wishes. Of considerable importance, too, was the appearance of an organized lobbying effort with a significant grassroots element provided by LPFM advocates, including the Future of Music Coalition and the Prometheus Radio Project. This campaign drew in a broad range of support, including organized labor, church groups, and civil rights organizations. This organizing effort was instrumental in mobilizing congressional support for the Kennard LPFM plan.

In the end, the NAB won—and the number of LPFM stations was reduced from one thousand to a few hundred. It was not through a majority vote on the Senate floor, but through a rider put on the budget bill in late December 2000.[5] "There were no hearings. It was done in the appropriations process at a time when all the special interests know that their power is greatly enhanced because it is done in the dark of night," Kennard later explained in an interview. "You know, you wake up the next day and legislation is written. The people who had the most to say about it are completely cut out of the process. If I sound bitter, I am."[6]

Media reform activists learned crucial lessons from the LPFM fight: organizing around tangible reform proposals could actually generate popular support and sustained attention on Capitol Hill. For the first time in memory, media policy making had been taken off the proverbial Havana patio. Organized people were challenging organized money. The industry had been forced to resort to a middle-of-the-night maneuver to get its way. Momentum for media reform continued to grow. In the spring of 2002, Representative Bernie Sanders of Vermont convened the first-ever "congressional town meetings" to address the problem of "corporate control of the media." Held on consecutive nights in Montpelier and Burlington, the events drew overflow crowds of several hundred people, to everyone's surprise. Sanders, who had held scores of town meetings in Vermont on a wide range of public policy issues since entering Congress in 1991, could not recall ever getting such an enthusiastic response. "I think this shows that the movement for democratic media reform strikes a chord among the citizenry. It is going to be a long-term process but, after these last two days, I really think we can win it."[7]

The issue that finally put the media reform movement on the map was media ownership regulations. The 1996 Telecommunications Act required the five-member FCC to review its media ownership rules every two years to see if they needed to be revised in view of changing circumstances. The FCC held these biennial reviews twice after 1996 as required and ruled each time that conditions had not changed sufficiently to warrant changes in ownership rules. New FCC chairman Michael Powell, chosen by President George W. Bush to replace Kennard, formed a media ownership working group of FCC staffers to study the matter in October 2001.[8] He was expressly committed to scrapping media ownership rules. Indeed, the hard work of the Consumers Union and the Consumers Federation of America to keep Congress aware of what the FCC was planning and to slow down Powell did keep him from moving quickly. As the Consumers Union's Gene Kimmelman recalls, "Industry was extremely angry that Powell 'wasted' six to nine months" in 2001 and 2002 before he got on track.[9]

Simultaneously, the corporate media lobbies were working the court system to have all the ownership rules thrown out. In February and April 2002, in two rulings, the Federal Appeals Court in Washington, known for its neoliberal bent, sided with industry lawyers. It pronounced that unless the FCC could prove that media ownership rules clearly served the public interest, the intent of Congress in the 1996 Telecom Act was that they be abolished.

The FCC announced its next biennial review of media ownership rules in September 2002. As a result of this review, ownership restrictions would have to be defended or else the rules would be tossed out and media ownership would be subject only to antitrust enforcement, like other industries. Six rules were under review, including the prohibition against newspaper-broadcast cross-ownership and the rules regulating the number of TV stations a single firm could own locally and nationally. At that point, firms were permitted to own only one TV station in a market, except in the very largest cities, where they could own two. Firms were also prohibited from owning TV stations that, in total, reached more than 35 percent of the population, though both Viacom and News Corporation had been granted waivers by the FCC to exceed that figure. These were the rules that the industry was most eager to see relaxed or eliminated.

POWELL AND COPPS TAKE THE STAGE

It was ironic that FCC chairman Michael Powell would be the official responsible for demonstrating to the courts that media ownership rules could be justified as serving the public interest. The son of Colin Powell, Michael Powell was being groomed for a career as a major player in the Republican Party. Long before the autumn of 2002, Powell had emerged as an enthusiastic, almost religious, proponent of neoliberal ideology and called for extending "full First Amendment rights" to commercial broadcasters.[10] In theory that meant unvarnished praise for free markets, in practice it meant giving the corporate media

lobbies whatever they wanted. For example, he opposed Kennard's
LPFM plan. Even if deregulation led to more concentration, even
monopoly, Powell's approach was to damn the torpedoes and plow full-
speed ahead: "I don't see why we have to tell companies they have to eat
their vegetables before they get their dessert." Powell saw the role of
the FCC as facilitating profit making for corporations, pure and simple:
"Government policy needs to follow the rule of capital and investment,
not always the other way around."[11]

Powell had never been especially concerned about media concentration. "Monopoly is not illegal by itself in the United States," Powell
commented in early 2002. "People tend to forget this. There is something healthy about letting innovators try to capture markets."[12]
While he acknowledged that a complete monopoly was problematic
legally, he characterized the duopoly of satellite television—with two
firms controlling the entire market—as "a vibrant competitive market."[13] Powell conceded that he found the very notion of public interest regulation dubious: "The public interest works with letting the
market work its magic."[14] In Powell's view, he was "working himself
out of a job" at the FCC by having public interest regulation eliminated, and the sooner he did it, the better.[15]

Having this corporate media enthusiast in charge of defending the
FCC's right to regulate media ownership in the public interest was
like putting Florida's Republican secretary of state, Katherine Harris,
in charge of Al Gore's Florida recount team in November 2000. The
other two Republican members of the FCC were, if anything, even
more devoted to advancing commercial media interests. Kathleen Q.
Abernathy had been a corporate lobbyist before joining the FCC and
was characterized as a "quiet warrior" for ownership deregulation.
She almost never appeared in public and was seen as a "reliable vote"
for Chairman Powell.[16] Abernathy was much appreciated among corporate media lobbyists; she lavished praise upon the corporate-controlled plan for digital radio as "a win-win for everyone."[17] The other
Republican, Kevin Martin, had worked as a lawyer in the powerhouse
Washington law firm of Wiley, Rein & Fielding, whose business was
representing corporate communication clients. Richard Wiley,

Martin's boss and a former FCC member, was a zealous advocate of eliminating media ownership rules. Wiley spent so much time in FCC headquarters that he was dubbed the "sixth member" of the FCC.[18] Martin also worked full-time on the Bush-Cheney election campaign as a general counsel from 1999 to 2001.[19]

Because the commission had a vacancy for a Democratic member in the fall of 2002, the one dissenting voice to a thoroughgoing relaxation of media ownership rules was Democrat Michael Copps, a history Ph.D. who had been appointed in 2001. Copps, too, was a patronage appointment, having served as an aide for many years to Senator Ernest "Fritz" Hollings, the ranking Democrat on the Senate Commerce Committee. Perhaps it was because the Democrats were out of power and therefore less deferential to the media lobby—or perhaps it was simply because Copps was cut from different cloth—but very early on it became clear that he was not at all like Kennard and the other Democrats who had recently served on the FCC. A self-described New Dealer, Copps was the one vote against approving Comcast's takeover of AT&T's cable systems in 2002: "The sheer economic power created by this mega-combination, and the opportunities for abuse that would accompany it, outweigh the very limited public interest benefits that either the Applicants or the majority find here." Copps rejected the Powell-Abernathy-Martin formulation that if a merger generated increased efficiencies (generally measured by profits) it meant the deal would be beneficial to the public: "It strikes me as bedrock that our review of proposed consolidations must venture beyond economic efficiencies if we are to ensure that combinations serve the public interest."[20]

Copps was adamant that the FCC's review of media ownership rules needed to reach out to the public. "We need much wider participation," he argued. "This is not an inside-the-Beltway issue."[21] Copps thought the Commission's plan to allow for sixty days of public comment was insufficient in view of the stakes involved. He suggested that the FCC hold a series of hearings around the nation to gauge public opinion on the issue. Powell, supported by the other commissioners, was "unenthusiastic" and formally rejected Copps's recommendation in November.[22] By this time, relations between Powell and Copps had already become frosty. Copps issued a release expressing "alarm" and "disappointment" at Powell's refusal to hold public hearings or to find other ways to generate increased public participation.[23]

By the end of 2002 all indications were that the Republican majority would get their way and ownership limits would be greatly relaxed, if not eliminated. The courts were on board. The FCC majority was on board. Only three votes would be required; Copps was treading deep water. Powell sent out a clear indication of his sentiment when the FCC elected not to appeal the court decision throwing out cross-ownership prohibitions on broadcast stations and cable TV systems in the same community. "It's finished," Kenneth Ferree, Powell's hand-picked chief of the FCC Media Bureau, announced.[24] The White House was on board. Congress was in the hands of the Republicans and gave few indications that it would present an obstacle. "There's a saying in Washington that a politician should never mess with the NAB," a writer for *Variety* reminded in November 2002, "which is considered one of the most powerful lobbying arms around."[25] Corporations such as the Tribune Company were already fantasizing about the deals they awaited.[26] When News Corporation, Viacom, and General Electric made their joint filing in December, they asked the FCC "to scrap all of the government's ownership rules."[27]

Following the long-standing pattern, there was virtually no media coverage.[28] As Marvin Kalb put it, "Powell is not making news. He flies under the radar of public concern or outrage."[29] And surveys showed that three-quarters of Americans had no idea what was going on, while only a few percent had much of a clue.[30] Sure, there would be some intracorporate jostling over national TV station ownership limits, where the NAB actually opposed relaxing the national cap because its small-station membership knew the cap was all that kept them economically competitive.[31] Otherwise, it was full steam ahead for the corporate media conglomerates.

In the fall and early winter of 2002, organized opposition to the relaxation of media ownership rules was already much greater than anyone had expected. The Consumers Union, the Consumer Federation of America, the Media Access Project, and the Center for Digital Democracy were the main players, though a number of new groups were beginning to surface. The *Wall Street Journal* even reported that the FCC had been "flooded with letters opposing media consolidation" during the comment period. Industry lobbyists dismissed the input, with no sense of irony, because the number of letters was "obviously somewhat ginned up" by the organized campaign to publicize the process.[32] An immense amount of organizing effort went to having the FCC extend the public comment period; Powell finally relented and allowed for another thirty days, until January 2, but he made it clear that it would not derail his plans to have the review complete by the late spring of 2003.[33]

In January 2003 the tide slowly but perceptibly began to change. Jonathan Adelstein, an aide to Senator Tom Daschle, joined the FCC as the second Democrat and immediately demonstrated that he shared Copps's concerns. "It violates every tenet of a free society to let a handful of powerful companies control our media," he stated.[34] The organizing effort against media consolidation began to get attention in Congress; several letters were sent by members of the House and Senate, by Republicans as well as Democrats, to Powell calling on him to open up the process, slow it down, and take concerns about media consolidation more seriously.

In particular, Powell and the FCC came in for a grilling on Capitol Hill in two January hearings.[35] Here the work of the Consumers Union and other activists to educate members of Congress on media owner-ship issues paid dividends. As Copps noted, members of Congress expressed considerable concern that Powell was planning to railroad through ownership rule changes without public or congressional input. Recounting a hearing before the Senate Commerce Committee in January that included testimony from FCC members, Copps explained, "This was supposed to be a hearing on telecommunica-tions. We weren't into that hearing two minutes, I'll bet, before one senator after another started asking about media consolidation and what's going on down there at the Commission. Equally interesting, it wasn't just the Democratic side, but it was also the Republican side."[36]

Copps fanned these flames of interest by encouraging a public hearing on media ownership at Columbia University in January. Powell, Adelstein, and Martin attended the informal hearing. Although the panels were evenly balanced with industry and nonindustry participants, the tenor in the audience was decidedly anxious about media consolidation.

BELTWAY OPPOSITION STIFFENS

By the end of January 2003, any hope that Michael Powell and the FCC majority were going to breeze through relaxation of media ownership rules was dashed. Powell's refusal to join Copps and Adelstein in a series of public hearings around the nation to solicit public input was becoming more and more of a PR problem. Finally, "clearly feeling the pressure," as one trade publication observed, Powell made an "unusual turnaround" and agreed to hold one official hearing in Richmond, Virginia, in February.[37] It was "a victory of sorts for Copps," and the trade press noted that Powell hoped this would put an end to talk about public hearings.[38] Powell dismissed the idea that additional FCC public hearings on media ownership would be necessary or beneficial. He selected Richmond for its proximity to Washington—it would make it a day trip for FCC officials and lobbyists—and he intimated to the trade publication *Broadcasting & Cable* that he thought the Richmond hearing would be a waste of time.[39] There was too much real work to be done in Washington studying the issue of media ownership, he argued, to gallivant around the country. Anyway, "in the digital age, you don't need a nineteenth-century whistle-stop tour to hear from America." Powell invited Americans to use the Internet to send him and the FCC their thoughts on the relaxation of media ownership rules.[40]

In truth, Powell had a pretty clear idea long before the Richmond hearing of how he wanted to change the rules. But the specifics would remain a closely guarded secret until May, three weeks before a final vote, when the law required Powell to disclose them to the other commissioners.[41] Powell and his staffers discussed the matter with Abernathy, Martin, and their staffers to make sure their votes were safe, but Adelstein and especially Copps were outside the loop.[42] Powell used much of the spring to sell media rule changes to Congress and the public, so the process would look like a legitimate undertaking, not a kowtowing to well-heeled corporate interests. Sure, he knew he was going to get his three votes no matter what, but the bumpier the ride at the FCC the harder the fight might be later in Congress and the more political fallout might hit the White House.

The problem was made much more desperate for Powell because Copps and Adelstein were both so openly contemptuous of how the FCC was proceeding. Copps was planning to hold public hearings in the spring of 2003 across the nation, without Powell if need be, and use them as a "bully pulpit" to bring media ownership "to the public's attention."[43] This was historically unprecedented for the FCC; in the past an FCC chair like Powell would have never had to worry about public dissent from other members or public concern about FCC operations. "I don't recall ever seeing before the level of open and very public dispute among the commissioners on these issues," a lobbyist for Clear Channel and News Corporation commented.[44] Powell was in uncharted and dangerous waters.

In a sense, Powell deserves some sympathy. His career had been built upon lavishing praise on the market and unbridled contempt for ownership rules or regulation in the public interest—but, as the response from Congress and the public made clear by January, that tack would be counterproductive in 2003. Powell began to present himself as an earnest pragmatist repelled by extremism and incendiary rhetoric. "I am absolutely a good middle-of-the-road moderate," he told an audience at Harvard in April.[45] His moderation, however, was not based on any moderation of his extreme views on regulation, but, rather, upon his willingness to proceed at a slower pace to get what he wanted.

Powell spent much of the first half of 2003 painting himself as the reluctant deregulator. "These rules, if I do nothing, will be dead soon," Powell remarked to an audience of investors organized by Goldman Sachs. Why? "Because the courts say so—the courts demand that a regulatory agency justify its rules."[46] "Keeping the rules exactly as they are, as some so stridently suggest," was "not a viable option."[47] As Powell's point man Ken Ferree put it, "Courts are saying, 'Hey, don't come here and tell us this rule is necessary because you believe it to be. You've got to come in with empirical evidence and show exactly what harms you're preventing, and how you do the balancing.'"[48]

The D.C. Appeals Court had based its 2002 ruling on the belief that Congress's intent in the 1996 Telecommunications Act was to eliminate media ownership rules unless incontrovertible and overwhelming evidence justified their continuation in the public interest. Powell accepted this view and elected not to appeal the court's interpretation. "Congress shifted the burden to the FCC, rather than the industry, to demonstrate the need for a rule," Powell explained. "The congressional bias is for deregulation and the standard for maintaining a rule is an enormous hill to climb."[49] To Copps and Adelstein, Powell's response defied logic, since the law that established the FCC mandated the commission to serve the public interest. As Copps observed, "That phrase, 'serving the public interest, convenience, and necessity,' appears 112 times in the statute. So I think Congress was serious about us serving the public interest."[50]

Had Powell elected to appeal the court's interpretation of the Telecommunications Act, he would have had a powerful legal case. The act merely states that every two years the FCC "shall determine whether any of such rules are necessary in the public interest as the result of competition. The Commission shall repeal or modify any regulation it determines to be no longer in the public interest."[51] Although the spirit of the law pushed toward relaxation of the rules, since competition was presumed to be increasing, Senator John McCain, chairman of the Senate Commerce Committee, argued that the law permitted the FCC to *tighten* media ownership rules if it found market conditions warranted doing so in the public interest.[52] At any rate, conditions had not changed much since 1996 when the law was passed. If Congress had wanted to throw out the ownership rules in 1996, it could have done so itself. Indeed, the evidence from Congress was clear: many who voted for the Telecommunications

Act intended ownership rules to remain unless striking, unforeseeable developments occurred. The FCC's job was to monitor these developments.

Few in Congress bought Powell's line that "the courts are making me do this." Literally scores of members of Congress wrote to Powell in 2003 making explicit their conviction that the appeals court interpretation of congressional intent was wrong. Powell and the FCC "could maintain limits if they wanted to," the media activist Jeff Chester maintained. "He doesn't want to."[53]

Powell reverted to his neoliberal roots on occasion despite his effort to appear moderate. In April, before an appreciative crowd of newspaper owners, he stated that the assumption that the public interest was served by regulating against concentrated media ownership "is simply false."[54] When Powell the moderate pragmatist disappeared, he typically became not so much a proponent of unregulated markets as a crusader for freedom of the press and democracy. Characterizing himself as among those who are "unapologetic defenders of the First Amendment," Powell framed the issue as one of whether the nation, in seeking to prevent Citizen Kane, would "justify the resurrection of King George."[55] Powell expressed his opposition to having the FCC—"unelected regulators who have no direct accountability" to the citizens—play any role in dictating content.[56]

Powell presented the defenders of media ownership rules as elitists who could not cut it in the marketplace and wanted to force their ideas about media content onto an unwilling public.[57] His opponents, Powell stated, want "to require that the public accept by law what it is uninterested in by choice."[58] The values Powell invoked have tremendous appeal in U.S. culture, but, interestingly, they did not seem to fly in 2003. Powell's noble rhetoric was irrelevant; the issue concerned whether the government was going to let a fairly small number of firms have an even larger number of government-granted monopoly licenses. Was Powell's letting fewer companies own more and more of the media any less a form of government intervention than requiring the same firms to own less?

POWELL'S THREE ARGUMENTS

In general, as Powell made his case for relaxing the media ownership rules, he seemed to be channeling Rupert Murdoch or Sumner Redstone as he spoke. This hardly helped his image as a moderate pragmatist determined to salvage what he could of public interest regulation in a hostile world . . . or at least, in the face of a hostile Appeals Court. Powell made three points over and over during the course of 2003. First, he argued that with the radical increase in media channels due to cable TV and the Internet, concerns over media concentration were quickly becoming "a moot issue."[59] "Today choices abound," Powell wrote in *USA Today*. "This abundance means more programming, more choice, and more control in the hands of citizens." In addition to hundreds of TV channels, "Americans now have access to a bottomless well of information called the Internet."[60] Powell maintained that this "democratization of technology" undermined traditional concerns about media concentration and any rationale for ownership regulation.[61] Here Powell echoed NBC CEO Robert Wright, who termed media ownership rules "ridiculous."[62] Indeed, Powell proclaimed that the problem with the media system was not too much concentration but "hyper-competitiveness" that led desperate firms to present vulgar fare they might not produce otherwise.[63]

Although Powell was correct about the emergence of new channels, the argument that this undermined the need for ownership regulation was far from convincing. Chris Murray of the Consumers Union pointed out, "Yes, there are 500 channels on cable television, but five companies control the same market share that the three networks did in the 1970s."[64] The degree to which the same large media corporations owned the TV networks, the cable TV channels, and the Hollywood film studios was a subject that Powell, with his purported obsession with quantitative data, never acknowledged. If the FCC relaxed the ownership rules further, those five companies would only increase their hold. Although there were a gazillion websites, that hardly qualified as genuine commercial competition.

But there was an even more fundamental problem with Powell's argument that the multitude of new media undermines concerns about media concentration. There *was* and *is* an empirical measure of truth behind this statement, a way to determine whether conditions had changed sufficiently to justify relaxing media ownership limits on broadcasters. The traditional justification for having media ownership rules was based on the idea that the government was granting firms beachfront property in the media system when they were given monopoly licenses to broadcast channels. Therefore the public had an interest in preventing firms from monopolizing these scarce licenses and dominating the media system. If the existence of so many new media channels through cable TV and the Internet had undermined the market power of the broadcast licenses, then having a TV or radio channel was no longer owning beachfront property but rather holding a mere grain of sand on the digital beach, as Michael Powell suggested.

In that scenario, one would rationally expect the value of radio and TV licenses to stagnate and eventually fall. After all, what rational capitalist would spend hundreds of millions of dollars to purchase a TV station if someone else could effectively compete with him by spending a pittance to produce a hundred websites? In fact, the value of radio and TV licenses had increased since 1996, and at a much greater rate than the rate of inflation. These licenses do indeed continue to confer tremendous market power or, as economists would say, monopolistic power. That is why large media companies lobby incessantly to relax the ownership rules: they want to purchase more stations. That is why media ownership rules continue to be necessary. When News Corporation and Viacom and Disney and General Electric are dumping their TV stations and the price of a license is going into the toilet, Powell will have a more convincing case.

Powell's second argument on behalf of relaxing media ownership rules was related to the first; he claimed that unless big media companies could own more and more TV stations they would not be able to make a profit and "free TV" would end.[65] The current media ownership rules were going to drive the major TV networks out of business.[66] In making this argument, Powell presented himself as a populist crusader focused on the needs of those who could not afford cable TV, satellite TV, or pay-per-view channels.[67] (This of course seemed to contradict his first argument about everyone having access to limitless choice on the Internet.) The hardship claim was straight out of the TV networks' playbook. Viacom president Mel Karmazin told the Senate Commerce Committee in May that network television is "not a very good business."[68] Viacom's lobbyists argued that media ownership rules had to be relaxed "to help ensure that free, over-the-air broadcasting continues to be available across America."[69] Rupert Murdoch told Congress that allowing broadcast companies to own more stations was necessary for over-the-air television to survive: "It's about impossible to run an entertainment network at a profit."[70]

There were two problems with this argument. First, even if true, is it rational public policy to protect firms in a dying industry? Shouldn't there be a broader debate about how best to deploy public resources, if the network TV structure had become outdated? Also, even if the networks were struggling, the parent companies were almost all doing very well and also owned most of the cable TV channels. What guarantee was there that these firms would maintain free television in the future? Perhaps these companies would get to own all the stations and then determine that there was a more profitable use of the public airwaves. Was Powell prepared to require these companies to broadcast free television in exchange for receiving more TV channels? In short, Powell's "policy" with regard to saving network TV seemed half-baked.

The second problem with Powell's campaign to "save free TV" was that it was premised on a bogus claim—in fact, an outright lie. Media mogul Barry Diller, who built the Fox TV network, scoffed at Powell's concerns about the networks' financial health: "Anybody who thinks they're in trouble hasn't read the profit statements of these companies. The only way you can lose money in broadcasting is if somebody steals it from you."[71] Ironically, exactly at the moment Powell was pressing this case, in May 2003, the same TV networks that claimed to be on their deathbed recorded the greatest wave of advance advertising sales in U.S. history. The head of Disney's ABC was ecstatic. "It's like being back in college and pulling those all-nighters," he said of their efforts to process all the sales.[72] "Broadcast Nets Hit the Jack-pot," one headline read, with the article concluding, "The market was red-hot everywhere this year."[73] "By the time you read this," one trade publication plastered on its front page, "many TV ad sales exec-utives will be on the golf course celebrating the record $21 billion upfront market."[74] Moreover, market research suggested that broad-cast advertising was expected to continue to climb at a healthy clip through 2007.[75] Their economic future was bright indeed.

Powell's third argument contradicted the logic of his second argu-ment, in which he suggested that media mergers might save free TV. He now claimed that the relaxation of media ownership rules that the FCC proposed would not amount to a big deal: "I think there will be an increase in mergers, but not to the extent that it would cause public policy concerns."[76] "The United States has the most diverse media marketplace in the world," Powell wrote, adding, "our nation's media landscape will not become significantly more concen-trated as a result of changes to the FCC rules."[77] Therefore, Powell sug-gested, his opponents were making much ado about nothing.

Powell provided no evidence for this argument. Indeed, there was considerable evidence that the largest media firms and Wall Street investment banking houses anticipated a major wave of media merg-ers once the rules were relaxed. "Everyone is waiting for the new rules; then they'll pounce," one banker predicted.[78] The trade press teemed with articles throughout the first half of 2003 in which industry insiders discussed the impending merger mania. The tone was often giddy.[79] "Major media companies are drawn and cocked," the *Denver Post* publisher and MediaNews Group CEO William Dean Singleton announced. Singleton was especially pleased because the FCC rule changes would make it possible for firms like his to grow so large as to assure their dominance of the Internet: "We are in the news and information business. In fact, we own it."[80]

The greatest wave of mergers was expected at the local level, where the profit potential of owning the daily newspaper, two or three TV stations, and eight radio stations was the stuff of media owner fan-tasies. After all, look at what Clear Channel had accomplished with radio since 1996. Imagine if you could toss in the daily newspaper and a few TV stations, too. As one investment analyst put it, "The media companies' top priority is more concentrated power in local markets."[81] "The big guys will get bigger," a leading media financial analyst concluded, sounding a bit like Don Corleone, "and the little guys will have to decide whether they want to exist anymore."[82] Or as Senator Ron Wyden of Oregon said, Powell's decision to loosen media ownership rules "rings the dinner bell for big media corporations who are salivating to make a meal out of the nation's many small media outlets."[83]

Of course, no one knew for certain what would happen. Perhaps time would prove Powell's third argument correct and there would not be all that many deals as a result of rules relaxation. But to Copps and Adelstein this was reckless policy making, when the prudent course was to be cautious. "Some argue that the concern about the threat to American democracy is overblown since it is so strong and resilient," Adelstein said. "While our democracy is strong and not about to crumble, does it mean we can afford to weaken it?"[84] "This is a huge and foolhardy gamble with the future," Copps warned.[85] "Suppose for a moment that the FCC votes to remove or significantly modify the concentration protections. Suppose that turns out to be a mistake," Copps observed. "How would we ever put the genie back in the bottle? The answer is we could not. That's why we need a national dialogue on the issue and better data and analysis."[86]

Powell did offer some research and evidence on behalf of relaxing the media ownership rules. In the fall of 2002 the FCC released a study made up of twelve research reports on media ownership that it had commissioned from an assortment of academics. By the spring of 2003 Powell was invoking this study as if it had established his case, but there was little evidence that he had read the reports.[87] In one, for example, over-the-air broadcasting was characterized as "remaining relatively strong" and therefore would "retain its relative audience-size edge and hence its basic source of support" into the future—a finding that contradicted Powell's argument that "free TV" was imperiled.[88] The most comprehensive analysis of the FCC reports

concluded that they actually provided "considerable basis for concern about the ongoing process of concentration in the media industry."[89] After rigorous review, some of the reports were subject to
scathing criticism. "The F.C.C. study," Commissioner Adelstein stated, "was basically blown out of the water."[90]

Leaving aside questions about of the quality of some of the reports,
by all accounts the study left crucial issues unexamined. None of the
reports examined the content of local TV news to see how local it really was.[91] None of the reports attempted to measure the extent to
which the commercial interests of media companies and their advertisers affected the content of news and entertainment. Nor did any of
the reports consider how ownership concentration might affect the
ability of various political groups or interest groups to reach a wider
public with their views.[92] The list goes on and on.

"I'm not going to critique the studies," Copps noted in a February
2003 interview. "I think some outside parties have already indicated
that there were some problems with some of the studies. I'm willing
to say that they were a good faith effort to do research, but it is plain
to me that not only do they not provide all of the answers, neither do
they ask all of the questions. The more comment that comes in here,
and the more input that we get, the more unanswered questions
there appear to be out there. We haven't really scratched the surface."[93] The person who coordinated the study for the FCC acknowledged that it would be incorrect to draw conclusions from the
reports: "We have not yet begun to understand the implications," he
conceded, calling for much more research to be done.[94]

OPPOSITION GROWS BEYOND THE BELTWAY

Michael Powell's campaign to advance the case for loosening media
ownership rules in the spring of 2003 was based upon contradictory
arguments constructed with dubious evidence. In the battle for public opinion, this put him at a decided disadvantage. His arguments
did not appear to convince people who were not invested in the system and did not share his euphoric attitude toward the U.S. commercial media system. In years past, that wouldn't have mattered

THE PROBLEM OF THE MEDIA

because Americans would have been clueless about the FCC's proceedings. But in 2003 many things had changed, not the least of which was that FCC member Michael Copps had taken it upon himself to rouse public interest and involvement in the issue.

"This is still, in my mind, very much an inside-the-Beltway issue," Copps explained in February, "It has not become one where the country is really plugged into it and knows what's going on here. That's because the country doesn't really know. If it did know, I think a lot of people would be vitally interested in the outcome." Copps was blunt about his mission: "I am trying to raise as much ruckus as I can about it."[95] In doing so, Copps found the public to be receptive; people had considerable concerns about media, and when they learned these concerns could be attached to a specific policy, their interest grew dramatically. Fairly soon, Copps had many more allies than he could have anticipated, far beyond the stalwart public interest groups in Washington, D.C.

The official FCC hearing in Richmond on February 27 was an omen. Four of the five hours were devoted to panelists, and most of the twenty-one experts were from out of town, including a large contingent of industry representatives. The public then had an hour to make statements—and every speaker opposed relaxing the media ownership rules. "What stood out most," Copps commented afterward, "was the level of concern on the issue and the level of dissatisfaction."[96] Powell immediately announced that the Richmond hearing provided "enough" input from the public and that it was imperative to get the process completed as quickly as possible. "This is one of the most extensively developed records in the history of the commission," Powell stated. You can hold hearings until "you're blue in the face but at some point people expect you to take a position."[97] Powell, Abernathy, and Martin would not attend any of the subsequent public hearings on media ownership.

Over the next three months twelve more public hearings were held across the nation, almost all attended by Copps and many by Adelstein, who termed this their "magical mystery tour." The events were always nonpartisan, organized by a local university or civic group, and featured representatives of the broadcasting industry. Numerous activist groups, like Jeff Chester's Center for Digital Democracy and the Benton Foundation, helped organize the events. There were also a number of smaller events, sometimes attended by Copps or Adelstein separately.[98] In most cases, members of Congress from the area participated. Some events were attended by fewer than 200 people, as in Detroit, Chicago, and Phoenix, but most of the rest became standing-room-only affairs with 400–1,000 attendees, as in Seattle, Philadelphia, Burlington, Atlanta, and San Francisco.[99] Even more than the turnout, it was the public's comments that caught the attention of Copps and Adelstein and energized them as they squared off with Powell and the Republicans back at FCC headquarters. "Of the hundreds of citizens I heard from, many extremely articulate, not one of them stood up to say, 'I want to see even more concentration in our media ownership.' Not one," Adelstein observed. "The public knows instinctively what the FCC is supposed to do—protect them from large entities gaining too much control over critical channels of communication."[100]

This attendance was all the more incredible because the local press gave little or no advance coverage and in most cases no follow-up coverage either—especially curious since local media often had executives on hearing panels.[101] "That people even found out about these meetings," Copps acknowledged, "is a miracle."[102] This pointed to a problem that faced the activists throughout 2003: the paucity of mainstream news coverage. As a study conducted for the *American Journalism Review* concluded, in the first five months of 2003, commercial TV and the cable networks offered "virtually no coverage" of the FCC deliberations on media ownership. Even the handful of newspapers that covered the story on occasion throughout the year, like the *Chicago Tribune*, "seemed to lose interest in the consumer and democracy angles, treating the story mainly as a business and investment issue." As the author of the study concluded, "you wouldn't have learned much about the controversy from the many news outlets that were eager to cash in."[103] Instead, the organizers had to rely upon alternative media and the Internet to do much of their outreach; one can only imagine what the

response would have been had the conventional news media given anything close to the attention that a story of such magnitude—but not
involving the corporate media—would have merited.

Despite the mainstream news blackout, the movement grew rapidly. What happened to radio following the relaxation of radio ownership rules in the 1996 Telecommunications Act spurred Americans'
concern about media policies. Radio was often invoked as the
"canary in the coal mine" that would predict what would happen
when ownership rules for television, cable, and newspapers were
relaxed. And the consensus about radio was almost universally negative. Local news had disappeared, musical variety had diminished,
and commercialism had increased.[104] "So television's going to be
more like radio now," the TV critic Tom Shales mused in a column on
Powell's media ownership plans. "Gosh, that's swell. Let's have a little
dancing in the streets, because this is no small accomplishment—
finding a means to make TV worse, I mean."[105]

"If you really like what happened in radio," Copps argued, "you'll
love what's barreling down the FCC track toward you."[106] Or, as he told
his colleagues, "this experience should *terrify* us."[107] As one reporter put
it, "The sorry state of the radio industry is sabotaging FCC chairman
Michael Powell's plans to let media conglomerates run wild." Much
opposition to ownership relaxation in the African American and
minority communities could be attributed to the bad experience with
radio, an industry that saw minority ownership collapse since 1996
and journalism for minority groups shrivel.[108] Indeed, Powell acknowledged that radio was in crisis, but he refused to let its condition influence his evaluation of ownership rules changes for other media.[109]

Another issue that mobilized citizens was the fate of journalism
under media concentration. The FCC had ignored or mangled this topic
in its study with its twelve reports; indeed, if one looked at who actually
wrote or produced news in local markets, the effects of concentrated
ownership on journalism would be apparent, as would the likely
impact of further relaxation of ownership.[110] A study released by the
Project for Excellence in Journalism in February 2003 concluded that
larger TV station-owning companies used their market power to reduce

their commitment to local journalism.[111] Powell not only defended the status quo but also argued that increased media concentration would improve journalism: "Scale and efficiency are becoming more vital to delivering quality news and public affairs."[112] Not many shared Powell's enthusiasm. Common Cause, the public interest citizens group, received so much concern from its several hundred thousand members about how concentrated media ownership would affect journalism and public life that it made fighting Powell its main organizing issue in 2003. Common Cause's president, Chellie Pingree, remarked that she had never seen so much rank-and-file interest in an issue. Common Cause, which had never worked in media policy before, had suddenly become a media reform organization.

Even more striking was the opposition to the relaxation of media ownership rules that came from working journalists. Their ire certainly undercut Powell's effort to wrap his media ownership plan in the guise of protecting the First Amendment. Those on the front lines saw what concentration had done to journalism and they did not want to see more of it. From the *Columbia Journalism Review* to avidly pro-deregulation trade publications such as *Broadcasting & Cable*, working journalists criticized relaxation of media ownership rules as bad for journalism.[113] Linda Foley, president of the Newspaper Guild, detailed the pronounced concern over media concentration among her members. The guild and AFTRA, the union representing broadcast journalists, made stopping the relaxation of media ownership rules central to their lobbying work in 2003.[114]

The National Association of Black Journalists and the National Association of Hispanic Journalists both came out against relaxing the rules. Working with the National Association of Black Owned Broadcasters, they were able to generate interest in this issue among members of the Congressional Black Caucus and the Hispanic Caucus, which would prove valuable down the road. For what may have been the first time in its history, the International Federation of Journalists, representing 500,000 journalists in more than 100 countries, weighed in on a U.S. media ownership policy matter, calling Powell's plan "a dangerous shift of power at the expense of democracy."[115]

Journalists were not the only ones closely connected to the media industries who spoke out. All the Hollywood unions worked to oppose Powell and the FCC, in combination with most of the independent producers.[116] "This is really unprecedented," the president of the West Coast branch of the Writers Guild of America noted. "It's remarkable how this one issue seems to have captured the entire community."[117] Driven by the media unions, the AFL-CIO Executive Council formally opposed the relaxation of media ownership rules in March 2003.[118] Even the Public Relations Society of America condemned Powell, and leading advertisers criticized media concentration.[119] Numerous independent media owners such as Frank Blethen, publisher of the *Seattle Times*, stepped forward to fight against rule relaxation. Even the huge conglomerate Sony expressed concerns about concentration in the TV industry.[120] The arguments invariably were that concentration produces lousier media content.

Powell and his supporters could rightly claim that much of this opposition within the media industries came from self-interested parties who had much to lose. But Powell's entire base of support also came from self-interested parties with much to gain. And it hardly helped Powell's cause that those on the inside of these industries, such as journalists, stated emphatically that concentration was bad for quality media content.

Two media moguls in particular proved embarrassing for Powell as he pressed his case. Ted Turner, the largest individual shareholder of Time Warner and founder of CNN, argued that CNN would not have gotten off the ground if Powell's new "marketplace" had been in effect. He criticized Powell's plans as terrible for free enterprise in media industries.

> Large media companies are far more profit-focused and risk-averse. They sometimes confuse short-term profits and long-term value. They kill local programming because it's expensive, and they push national programming because it's cheap—even if it runs counter to local interests and community values. For a corporation to launch a new idea, you have to get the backing of executives who are obsessed with quarterly

earnings and afraid of being fired for an idea that fails. They often prefer to sit on the sidelines waiting to buy the businesses or imitate the
models of the risk-takers who succeed.[121]

Barry Diller was every bit as unsparing, and he specifically went after
Powell's secretive process: "I'm opposed to the changes, but I'm much
more upset that this has not produced enough conversation and dialogue. The way Michael Powell has gone about it is to hide the issue as
much as possible, organizing it to avoid debate and hearings, and getting it done under the cover of night."[122] "The conventional wisdom is
wrong," concluded Diller, one of the most successful media moguls of
his generation. "We need more regulation, not less."[123]

LEFT AND RIGHT UNITE

As impressive as this opposition to Powell looked, two additional developments generated what would be the lion's share of some two or
three million Americans who would formally oppose the relaxation of
media ownership rules in 2003. First was the U.S. invasion and subsequent occupation of Iraq. During the buildup to the war, in the first
three months of 2003, the burgeoning anti-war movement spent considerable time castigating what it regarded as the uncritical and propagandistic nature of TV news coverage of the Bush administration's war
rationale. Phil Donahue's program was terminated by MSNBC in February; its cancellation came in the wake of an internal NBC report
claiming that Donahue projected a "difficult public face for NBC in
time of war. He seems to delight in presenting guests who are antiwar,
anti-Bush, and skeptical of the administration's motives." The report
worried that Donahue would become "a home for the liberal antiwar
agenda at the same time that our competitors are waving the flag at
every opportunity."[124] Cable giant Comcast refused to air an anti-war
ad during Bush's State of the Union address.[125]

The concentrated world of radio was seen as being particularly hostile to all who did not support the Bush administration.[126] Clear Channel's DJs led pro-war rallies, fired the South Carolina 2002 "Radio
Personality of the Year" allegedly for her anti-war politics, and, along

with fellow radio giant Cumulus, dropped the Dixie Chicks from its playlists after a member of the band criticized Bush at a concert in England.[127] When activists learned that the same companies that seemed most aggressively pro-war—e.g., Clear Channel and Rupert Murdoch's News Corporation—were leading the lobbying fight to acquire even more media, activists started publicizing the FCC issue. Around this time, Murdoch announced his intention to purchase DirecTV, the firm that dominated U.S. satellite television delivery.

When Powell praised the outstanding and "thrilling" TV news coverage of the Iraq war as justifying his contention that media concentration actually promotes better journalism, it was like waving a red flag in front of a bull.[128] (Copps, on the other hand, observed that TV news coverage of the war lacked "clash and a diversity of ideas.")[129] The liberal online activist group MoveOn.org was deluged with comments from many of its million-plus members demanding that MoveOn organize to oppose Powell and the FCC. With its huge e-mail lists, MoveOn was able to generate hundreds of thousands of supporters for media reform during the course of 2003.

The second striking development was the emergence of conservative opposition to the relaxation of media ownership rules.[130] Some of it grew from public distaste with the vulgarity of radio and television— what conservative media activist Brent Bozell termed "the raw sewage, the ultraviolence, the graphic sex, the raunchy language that is flooding their living rooms day and night."[131] This persistent lewdness was exacerbated by media concentration, because huge firms provided the cheapest fare possible and were unaccountable to local communities. Conservatives also disliked the decline of local ownership and localism in commercial media. "I am a conservative. I believe in free markets and limited government," Representative Richard Burr of North Carolina said in explaining his opposition to Powell. "But I also believe in another important conservative ideal—the right of local citizens to influence decisions that impact their communities."[132]

The National Rifle Association shared these concerns—it regarded the big media conglomerates as unsympathetic to gun owners—and, at the urging of its membership, became an aggressive force against the FCC in the spring of 2003. The NRA generated several hundred thousand postcards in opposition to relaxing media ownership rules.[133] People were astounded by the emerging alliance, with Jesse Helms in tandem with Jesse Jackson.[134] "When all of us are united on an issue, then one of two things has happened," Bozell observed. "Either the earth has spun off its axis and we have all lost our minds or there is universal support for a concept."[135]

Probably no conservative did more to legitimize the opposition than William Safire. Over the course of 2003, Safire wrote eight columns in the *New York Times* countering Powell. At key moments in the struggle, Safire produced column after column poking holes in Powell's arguments and demanding that he be stopped.[136] Mixed in with numerous columns supporting the war in Iraq, Safire repeatedly explained why opposition to media consolidation was a bedrock principle for conservatives: "The *concentration* of power—political, corporate, media, cultural—should be anathema to conservatives. The *diffusion* of power through local control, thereby encouraging individual participation, is the essence of federalism and the greatest expression of democracy."[137] "Concentration of power in media," Safire wrote in December, "enables a political clique to concentrate its power. We have to resist this everywhere."[138] As Safire noted, his FCC columns struck a positive nerve among readers. "When I weighed in against this impending sellout a couple of weeks ago," he wrote in June, "thousands—no kidding, an unprecedented torrent—of e-mails came roaring in," virtually unanimous in support. His conclusion: "Listeners, viewers and readers are interested."[139]

As popular opposition grew, increased attention turned to what, exactly, the FCC was doing. Although Powell claimed he was too busy to attend any of the public hearings in the spring, he apparently was able to carve out time to attend major conferences of media owners. In his speech before the NAB in Las Vegas in April he dropped the role of the moderate pragmatist and technocrat and urged broadcasters to support "comprehensive deregulation of the broadcast industry."[140] Three weeks later, in Seattle, Powell told the nation's newspaper owners that they were "likely to fare well" under his media ownership rule changes. "I could have written the speech myself," CEO William Dean Singleton of Media News announced ecstatically.[141]

Then, in May, a revealing report from the nonpartisan Center for Public Integrity (CPI) disclosed what Powell and FCC staffers had been doing most of the spring. Since the formal review of media rules had been announced in September 2002, FCC officials had held seventy-one closed-door, off-the-record meetings with corporate media CEOs and their lobbyists, but only five such meetings with public interest groups. Rupert Murdoch and Viacom's Mel Karmazin had each had series of meetings with commissioners and staffers in late January and early February, precisely when the FCC was crafting its new ownership rules.[142] On March 11, a group of Disney executives met with eighteen different FCC officials in six different closed-door meetings. That was probably more contact than most consumer groups had had with the FCC in a decade.

The CPI also reported that corporate interests had lavished $2.8 million on FCC members for junkets over the previous eight years and that much of the data the FCC used to make its determinations of policies was provided by industry.[143] Finally, on June 2, a *Wall Street Journal* investigative report disclosed that Bear Stearns media analyst Victor Miller, whose job is to advise large investors concerning media stocks, played a central role in helping the FCC draft the new ownership regulations. Michael Powell's top aide, Susan Eid, defended Miller's role: "His analysis is rock-solid."[144] (Before the end of 2003, Michael Powell's chief of staff, who helped craft the new ownership rules, left the FCC to become a top lobbyist for the NAB.)[145] As Charles Lewis, CPI's director, concluded: "The idea that the FCC can render an objective, independent judgment about media ownership is laughable."[146]

In February Powell had encouraged Americans to use the Internet to let the FCC know their thoughts on media ownership. In the past, on its most controversial issues, the FCC had received about 5,000 calls and letters.[147] With interest picking up speed like a hurricane crossing the open sea, the number of e-mail messages, letters, and petition signatures reaching the FCC had climbed to an extraordinary 750,000 by the end of May. There was so much incoming e-mail that the FCC's computers crashed. All examinations of the contents indicated that a good 99.9 percent opposed relaxing the media ownership rules, and many citizens favored tightening them.[148] There was almost no indication that anyone in the country, aside from big media owners, strongly favored relaxing the rules.

When the CNN business program *Moneyline with Lou Dobbs* ran an on-air poll in May asking whether "too few corporations own too many media outlets," fully 98 percent said yes.[149] The city councils in Chicago and Seattle passed resolutions against the relaxation of media ownership rules—Chicago by a unanimous vote.[150] What was most astonishing, as a *Christian Science Monitor* study determined, was that this resistance had developed with very little press coverage, especially for a story of this magnitude.[151] Shamelessly, Powell boasted about the "extraordinary amount of public comment" the FCC had received, enabling it to address the issues "through the eyes and ears of the American public."[152] But no matter how Powell tried to spin it, he had decisively lost the battle for public opinion.

FROM FCC TO CONGRESS

Throughout the spring as public attention was being drawn to the issue of media ownership, a sense of impending doom hung over the opposition since it was obvious that Powell was determined to ram the changes through. The counsel Powell was getting from the Bush administration fortified his resolve. In April, Commerce Secretary Don Evans informed Powell in no uncertain terms that the White House expected the ownership rules to be relaxed as planned and without delay.[153] The Bush administration's interest in delivering relaxed media ownership rules to the media giants could be explained by its ideological commitment to "deregulation." It was possibly influenced as well by media corporations' large political donations, especially toward Republicans. Certainly the Bush administration's stance did nothing to discourage such donations.[154]

In addition, the Bush administration counted some close political friends in the corporate media community. Some of the media firms most aggressively lobbying against the ownership rules were strong ideological allies. Clear Channel had a close relationship with Bush going back to his stint as Texas governor, and its stations were notorious for their pro-Republican slant. Rupert Murdoch's Fox News Channel was similarly well-known as a bastion of Republican support; in October 2003, Charles Reina, who worked as a producer and writer at Fox News Channel from 1997 until he resigned in 2003, revealed that the station's management gave daily directives on issues and angles to cover that tended to correlate with White House spin.[155] Indeed, Roger Ailes, head of Fox News Channel, had offered advice to President Bush about how to react to the 9/11 attacks.

There were even suggestions in the trade press that the administration's FCC stance was payback to the media for its treatment of Bush during the 2000 election and after, with an eye toward encouraging continued favorable coverage in the future.[156] Generally soft media coverage extended beyond news reporting: In September 2003, Viacom's Showtime aired a docudrama, DC 9/11: Time of Crisis, which portrayed George W. Bush as a cross between Winston Churchill and Abraham Lincoln. Only two months later, Viacom's CBS canceled a miniseries on Ronald Reagan when Republican critics charged it was unsympathetic; the station then passed a watered-down version to Showtime to fend off critics charging censorship.[157] The Financial Times noted that News Corporation's Fox News Channel hammered CBS on this issue and Viacom caved in exactly as the media ownership rules were in jeopardy on Capitol Hill.[158] Even the rabidly anti-regulation trade publication Broadcasting & Cable was appalled by CBS's cave-in, paraphrasing Viacom's position as "We'd better do what we're told by the D.C. powers that be—in this case, the Republican National Committee—if we want to be able to buy more stations."[159]

While we may never know the Bush administration's precise motives, it was clear that relaxation of media ownership rules had become a high priority. From its vantage point, supporting the media giants seemed to be a no-lose proposition.

On the opposing side, in the spring of 2003, activists intensified their pressure on Powell to disclose the proposed rules changes so that the public could provide input before the FCC vote.[160] Even the trade publication *Television Week* urged Powell to "bring the public into the process."[161] "We don't know what we're going to be working on," a frustrated Copps said in early May. "It's like a state secret."[162] The new rules were finally turned over to Copps and Adelstein on May 12, exactly three weeks before the planned June 2 vote, the legal minimum notice. As expected, the rules called for eliminating the ban on cross-ownership, permitting companies to purchase two TV stations in most markets and three TV stations in the largest markets, and letting the biggest TV station-owning companies increase their market coverage from 35 percent to 45 percent of the population. Copps and Adelstein immediately asked for a delay of the vote, a "traditional right of commissioners," which had never been denied in anyone's memory.[163] Powell rejected the request, citing counsel by Abernathy and Martin. Over Memorial Day weekend, for yet another first in U.S. media history, demonstrations protesting the FCC's impending relaxation of media ownership rules took place in fourteen cities.[164]

The outcome of the June 2 FCC meeting was a foregone conclusion, but the debate was far from anticlimactic. Copps and Adelstein each delivered long and meticulous dissenting statements that exposed the majority's arguments to be baseless and the FCC's review to be nothing short of fraudulent. As Adelstein put it, the review was a "results-driven process" in which principles were nonexistent and evidence was emphasized or ignored depending upon whether it justified the desired end. (When analysts for the Consumers Union and the Consumer Federation of America were finally able to spend weeks inspecting the FCC's 257-page order, the federation's research director concluded, "The FCC cooked the books to come up with the result they wanted—and the books aren't even half baked.")[165] Copps and Adelstein both were clearly moved by the outpouring of popular support during the process. "We'll look back upon this 3–2 vote as a Pyrrhic victory," Copps concluded. "The Commission faces a far more informed and involved citizenry. The obscurity of the issue that many have relied upon in the past, where only a few dozen inside-the-Beltway lobbyists understood the issue, is gone forever."[166] Adelstein ended his statement by paraphrasing Winston Churchill: "This is not the end, or even the beginning of the end, but just the end of the beginning."[167]

Adelstein was more accurate than he may have realized. In all the commotion surrounding Powell and the FCC during the first half of 2003, Congress's role had received little attention. In fact, the FCC is not a body like the Supreme Court, established to be independent of the legislative branch. To the contrary, the FCC was created by Congress, funded by Congress, and expected to fulfill the interests of the American people as specified by Congress. The court decision shifting the burden of proof to the FCC to justify the continuation of media ownership rules was predicated on that being the will of Congress. Powell acknowledged at all times that if Congress was dissatisfied with the FCC's actions, all it had to do was pass legislation instructing him to do something else.

Under normal circumstances, Congress would be unlikely to pester the FCC to act against powerful media interests, due to the media industry's massive lobbies, control over the news, and hefty campaign contributions. The legendary chair of the House Energy and Commerce Committee that oversees the FCC was Louisiana's Billy Tauzin, and no member of Congress was more devoted to serving corporate media interests than he was. Tauzin had been pushing Powell throughout the spring to proceed full speed ahead on relaxing the media ownership rules, and he would fall on his sword before he would let his committee consider any legislation that might overturn what Powell had done. Tauzin was notorious for being ethically challenged. According to one trade publication, for example, Tauzin purchased a million-dollar ranch in Texas that he planned to pay for by starting a "hunting club" to which he would sell memberships to lobbyists and campaign contributors.[168] By the end of 2003 Tauzin was in negotiations to quit Congress and replace Jack Valenti as head of the Motion Picture Association of America, the film industry's lobbying arm. Then he could make some serious money lobbying for the industry he used to "regulate."

Another reason that activists did not regard Congress as a route for dissent was that Republicans controlled it, and the Republican leaders of both the House and Senate dutifully served the White House. If George W. Bush or Karl Rove said "Jump", Senate Majority Leader Bill Frist and Speaker of the House Dennis Hastert asked, "How high?" House Majority Leader Tom DeLay had a single-minded focus on serving corporate interests that made Billy Tauzin look like Ralph Nader, and DeLay brooked no dissidence within Republican ranks. So the conventional wisdom, as the FCC vote approached, was that Congress could never overturn what the FCC had done, and, in fact, the issue would almost certainly die a quiet death since the Republican leadership would kill it off long before any vote could reach the floor.

But these were not normal circumstances. Even if Bush's FCC appointees Powell, Abernathy, and Martin could afford to ignore the input of 750,000 Americans, members of Congress had to pay closer attention to their constituents. And Congress was getting the message. Two days after the FCC vote, the Senate Commerce Committee called all five FCC commissioners to the Hill to explain the vote and spewed unbridled contempt. "We are moving to roll back one of the most complete cave-ins to corporate interests I've ever seen by what is supposed to be a federal regulatory agency," Senator Byron Dorgan of North Dakota declared.[169] Ranking Democrat Ernest Hollings of South Carolina accused Powell of "spin and fraud" and slammed the FCC as an "instrument of corporate greed."[170]

A few days later, Republican committee chairman John McCain remarked that the media ownership issue had "sparked more interest than any issue I've ever seen that wasn't organized by a huge lobby."[171] A handful of conservative Republicans such as Trent Lott and Representative Frank Wolf of Virginia came out strongly against the FCC changes, despite pressure from on high. "I did not get elected to be a potted plant," Wolf asserted, "and I don't care what the White House thinks."[172] "In all the years I've been here," California senator Barbara Boxer observed, "I've not seen such deeply held feelings across ideologies."[173] "It's an issue that has huge momentum," McCain concurred. "It's a classic populist issue."[174] The politicians with their fingers firmly on the national pulse, the nine candidates campaigning for the Democratic presidential nomination, all came out strongly against Powell and the FCC.[175] By the end of June the Senate Commerce Committee, with significant Republican support, voted to overturn key elements of the FCC rule changes. The vote shocked the political establishment and demonstrated that the issue was in play on the Hill.

Public opinion research confirmed what members of Congress were sensing. A Pew Research Center Poll conducted in summer 2003 found that the number of Americans who had heard "a lot" or "a little" about the FCC's review of media ownership rules had doubled to nearly 50 percent since February. Most striking, the figures showed dramatically that the more people knew about what the FCC was doing the less likely they were to support it. Of those 12 percent of Americans who had "heard a lot," seven in ten believed that the effects of relaxing media ownership rules would be negative, while only 6 percent thought they would be positive.[176]

By now Powell and the commercial media had quit suggesting that rule relaxation had popular support. To the contrary, they started arguing that most Americans were apathetic and that apathy should be interpreted as support for the status quo.[177] Powell asserted that he represented the "silent majority" of Americans, those who "yawn at the whole thing."[178] His constituency was made up of those who "are in a fraternity watching TV and drinking beer and happy" and oblivious to the debate. Powell presented a contradictory stance: he announced that support for his ownership plan was minuscule only because the public debate had been "lopsided" against him—yet he had done everything possible to avoid public debate because, as surveys showed, the more people knew, the more ground he lost.[179] His strategy, as he tacitly acknowledged, was to keep people ignorant—the FCC's modus operandi—so he could then claim their support for whatever he did.

TRENCH WARFARE

The poll energized activists, who knew that the more people learned about the issue and the more members of Congress heard from their constituents, the more likely Congress could be persuaded to overturn what the FCC had done. Russ Feingold related a story about a trip home to Wisconsin, where the popular opposition to the FCC over-whelmed him. "When they heard that these rules came out," Feingold recalled, "they were angry."[180] For the balance of the summer and fall activist attention went toward generating more public pressure upon members of Congress. On Capitol Hill, a wide range of public interest groups conducted the lobbying effort, led by Consumers Union, Free Press, Common Cause, MoveOn.org and organized labor. On numer-ous occasions MoveOn.org used its vast subscriber list to generate peti-tion signatures and telephone calls by constituents to Congress. In one afternoon alone, House members received an estimated 40,000 dissenting telephone calls from constituents. As Democratic Repre-sentative David Price of North Carolina put it, his colleagues were say-ing, "Call off the dogs, my office is being flooded with constituent calls on this issue."[181] By the calculation of the FCC commissioner Adelstein, some 2.3 million comments or petition signatures oppos-ing media concentration had been registered with either the FCC or Congress by the end of the summer.

This response convinced Democrats that the issue was a winner for them, and the vast majority of them committed to overturning the FCC's media ownership rules. On the other side of the aisle, the Republican leadership had reason to be nervous. An aide to a senior Republican senator cautioned, "We have to be careful that Republi-cans aren't seen as giving something away to big business." A Repub-lican FCC staffer observed, "If there was an issue that generated 750,000 letters from the [NRA] and the Christian right like this one has, then I'd be pretty worried if I was the president."[182] The corpo-rate media lobbies came out in force, as seventy-five general man-agers from TV stations around the country flew into Washington in July to convince Congress of the FCC plan's wisdom.[183] In early August the Newspaper Association of America sent an action item to its members urging the "critical" need for editors and publishers to contact their representatives on the Hill and explain the importance of scrapping the cross-ownership rule.[184]

In a major shift, the NAB announced in July that it would not attempt to overturn the FCC's rule change to permit the largest TV station-owning companies to increase their market share to 45 percent of the country, although this had been seen as mission critical to its small station-owning members. The reason? It might undermine the broader goal of relaxing all the other media ownership rules, especially the one restricting cross-ownership.[185] Then in August, the NRA elected not to work on overturning the FCC changes, despite anti-FCC sentiment from its membership and even NRA Executive Vice President Wayne LaPierre. As an aide to Tauzin acknowledged, "It's trench warfare."[186]

Michael Powell played a role in the campaign to salvage his handiwork as well. Although he periodically made bellicose comments about his opponents creating "hysteria" and attempting to "censor the most popular TV programming," he also pursued a more conciliatory path in an effort to undercut the mounting opposition.[187] In May he established an advisory committee to study ways the government could encourage minority media ownership.[188] Then the FCC's press release announcing the relaxation of media ownership rules was headlined: "FCC Sets Limits on Media Concentration." Even *Variety* termed this "almost Orwellian."[189] At the end of the summer, after members of Congress demanded an explanation for the exposé of FCC junkets by the CPI, Powell announced that the commission would "study" the ethics of industry-supported trips for agency officials.[190] He was also making numerous TV appearances to defend the new rules.[191]

Finally, in late August, Powell announced that he would hold public hearings around the nation aimed at promoting localism in broadcast media. Powell described the initiative as "an honest attempt to address the concerns raised by the public about localism during the media ownership proceeding," but he insisted that localism would not be harmed by the rules changes. The FCC plan would not be delayed.[192] Powell's opponents countered that if he was sincere, he would issue a stay on media ownership rules changes until the localism hearings had been conducted; that way any damage from the policies would be minimized.[193] Michael Copps responded, "I don't believe this diversionary tactic will divert either the American people or their representatives in Congress."[194]

The problem facing opponents of the FCC ownership plan was getting legislation through Congress. Bills had to go through committees to reach a vote on the floor, and the bills had to pass both the House and Senate to be sent to the president for his signature. The traditional route, and the cleanest route, would be for the commerce committees in both the Senate and the House to pass similar bills overturning the FCC's changes and then bring them to the floor for a vote. The Senate Commerce Committee had done that in June, but House Commerce Committee chairman Tauzin refused to let any FCC bill come before his committee, so that road was closed.

In cases where the primary committee blocks legislation, the standard recourse in Congress is to proceed through the appropriations committees and have them add amendments to budget bills that would block implementation funds for the rule changes. This was meant to be an end run around usually all-powerful Tauzin, and he let his colleagues know he thought it "wretched" for another committee to usurp his committee's role.[195] Nevertheless, the House Appropriations Committee proceeded to vote 40–25 to overturn the rule changing the TV ownership cap to 45 percent.[196] When the measure came to the floor of the House on July 23, opponents of raising the cap won by an incredible 400–21 vote. As one member said during the floor debate, members would be facing a public armed with "pitchforks and torches" if they did not overturn the rules.[197]

But the appropriations route had liabilities: even if Congress stopped funding measures to enforce the rules, the rules would nevertheless be in place and would go into effect a year later unless Congress acted again. The appropriations process offered a torturous route, even if both the House and Senate passed amendments overturning the FCC rule changes. The budget would inevitably be hammered out in a conference to reconcile the House and Senate bills, and those conferences were notorious for two things—White House pressure and enabling powerful special interests to get their way with almost no public awareness.

And then, of course, even if something did clear Congress, it faced the threat of a presidential veto. One advantage of going the appropriations route was that the president would be less likely to veto an entire multi-billion-dollar budget bill to take out a single clause. Bush made no public statements on the matter other than to say that he supported the FCC. In July, his senior policy advisors released a "Statement of Administration Policy" indicating they would recommend a veto of any legislation that reversed the FCC's rule changes.

When it became clear that a majority in both the Senate and the House backed some sort of rule change rollback, industry supporters on the Hill drafted a letter to gather signatures; their intent was to demonstrate to Bush that they held enough votes in Congress to sustain a veto—it takes a two-thirds vote to overturn a veto—should he elect to wield his presidential power. The goal was not only to convince Bush, but to demonstrate to congressional leaders that efforts to overturn the FCC's media ownership rules were futile. The media industry enjoyed most of its support in the House, and the letter needed 146 signatures to sustain a veto. After a round of furious activity, with corporate media lobbyists doing much of the footwork, the letter did not tally even 100 members' names.[198] "The president will never veto the bill because he just found out from this letter that Congress would override it," former FCC chairman Reed Hundt concluded. "There's no popular support for what the FCC did."[199]

The White House strategy was now aimed at extricating Bush from a position where he would have to veto an appropriations bill. Instead of having the Senate vote on the floor for any of the amendments to overturn the FCC rules changes—some of which would have certainly passed—Senate Majority Leader Frist opted for an "omnibus" appropriations bill where all the budget amendments would be hammered out in back-room meetings before they came to a floor for a vote. The FCC issue was but one of several contentious provisions—not necessarily the primary one—that pushed Frist and the congressional leadership into the omnibus. (Needless to say, this is where the real action takes place on Capitol Hill, and these secretive budget negotiations are the pork belly Olympics.) The resulting conference report would then emerge from this high-level, high-pressure committee for up or down votes in the House and Senate on several hundred billion dollars' worth of federal funding—including the funds earmarked for the districts of cooperative members. Then the bill would proceed directly to the White House for the president's signature.

The one concession in the omnibus bill the Republican conferees made to the Democrats was to retain the TV station ownership limit at 35 percent of the nation, instead of loosening the figure to 45 percent as the FCC proposed. Otherwise the FCC's ownership rules changes would sail through. But even here, the Republican leadership changed the deal and raised the figure for what percentage of the nation a company could reach with its TV stations to 39 percent. "The Republicans' decision to make the broadcast ownership cap 39% was no 'compromise' at all," Senator Hollings commented when the change was announced in late November. "It was a total violation of the conference agreement. Both Houses included the exact same wording. The item was not in dispute. All had agreed to the 35% cap. The Republicans went into a closet, met with themselves, and announced a 'compromise.' The Democrats and the conferees were ignored."[200]

Why 39 percent? This figure would mean that Viacom and News Corporation, both of which reached more than 35 percent of the nation with their TV stations, would be in compliance with the law and not have to sell off any of their stations. "On the face of it," Rupert Murdoch commented, "it suits us just fine." The head lobbyist for Disney was "pleased," because it "leaves ABC substantial room to acquire additional stations."[201] Frist made it clear that to the people at the White House, allowing the networks to own more stations was one of the "three or four issues" in the entire budget "that were very important to them."[202] The omnibus budget bill passed the House in December and was scheduled for a hotly debated vote in the Senate in late January 2004. For media activists across the nation it seemed like the fix was in. Big money rigged the system to foil the will of the people.

But all was not lost, not at all. In August, a third track to defeat the FCC's ownership rules changes was launched in the Senate, when a group of Senators collected enough names to invoke a congressional "resolution of disapproval," a provision in the Congressional Review Act, a government oversight law. This rarely used procedure permitted senators to bypass the committee structure altogether if they gathered 30 signatures in support of a vote to disapprove a regulatory agency's actions, such as the FCC's media ownership rule changes. Led by the Democrat Dorgan and the Republican Lott, more than enough signatures were collected, and the matter came to a vote on the Senate floor on September 16. The Senate voted 55–40 to overturn the entirety of the FCC rule changes.[203]

In the House, the rules permitted the Speaker to keep the vote from the floor in the fall session. Because the last thing the White House wanted was to be put in the position of having to veto such a popular bill, Speaker Hastert was placed under significant pressure to keep the Senate measure from reaching the floor. By November, House supporters of the effort to invoke the Congressional Review Act "resolution of disapproval" had collected over 200 signatures on a letter demanding that the matter be brought to a vote. Combined with earlier votes on the appropriations amendments, a clear majority of the House was on record as opposing what the FCC had done. The House could act on the CRA at any point until the congressional session ended in January 2005, so it looked to be a live issue throughout 2004.

The corporate media lobby had one final card to play: the pro-business U.S. Circuit Court of Appeals in the District of Columbia, which had repeatedly shown sympathy for the concerns of corporate media and contempt for the notion of broadcast regulation in the public interest. "The D.C. Circuit Court has been very predictable in favoring greater media-ownership deregulation," a media financial analyst observed.[204] Indeed, the industry had been planning all along to return to the court of appeals to get even Powell's weak rules eliminated. The only thing that could stop the D.C. court, it seemed, was a firm statement from Congress supporting broadcast ownership regulations.

But then events took another turn. The Media Access Project filed a petition with the Third Circuit Court of Appeals in Philadelphia on behalf of the Philadelphia-based Prometheus Radio Project arguing that the media ownership rule changes violated federal statutes and were generated improperly. To get the case out of the dreaded D.C. court of appeals, activists had filed lawsuits in federal courts around the country. When all the cases were consolidated, a lottery was used to pick a federal appeals court to adjudicate. The D.C. court had three-to-one odds stacked against it, and Philadelphia won.[205] Even so, winning the case was regarded as a long shot, but on September 3, the court agreed to hear the case. More important, the court issued an immediate stay so that the rule changes would not be put into effect. "The harm to petitioners absent a stay would be the likely loss of an adequate remedy should the new ownership rules be declared invalid in whole or in part," the court wrote. "In contrast to this irreparable harm, there is little indication that a stay pending appeal will result in substantial harm to the commission or to other interested parties."

Copps was satisfied by the turn of events: "The court has done what the commission should have done in the first place."[206] As the *New York Times* noted, "The court raised tough questions for the commission and its industry supporters" that suggested the future could not be predicted.[207] Although the case would not be settled until sometime in 2004, it constituted an enormous victory for opponents of media concentration. It bought time to work the halls of Congress to get the FCC's rules overturned before they could go into effect.

EPILOGUE: THE HARDEST BATTLE HAS BEEN WON

If the best solution to the problem of the media is widespread informed public participation in fundamental media policy debates, this book offers readers a happy ending. Regardless of the outcome of the media ownership fight of 2003, the episode was a remarkable and unprecedented moment in U.S. media history. For the first time in generations, media policy issues were taken from behind closed doors and made the stuff of democratic discourse and political engagement. In January 2003 Senator John Ensign, a Republican from Nevada, informed the Senate Commerce Committee that he had never had a constituent raise the issue of media policy with him, implying that the average person was uninterested in the topic. By the end of the year, not a single congressperson could make Ensign's claim. Indeed, members of Congress agreed that in 2003, media ownership was their constituents' second most discussed issue, trailing only the war in Iraq. It is unlikely that a media policy issue has cracked Congress's top twenty list in the previous half century.

For perhaps the first time ever, members of Congress faced the prospect of losing votes, maybe even elections, because of their stance on media policy issues. The change in climate since 1996—when the corrupt Telecommunications Act had been drafted, debated, and passed in almost total silence—could not have been more dramatic. Most incredible of all, in January 2003 nobody anticipated this transformation.

It remains to be seen where, exactly, this movement is going. By the end of 2003, what little mainstream news media coverage attended the story had disappeared, and there were considerable pressures to have the issue return to the proverbial Havana patio. But there was no reason to think public opinion had shifted back. In December the CNN *Lou Dobbs Tonight* ran another informal poll on the question "Do you agree big media companies should be broken up?" Over 96 percent of the 5,000-plus respondents said yes.[208] At the same time, Democratic candidates for president ranging from John Kerry and Wesley Clark to Howard Dean and Dennis Kucinich each came out forcefully for media reform, even breaking up the big media companies. It was another first for recent U.S. politics.[209]

As the dust clears, we can see that the fight that galvanized the nation in 2003 was a defensive one; even if it had been successful, it still left the media system where it had been on June 1, 2003. For most Americans involved, it was the severe problems with the existing media system that drove them to organize to keep matters from getting worse—so it was predicated on a belief that the status quo is no longer acceptable. The challenge for those who support democratic media policy making, and a democratic solution to the problem of the media, is to harness this energy and not allow it to dissipate. But the most important struggle is simply to convince people that the media are political forces that can be shaped, not natural ones that must be endured. Once people grasp that, as they did in 2003, the possibilities for change and for democracy suddenly become much greater. With this in mind, people can also see how much of the status quo's power lies in keeping them ignorant of their basic democratic rights and responsibilities.

Whether the United States is approaching a critical juncture with regard to media policy making is yet to be seen. That will depend on the ability of the media reform movement to connect with many other organized political forces in the nation—for example, labor, civil rights, feminism, environmentalism—and draw them deeper into the battle. These groups need to understand that as long as the media system remains as it is, the prospects for viable social change are limited elsewhere. Media reform and campaigns for social justice are inexorably linked.

In November 2003 the first National Conference on Media Reform was held in Madison, Wisconsin. The conference organizers expected a turnout of two hundred when the conference was originally proposed in December 2002. Eleven months later it drew nearly two thousand people from all over the nation, including the FCC's Copps and Adelstein, John Sweeney of the AFL-CIO, Jesse Jackson, Bill Moyers, PBS president Pat Mitchell, Ralph Nader, scores of journalists and entertainers, and a half-dozen members of Congress. It is amazing what a little political success does to a movement's self-confidence and ambitions. Media reform has gone from being an abstract issue with no sex appeal to one that is downright populist. It cuts across the political spectrum. It allows for incremental victories—unlike, say, campaign finance, for which any piecemeal reform invariably leaves destructive loopholes. It can draw in allies for help on specific measures, even though they might not support others. It is politically flexible.

A whole cohort of media activist groups entered 2004 energized. They drew up media reform proposals that were proactive, and not merely defensive, and that covered a broad range of issues. I do not mean to exaggerate the position we are in today; many will argue that the power of organized money will overwhelm efforts to organize people. We have a very long way to go. But the very hardest battle has been won. Media reform is now thinkable. Nothing will ever be the same again.

NOTES

CHAPTER 1

1 George Melloan, "'Limits to Growth': A Dumb Theory That Refuses to Die," *Wall Street Journal Online*, 27 August 2002.

2 Patricia Aufderheide, *Communications Policy and the Public Interest: The Telecommunications Act of 1996* (New York: Guilford Press, 1999), p. 5.

3 For an enlightening discussion of this point, see Lawrence Lessig, *Code and Other Laws of Cyberspace* (New York: Basic Books, 1999), ch. 7.

4 "The World's 500 Largest Corporations," *Fortune*, 21 July 2003, pp. 105–12; "The Forbes Sales 500," *Forbes*, 15 May 1975, pp. 159–65.

5 "The World's Top 200 Companies," *Business Week*, 14 July 2003, pp. 61–62.

6 See Kevin Phillips, *Wealth and Democracy* (New York: Broadway Books, 2002), chap. 2.

7 Jane L. Levere, "A Forecaster Predicts a Recovery in the Media Sector, but Not of the Vigor Seen in the Past," *New York Times*, 5 August 2002; "Lights! Camera! No Profits!" *The Economist*, 18 January 2003, pp. 11–12.

8 Michael J. Wolf, "These Are Not the Dark Ages for Media's Brightest Lights," *Wall Street Journal Online*, 23 July 2002.

9 "2002 Forbes 400 List," www.hollywoodreporter.com, 13 September 2002.

10 Janet Wasko, *Movies and Money: Financing the American Film Industry* (Norwood, N.J.: Ablex, 1982); Aron Moore, "Entangling Alliances," *Columbia Journalism Review*, March-April 2003.

11 AdAge.com, "100 Leading National Advertisers Ranked by Total U.S. Advertising Spending in 2001," http://www.adage.com/page.cms?pageId=913.

12 See Bernard Miege, *The Capitalization of Cultural Production* (New York: International General, 1989).

13 Cited in Robin Blackburn, "The Bourgeois Revolutionary," *The Nation*, 4/11 August 2003, p. 34.

14 Alexander Keyssar, *The Right to Vote: The Contested History of Democracy in the United States* (New York: Basic Books, 2000).

15 Andrew Davidson, "A Tall Order," *Financial Times*, 31 August 31–1 September 2002, p. 3.

16 For an elaboration of this notion, see Ruth Berins Collier and David Collier, *Shaping the Political Arena: Critical Junctures, the Labor Movement, and Regime Dynamics in Latin America* (Princeton, N.J.: Princeton University Press, 1991).

17 See Ithiel de Sola Pool, *Technologies of Freedom* (Cambridge, Mass.: Belknap Press, 1983), pp. 16–17.

18 For a discussion of copyright and the political economy of communication, see Ronald V. Bettig, *Copyrighting Culture: The Political Economy of Intellectual Property* (Boulder, Colo.: Westview, 1996).

19 Some of the most influential and outstanding works on the First Amendment and democracy in recent times have accordingly emphasized free speech, though they suggest clear implications for free press. See Steven H. Shiffrin, *The First Amendment, Demcocracy, and Romance* (Cambridge, Mass.: Harvard University Press, 1990); David M. Rabban, *Free Speech in Its Forgotten Years* (New York: Cambridge University Press, 1990).

20 See Milton R. Konvitz, *Fundamental Liberties of a Free People: Religion, Speech, Press, Assembly* (New Brunswick, N.J.: Transaction Press, 2003). First published by Cornell University Press in 1957.

21 Michael Kent Curtis, *Free Speech, "The People's Darling Privilege": Struggles for Freedom of Expression in American History* (Durham, N.C.: Duke University Press, 2000).

22 See Culver H. Smith, *Press, Politics, and Patronage: The American Government's Use of Newspapers, 1789–1875* (Athens, Ga.: University of Georgia Press, 1977).

23 See Jeffrey L. Pasley, *"The Tyranny of Printers": Newspaper Politics in the Early American Republic* (Charlottesville, Va.: University Press of Virginia, 2001).

24 Timothy E. Cook, *Governing with the News: The News Media as a Political Institution* (Chicago: University of Chicago Press, 1998), pp. 26–32.

25 William E. Ames, *A History of the National Intelligencer* (Chapel Hill, N.C.: University of North Carolina Press, 1972), p. 345.

26 Robert W. T. Martin, *The Free and Open Press: The Founding of American Democratic Press Liberty, 1640–1800* (New York: New York University Press, 2001), pp. 8, 168.

27 Akhil Reed Amar, *The Bill of Rights* (New Haven: Yale University Press, 1998), chap. 2.

28 For several of these quotes, see Robert W. McChesney and John Nichols, *Our Media, Not Theirs: The Democratic Struggle Against Corporate Media* (New York: Seven Stories Press, 2002).

29 Adrienne Koch and William Peden, eds., *The Life and Selected Writings of Thomas Jefferson* New York: Modern Library, 1944), p. 412. Quote taken from a letter to Edward Carrington, 16 January 1787.

30 Cited in Jay Inslee, "Media Mergers Endanger Democracy, Diversity of News," *Seattle Times*, 7 March 2003.

31 Richard R. John, "Private Enterprise, Public Good? Communications Deregulation as a National Political Issue, 1839–1851," unpublished paper, January 2002.

32 *Whitney v. California*, 274 U.S. 357 (1927), cited in Gene Kimmelman, "Deregulation of Media: Dangerous to Democracy," text of speech given at University of Washington Law School, Seattle, Wa., 6 March 2003.

33 Cited in Harold L. Nelson and Dwight L. Teeter Jr., eds., *Law of Mass Communications* (Mineola, N.Y.: Foundation Press, 1969), p. 488.

34 C. Edwin Baker is perhaps the most articulate in this regard. See his *Media, Markets and Democracy* (New York: Cambridge University Press, 2001).

35 Burt Neuborne, "First Amendment for the Rich?" *The Nation*, 9 October 2000, p. 25.

36 Richard R. John, *Spreading the News: The American Postal System from Franklin to Morse* (Cambridge, Mass.: Harvard University Press, 1995).

37 Theda Skocpol, "The Tocqueville Problem: Civic Engagement in American Democracy," *Social Science History* 21(4) (1997): 455–79.

38   Cited in Richard B. Kielbowicz, *News in the Mail: The Press, Post Office, and Public Information, 1700-1860s* (Westport, Conn.: Greenwood Press, 1989), p. 35.

39   Pool, *Technologies of Freedom*, p. 77.

40   Cook, *Governing with the News*, pp. 40-44.

41   John, *Spreading the News*, chap. 2.

42   Alexis de Tocqueville, *Democracy in America* (New York: Signet Classic, 2001), p. 93.

43   Cook, *Governing with the News*, p. 44.

44   John, "Private Enterprise, Public Good?."

45   Dan Schiller, *Theorizing Communication: A History* (New York: Oxford University Press, 1996).

46   See Richard Du Boff, "The Rise of Communications Regulation: The Telegraph Industry, 1844-1880," *Journal of Communication* 34, no. 2 (Summer 1984): 52-66; Richard B. Du Boff, "The Telegraph and the Structure of Markets in the United States, 1845-1890," in *Research in Economic History: A Research Annual*, vol. 8, ed. Paul Uselding (Greenwich, Conn.: JAI Press, Inc., 1983), pp. 253-277.

47   Menahen Blondheim, *News Over the Wires: The Telegraph and the Flow of Public Information in America, 1844-1897* (Cambridge, Mass.: Harvard University Press, 1994).

48   Richard B. Du Boff, "The Telegraph in Nineteenth-Century America: Technology and Monopoly," *Comparative Studies in Society and History* 26, no. 4 (October 1984): 571-86.

49   Ibid., p. 582.

50   Dan Schiller, "Telecommunications and the Cooperative Commonwealth: The Challenge from Below and Its Containment, 1894-1919," unpublished manuscript, 2003, part of longer book project. http://leep.lis.uiuc.edu/publish/dschille/Telecommunications_And_The_Cooperative_Commonwealth.pdf

51   Harry G. Good and James D. Teller, eds., *A History of American Education*, 3rd ed.(New York: Macmillan, 1973), chap. 3; quotation, p. 85.

52   See Sarah Mondale and Sarah B. Patton, *School: The Story of American Public Education* (Boston: Beacon Press, 2001).

53   Willis G. Regier, "5 Problems and 9 Solutions for University Presses," *The Chronicle of Higher Education*, 13 June 2003.

54   Janet Wasko, *Understanding Disney* (Cambridge, Mass.: Polity, 2001), p. 19.

55   See Robert W. McChesney, *Telecommunications, Mass Media, and Democracy: The Battle for the Control of U.S. Broadcasting, 1928-1935* (New York: Oxford University Press, 1993). All of the material in this particular discussion is drawn from this book.

56   See Vincent Mosco, *Broadcasting in the United States* (Norwood, N.J.: Ablex, 1979).

57   See Gerd Horten, *Radio Goes to War: The Cultural Politics of Propaganda During World War II* (Berkeley: University of California Press, 2002), p. 181.

58   "Who Owns Who in Cable," *Electronic Media*, 24 January 2000, p. 112.

59   See Michael E. Kinsley, *Outer Space and Inner Sanctums: Government, Business, and Satellite Communication* (New York: John Wiley & Sons, 1976); Dallas Smythe, *Counterclockwise: Perspectives on Communication*, ed. Thomas Guback (Boulder, Colo.: Westview, 1994), chap. 10.

60   William Kennard, "'What Does $70 Billion Buy You Anyway?': Rethinking Public Interest Requirements at the Dawn of the Digital Era," speech delivered at Museum of Television and Radio, New York, N.Y., 10 October 2000.

61   "The Blue Book: Public Service Responsibility of Broadcast Licensees," in *Documents of American Broadcasting*, 3rd ed.

(Englewood Cliffs, N.J.: Prentice-Hall, 1978), pp. 132–216.

62 See, for example, Charles A. Siepmann, *Radio, Television, and Society* (New York: Oxford University Press, 1950); Susan L. Brinson, *Personal and Public Interests: Frieda B. Hennock and the Federal Communications Commission* (Westport, Conn.: Praeger, 2002).

63 "The Fairness Doctrine: In the Matter of Editorializing by Broadcast Licensees," in *Documents of American Broadcasting*, ed. Frank J. Khan (Englewood Cliffs, N.J.: Prentice-Hall, 1978), pp. 217–31; Ford Rowan, *Broadcast Fairness: Doctrine, Practice, Prospects* (New York: Longman, 1984); William B. Ray, *FCC: The Ups and Downs of Radio-TV Regulation* (Ames, Iowa: Iowa State University Press, 1990), chap. 4.

64 Douglas Gomery, *The FCC's Newspaper-Broadcast Cross-Ownership Rule: An Analysis* (Washington, D.C.: Economic Policy Institute, 2002).

65 Steve McClellan, "Fin-Syn," *Broadcasting & Cable*, 24 January 2000. pp. 30–36.

66 See Charles Goldsmith, "U.S. Is Unlikely to Copy U.K. Move to Ease Media Ownership Controls," *Wall Street Journal Online*, 13 May 2002.

67 See Charles H. Tillinghast, *American Broadcast Regulation and the First Amendment: Another Look* (Ames, Iowa: Iowa State University Press, 2000).

68 Erwin G. Krasnow, Lawrence D. Longley, and Herbert A. Terry, *The Politics of Broadcast Regulation*, 3rd ed. (New York: St. Martin's Press, 1982), chap. 8.

69 Michael J. Copps, "Remarks," Everett Parker Ethics in Communications Lecture, Washington, D.C., 24 September 2002.

70 Todd Shields, "Copps Criticizes Broadcast License Renewals," www.mediaweek.com, 23 July 2003.

71 Paige Albinek, "Service with an $8B Smile," *Broadcasting & Cable*, 10 April 2000, p. 24.

72 David Hatch, "Report: PSA's Air in Worst Daypart," *Electronic Media*, 25 February 2002, p. 6.

73 "All Politics Is Local, But You Wouldn't Know It by Watching Local TV," Report of the Alliance for Better Campaigns, October 2003; see also Jennifer Harper, "Study Finds 'Near Blackout' of Local Public Issues on TV," *Washington Times*, 28 October 2003.

74 Christine Y. Chen, "The Bad Boys of Radio," *Fortune*, March 3, 2003, p. 119.

75 Bill McConnell, "Merger-Modeling Debut," *Broadcasting & Cable*, 10 June 2002, p. 22.

76 See, for example, James C. Foust, *Big Voices of the Air: The Battle Over Clear Channel Radio* (Ames, Iowa: Iowa State University Press, 2000),

77 Robert W. McChesney interview with William Kennard, February 2001. For a small section of the interview, see Robert W. McChesney, "Kennard, the Public, and the FCC," *The Nation*, 14 May 2001, pp. 17–20.

78 Julie Wakefield, "Telecom's Man of the Moment," *Scientific American*, February 2002.

79 For a good overview of this episode, see Erwin G. Krasnow, Lawrence D. Longley, and Herbert A. Terry, *The Politics of Broadcast Regulation*, 3rd ed. (New York: St. Martin's Press, 1982), pp. 206–20.

80 See, for a related example, Ira Tienowitz, "Black Leaders Turn Up Heat," *Advertising Age*, 16 September 2002, p. 4.

81 See Milton Mueller, "Reinventing Media Activism: Citizen Activism as a Socio-Economic and Political Phenomenon," unpublished paper, 2003.

82   For an excellent treatment of this sub-
      ject, see Robert Pollin, *Contours of Descent:
      U.S. Economic Fractures and the Landscape
      of Global Austerity* (New York: Verso, 2003).

83   Quotation of Professor Thomas W.
      Hazlett, a leading figure in the move-
      ment to have free market principles
      guide communications policy making.
      Taken from the back cover of Peter
      Huber, *Law and Disorder in Cyberspace:
      Abolish the FCC and Let Common Law Rule
      the Telecosm* (New York: Oxford University
      Press, 1997). See also Bruce M. Owen, *The
      Internet Challenge to Television* (Cambridge,
      Mass.: Harvard University Press, 1999).

84   Lee C. Bollinger, *Images of a Free Press*
      (Chicago: University of Chicago Press,
      1991), p. 121.

85   David Hatch, "Independents Fight the
      Good Fight," *Electronic Media*, 29 January
      2001, p. 3; Doug Halonen, "FCC Sets
      Its Sights on 'Total Carriage,'" *Electronic
      Media*, 19 August 2002, p. 1A.

86   Cited in Lucas A. Powe Jr., *The Fourth
      Estate and the Constitution* (Berkeley:
      University of California Press, 1991).

87   Herbert I. Schiller, *Culture, Inc.: The Corpo-
      rate Takeover of Public Expression* (New York:
      Oxford University Press, 1989), chap. 3.

88   Thomas Frank, *One Market Under God:
      Extreme Capitalism, Market Populism, and
      the End of Market Democracy* (New York:
      Doubleday, 2000).

89   See Robert W. McChesney, *Rich Media,
      Poor Democracy: Communication Politics in
      Dubious Times* (New York: New Press,
      2000). Also see Patricia Aufderheide,
      *Communications Policy and the Public
      Interest: The Telecommunications Act of 1996*
      (New York: Guilford Press, 1999).

90   See, for example, Matt Richtel, "Time
      Warner to Use Cable Lines to Add Phone

      to Internet Service," *New York Times*,
      9 December 2003; Matt Richtel,
      "Phone Service Over Internet Revives
      Talk of Regulation," *New York Times*,
      15 December 2003.

91   Poll conducted by Pew Research Center
      for the People and the Press, May 2002.
      See www.people-press.org.

92   "Consumer Group Says Deregulation
      of Cable Industry Hasn't Cut Rates,"
      Wall Street Journal Online, 24 July 2002;
      Jon Groat, "Cable Not Competitive,
      Congress Told," http://cbs.market-
      watch.com, 6 May 2003.

93   Several exceptions to the cross-
      ownership prohibition existed, such
      as News Corporation owning the *New
      York Post* as well as having a Fox TV
      station in New York. Likewise the
      Chicago Tribune owned WGN radio and
      television stations in Chicago.

94   Juliana Ratner, "Regulator Steps Out
      Into the Market," *Financial Times*,
      22 August 2002, p. 8.

95   Meg James, "TV Networks Find Ways
      to Stretch Educational Rules,"
      Los Angeles Times, 23 February 2003.

96   Doug Halonen, "Watchdogs Label
      Kennard a 'Failure,'" *Electronic Media*,
      17 July 2000, p. 3.

97   Dab Briody, *The Iron Triangle: Inside
      the Secret World of the Carlyle Group*
      (Hoboken, N.J.: John Wiley & Sons,
      2003), pp. 106–10; Tim Shorrock,
      "Crony Capitalism Goes Global," *The
      Nation*, 1 April 2002, pp. 11–15.

98   McChesney, "Kennard, the Public,
      and the FCC."

99   Charles Lewis, "Media Money,"
      Columbia Journalism Review,
      September/October 2000, pp. 20–27.

100 Derrick Wetherell, "The Bush/Gore

Scorecard," *Columbia Journalism Review*, September/October 2000, p. 23.

101 Mark Fitzgerald, "Bush? Gore? It Doesn't Matter!" *Editor & Publisher*, 5 June 2000, p. 12.

CHAPTER 2

1   See Jeffrey L. Pasley, *"The Tyranny of Printers": Newspaper Politics in the Early American Republic* (Charlottesville: University Press of Virginia, 2001).

2   Harry J. Maihafer, *War of Words: Abraham Lincoln and the Civil War Press* (Washington, D.C.: Brassey's, Inc., 2001).

3   Michael Schudson, *The Sociology of News* (New York: W.W. Norton, 2003), p. 80.

4   See Lawrence Goodwyn, *The Populist Moment* (New York: Oxford University Press, 1978), pp. 206–12, 288.

5   Edward Bellamy, *Looking Backward: 2000–1887* (New York: Signet Classic, 2000).

6   Goodwyn, *The Populist Moment*, pp. 206–212, 288.

7   See, for example, Elliott Shore, Ken Fones-Wolf, and James P. Danky, eds., *The German-American Radical Press* (Urbana, Ill.: University of Illinois Press, 1992).

8   See Rodger Streitmatter, *Voices of Revolution: The Dissident Press in America* (New York: Columbia University Press, 2001).

9   See Gerald J. Baldasty, *E. W. Scripps and the Business of Newspapers* (Urbana, Ill.: University of Illinois Press, 1999).

10   Matthew Engel, "How to Squeeze the Life Out of a Newspaper," www.timesonline.co.uk, 7 March 2003.

11   This leaves aside newspapers launched in suburban areas that emerged as markets over the course of the twentieth century or national markets made possible by satellite communication. *USA Today* falls in the latter category.

12   See, for example, Paul Milkman, *PM: A New Deal in Journalism* (New Brunswick, N.J.: Rutgers University Press, 1997).

13   See Daniel Cohen, *Yellow Journalism* (Brookfield, Conn.: Twenty-First Century Books, 2000).

14   This analysis comes from the research done for the introduction to Robert W. McChesney and Ben Scott, eds., *Our Unfree Press: 100 Years of Radical Media Criticism* (New York: The New Press, 2004).

15   Richard Hofstadter, *The Age of Reform* (New York: Alfred A. Knopf, 1955), p. 238.

16   John Graham, ed., *"Yours for the Revolution": The Appeal to Reason, 1895–1922* (Lincoln, Neb.: University of Nebraska Press, 1990).

17   Will Irwin, *The American Newspaper: A Series First Appearing in* Collier's, *January–July, 1911* (Ames, Iowa: Iowa State University Press, 1969), p. 8. This particular quote is from Irwin's first installment.

18   See Upton Sinclair, *The Brass Check* (Urbana, Ill.: University of Illinois Press, 2003), with an introduction by Robert W. McChesney and Ben Scott.

19   Ibid., p. 241.

20   This rich tradition of press criticism is collected in McChesney and Scott, *Our Unfree Press*.

21   See Edwin Emery, *History of the American Newspaper Publishers Association* (Minneapolis, Minn.: University of Minnesota Press, 1950); Linda Lawson, *Truth in Publishing: Federal Regulation of the Press's Business Practices, 1880–1920* (Carbondale, Ill.: Southern Illinois University Press, 1993).

22   See McChesney and Scott, *Our Unfree Press.*

23   For the classic statement on professional journalism, see Joseph Pulitzer, "Selection from the College of Journalism," in *Killing the Messenger: 100 Years of Press Criticism,* ed. Tom Goldstein (New York: Columbia University Press, 1989), pp. 190–99. Originally published in *North American Review,* May 2004.

24   Paul Alfred Pratte, *Gods Within the Machine: A History of the American Society of Newspaper Editors, 1923–1993* (Westport, Conn.: Praeger, 1995).

25   See Ben H. Bagdikian, *The Media Monopoly,* 6th ed. (Boston: Beacon Press, 2000).

26   Some of these issues were of tremendous importance for journalism, regardless of the overall nature of the system. It was, for example, an enormous victory to have the Supreme Court order relaxation of onerous libel laws, which once made it prohibitive for journalists to do hard-hitting and controversial exposés of powerful public figures. See Anthony Lewis, *Make No Law: The Sullivan Case and the First Amendment* (New York: Random House, 1991). Indeed, the fear of libel law suits has had a distinct "chilling effect" on news coverage of the well-heeled corporate sector, which has been granted by law more libel protection than that afforded government officials. Lois G. Foner, *A Chilling Effect: The Mounting Threat of Libel and Invasion of Privacy Actions to the First Amendment* (New York: W. W. Norton, 1987); Richard Labunski, *Libel and the First Amendment: Legal History and Practice in Print and Broadcasting* (New Brunswick, N.J.: Transaction Books, 1987).

27   George Seldes, *Freedom of the Press* (New York: Bobbs-Merrill, 1935), pp. 358, 360.

28   See Frank C. Waldrop, *McCormick of Chicago* (Englewood Cliffs, N.J.: Prentice-Hall, 1966).

29   Horst J. P. Bergmeier and Rainer E. Lotz, *Hitler's Airwaves: The Inside Story of Nazi Radio Broadcasting and Propaganda Swing* (New Haven: Yale University Press, 1997), pp. 70–73.

30   Cited in John Taylor Gatto, "Against School," *Harper's,* September 2003, p. 37.

31   Jeff Schmidt, *Disciplined Minds* (Lanham, Md.: Rowman & Littlefield, 2000).

32   See Norman E. Isaacs, *Untended Gates: The Mismanaged Press* (New York: Columbia University Press, 1986), chap.1.

33   Christopher Lasch, *The Revolt of the Elites and the Betrayal of Democracy* (New York: W. W. Norton, 1995), chap. 9.

34   James Carey, "The Press, Public Opinion, and Public Discourse: On the Edge of the Postmodern," in *James Carey: A Critical Reader,* ed. Eve Stryker Munson and Catherine A. Warren (Minneapolis, Minn.: University of Minnesota Press, 1997), p. 247.

35   The classic treatments of this topic include: Gaye Tuchman, *Making News: A Study in the Construction of Reality* (New York: The Free Press, 1978); Herbert J. Gans, *Deciding What's News* (New York: Pantheon Books, 1979); Mark Fishman, *Manufacturing the News* (Austin: University of Texas Press, 1980). For a more recent critique, from a Canadian perspective, see Robert A. Hackett and Yuezhi Zhao, *Sustaining Democracy?: Journalism and the Politics of Objectivity* (Toronto: Garamond Press, 1998).

36   I am indebted to Ben Bagdikian for much of what follows. See Bagdikian, *The Media Monopoly.*

37 Brent Cunningham, "Rethinking Objectivity," *Columbia Journalism Review*, July/August 2003, p. 27.

38 See Stephen Ponder, *Managing the Press: Origins of the Media Presidency, 1897–1933* (New York: Palgrave, 1998).

39 See Robert C. Cottrell, *Izzy: A Biography of I. F. Stone* (New Brunswick, N.J.: Rutgers University Press, 1992).

40 Russell Mokhiber and Robert Weissman, "A Dull and Largely Uncritical Recitation of Official Sources," www.commondreams.org, 24 October 2003.

41 Ina Howard, "Power Sources," *Extra!*, June 2002.

42 See Commission on Civil Disorders, "The Role of the Mass Media in Reporting of News About Minorities," in Goldstein, *Killing the Messenger*, pp. 200–27.

43 See Sheldon Rampton and John Stauber, *Trust Us, We're Experts: How Industry Manipulates Science and Gambles with Your Future* (New York: Tarcher, 2000); Alicia Mundy, *Dispensing with Truth: The Victims, the Drug Companies, and the Dramatic Story Behind the Battle Over Fen-Phen* (New York: St. Martin's Press, 2001); Stuart Ewen, *PR! A Social History of Spin* (New York: Basic Books, 1996).

44 Suzanne Vranica, "Publicis Groupe Bolsters Its PR Holdings," *Wall Street Journal*, 30 May 2001.

45 Joseph N. Cappella and Kathleen Hall Jamieson, *Spiral of Cynicism: The Press and the Public Good* (New York: Oxford University Press, 1997).

46 See James Fallows, *Breaking the News: How the Media Undermine American Democracy* (New York: Vintage, 1996).

47 Bagdikian, *The Media Monopoly*.

48 C. Edwin Baker, *Media, Markets, and Democracy* (New York: Cambridge University Press, 2002), p. 106.

49 See George Farah and Justin Elga, "What's *Not* Talked About on Sunday Morning? Issue of Corporate Power Not on the Agenda," *Extra!*, September/October 2001, pp. 14–17.

50 Interview with Charles Lewis, in *Orwell Rolls Over in his Grave*, documentary by Robert Pappas, 2002.

51 For examples of the CPI's work, see www.publicintegrity.org.

52 The classic treatment of this subject is Edward S. Herman and Noam Chomsky, *Manufacturing Consent: The Political Economy of the News Media*, 2nd ed. (New York: Pantheon, 2002).

53 Cited in *World Editorial & International Law*, October 2003, p. 2.

54 See, for example, Edward Jay Epstein, *News from Nowhere: Television and the News* (New York: Vintage Books, 1973); Bill Kovach and Tom Rosenstiel, *Warp Speed: America in the Age of Mixed Media* (New York: The Century Foundation Press, 1999); W. Lance Bennett, *News, The Politics of Illusion*, 4th ed. (New York: Longman, 2001); Jeffrey Scheuer, *The Sound Bite Society: Television and the American Mind* (New York: Four Walls Eight Windows, 1999).

55 See "Lost in the Margin: Labor and the Media," *Extra!*, special issue, Summer 1990; Harold Meyerson, "If I Had a Hammer: Whatever Happened to America's Working Class?" *Los Angeles Times*, 2 September 2001.

56 Jon Fine, "California Dreaming, Scheming," *Advertising Age*, 30 April 2001, p. S1; for the classic work on this, see Robert Gottlieb, *Thinking Big: The Story of the Los Angeles Times, Its Publishers, and Their Influence on Southern California* (New York: Putnam, 1977).

57 See, for example, Judith Serrin and William Serrin, eds., *Muckraking! The Journalism that Changed America* (New York: The New Press, 2002); Nancy J. Woodhull and Robert W. Snyder, eds., *Defining Moments in Journalism* (New Brunswick, N.J.: Transaction Publishers, 1998).

58 For a collection of their reports gathered into a book, see Donald L. Bartlett and James B. Steele, *America: What Went Wrong* (Kansas City, Mo.: Andrews and McMeel, 1992).

59 Bill Kovach and Tom Rosenstiel, *Warp Speed: America in the Age of Mixed Media Culture* (New York: Century Foundation Press, 1999).

60 See, for example, George W. Pring and Penelope Canan, *SLAPPs: Getting Sued for Speaking Out* (Philadelphia: Temple University Press, 1996); *First Amendment and Libel: The Experts Look at Print, Broadcast & Cable* (New York: Harcourt Brace Jovanovich, 1983).

61 Much of this has been written by prominent journalists like Bagdikian. See also James D. Squires, *Read All About It! The Corporate Takeover of America's Newspapers* (New York: Times Books, 1993); Doug Underwood, *When MBAs Rule the Newsroom* (New York: Columbia University Press, 1993); John H. McManus, *Market-Driven Journalism: Let the Citizen Beware?* (Thousand Oaks, Calif.: Sage, 1994).

62 Michele Greppi, "All's Not Well at ABC News," *Electronic Media*, 28 May 2001, p. 3. The definitive work on this issue is Penn Kimball, *Downsizing the News: Network Cutbacks in the Nation's Capital* (Baltimore: Johns Hopkins University Press, 1994).

63 Dan Trigoboff, "No Good News for Local News," *Broadcasting & Cable*, 18 November 2002, p. 12.

64 Paul Tharp, "Kann Gives Angry WSJ-ers a New Lesson in Capitalism," www.nypost.com, 5 December 2002.

65 David Laventhol, "Profit Pressures," *Columbia Journalism Review*, May/June 2001, pp. 18–22; Felicity Barringer, "Publisher Who Resigned Urges Editors to Put Readers First," *New York Times*, 7 April 2001.

66 Wayne Walley, "Fox News Sweeps to TV Marketer of Year," *Advertising Age*, 4 November 2002, pp. 1, 22.

67 Robert W. McChesney interview of Rick Kaplan, former president of CNN, March 2001.

68 "It Pays to Be Right," *The Economist*, 7 December 2002, p. 60.

69 Jill Goldsmith and Pamela McClintock, "Extra! TV Mavens Eye Paper Route," *Variety*, 12–18 March 2001, pp. 1, 58.

70 See Meg Campbell, "Newsplex Puts the New in Newsroom," *Editor & Publisher*, 12 December 2002.

71 Christina Hoag, "CBS 4 and Herald Form Media Alliance," www.miami.com, November 24, 2002.

72 Dan Trigoboff and Steve McClellan, "Watchdogs Howl Over ABC/CNN," *Broadcasting & Cable*, 25 November 2002, p. 1.

73 Tom Lowry, "Online Extra: The Case Against an ABC/CNN Merger," www.businessweek.online, 2 December 2002.

74 Av Westin, "'Minutes' Master Misses Mark," *Variety*, 16–22 April 2001, p. 35.

75 "Editor Is Dismissed Over Truth of Article," *New York Times*, 19 November 2002; Felicity Barringer, "Wire Service Says Reporter It Fired Invented His Sources," www.nytimes.com, 22 October 2002.

76 Seth Mnookin, "The Secret Life of Jayson Blair," *Newsweek*, 26 May 2003, pp. 1, 40–51.

77 Trudy Lieberman, "You Can't Report What You Don't Pursue," *Columbia Journalism Review*, May–June 2000.

78 Nolan Reeds and Freda Colbourne, "Fewer Gatekeepers, More Open Gates," *Strategy Magazine*, 6 November 2000, p. 25.

79 I develop this point more in Robert W. McChesney, *Rich Media, Poor Democracy: Communication Politics in Dubious Times* (New York: The New Press, 2000).

80 Marion Just, Rosalind Levine, and Kathleen Regan," Investigative Journalism Despite the Odds," *Columbia Journalism Review*, November–December 2002, p. 103.

81 Interview with Charles Lewis, *Orwell Rolls Over in His Grave*, documentary film by Robert Pappas, 2002.

82 Brett Schaeffer, "Minority Reporter," *In These Times*, 19 August 2002, p. 8.

83 Sheldon Rampton and John Stauber, *Trust Us, We're Experts: How Industry Manipulates Science and Gambles with Your Future* (New York: Putnam, 2001).

84 Elisabeth Bumiller, "Bush Criticized by Lawmakers on Corporate Governance," *New York Times*, 1 August 2002.

85 David Greenberg, "Calling a Lie a Lie," *Columbia Journalism Review*, September–October 2003.

86 Paul Waldman, "Why the Media Can't Call It as They See It," *Washington Post*, 29 September 2003.

87 See, for example, Richard W. Stevenson and Elisabeth Bumiller, "Parties Jousting Over Wrongdoing by U.S. Businesses," *New York Times*, 8 July 2002; Alison Mitchell, "Democrats See Scandals as Chance to Attack Privatizing Social Security," *New York Times*, 13 July 2002.

88 See, for example, Patricia Moy and Michael Pfau, *With Malice Toward All? The Media and Public Confidence in Public Institutions* (Westport, Conn.: Praeger, 2000).

89 Av Westin, *Best Practices for Television Journalists* (Arlington, Va.: The Freedom Forum, 2000), p. 5.

90 Louis Chunovic, "News Departments Boost Bottom Line," *Electronic Media*, 7 January 2002, p. 6.

91 Pew Research Center, "Self Censorship: How Often and Why," 30 April 2000. Available at: http://peoplepress.org/reports/display.php3?ReportID=39.

92 See, for example, Janine Jackson, Peter Hart, and Rachel Coen, "Fear & Favor 2002: How Power Shapes the News," *Extra!*, April 2003, pp. 18–24.

93 Erin White, "P&G to Use Plugs in TV News Stories to Send Viewers to Its Web Sites," *Wall Street Journal*, 7 March 2001.

94 "CNN Headline News to Display Ad Logos," www.accessatlanta.com, 1 August 2001; Bruce Orwall, "Dinosaur Ad Crosses a Line at Newspapers," *Wall Street Journal*, 18 July 2001; "Gannett Allows Front-Page Ads at Local Papers," *Wall Street Journal*, 25 May 2000; Felicity Barringer, "Concerns on Space and Revenue Spur Growth of Paid Obituaries," *New York Times*, 14 January 2002.

95 Paul Raeburn, "The Corruption of TV Health News," *Business Week*, 28 February 2000, pp. 66, 68; Karissa S. Wang, "WCBS in Ethics Firestorm Over Ad," *Electronic Media*, 17 April 2000, pp. 3, 44; Robert Feder, "Is Medical Magazine Healthy for Journalism?" *Chicago Sun-Times*, 23 October 2002; Diana Zuckerman, "Hype in Health Reporting," *Extra!*, September/October 2002, pp. 8–11.

96   "Releases Go into the Garbage,"
     O'Dwyer's PR Daily, 13 November 2002.

97   Howard Kurtz, "Local TV News:
     Now Part of Sales?" *Washington Post*,
     2 November 2003; John Eggerton,
     "Media General Supports 'Infopayment'
     Practice,' *Broadcasting & Cable*,
     3 November 2003, p. 14.

98   Joe Strupp, "New Advertorials Raise
     Old Ethical Questions," *Editor & Publisher*,
     17 November 2003, pp. 6-7.

99   Mark Jurkowitz, "When Journalists
     Become Pitchmen," *Boston Globe*,
     10 February 2000.

100 Lloyd Grove, "For CBS Correspondent
     Rose, Things Go Better With Coke,"
     Washington Post, 23 April 2002.

101 Kim Campbell, "TV News Moves Toward
     Hollywood Star System," *Christian
     Science Monitor*, 25 January 2002; Paula
     Bernstein, "CNN to Revamp Format,
     Highlight Personalities," *Variety*, 11-17
     December 2000, p. 60; Sally Beatty,
     "As Hard News Gets Even Harder,
     CNN Segues to Glossier Format,"
     Wall Street Journal Online, 5 July 2002.

102 Richard Huff, "Singles to See if Fox's
     Price is Right," *New York Daily News*,
     21 November 2002.

103 Richard Huff, "Doc Quits ABC for
     Tylenol," www.nydailynews.com,
     10 December 2002.

104 David Folkenflik, "Medical Show
     Packages Stories and Sponsors,"
     Baltimore Sun, 8 May 2002.

105 J. D. Lasica, "Synergy and the Day of
     Infamy," *Online Journalism Review*, 31 May
     2001; Lisa de Moraes, "When 'Push' Comes
     to Shove," *Washington Post*, 6 September
     2002; for a longer discussion of the cor-
     porate influence over ABC News, see Jane
     Meyer, "Bad News: What's Behind the

     Recent Gaffes at ABC?" *The New Yorker*,
     14 August 2000, pp. 30-36.

106 Norman Solomon, "Announcing the
     P.U.-litzer Prizes for 2002," syndicated
     column, www.commondreams.org,
     3 January 2003.

107 Bill Carter, "At CBS, the Lines between
     News and Entertainment Grow
     Fuzzier," *New York Times*, 26 June 2000.

108 Matt McAllister, "Selling *Survivor*:
     The Use of TV News to Promote
     Commercial Entertainment," in *A
     Companion to Media Studies*, ed. Angharad
     N. Valdivia (Oxford: Blackwell, 2003).

109 *Tyndall Report*, cited in www.tvguide.
     com/magazine/robins/030113.asp,
     13 January 2003.

110 Elizabeth Jensen, "Headline News Faces
     Criticism for Channeling Viewers,"
     Los Angeles Times, 20 August 2001.

111 "Ken Auletta: 'The Drive to Achieve
     Synergy Is Often Journalism's
     Poison','" www.iwantmedia.com,
     19 December 2002.

112 See, for example, Alex Kuczynski,
     "Newsweeklies Turn a Cold Shoulder to
     Hard News," *New York Times*, 14 May 2001.

113 Dan Trigoboff, "It Depends On What
     'Hard' Is," *Broadcasting & Cable*,
     27 May 2002, p. 18.

114 Will Lester, "Media Coverage
     of Government Is Declining," *Editor
     and Publisher*, 24 July 2003.

115 Tom Shales, "When Serious News
     Goes Pop," *Electronic Media*, 18 November
     2002, p. 23.

116 Lisa de Moraes, "Exclusive Perks:
     CNN's Red-Carpet 'Get' in the Blake
     Story," *Washington Post*, 23 April 2002.

117 Tom Shales, "News Gone Wild:
     All Jackson, All the Time," *Television
     Week*, 24 November 2003, p. 31.

118 Michele Greppi, "Newsmags Hold Key to ABC's Sweeps Bump," *Electronic Media*, 18 November 2002, p. 2.

119 Karissa S. Wang, "Study: TV News Big on Violence," *Electronic Media*, 10 December 2001, p. 16.

120 Brian Lowry, "Newscasts Too Often Employ Scare Tactics," *Los Angeles Times*, 16 October 2002.

121 Tim Wise, "Coloring Crime: Violence, Deviance, and Media Manipulation," Znet Commentary, www.zmag.org, 23 June 2003; Eric Alterman, *What Liberal Media?* (New York: Basic Books, 2003), pp. 114–17; Robert Entman and Andrew Rojecki, *Black Image in the White Mind* (Chicago: University of Chicago Press, 2000).

122 This research is discussed in Salim Muwakkil, "Racial Bias Still Haunts Media," *In These Times*, 17 November 2003, p. 10.

123 See, for example, Lee Hall, "20th Anniversary: CNN Headline News; Q&A: Larry Goodman, President, Sales and Marketing," *Electronic Media*, 16 December 2002, pp. 26, 32.

124 Patricia Callahan and Kevin Helliker, "Knight Ridder Loses Readers but Charges More to Reach Them," *Wall Street Journal*, 18 June 2001.

125 Louis Chunovic, "Taking the High-Income Road," *Television Week*, 17 March 2003, p. 6.

126 See, for example, William J. Puette, *Through Jaundiced Eyes: How the Media View Organized Labor* (Ithaca, N.Y.: ILR Press, 1992). For a concrete analysis of the way in which labor issues are poorly covered in the news media, see Christopher R. Martin, *Framed! Labor and the Corporate Media* ((Ithaca: Cornell University Press, 2004).

127 See Peter Johnson, "Few TV News Stories Focus on Hispanics," *USA Today*, 16 December 2002.

128 Ben H. Bagdikian, "A Secret in the News: The Country's Permanent Poor," www.zmag.org, 2 April 2001.

129 "Public Misconception about Poverty Continues," U.S. Newswire, www.usnewswire.com, 7 January 2003.

130 Joan Oleck, "Training Scribes for the Biz Beat," *Business Week*, 28 May 2001, p. 16.

131 "Sunday Morning Talk Shows Ignore Corporate Power Issues," www.essentialaction.org, undated, ca. 2000.

132 Norman Solomon, "Bloomberg's Victory and the Triumph of Business News," syndicated column, Creators Syndicate, 8 November 2001.

133 Dan Fost, "When Scoops Are Product Placements, Press 'Leaks' Can Serve a Corporate Agenda," *San Francisco Chronicle*, 1 September 2002; Dan Fost, "Strained Relations: Business Magazines Struggle to Maintain Objectivity Under Pressure from Their Biggest Tech Advertisers," *San Francisco Chronicle*, 16 January 2002.

134 Vincent Boland, "Media Face Clash with Regulators Over Analysts," *Financial Times*, 23–24 November 2002, p. 1.

135 Phillip J. Longman, "Bad Press: How Business Journalism Helped Inflate the Bubble," *Washington Monthly*, October 2002; Howard Kurtz, "On CNBC, Boosters for the Boom," *Washington Post*, 12 November 2002.

136 Norman Solomon, "The Old Spin on the 'New Economy'," www.alternet.org, 18 July 2002.

137 Simon Romero and Riva D. Atlas, "WorldCom Files for Bankruptcy; Largest U.S. Case," *New York Times*, 22 July 2002.

138 William Greider, "The Enron Nine," *The Nation*, 13 May 2002, pp. 18–22.

139 Robert Weissman and Russell Mokhiber, "Cracking Down on Corporate Crime, Really," www.zmag.org, 23 July 2002.

140 Bob Herbert, "Joined at the Hip," *New York Times*, 10 January 2002.

141 Andrew Wheat, "System Failure: Deregulation, Political Corruption, Corporate Fraud and the Enron Debacle," *Multinational Monitor*, January/February 2002, pp. 34–42; Joshua Chaffin, "Enron in California: A Titanic Error," *Financial Times*, 22 November 2002, p. 20.

142 "Andersen, Politics and Money: By the Numbers," *Multinational Monitor*, January/February 2002, p. 44; Matt Bliven, "Enron's Washington," www.thenation.com, 24 January 2002; Charles Lewis, "Enron Scandal Goes Deep," Wilmington *Sunday News Journal*, 24 February 2002.

143 Amy Borrus, "Global Crossing Tossed More Cash around Town than Enron," *Business Week*, 11 February 2002, p. 49.

144 Orville Schell, "How Big Media Missed the Big Story," www.msbnc.com, 19 July 2002.

145 "From Enron to Black Hawk Down," *CounterPunch*, 1–15 January 2002, pp. 1, 2.

146 Kurt Eichenwald, "For WorldCom, Acquisitions Were Behind Its Rise and Fall," *New York Times*, 8 August 2002. For what the media missed at the time, see "Before the Fall: How, from the Outset, Bernie Ebbers' Character and Business Methods Sowed the Seeds of Disaster," *Financial Times*, 19 December 2002, p. 11.

147 Ben Schiller, "Where Did All the Reporters Go?" www.alternet.org, 13 February 2002.

148 James Ledbetter, "The Boys in the Bubble," *New York Times*, 2 January 2003.

149 Howard Kurtz, "Enron-N.Y. Times Co. Deal Highlights Media's Dilemma," *Washington Post*, 18 July 2002; Rebecca Smith, "Blockbuster, Enron Agree to Movie Deal," *Wall Street Journal*, 20 July 2000; Richard Blow, "Money, Power and Influence: Muckrakers Become Buckrakers," www.tompaine.com, 31 January 2002.

150 FAIR Media Advisory, "PBS's 'Commanding' Conflict of Interest: Enron and Other Corporate Giants Sponsored New Globalization Series," www.fair.org, 3 April 2002.

151 See David Corn, *The Lies of George W. Bush* (New York: Crown Publishers, 2003), chap. 11.

152 Bob Herbert, "Joined at the Hip," *New York Times*, 10 January 2002; John Dunbar, Robert Moore, and MaryJo Sylwester, "Enron Executives Who Dumped Stock Were Heavy Donors to Bush," *The Public I*, February 2002, pp. 1, 2, 6.

153 The party was videotaped and released in December 2002. See Associated Press, "Enron Video from 1997 Reportedly Parallels Future Scandal," 16 December 2002.

154 Jason Leopold, "Secrets and Lies: Bush, Cheney and the Great Rip-Off of California Ratepayers," www.counterpunch.org, 21 November 2002.

155 See, for example, Richard A. Oppel Jr., "Senator Releases Documents on Gore Aide's Enron Ties," *New York Times*, 13 November 2002.

156 "Dirty Money: Corporate Criminal Donations to the Two Major Parties," released by *Corporate Crime Reporter*, 3 July 2003.

157 Richard A. Oppel Jr., "Senate Report Clears Rubin of Illegality in Enron Matter," *New York Times*, 3 January 2003.

158 Russ Lewis, "The Press's Business...," *Washington Post*, 30 January 2002.

159 Tom Shales, "Too Entertained to Be Outraged," *Electronic Media*, 22 July 2002, p. 33.

160 Adolph Reed, "The Road to Corporate Perdition," *The Progressive*, September 2002, p. 31.

161 Jill Goldsmith, "H'Wood's High-Priced Suits," *Variety*, 23–29 April 2001, pp. 1, 48; Paul Krugman, "The Outrage Constraint," *New York Times*, 23 August 2002.

162 Mark Gimein, "You Bought, They Sold," *Fortune*, 2 September 2002, pp. 64–74; Peter Thal Larsen, Adrian Michaels, Ien Cheng, and Christopher Grimes, "SEC to Probe Forecasts Made as AOL Chiefs Sold Shares," *Financial Times*, 23 August 2002, p. 1; Diane Mermigas, "Investigation Dampening News of Deal," *Electronic Media*, 26 August 2002, p. 20.

163 Nanette Byrnes and Tom Lowry, "A Different Yardstick for Cable," *Business Week*, 2 September 2002, p. 56; Tamara Conniff, "Labels Upbraided at State Hearings on Accounting," www.hollywoodreporter.com, 25 September 2002.

164 "Eisner's Participation in IPO Under Review," Reuters dispatch, www.latimes.com, 18 December 2002; "Gemstar Announces Transition of SEC Probe to Formal Status," *Wall Street Journal Online*, 21 October 2002; David Streitfeld, "Feds Subpoena Firm Controlled by News Corp.," www.latimes.com, 3 October 2002; Sallie Hofmeister, "Charter to Slash Jobs in Wake of U.S. Probe," www.latimes.com, 11 December 2002;

Victor Mallet and Peter Thal Larsen, "Criminal Proble Deals Fresh Blow to Vivendi," *Financial Times*, 5 November 2002, p. 1; "Messier's Mess," *The Economist*, 8 June 2002, pp. 55–57; Jo Johnson and Peter Thal Larsen, "Vivendi Prepares to Face Legal Scrutiny," *Financial Times*, 10 January 2003, p. 20.

165 Peter Thal Larsen, Tally Goldstein, Jonathan Moules, and Peter Spiegel, "Former Adelphia Chiefs Arrested," *Financial Times*, 25 July 2002, p. 1. In 2003 newspaper baron Conrad Black became the subject of criminal investigations as well. See Tim Ariano and John Lehman, "FBI, U.S. Attorney Target Hollinger," *New York Post*, 17 December 2003.

166 Christopher Grimes, "AOL Inflated Advertising Revenues by Nearly $200M," *Financial Times*, 24 October 2002, p. 1; Peter Thal Larsen, "AOL Time Warner Sued Over Homestead Deals," *Financial Times*, 18 November 2002, p. 19; David R. Kirkpatrick, "New Charges Made in Suit On Homestore," *New York Times*, 16 November 2002; "A Steal?" *The Economist*, 26 October 2002, pp. 57–58; Martin Peers and Laurie P. Cohen, "SEC Probes AOL-Oxygen Pact for Double-Booking of Revenue," *Wall Street Journal Online*, 7 October 2002; Julia Angwin and Martin Peers, "Investment in Advertisers Was Key to AOL Income," *Wall Street Journal Online*, 26 August 2002; David D. Kirkpatrick and Saul Hansell, "U.S. Initiates Investigation of Accounting at AOL Unit," *New York Times*, 1 August 2002.

167 David D. Kirkpatrick and Simon Romero, "AOL's Swap Deals with 2 Others Said to Be a Focus of the S.E.C.," *New York Times*, 23 August 2002.

168 Kurt Eichenwald, "Fraud Charges Filed Against 2 Employees of Enron Unit," *New York Times*, 13 March 2003.

169 Miles Maguire, "Business as Usual," *American Journalism Review*, October 2002.

170 Bethany McLean and Peter Elkind, "Partners in Crime," *Fortune*, 27 October 2003, pp. 78–100.

171 Adrian Michaels and Joshua Chaffin, "Banks 'Were Aware of Enron Fraud,'" *Financial Times*, 29 July 2003, p. 1; Bethany McLean and Peter Elkind, "Enron Banks Dodge a Bullet," *Fortune*, 1 September 2003, p. 46.

172 Stephanie N. Mehta, "Well Connected," *Fortune*, 9 June 2003, p. 40.

173 "The Corporate Crime Wave: The Response," *Multinational Monitor*, December 2002, p. 5.

174 Evelyn Nieves and Elisabeth Bumiller, "In Twin Speeches, Bush and Cheney Vow to Fight Fraud," *New York Times*, 8 August 2002.

175 Richard S. Dunham, Amy Borrus, and Mike McNamee, with Lorraine Woellert, "Reform Lite," *Business Week*, 1 April 2002, pp. 30–32; Robert Kuttner, "So Much for Cracking Down on the Accountants," *Business Week*, 18 November 2002, p. 24.

176 Molly Ivins, "Surprise! Real Corporate Reform Isn't Happening," *Boulder Daily Camera*, 9 October 2002.

177 Mark Weisbrot, "Making Accountants Liable for Corporate Fraud," www.counterpunch.org, 2 January 2003.

178 Jennifer Loven, "Newspapers Warned about Bottom Line," Associated Press, 10 April 2002.

179 "Come Back, Ed Murrow," *The Economist*, 7 October 2000, p. 42; Paula Bernstein, "Serious Newscast Puffed Out," *Variety*, 6–12 November 2000, pp. 13, 17; Jacques Steinberg, "To Grab Young Readers, Newspapers Print Free, Jazzy Editions," *New York Times*, 1 December 2003.

180 Susan J. Douglas, "Navel-Gazing the News," *In These Times*, 20 January 2003, p. 9.

181 Felicity Barringer, "An Old-Times Newspaper War for Young Loyalists," *New York Times*, 31 October 2002; Oliver Burkman, "US Press Move to Youth Groove," *Guardian* (U.K.), 14 November 2002; Peter Johnson, "News Channels Losing Battle for Young Viewers," www.usatoday.com, 10 December 2002.

182 Jacques Steinberg, "New Papers Hope Free and Brief Will Attract Younger Readers," *New York Times*, 13 October 2003.

183 Bruce A. Williams and Michael X. Delli Carpini, "Heeeeeeeeeeeeere's Democracy!" *Chronicle of Higher Education*, 19 April 2002, p. B14; Don Kaplan, "Don't Trust Daily News," www.nypost.com, 23 November 2002.

184 Michael Schneider, "Local Newscasts Fall Victim to Cost Cuts," *Variety*, 25 January–3 February 2002, p. 22; Dan Trigoboff, "Live at 11? Maybe Not for Long," *Broadcasting & Cable*, 11 February 2002, p. 29.

185 Jaime McLeod, "Media Icon Walter Cronkite Remains as Sharp as Ever," www.moonrecordstar.com, 30 October 2002; David Halberstam, "The Powers That Were," *Brill's Content*, September 2000, pp. 23–26; Cris Ramon, "'Dateline' Reporter: Remain Critical of Media," www.dailynorthwestern.com, 13 November 2002; Michael Margolis, "PBS President Speaks on U.S., World Media," *Cornell Daily Sun*, 14 November 2002.

186 See, for example, William Serrin, ed., *The Business of Journalism* (New York: The New Press, 2000); Kristina Borjesson, ed., *Into the Buzzsaw: Leading Journalists Expose*

the Myth of a Free Press (Amherst, N.Y.: Prometheus Books, 2002).

187 Leonard Downie Jr. and Robert G. Kaiser, The News about the News: American Journalism in Peril (New York: Alfred A. Knopf, 2002).

188 Howard Gardner, Mihaly Csikszentmihalyi, and William Damon, Good Work: When Excellence and Ethics Meet (New York: Basic Books, 2001), chap. 7.

189 Deborah Potter, "Pessimism Rules in TV Newsrooms," Columbia Journalism Review, November–December 2002, p. 90.

190 Robert W. McChesney interview with Linda Foley, Washington D.C., July 2002.

191 Paul Simon, "The Pandering Trap," Editor & Publisher, 24 November 2003, p. 22.

192 Stebe Hinnefeld, "Survey Finds Journalists Happier with Jobs, Older," www.hoosiertimes.com, 11 April 2003.

193 Danielle M. Parker, "Study Asks Whether TV News Is Slipping," Electronic Media, 9 October 2000, p. 20; Rich Opel, "The Anticorporate Crowd's Foolish Self-Destruction," Austin American-Statesman, 8 December 2002.

CHAPTER 3

1   Bernard Goldberg, Bias: A CBS Insider Exposes How Media Distort the News (Regnery, 2001); Ann Coulter, Slander: Liberal Lies About the American Right (New York: Crown, 2002); Sean Hannity, Let Freedom Ring: Winning the War of Liberty Over Liberalism (New York: Regan Books, 2002).

2   Warren Breed. "Social Control in the Newsroom: A Functional Analysis," Social Forces 33, no. 4 (1955): 326–35.

3   Alexander Cockburn, "The Jayson Blair Affair," CounterPunch, 1–15 May 2003, p. 1.

4   Personal communication to author, 1 November 2003.

5   See, for a recent example, Kathleen Hall Jamieson and Paul Waldman, The Press Effect (New York: Oxford University Press, 2003).

6   Gingrich interview, Broadcasting & Cable, 20 March 1995.

7   Mike Mills, "Meeting of the Media Giants," Washington Post, 21 January 1995.

8   Lawrence Jarvik, PBS: Behind the Screen (Rocklin, Calif.: Forum, 1997).

9   Eric Alterman, What Liberal Media? (New York: Basic Books, 2003), pp. 19–20.

10   Greg Mitchell, "Readers Support Bush, Say Coverage Was Good," Editor & Publisher, 6 November 2000, pp. 7–9.

11   Goldberg, Bias, p. 25.

12   Alexander Stille, "Thinkers on the Left Get a Hearing Everywhere but at Home," New York Times, 11 November 2000; Antonia Zerbisias, "American Media Keep the Liberals Invisible," Toronto Star, 1 October 2002.

13   Christi Parsons, "Poll Says Many Back Gay Rights, ERA, Gun Limits," Chicago Tribune, 17 June 2003.

14   Nicholas D. Kristoff, "God, Satan, and the Media," New York Times, 4 March 2003; Alterman, What Liberal Media?, pp. 104–5.

15   David Croteau, "Challenging the 'Liberal Media' Claim: Journalists' Views on Politics, Economic Policy and Media Coverage," Extra!, July–August 1998, pp. 4–9.

16   Goldberg, Bias, pp. 21–24, 221–23.

17   Ibid., p. 167.

18   David Shaw, "Journalists Losing Touch with the Man on the Street," www.latimes.com, 8 December 2002.

19   Jamie Passaro, "Fingers to the Bone: Barbara Ehrenreich on the Plight of the Working Poor," The Sun, January 2003, p. 8.

20 Cited in Vicente Navarro, "The Inhuman State of U.S. Health Care," *Monthly Review*, September 2003, p. 56.

21 Cited in Tim Rutten, "Affluence Remakes the Newsroom," *Los Angeles Times*, 13 December 2003.

22 Croteau, "Challenging the 'Liberal Media' Claim," pp. 4–9.

23 John R. MacArthur, *The Selling of "Free Trade"* (New York: Hill and Wang, 2000).

24 An excellent discussion of this appears in Alterman, *What Liberal Media?*, chap. 8.

25 William McGowan, *Coloring the News: How Crusading for Diversity Has Corrupted American Journalism* (San Francisco: Encounter Books, 2001).

26 Alterman, *What Liberal Media?*, pp. 114–15.

27 Martin Gilens, *Why Americans Hate Welfare* (Chicago: University of Chicago Press, 1999).

28 Andrew Grossman, "Study Finds TV, Radio Newsrooms Lack Diversity," Reuters dispatch, 1 August 2003.

29 Goldberg, *Bias*, pp. 160–63.

30 Alterman, *What Liberal Media?*, p. 106.

31 Telephone interview with Jeff Cohen, senior producer, *Donahue*, MSNBC, December 2002.

32 Robert Parry, "Media-Homeless Liberals," www.consortiumnews.com, 13 November 2002.

33 Herbert Gans, *Deciding What's News* (New York: Pantheon, 1979), p. 190–93.

34 Cited Rutten, "Affluence remakes the Newsroom," 13 December 2003.

35 Greg Mitchell, "'Liberal' Papers More Likely to Criticize Clinton," *Editor & Publisher*, 11 August 2003.

36 Richard Blow, "Conservative Journalists' Dirty Little Secret," www.tompaine.com, 29 May 2003.

37 For an example of the slipshod evidence that brings discredit to the conservative argument, see L. Brent Bozell III and Brent H. Baker, eds., *And That's the Way It Isn't: A Reference Guide to Media Bias* (Alexandria, Va.: Media Research Center, 1990). For example, to establish that even media corporations like General Electric have a "liberal" bias, the authors point to how GE's philanthropic arm gives a few hundred thousand dollars annually to numerous mainstream groups (e.g., the NAACP, the Council on Foreign Relations, the Audubon Society). GE's enormous contributions to politicians and multimillion-dollar lobbying armada do not rate any mention whatsoever. Journalist bias is proven by taking short quotations by reporters out of context. By this crackerjack methodology one could probably make Rush Limbaugh, Oliver North, and Dick Cheney into Bolsheviks.

38 Greg Palast, "The Screwing of Cynthia McKinney," www.AlterNet.org, June 2003.

39 Quoted in *Washington Post*, 20 August 1992. Cited in Alterman, *What Liberal Media?*, p. 2.

40 See *Buying a Movement: Right-Wing Foundations and American Politics* (Washington, D.C.: People for the American Way, 1996).

41 Matt Bai, "Notion Building," *New York Times Magazine*, 12 October 2003, p. 85.

42 Joe Conason, "The BBC's Bullies Can Dish It Out, but They Can't Take It," *Guardian*, 18 September 2003.

43 Emma Ruby-Sachs and Timothy Waligore, "Alternative Voices on Campus," *The Nation*, 17 February 2003, pp. 27–29.

44 Sam Husseini, "Checkbook Analysis: Corporations Support Think Tanks— and the Favor Is Returned," *Extra!*, May/June, 2000, p. 23; Michael Dolny, "The Rich Get Richer," *Extra!*, May/June

2000, p. 23; Kim Campbell, "A Call to the Right," *Christian Science Monitor*, 25 July 2002; Kimberley Conniff, "All the Views Fit to Print," *Brill's Content*, March 2001; Blaine Harden, "In Virginia, Young Conservatives Learn How to Develop and Use Their Political Voices," *New York Times*, 11 June 2001.

45 Michael Dolny, "Spectrum Narrows Further in 2002," *Extra!*, July/August 2003, p. 29.

46 Robert Kuttner, "Comment: Philanthropy and Movements," *American Prospect*, 15 July 2002.

47 John F. Harris, "Mr. Bush Catches a Washington Break," *Washington Post*, 6 May 2001.

48 Bai, "Notion Building," p. 84.

49 Comment of Joesph Farah, in Mark O'Keefe, "Right Wing's Strength in Talk Radio, New Media Frustrates Democrats," Newhouse News Service, 24 November 2002.

50 Geoffrey Nunberg, "How Conservatives Pigeonholed Those Poor Liberals," *New York Times*, 2 March 2003.

51 Geoffrey Nunberg, "Label Whores," *The American Prospect*, 6 May 2002.

52 See, for example, Parry, "Media-Homeless Liberals"; Bill Carter and Jim Rutenberg, "Fox News Head Sent a Policy Note to Bush," *New York Times*, 19 November 2002; Steve Rendall, "Fox's Slanted Sources," *Extra!*, July–August 2001, p. 13.

53 Joe Conason, *Big Lies* (New York: St. Martin's Press, 2003), p. 42.

54 E. J. Dionne Jr., "The Rightward Press," *Washington Post*, 6 December 2002.

55 See *Washington Post* syndicated columnist Michael Kelly, "Media Now More Like the Public: Democratic," *News-Gazette*

(Champaign, Ill.), 20 December 2002.

56 Conason, *Big Lies*, p. 34.

57 The balance was, in effect, a balance of mainstream political positions.

58 Paul Fahri, "Talk Radio, Top Volume on the Right," *Washington Post*, 8 May 2002.

59 Bai, "Notion Building," pp. 84–85.

60 Point discussed in Steven Rendall, Jim Naureckas, and Jeff Cohen, *The Way Things Aren't: Rush Limbaugh's Reign of Error* (New York: The New Press, 1995), p. 116.

61 Steve Carney, "22% of Americans Get News from Talk Jocks," www.latimes.com, 10 January 2003.

62 Pamela McClintock and Michael Schneider, "Yakkers Get New Backers," *Variety*, 3–9 February 2003, p. 25.

63 Molly Ivins, "Media Concentration Is a Totalitarian Tool," *Boulder Daily Camera*, 31 January 2003.

64 Kimberley Pohlman, "Solid Ratings Don't Protect Progressive Radio Voices," *Extra!*, July/August 2000, p. 22.

65 Statistic provided by Paul Begala. Cited in "UAW CAP Conference Delegates Engage in Lively Discussion with Media Panel," www.uaw.org, 6 February 2001.

66 Robert W. McChesney interview with Rick Kaplan, Urbana, Ill., March 2002.

67 Conason, *Big Lies*, p. 43.

68 David Teather, "Memo Emerges to Haunt President," *Guardian*, 2 November 2002; Harold Evans, "The Watchdog Didn't Bark," www.salon.com, 16 July 2002; Paul Krugman, "The Insider Game," *New York Times*, 12 July 2002.

69 See reference in Alterman, *What Liberal Media?*, chap. 10; Conason, *Big Lies*, pp. 43–46.

70 Conason, *Big Lies*, p. 46; *Hardball with Chris Matthews*, MSNBC, 18 November 2003.

71 See Alterman, *What Liberal Media?*; Conason, *Big Lies*; Paul Krugman, *The Great Unraveling* (New York: W. W. Norton, 2003). In particular, Al Franken goes directly after Coulter and O'Reilly. Despite being marketed as a humor book, the case Franken makes that Coulter and O'Reilly are frauds is powerful. See Al Franken, *Lies and the Lying Liars Who Tell Them* (New York: Dutton, 2003).

72 Paul Krugman, "Lessons in Civility," *New York Times*, 10 October 2003.

73 "Watchdogs of War?" *Editor & Publisher*, 8 September 2003, p. 20; Greg Mitchell, "Why We Are in Iraq," *Editor & Publisher*, 8 September 2003, p. 26.

74 John L. Hess, *My Times: A Memoir of Dissent* (New York: Seven Stories Press, 2003), p. 7.

75 David D. Kirkpatrick, "Jessica Lynch Criticizes U.S. Accounts of Her Ordeal," *New York Times*, 7 November 2003; Lynda Hurst, "Jessica Lynch's Story Is Turning 'Into a Monster' for the Bush Administration," *Toronto Star*, 16 November 2003.

76 William E. Jackson Jr., "Now It's Miller Time," *Editor & Publisher*, 16 June 2003, p. 33.

77 Steve Pittelli, "When Will House Republicans Call for Bush's Impeachment?" www.commondreams.org, 17 June 2003.

78 Jim Rutenberg, "Left and Right Look for Signs of Bias in Reporting," *New York Times*, 19 March 2003.

79 Eric Margolis, "Bush's Tame Media May Yet Have Teeth," *Toronto Sun*, 21 September 2003.

80 Richard Wolffe and Rod Nordland, "Bush's New War," *Newsweek*, 27 October 2003.

81 Julia Day, "BBC's Dyke Attacks US War Coverage," www.mediaGuardian.co.uk, 25 November 2003.

82 Dana Milbank and Claudia Deane, "Hussein Link to 9/11 Lingers in Many Minds," *Washington Post*, 6 September 2003.

83 MSNBC, 24 February 2003.

84 Seth Porges, "Truth Was the First Casualty, Not Last," *Editor & Publisher*, 29 September 2003, p. 48.

85 Jim Lobe, "The Hazards of Watching Fox News," *Inter Press Service*, 6 October 2003; Jeff Cohen, "Bush and Iraq: Mass Media, Mass Ignorance," www.commondreams.org, 1 December 2003.

86 Terrence McNally, "Democracy in Deep Decay," AlterNet.org, www.alternet.org, 17 September 2002.

87 See Richard A. Posner, *Breaking the Deadlock* (Princeton, N.J.: Princeton University Press, 2001), p. 20.

88 Richard W. Stevenson, "Study Details Income Gap Between Rich and the Poor," *New York Times*, 31 May 2002.

89 Paul Krugman, "For Richer: How the Permissive Capitalism of the Boom Destroyed American Equality," *New York Times Magazine,* 20 October 2002, p. 65.

90 Cited in Paul Street, "Labor Day Reflections: Time as a Democracy Issue," ZNet Commentary, www.zmag.org, 3 September 2002.

91 Kevin Phillips, *Wealth and Democracy* (New York: Broadway Books, 2002).

92 Center for Public Integrity, *Our Private Legislatures: Public Service, Private Gain* (Washington, D.C.: The Center for Public Integrity, 2000), p. 1.

93 Two outstanding recent books that chronicle this decline in political participation are Thomas E. Patterson, *The Vanishing Voter: Public Involvement in an Age of Uncertainty* (New York: Alfred A. Knopf, 2002); Matthew A. Crenson and Benjamin Ginsberg, *Downsizing*

Democracy: How America Sidelined Its Citizens and Privatized Its Public (Baltimore: Johns Hopkins University Press, 2002).

94 Steve Basco, "The Vanishing Voter: Why Does This Describe Half of the U.S. Electorate? An Interview with Professor Thomas Patterson," www.tompaine. com, October 2002.

95 Steven Hill and Rashad Robinson, "Are Young People Too Smart to Vote?" article distributed by e-mail, October 2002.

96 For a recent treatment that emphasizes media, see Robert D. Putnam, *Bowling Alone: The Collapse and Revival of American Community* (New York: Simon & Schuster, 2000).

97 For a nice overview of the limitations of contemporary U.S. electoral journalism, see Thomas E. Patterson, *The Vanishing Voter: Public Involvement in an Age of Uncertainty* (New York: Alfred A. Knopf, 2002), chap. 3.

98 See Heather Maher, "11 O'Clock Blues," *Brill's Content*, February 2001.

99 Richard L. Berke, "Freshman Senator Sees the Presidency as His Next, and Second, Office," *New York Times*, 30 December 2002.

100 Basco, "The Vanishing Voter."

101 Howard Kurtz, "Local TV News and the Elections: Ads Infinitum, but Few Stories," *Washington Post*, 2 November 2002; Daisy Whitney, "Study: Stations Dropped Ball in Election Coverage," *Electronic Media*, 21 October 2002, p. 2.

102 See Maher, "11 O'Clock Blues."

103 "The Broadcast Industry and a Watchdog Group Trade Charges over Study of Publicized Debates," *The Political Standard*, July 2002, p. 6.

104 Steven Rosenfeld, "Is This News? Most TV Stations Aren't Covering the Elec-

tion: An Interview With Martin Kaplan, www.tompaine.com, October 2002.

105 Mary Carey, "Barney Frank Takes Media Coverage to Task," www.gazettenet.com, 6 May 2003.

106 Cited in Norman Solomom, "California's Populist Revival," www.commondreams.org, 28 September 2003.

107 Alliance for Better Campaigns, *Gouging Democracy: How the Television Industry Profiteered on Campaign 2000* (Washington, D.C.: n.d.), p. 15; Alliance for Better Campaigns press release, 11 November 2002.

108 Paul Taylor, "TV's Political Profits," *Mother Jones*, May–June 2000, p. 31.

109 Jennifer Harper, "Local Hopefuls Receive Little Coverage in Newscasts," *Washington Times*, 17 October 2002.

110 Stuart Elliott, "Advertising," *New York Times*, 18 June 2003.

111 "Media Advertising: Huge '04 Seen for Politicals; $1.6 Billion to TV Stations; Viacom Benefits Most," *Bernstein Research Call*, 1 December 2003.

112 Alliance for Better Campaigns press release, November 11, 2002.

113 Jim Rutenberg, "TV's Intense Glare Makes the Odd California Campaign Seem Even Odder," *New York Times*, 2 October 2003.

114 Jim Rutenberg, "Early Flood of Political Ads Saturates Airwaves in Iowa," *New York Times*, 4 December 2003.

115 Paul Janensch, "Media Partly at Fault for Poor Turnout," www.ctnow.com, 7 November 2002.

116 Peter Marks, "Commercials Dominating Politics on TV, Studies Find," *New York Times*, 13 June 2000.

117 See, for example, "Aided by Political Ads, Belo Shows a Profit," *New York Times*, 8 February 2003.

118 Paul Taylor, "Too Little Time,"
     The Washington Monthly, September 2000.

119 Kathy Haley, "A Candidate for Growth,"
     Broadcasting & Cable, 24 November 2003,
     p. 16.

120 Barbara Bliss Osborn, "Election
     Neglected on L.A.'s Local TV," *Extra!*,
     July/August 1997, p. 14.

121 "Campaign-Season Newscasts Contained
     Little Campaign News," *The Political
     Standard*, May 2003, p. 4.

122 John Dunbar, "Broadcast Lobby Defeats
     Provision of Campaign Finance Reform
     Bill," www.public-i.org, 7 March 2002;
     Howard Kurtz, "The Story that Wouldn't
     Live," *Washington Post*, 25 February 2002.

123 See, for example, David M. Haldfinger,
     "Veteran Battles Charge He's Soft on
     Defense," *New York Times*, 28 October
     2002; Peter Marks, "G.O.P. Counterat-
     tacks Quickly after Democrats' TV AD,"
     New York Times, 11 June 2000; Helene
     Cooper, "Gore, Bush to Step Up Their
     Campaigns with Competing TV-
     Advertising Blitzes," *Wall Street Journal*,
     21 August 2000.

124 See, for example, Stephen Ansolabehere
     and Shanto Iyengar, *Going Negative:
     How Political Advertisements Shrink and
     Polarize the Electorate* (New York:
     The Free Press, 1995).

125 John Buell, "Looking to Paul Wellstone's
     Legacy," www.commondreams.org,
     6 November 2002.

126 Jennifer 8. Lee, "A Call for Softer, Greener
     Language," *New York Times*, 2 March 2003.

127 Ira Teinowitz, "Political Ads Hit $1 Bil
     Mark," *Advertising Age*, 4 November 2002,
     pp. 3, 50; Stefano Hatfield, "The Vitriol
     in Political Ads Badly Serves U.S.
     Elections," *Advertising Age*, 11 November
     2002, p. 20.

128 See, for example, Ira Teinowitz, "No Ad
     Victory in 2000 Race for Bush, Gore,"
     Advertising Age, 30 October 2000, p. 12;
     Jodi Wilgoren, "Ad-Weary Ask, 'Is It
     Wednesday Yet?,'" *New York Times*,
     4 November 2000.

129 Mark Green, "The Evil of Access," *The
     Nation*, 30 December 2002, p. 16.

130 Alliance for Better Campaigns, *The Case
     for Free Air Time* (Washington, D.C.:
     Alliance for Better Campaigns, 2002).

131 David J. Garrow, "Ruining the House,"
     New York Times, 13 November 2002.

132 "How to Rig an Election," *The Economist*,
     27 April 2002, p. 29.

133 Alliance for Better Campaigns, *The Case
     for Free Air Time* , p. 36.

134 Richard A. Oppel Jr., "Governors' Races
     Reach New Highs in Expenditures,"
     New York Times, 17 September 2002.

135 Adam Nagourney, "Politicians Turn to
     Alternatives to TV Advertising," *New York
     Times*, 5 September 2002.

136 See, for example, Larry Makinson,
     *Speaking Freely: Washington Insiders Talk
     about Money in Politics*, 2nd ed.
     (Washington, D.C.: Center for
     Responsive Politics, 2003).

137 Rick Pearson, "Political Ads on TV Early
     and Often, Study Finds," *Chicago Tribune*,
     31 July 2003.

138 Ellen S. Miller, "The Elephant in the
     Living Room," www.tompaine.com,
     December 2002.

139 Nick Nyhart and Joan Claybrook,
     "The Dash for Cash," *Los Angeles Times*,
     27 April 2003.

140 James Harding, "As 2004 Looms, Bush
     Sets Out to Double His Campaign Funds,"
     Financial Times, 20 May 2003, p. 13.

141 Nyhart and Claybrook, "The Dash for
     Cash."

142 Alan B. Krueger, "Lobbying by Business Overwhelms Their Campaign Contributions," *New York Times*, 19 September 2002.

143 For a recent example, see Mark Green, *Selling Out: How Big Corporate Money Buys Elections, Rams Through Legislation, and Betrays Our Democracy* (New York: Regan Books, 2002). See also, for example, Donald L. Bartlett and James B. Steele, "How the Little Guy Gets Crunched," *Time*, 7 February 2000; "The Corporate Tax Break Feeding Frenzy," *Multinational Monitor*, November 2001, pp. 24–25; Amy Borrus and Lorraine Woellert, "Populism Takes a Bank Holiday," *Business Week*, 16 September 2002, p. 62; Tom Hanburger, Laurie McGinley and David S. Cloud, "Industries that Backed Bush Are Now Seeking Return on Investment," *Wall Street Journal*, 6 March 2002; Stephen A. Labaton, "Bush Is Putting Team in Place for a Full-Bore Assault on Regulation," *New York Times*, 23 May 2001.

144 Edmund L. Andrews, "Economic Inequality Grew in 90s Boom, Fed Reports," *New York Times*, 23 January 2003.

145 Gar Alpcrovitz, "Tax the Plutocrats!" *The Nation*, 23 January 2003, p. 15.

146 Huck Gutman, "Corporate Tax Evasion on an Enormous Scale," www.commondreams.org, 28 February 2003.

147 David Cay Johnston, "Departing Chief Says the I.R.S. Is Losing Its War on Tax Cheats," *New York Times*, 5 November 2002.

148 See Charles Lewis and the Center for Public Integrity, *The Buying of the President 2000* (New York: Avon Books, 2000); Charles Lewis and the Center for Public Integrity, *The Buying of the Congress* (New York: Avon Books, 1998). See also Don Van Natta Jr. and John M. Broder, "The Few, the Rich, the Rewarded Donate the Bulk of G.O.P Gifts," *New York Times*, 2 August 2000.

149 Don Van Natta Jr. and John M. Broder, "Among Lobbyists, a Trend Toward Ambidextrous Aid," *New York Times*, 16 August 2000.

150 Robert B. Reich, "Corporate Power in Overdrive," *New York Times*, 18 March 2001.

151 Bill Moyers, "Where Are the Democrats?," www.commondreams.org, 7 March 2003.

152 Philip Meyer, "Lax Media Let Legislators Hide Ties," *USA Today*, 30 October 2002; Diane Renzulli and the Center for Public Integrity, *Capitol Offenders: How Private Interests Govern Our States* (Washington: Public Integrity Books, 2000).

153 Consider the common pattern of public officials becoming lobbyists to capitalize upon their contacts and knowledge, or the use of relatives of politicians to serve as lobbyists. Once regarded with suspicion, if not considered unethical, it is now commonplace. See Leslie Wayne, "Trading Their Names: Turning Government Experience into Corporate Advice," *New York Times*, 23 May 2001; Carl Hulse, "In Capitol, Last Names Link Some Leaders and Lobbyists," *New York Times*, 4 August 2002.

154 See Matthew Miller, "Tyranny of Symbols," *Columbia Journalism Review*, November/December 2003, pp. 26–33.

155 See Steven Hill, *Fixing Elections: The Failure of America's Winner Take All Elections* (New York: Routledge, 2002).

156 Jim Rutenberg, "Some Democratic Hopefuls Question Value of Debates," *New York Times*, 25 October 2003.

157 See John Nichols, *Jews for Buchanan* (New York: The New Press, 2001); Alterman, *What Liberal Media?*, chap. 11. Even arguments on behalf of Bush winning Florida and the election are not predicated on the claim that he was the choice of a plurality or majority of Florida voters, but, rather, legalistic claims about whether votes should be included that would have almost certainly made Gore the winner. See Richard A. Posner, *Breaking the Deadlock* (Princeton, N.J.: Princeton University Press, 2001).

158 See Nichols, *Jews for Buchanan.*

159 Richard L. Berke, "Lieberman Put Democrats In Retreat on Military Vote," *New York Times*, 15 July 2001. See also John Lantigua, "How the GOP Gamed the System in Florida," *The Nation*, 30 April 2001, pp. 11–17.

160 Posner, *Breaking the Deadlock,* makes a case for justifying the decision, but does so by offering an alternative justification than the one provided by the court. Other evaluations have been savage and devastating in their criticism of the opportunism and corruption of the Supreme Court in overturning the ruling of the Florida Supreme Court. See Alan Dershowitz, *Supreme Injustice: How the High Court Hijacked Election 2000* (New York: Oxford University Press, 2001); Vincent Bugliosi, *The Betrayal of America* (New York: Thunder's Mouth Press, 2001).

161 See, for example, Lisa Getter, "Florida Net Too Wide in Purge of Voter Rolls," *Los Angeles Times*, 21 May 2002; David Barstow and Don Van Natta Jr., "How Bush Took Florida: Mining the Overseas Absentee Vote," *New York Times*, 15 July 2001.

162 See, for example, Jackie Calmes and Edward P. Foldessy, "In Election Review, Bush Wins without Supreme Court Help," *Wall Street Journal*, 21 November 2001; Ford Fessenden and John M. Broder, "Study of Disputed Ballots Finds Justices Did Not cast the Deciding Vote," *New York Times*, 12 November 2001.

163 "Read All About It? Bush Was Winner," *News-Gazette* (Champaign, Ill.), 13 November 2001.

164 Miranda Spencer, "Who Won the Election? Who Cares?" *Extra!*, January–February 2002, pp. 21–24; Gore Vidal, "*Times* Cries Eke! Buries Al Gore," *The Nation*, 17 December 2001, pp. 13–15;

165 Jay T. Harris, "News and Profits," *The Nation*, 28 May 2001, p. 6.

166 James Carey, "American Journalism on, before, and after September 11," in *Journalism after September 11,* ed. Barbie Zelizer and Stuart Allan (London and New York: Routledge, 2002), p. 89.

CHAPTER 4

1 See Daniel Pope, *The Making of Modern Advertising* (New York: Basic Books, 1983), chap. 2.

2 Stuart Elliott, "Forecasters Expect End to Ad Industry's Recession in 2004," *New York Times*, 9 December 2003.

3 Statistics can be found at www.adage.com.

4 Stuart Elliott, "Advertising's Big Four: It's Their World Now," *New York Times*, 31 March 2002.

5 "Five Claim 76% of Ad Revenue," *Advertising Age*, 21 April 2003, p. S1.

6 "World's Top 25 Ad Organizations," *Advertising Age*, 21 April 2003, p. S4.

7 "Star Turn," *The Economist*, 11 March 2000, p. 67.

8 Meg James, "Disney Sells a $1-Billion Ad Package," www.latimes.com, 11 June

2002; Christopher Grimes, "Cross-Plat-form Clout," *Financial Times*, 4 February 2002; Julia Angwin, "AOL Lands Toyota for Multimedia Pact," *Wall Street Journal*, 28 August 2001; Richard Tomkins, "A Deal that Sends a Message to the World," *Financial Times*, 1 June 2001, p. 19; Emily Nelson and Vanessa O'Connell, "P&G and Viacom Sign Broad Ad Accord," *Wall Street Journal*, 31 May 2001; Chuck Ross, "OMD Doing $1 Billion Deals," *Electronic Media*, 6 May 2002, pp. 1, 46; Eric Garland, "Disney Enters Into a New Kind of Advertising Deal," *New York Times Online*, 21 June 2002.

9   Jennie L. Phipps, "Firm Breathes New Life into Old Commercials," *Television Week*, 15 December 2003, p. 18.

10   For a critical view of advertising's negative externalities, see Paul Rutherford, *Endless Propaganda: The Advertising of Public Goods* (Toronto: University of Toronto Press, 2000).

11   Oliver James, "Materially Richer but Emotionally Poorer: Consumer Society Is Wrecking Our Minds as well as the Planet," *The CCPA Monitor*, April 2001.

12   Alissa Quart, *Branded: The Buying and Selling of Teenagers* (Cambridge, Mass.: Perseus Publishing, 2003), chap. 9.

13   Rance Crain, "Take Me Out to the Ball Game, If Only to Escape Fox Promos," *Advertising Age*, 4 November 2002, p. 20.

14   Charles Pappas, "Ad Nauseum," *Advertising Age*, 10 July 2000, p. 16.

15   Brian Steinberg, "Staid U.S. Marketers Try Racier Ads," *Wall Street Journal*, 31 July 2003.

16   Naomi Klein, *No Logo* (New York: Picador USA, 2000), p. 9.

17   Joe Flint and Emily Nelson, "CBS's Pulling of 'Family Law' Rerun Underscores Advertiser's Current Clout,"

Wall Street Journal, 20 August 2001.

18   See chapter 2, "Understanding U.S. Journalism I: Corporate Control and Professionalism."

19   See, for example, Ronald K. L. Collins, *Dictating Content: How Advertising Pressure Can Corrupt a Free Press* (Washington, D.C.: Center for the Study of Commercialism, 1992).

20   Theodore Peterson, *Magazines in the Twentieth Century* (Urbana, Ill.: University of Illinois Press, 1964).

21   The classic work on this is Erik Barnouw, *The Sponsor: Notes on a Modern Potentate* (New York: Oxford University Press, 1978).

22   J. Max Robins, "Increasingly, TV's a Mess of Messages," www.tvguide.com, 3 February 2002.

23   Vanessa O'Connell, "Amount of Ad 'Clutter' on Prime-Time TV Drops," *Wall Street Journal*, 1 March 2001; Chuck Ross, "Peacock Clutters Up Airwaves," *Electronic Media*, 7 August 2000, pp. 1, 39; Louis Chunovic, "ABC Again No. 1 on Clutter List," *Electronic Media*, 2 September 2002, pp. 1, 39; Joe Flint, "Commercial Clutter on TV Networks Rises to Record," *Wall Street Journal*, 2 March 2000.

24   Paul Taylor, "Too Little Time," *The Washington Monthly*, September 2000.

25   Louis Chunovic, "TV Clutter Reaches All-Time High," *Electronic Media*, 11 March 2002, pp. 1, 29.

26   Andrew Green, "Clutter Crisis," *Advertising Age*, 21 April 2003, p. 22.

27   J. Max Robins, "Increasingly, TV's a Mess of Messages," www.tvguide.com, 3 February 2002.

28   Dan Trigoboff, "Spot Squeeze Play in Nashville," *Broadcasting & Cable*, 21 October 2002, pp. 6–7; Michelle Greppi,

"Squeezed Shoes Upset Agencies," *Electronic Media*, 19 November 2001, pp. 1, 20; Michelle Greppi, "CBS Time Squeeze Scandal Widens," *Electronic Media*, 12 November 2001, pp. 1, 43; Dan Trigoboff, "Squeeze Play in Pittsburgh?" *Broadcasting & Cable*, 5 November 2001, p. 14.

29   Adam Bruckman, "Time to Cut Clueless Clutter," www.nypost.com, 21 August 2001.

30   Roger Baron, "Missing in Action: The 2002 Clutter Report," *Television Week*, 28 April 2003, p. 21.

31   Matthew Boyle, "Brand Killers," *Fortune*, 11 April 2003, p. 94.

32   Kate MacArthur, "Turner CEO Lambasts Ad-Avoiding Technologies," www.adage.com, 11 October 2002.

33   Richard Tomkins, "As Television Audiences Tire of Commercials, Advertisers Move into Making Programmes," *Financial Times*, 5 November 2002, p. 15.

34   Bill Carter, "NBC Is Hoping Short Movies Keep Viewers from Zapping," *New York Times*, 4 August 2003, pp. C1, C7; Richard Linnett, "NBC Uses Films to Boost Ad Viewership," *Advertising Age*, 18 August 2003, p. 27.

35   Wayne Friedman, "Coming to a Theater Near You: Targeted, Digital Ad Buying," *Advertising Age*, 21 October 2002, pp. 4, 57.

36   Russell Scott Smith, "When Ads Attack," www.nypost.com, 7 March 2003.

37   Wayne Friedman, "Cinema-Ad Seller Offers Big-Screen Creative via Aspect," *Advertising Age*, 3 February 2003, p. 6.

38   Hank Kim, "Madison Ave. Melds Pitches and Content," *Advertising Age*, 7 October 2002, p. 16.

39   Vernon Scott, "'E.T.' Invades Five More Continents," United Press International, 2 November 1982.

40   Michael McCarthy, "Digitally Inserted Ads Pop Up in World Series," www.usatoday.com, 18 October 2002.

41   Michael McCarthy, "Ads Show Up in Unexpected Places," *USA Today*, 23 March 2001.

42   David Goetzl, "TBS Tries Virtual Advertising," *Advertising Age*, 21 May 2001, p. 8; Stuart Elliott, "Advertising: Reruns May Become Testing Ground for Digital Insertion," www.nytimes.com, 23 May 2001.

43   Christy Grosz and Dan Bronson, "When Worlds Collide," *Hollywood Reporter*, 28 April 2003.

44   Kate MacArthur, "Coke Consolidation in Line with Strategy," *Advertising Age*, 1 December 2003, p. 3.

45   Matthew Rose and Suzanne Vranica, "Prolonged Ad Slump Puts Media In the Mood to Pander to Buyers," *Wall Street Journal Online*, 9 May 2002.

46   Chuck Ross, "USA Cozies Up to Advertisers," *Electronic Media*, 18 December 2000, pp. 1, 35.

47   Corie Brown, "Advertisers Seek a Bigger Role in TV Programming," www.latimes.com, January 15, 2002.

48   Laurie Freeman, "If the Product Fits a Series, TNT Wants It," *Electronic Media*, 27 November 2000, pp. 12, 59.

49   Debra Aho Williamson, "G4 Widens Playing Field for Advertisers," *Advertising Age*, 10 June 2002, p. S-14.

50   Andrew Wallenstein, "Brands Taking Place in Spotlight," *Hollywood Reporter*, 13 October 2003.

51   "ABC, Ad Agency to Develop TV Shows," Reuters, 2 December 2003. See also Richard Linnett, "ABC, Mindshare Looking for Scripts," *Advertising Age*, 8 December 2003, p. 35.

52 "ABC Partners with Advertisers Beyond
    Commercials," *Advertising Age*, special
    advertising section, 15 September 2003,
    p. S1.

53 "*Alias* Is Ford Focused," Robins Report,
    www.tvguide.com, 24 February 2003.

54 "A Coke and a Smile," *Variety*, 17–23
    July 2000, p. 5.

55 Anna Wilde Mathews, "Ford Motor
    Gets Starring Role on WB Network,"
    Wall Street Journal, 21 March 2001.

56 Dan Bronson, "Figured Out," *Hollywood
    Reporter*, 28 April 2003.

57 Richard Tomkins, "As Television
    Audiences Tire of Commercials,
    Advertisers Move into Making Pro-
    grammes," *Financial Times*,
    5 November 2002, p. 15.

58 Stuart Elliott, "On ABC, Sears Pays to Be
    Star of New Series," *New York Times*,
    3 December 2003.

59 Bill Carter, "Survival of the Pushiest,"
    New York Times Magazine, 28 January
    2001, p. 25.

60 Wayne Friedman, "Magna Sells NBC on
    Reality Series," *Advertising Age*,
    18 November 2003, p. 3.

61 Tony Wilbert, "Home Depot to Sponsor
    New Reality Show (Among Others),"
    Atlanta Journal-Constitution, 3 October 2003.

62 The producers of *Seinfeld* may well have
    done the program independent of
    compensation from the candy bar, but
    the point here is not about *Seinfeld* but
    about the value of product placement.

63 Louis Chunovic, "Placing Value on
    Placement," *Electronic Media*, 2 December
    2002, p. 6.

64 Meg James, "Nielsen to Follow Popularity
    of Product Placement on Prime-Time
    Television," *Los Angeles Times*, 5 December
    2003; Joe Mandese, "Nielsen Unveils

New Service," *Television Week*, 8 December
    2003, p. 17.

65 Claire Atkinson, "Absolut Nabs Sexy HBO
    Role," *Advertising Age*, 4 August 2003, p. 6.

66 Joe Flint and Emily Nelson, "TV 'Plot
    Placement' Yields ABC a Big Advertising
    Buy," *Wall Street Journal Online*,
    15 March 2002.

67 Andrew Wallenstein, "ESPN Looks into
    Longer, Hybrid Ads," www.holly-
    woodreporter.com, 24 September 2002.

68 Kate MacArthur, "Wendy's, ESPN Ink
    Promo," *Advertising Age*, 14 April 2003, p. 4.

69 Alice Z. Cuneo, "Ace Ads on 'MNF'
    Starring Madden Blur Content Line,"
    Advertising Age, 2 September 2002, p. 3.

70 Nat Ives, "Still More Brand Names to Get
    Star Roles in a Fox Sports Show," *New
    York Times*, 3 January 2003.

71 Richard Linnett, "Fox Sports Specialty:
    Product 'Immersion,'" *Advertising Age*,
    20 January 2003, p. 3.

72 Jon Fine, "On-Air Plug Pact Creates
    Debate," *Advertising Age*, 16 June 2003, p. 3.

73 See David Desser and Garth S. Jowett,
    eds., *Hollywood Goes Shopping* (Minneapo-
    lis, Minn.: University of Minnesota
    Press, 2000).

74 Wayne Friedman, "'Minority Report'
    Stars Lexus, Nokia," *Advertising Age*,
    17 June 2002, p. 41.

75 Bruce Orwall, "Miramax Coors Deal
    Married Entertainment and Advertis-
    ing," *Wall Street Journal Online*, 8 August
    2002; Kate MacArthur, "Coors Slammed
    for Targeting Kids," *Advertising Age*,
    3 November 2003, pp. 1, 59.

76 Lee Pfeiffer, "License to Shill," *Variety*,
    11–17 November 2002; "James Bond
    at 40" special section, p. A13.

77 Marc Graser, "007's Bid Ad-Venture,"
    Variety, 7–13 October 2002, pp. 1, 105;

Tim Burt, "His Name's Bond, James Bond and He's Been Licensed to Sell," *Financial Times*, 5–6 October 2002, p. 22.

78 Nicholas Foulkes, "James Bond," *Financial Times*, 16–17 November 2002, Weekend FT section, p. x.

79 Wayne Friedman, "Goss Ties It All Together at Universal's Brand Group," *Advertising Age*, 9 December 2002, p. 38.

80 T. L. Stanley, "New Line Forms Marketing Group," *Advertising Age*, 29 September 2003, p. 8.

81 T. L. Stanley, "Universal Asks Brands: Can We Be Co-Creators?" *Advertising Age*, 24 November 2003, p. 10.

82 Jon Lafayette, "VH1 Plans to Serve Up Liquor Ads," *Television Week*, 8 December 2003, p. 4.

83 Stuart Elliott, "Thanks to Cable, Liquor Ads Find a TV Audience," *New York Times*, 15 December 2003.

84 Matt Richtel, "Product Placements Go Interactive in Video Games," *New York Times*, 17 September 2002.

85 Stephanie N. Mehta, "Ads Invade Videogame!" *Fortune*, 26 May 2003, p. 46.

86 David D. Kirkpatrick, "Words from Our Sponsor: A Jeweler Commissions a Novel," www.nytimes.com, 3 September 2001; Tim Rutten, "Read Between the Lines and You Might See Commercials," www.latimes.com, 19 June 2002.

87 David Carr, "Magazine Imitates a Catalog and Has a Charmed Life, So Far," *New York Times*, 16 September 2002.

88 David Carr, "Men's Shopping Magazine Is Under Study," *New York Times*, 7 March 2003.

89 Vanessa O'Connell, "Omnicom, NBC Discuss Unusual TV Deal," *Wall Street Journal*, 5 July 2001; Richard Linnett, "McCann Creates Sponsor-Friendly TV Program Unit," *Advertising Age*, 21 August 2000, p. 4; Richard Linett, "Content Contenders," *Advertising Age*, 9 October 2000, pp. 20, 22.

90 Bill Carter, "Skipping Ads? TV Gets Ready to Fight Back," *New York Times*, 10 January 2003.

91 Erin White, "Movie-Trailer Ads Blur the Lines of Entertainment and Advertising," *Wall Street Journal Online*, 22 July 2002; Sheila Muto, "Theaters Showcase Product Pitches," *Wall Street Journal*, 29 August 2001.

92 Michael Schneider, " 'Wild' Infomercial Struts Its Stuff," *Variety*, 9–15 December 2002, p. 32.

93 Brad Pomerance, "Infomercials Take Soft-Sell Approach," *Television Week*, 29 September 2003, p. 12.

94 Louis Chunovic, "Stretching Beer Spots to 7 1/2 Minutes," *Electronic Media*, 10 February 2003, p. 3.

95 Wayne Friedman, "Chrysler Seeks Influence with Young Filmmakers," *Advertising Age*, 3 February 2003, p. 3; Grosz and Bronson, "When Worlds Collide."

96 White, "Movie-Trailer Ads Blur the Lines of Entertainment and Advertising"; Sheila Muto, "Theaters Showcase Product Pitches," *Wall Street Journal*, 29 August 2001.

97 Mark Gimien, "Program-Free Commercials," www.fortune.com, 1 April 2002.

98 David Goetzl, "BMW Rolls Out DirecTV Channel," *Advertising Age*, 23 September 2002, p. 55.

99 Nat Ives, "Advertising," *New York Times*, 4 November 2002.

100 Mark A. Stein, "Standing Up for Herself, If Somewhat Reluctantly," *New York Times*, 11 May 2003.

101 Richard Tomkins, "As Television Audiences Tire of Commercials, Advertisers

Move Into Making Programmes," *Financial Times*, 5 November 2002, p. 15.

102 Jane Weaver, "That's Advertainment," www.msnbc.com, 9 October 2002.

103 Scott Donaton, "Steve Berman Hears Music in Alliances with Advertisers," *Advertising Age*, 7 April 2003, p. 18.

104 Sherri Day, "Advertising," *New York Times*, 12 November 2002.

105 Jean Halliday, "Toyota Links with Phil Collins," *Advertising Age*, 14 October 2002, p. 8.

106 Jean Halliday, "Automakers Turn to Music," *Advertising Age*, 19 Aug. 2002, p. 6.

107 "Chevrolet Is 'Religiously' Supporting 'Rolling Stone,' Too," www.minonline. com, November 2002.

108 Nat Ives, "Advertising," *The New York Times*, November 6, 2002, p. C3.

109 Wayne Friedman, "Music Labels Court Brands," *Advertising Age,* 16 September 2002, p. 19 (emphasis added).

110 Claire Atkinson and Jean Halliday, "Corporate America Cozies Up to Hip-Hop," *Advertising Age*, 13 October 2003, p. 4.

111 Lynette Holloway, "Hip-Hop Sales Pop: Pass the Courvoisier and Count the Cash," *New York Times*, 2 September 2002.

112 Hank Kim, "Def Jam, H-P Explore Branded Music Alliance," *Advertising Age*, 9 September 2002, pp. 4, 28.

113 Rich Thomaselli and Cara B. DiPasquale, "Keeper of the Flame," *Advertising Age*, 23 September 2002, p. 16.

114 See, for examples of this, "Got Something to Sell? Sign a Rapper," *Business Week*, 27 October 2003, p. 94.

115 Erik Parker, "Hip-Hop Goes Commercial," *Village Voice*, 11–17 September 2002. Online at www.villagevoice.com.

116 Brian Lowry, "Now, A Column from Our Sponsors," *Los Angeles Times*, 18 May 2003.

117 Wayne Friedman, "MasterCard, Universal Eye $100 Mil Deal," *Advertising Age*, 2 December 2002, pp. 1, 56.

118 Scott Donaton, "'Restaurant' Serves Up Lesson in How Not to Integrate Brands," *Advertising Age*, 11 August 2003, p. 14.

119 "How Hollywood Brings Brands Into Your Home," *Financial Times*, 5 November 2002, p. 15.

120 Brian Lowry, "Going Far Beyond Product Placement," www.latimes.com, 10 July 2002.

121 Lowry, "Now, a Column from Our Sponsors."

122 Janet Stilson, "Placements Push to Front," *Advertising Age*, 9 June 2003, p. S-8.

123 See David Bollier, *Silent Theft: The Private Plunder of our Common Wealth* (New York: Routledge, 2002).

124 See, for example, Stephanie Thompson, "Pepsi Hits High Note with Schools," *Advertising Age*, 9 October 2002, p. 30; Karen W. Arenson, "Columbia Leads Academic Pack in Turning Profit from Research," *New York Times*, 2 August 2000; Joan Obra, Stacy Schwandt, and Peter Woodall, "Corporate Donors' Influence Spilling into UC Classrooms," *San Francisco Chronicle*, 26 June 2002; Eyal Press and Jennifer Washburn, "The Kept University," *Atlantic Monthly*, March 2000; Henry Giroux and Kostas Myrsiades, eds., *Beyond the Corporate University: Culture and Pedagogy in the New Millennium* (Lanham, Md.: Rowman & Littlefield, 2001); Chin-tao Wu, *Privatising Culture: Corporate Art Intervention since the 1980s* (London: Verso, 2002).

125 See www.commercialalert.org.

126 Derek Bok, *Universities in the Marketplace* (Princeton, N.J.: Princeton University Press, 2003), p. 12.

127 Sheldon Krimsky, *Science in the Private Interest* (Lanham, Md.: Rowman & Littlefield, 2003), p. 3.

128 Sharon J. Kahn, "Corporate America Discovers Key Demos in Indie Scene," *Variety*, 26 August–1 September 2002, Film Fest Guide, p. 5.

129 Thomas Frank and Matt Weiland, eds., *Commodify Your Dissent: Salvos from the Baffler* (New York: W. W. Norton, 1997).

130 Inger L. Stole, "The Gift that Keeps on Giving: Cause Related Marketing in the 1990s," paper presented to the Association for Consumer Research annual convention, Atlanta, Ga., October 2002.

131 See Al Ries and Lauar Ries, *The Fall of Advertising and the Rise of PR* (New York: HarperCollins, 2002); Sergio Zyman with Armin Brott, *The End of Advertising as We Know It* (Hoboken, N.J.: John Wiley & Sons, 2002).

132 Joe Mandese, "It's PR Time for Miller," *Television Week*, 1 December 2003, p. 15.

133 Kenneth Wylie, "Integrated Agencies," *Advertising Age*, 19 May 2003, p. S1.

134 See Todd Gitlin, *Media Unlimited* (New York: Metropolitan Books, 2001); Anna McCarthy, *Ambient Television* (Durham: Duke University Press, 2001).

135 R. J. Smith, "Among the Mooks," *New York Times Magazine*, 6 August 2000, pp. 34–41; John De Graaf, David Wann, Thomas H. Naylor, *Affluenza: The All-Consuming Epidemic* (San Francisco: Berrett-Koehler Publishers, 2001).

136 David Shaw, "A Nation Under Siege . . . by Product Placement," www.latimes.com, 3 November 2002; David W. Dunlap, "New York Tells Microsoft to Get Its Butterfly Decals Out of Town," *New York Times*, 25 October 2002.

137 Sheila Muto, "Signage It Is: More Buildings Sport Billboards," *Wall Street Journal*, January 10, 2001, p. B10.

138 Randy Kennedy, "Hail a Cab, Read a Commercial," *New York Times*, 26 August 2001; Motoko Rich, "Firms Pitch New Place to Park Ads," *Wall Street Journal*, 11 July 2001; Anna Wilde Mathews, "Clear Channel Readies Plan for Video Ads in Subways," *Wall Street Journal Online*, 23 December 2002; Gerard O'Dwyer and Bill Britt, "The New Billboards: Buggies," *Advertising Age*, 19 August 2002, p. 11; Reed Tucker, "Would You Put Your Ad on Toilet Paper?" *Fortune*, 4 March 2003.

139 Robert Johnson, "Ad-packed TVs May Soon Be Boarding City Buses," *Wall Street Journal*, 21 February 2001; Jack Neff, "Vendors Seek to Become Checkstand Media Moguls," *Advertising Age*, 6 March 2000, p. 36; Louis Chunovic, "These TV Channels Can't Be Turned Off," *Electronic Media*, 25 June–2 July 2001, p. 16; Geraldine Baum, "Taking News Overload to the Next Level," www.calendarlive.com, 14 October 2002.

140 Stuart Elliott, "A 'Brand Experience' on the Monorail as Ads Infiltrate New Arenas," *New York Times*, 18 November 2003.

141 Louis Chunovic, "GE Goes to Hospitals with Patient Channel," *Electronic Media*, 16 September 2002, p. 8.

142 Greg Johnson, "Nowhere to Run, Nowhere to Hide from Ad Barrage," www.latimes.com, 24 July 2001.

143 Alice Z. Cuneo, "Challenge for Wal-Mart TV: Getting Shoppers' Attention," *Advertising Age*, 6 October 2003, p. 30; Mercedes M. Cardona, "Retailers Cast Themselves as an Ad Medium," *Advertising Age*, 15 September 2003, p. 4.

144 Matthew Boyle, "Hey, Shoppers: Ads on Aisle 7!" *Fortune*, 24 November 2003, p. 50.

145 Michael McCarthy, "Ad Tattoos Get under Some People's Skin; Boxers Get Paid to Plaster Messages on Their Backs," www.usatoday.com, 4 April 2002.

146 Wayne Friedman, "Integration Front and Center as Alternate Revenue Source," *Television Week*, 15 September 2003, p. 16.

147 Rich Tomaselli, "Reebok's Terry Tate Set to Play Dirty Ball," *Advertising Age*, 21 April 2003, p. 4.

148 Stuart Elliott, "Short on Cash, Municipalities Are Renting Out Public Spaces to Marketers," *New York Times*, 23 June 2003.

149 John Chase and Ray Long, "Illinois: Brought to You by Sponsors," *Chicago Tribune*, 5 September 2003.

150 Information available at www.governmentacquisitions.com. Criticism of the practice is available at www.commercialalert.org.

151 Stuart Elliott, "A 'Brand Experience' on the Monorail as Ads Infiltrate New Arenas," *New York Times*, 18 November 2003.

152 Roger van Bakel, "Your Ad Here," *Christian Science Monitor*, 20 September 1999.

153 "Consumers in the Mist," *Business Week*, 26 February 2001, p. 92.

154 Gerry Khermouch and Jeff Green, "Buzz Marketing," *Business Week*, 30 July 2001, pp. 50–56.

155 Alissa Quart, *Branded: The Buying and Selling of Teenagers* (Cambridge, Mass.: Perseus Publishing, 2003).

156 Stephanie Thompson, "Targeting Teens Means Building Buzz," *Advertising Age*, 27 March 2000, pp. 26–27.

157 Gerry Khermouch and Jeff Green, "Buzz Marketing," *Business Week*, 30 July 2001, p. 53.

158 Daniel Eisenberg, "It's an Ad, Ad, Ad World," *Time*, 2 September 2002. Available at www.time.com.

159 Kate MacArthur and Hillary Chura, "Urban Warfare," *Advertising Age*, 4 September 2000, p. 16.

160 Jon Lafayette, "Internet, TV, Phone Vie for Kids' Attention," *Television Week*, 6 October 2003, p. 14.

161 "The Spider's Bite," *The Economist*, 11 May 2002, p. 57.

162 Commercial Alert, news release, 7 May 2001, "Commercial Alert Criticizes Movie-Length Ad Targeted at Kids," www.commercialalert.org.

163 David K. Kirkpatrick, "Snack Foods Become Stars of Books for Children," *New York Times*, 22 September 2000.

164 Courtney Kane, "TV and Movie Characters Sell Children Snacks," *New York Times*, 8 December 2003.

165 Gary Ruskin, "Why They Whine: How Corporations Prey on Our Children," *Mothering Magazine*, January/February 2003.

166 Courtney Kane, "TV and Movie Characters Sell Children Snacks," *New York Times*, 8 December 2003.

167 John Schwartz, "Alcohol Ads on TV Find a Young Audience," *New York Times*, 18 December 2002.

168 Wayne Friedman, "Nick Signs Up Embassy Suites for $20 Mil Deal," *Advertising Age*, 20 November 2000, p. 53.

169 Sheree R. Curry, "A Seller's Market," *Television Week*, 14 April 2003, p. 24.

170 Brooke Shelby Biggs, "Sesame Street Meets Madison Avenue," www.motherjones.com, 30 March 2001; Daniel Golden, "Channel One Aims to Involve Teachers in Marketing Push," *Wall Street Journal*, 28 August 2001; Geov Parrish, "Ads Creep in the Classroom," www.

workingforchange.com, 6 February 2002. See United States General Accounting Office, *Public Education: Commercial Activities in Schools* (Washington, D.C.: General Accounting Office, September 2000).

171 Ruskin, "Why They Whine."

172 Constance L. Hays, "Aided by Clifford and the Care Bears, Companies Go After the Toddler Market," *New York Times*, 11 July 2003.

173 Suzanne Vranica, "CDC Launches Ads Pushing Children to Be More Active," *Wall Street Journal Online*, 18 July 2002.

174 Paul Raeborn with Julie Forster, Dean Foust, and Diane Brady, "Why We're So Fat," *Business Week*, October 21, 2003, p. 114.

175 Courtney Kane, "TV and Movie Characters Sell Children Snacks," *New York Times*, 8 December 2003.

176 See, for example, James P. Steyer, *The Other Parent: The Inside Story of the Media's Effect on Our Children* (New York: Atria Books, 2002).

177 Ruskin, "Why They Whine."

178 Ruskin, "Why They Whine."

179 Ibid.

180 Claire Atkinson, "Ad Intrusion Up, Say Consumers," *Advertising Age*, 6 January 2003, pp. 1, 19.

181 David Carr, "Men's Shopping Magazine Is under Study," *New York Times*, 7 March 2003.

182 Brian Lowry, "Shows Reach Out and Pitch Someone, 24/7," www.latimes.com, 8 January 2003.

183 Alexander Meiklejohn, *Free Speech and Its Relation to Self-Government* (New York: Harper and Brothers, 1948).

184 Paul A. Baran and Paul M. Sweezy, "Theses on Advertising," *Science & Society*, Winter 1964. In Paul A. Baran, *The Longer View* (New York: Monthly Review Press, 1969), p. 232.

185 See James Twitchell, *Adcult* (New York: Columbia University Press, 1997).

186 James Rorty, *Advertising: Our Master's Voice* (New York: John Day & Company, 1934).

187 "Read This Ad. Or, Don't. An Exercise in Freedom." Advertising Council advertisement, *New York Times*, 12 September 2002.

188 Inger Stole, *Advertising on Trial: The Consumer Movement Versus Corporate Public Relations in the 1930s*, book manuscript forthcoming.

189 This still goes on: See Ira Teinowitz, "$700,000 Ad Council Spots Promote Patriotism," www.AdAge.com, 1 July 2002.

190 As Stole points out, this was a major fight during the Second World War. It periodically reemerges. See Ira Teinowitz, "FTC Report on Violence Stokes Regulatory Fires," *Advertising Age*, 18 September 2000, p. 3.

191 Ira Teinowitz, "Ad Tax Threat in Tennessee," *Advertising Age*, 21 May 2001, pp. 1, 42.

192 Erik Barnouw, *The Sponsor: Notes on a Modern Potentate* (New York: Oxford University Press, 1978), pp. 87–88.

193 "A Wise FTC," *Advertising Age*, 4 December 2000, p. 32.

194 Doug Halonen, "Group Seeks Curbs on Kids Advertising," *Advertising Age*, 23 October 2000, p. 93.

195 Claire Atkinson, "Watchdog Group Hits TV Product Placement," *Advertising Age*, 6 October 2003, p. 12.

196 For a classic presentation of the case, see Richard T. Kaplar, *Advertising Rights: The Neglected Freedom* (Washington, D.C.: The Media Institute, 1991).

197 This conviction is central to neoliberal thought. Since the market is the basis for all freedom, and freedom cannot exist except in a market economy, market freedoms, such as the right to advertise, are the foundation upon which other freedoms, such as free speech and free press, are built. See Milton Friedman, *Capitalism and Freedom* (Chicago: University of Chicago Press, 1962), ch. 1.

198 Robert Weissman, "Advertise This!" *Multinational Monitor*, September 2002, pp. 7–8.

199 Stanley Holmes, "Free Speech or False Advertising?" *Business Week*, 28 April 2003, pp. 69–70.

200 Joe Mandese, "Shifting Ad Accountability to Media," *Television Week*, 6 October 2003, p. 15; Louis Chunovic, "When Audiences Intersect," *Television Week*, 2 June 2003, p. 18; Jack Neff, "P&G Products to Wear Wire," *Advertising Age*, 15 December 2003, pp. 1, 32.

201 Richard Linnett and Tobi Elkin, "Nielsen Tracks Cinema Ads," *Advertising Age*, 6 October 2003, p. 4.

202 Brian Steinberg, Suzanne Vranica, and Yochi J. Dreazen, "Telemarketers Plan New Pitch," *Wall Street Journal*, 2 June 2003.

203 Janine Jackson, "Ads Gone Mad," *Extra!*, September/October 2002, p. 7.

CHAPTER 5

1 Cynthia Littleton, "FCC Review Hinges on Questions of Diversity, Competition," *Hollywood Reporter*, 18 February 2003.

2 For a discussion of the effects of concentrated markets in book publishing, see André Schiffrin, *The Business of Books* (New York: Verso, 2000).

3 Christopher Gaines, "Music Groups to Pay $143m to Settle Suit," *Financial Times*, 1 October 2002, p. 9.

4 Joe Flint and Peter Grant, "Comcast: Newfound Clout and Bare-Knuckle Tactics," *Wall Street Journal*, 27 June 2003.

5 Richard Linnett and Ira Teinowitz, "Media Merge, Marketers Pay," *Advertising Age*, 17 February 2003, pp. 1, 37; John Eggerton, "Mandel Cites 'Consolidation Tax,'" *Broadcasting & Cable*, 14 July 2003, p. 6.

6 Justin Oppelaar, "WalMart: Hicks Mix with Pix," *Variety*, 2–8 December 2002, p. 1.

7 David Shaw, "At Wal-Mart, a Curiously Selective Reading List," *Los Angeles Times*, 25 May 2003. www.calendarlive.com; Kathy Haley, "Shaking Up the Magic Kingdom," *Multichannel News*, supplement, 14 April 2003.

8 Jeffrey A. Trachtenberg, "Barnes & Noble Pushes Books from Ambitious Publisher: Itself," *Wall Street Journal*, 18 June 2003.

9 Tim Burt and Peter Thal Larsen, "Sony and BMG Sign Music Merger Deal," *Financial Times*, 12 December 2003.

10 Yochi Dreazen, Greg Ip, and Nicholas Kulish, "Oligopolies Are on the Rise as the Urge to Merge Grows," *Wall Street Journal Online*, 25 February 2002.

11 David D. Kirkpatrick, "A Merger of Book Middlemen Could Deeply Influence Sales," *New York Times*, 17 January 2002; Peter Lauria, "Magazine Consolidation Quickens," TheDeal.com, 17 July 2001; Alex Kuczynski, "Big Magazines Get Bigger as Small Ones Get Gobbled Up," *New York Times on the Web*, 30 July 2001.

12 "Chart Toppers," *Broadcasting & Cable*, 29 September 2003, p. 10.

13 Emily Nelson, "CBS Now Eyes Local Stations as Part of Turnaround Effort," *Wall Street Journal Online*, 26 August 2002.

14 Bruce Orwall, Deborah Solomon, and
    Sally Beatty, "Why the Possible Sale of
    AT&T Broadband Spooks 'Content'
    Firms," *Wall Street Journal*, 27 August 2001.

15 Yochi Dreazen, Greg Ip, and Nicholas
    Kulish, "Oligopolies Are on the Rise As
    the Urge to Merge Grows," *Wall Street
    Journal Online*, 25 February 2002.

16 Diane Mermigas, "Comcast Post-Merger
    Strategy Under Way," *Electronic Media*,
    15 July 2002, p. 4; Doug Halonen, "FCC
    Report a Mixed Bag for Comcast-AT&T
    Merger," *Electronic Media*, 10 June 2002,
    p. 26; Sallie Hofmeister, "Merger Could
    Drive a New Round of Consolidation,"
    LATimes.com, 21 December 2001.

17 John Dempsey and Meredith Amdur,
    "Clash of the Titans," *Variety*, 17–23
    March 2003, p. 25.

18 John Dempsey and Meredith Amdur,
    "Cable Biz Carps Over Carriage Fees,"
    Variety, 21–27 April 2003, p. 18.

19 Geraldine Fabrikant and Bill Carter,
    "Cable's New Giant Flexes His Muscles,"
    New York Times, 20 October 2003; Peter
    Thal Larsen, "How Cable Is Unravelling
    for Programmers," *Financial Times*,
    17 November 2003, p. 6.

20 Peter Thal Larsen, "Moguls Make Merry
    in Sun Valley," *Financial Times*, 14 July
    2003, p. 20.

21 Meredith Amdur and John Dempsey,
    "Congloms Bet Their Bottom Dollar
    on Orphan Cablers," *Variety*, 26 May–
    1 June 2003, p. 20.

22 Allison Romano, "How About the Fat
    Chance Channel?" *Broadcasting & Cable*,
    1 December 2003, p. 1.

23 Diane Mermigas, "Turner on War,
    Murdoch, Media," *Television Week*,
    21 April 2003, p. 47.

24 Jennifer 8. Lee, "Small Cable Operators

Worry about Life after Big Mergers,"
    New York Times, 26 December 2001.

25 Nicholas Garnham, *Emancipation, the
    Media, and Modernity: Arguments about the
    Media and Social Theory* (Oxford, U.K.:
    Oxford University Press, 2000), p. 52.

26 Michael Wolf, "In TV Land, Bigger Is
    Better," *Wall Street Journal*, 21 August
    2000; Justin Oppelaar, "Echostar Merger
    Plan Raises Media Congloms' Hackles,"
    Variety, 14–20 January 2002, p. 44.

27 Sallie Hofmeister, "Murdoch Empire's
    Chief Engineer," *LATimes.com*,
    2 September 2001.

28 "Changing Definitions of Syndie
    Success," *Television Week*, 15 December
    2003, p. 30.

29 Chris Pursell, "Partnering for Vertical
    Integration," *Television Week*, 24 March
    2003, p. 30.

30 Paul F. Duke, "D'Works: What Lies
    Beneath?" *Variety*, 24–30 July 2000. pp. 1,
    68. In 2002, DreamWorks and NBC
    agreed to team up and have Dream-
    Works produce programs for NBC, simi-
    lar to how the other TV networks use
    their film studios to generate TV shows
    for them. See Meg James, "DreamWorks
    to Develop TV Shows for NBC,"
    www.latimes.com, 8 August 2002;
    Michael Freeman, "NBC Firms Up
    Alliance with DreamWorks," *Electronic
    Media*, 12 August 2002, p. 2.

31 Marc Graser, "Better Unwed than in the
    Red," *Variety*, 5 October 2003, p. 11.

32 Jeff Leeds, "Vivendi, DreamWorks SKG
    Conclude Deal," *Los Angeles Times*, 12
    November 2003; Laura M. Holson, "With
    'Sand and Fog' Can Year Be Salvaged?"
    New York Times, 15 December 2003.

33 Jill Goldsmith, "Land of the Giants,"
    Variety, 15–21 May 2000, p. 56.

34 Diane Mermigas, "Deal-Making Goes into a Deep Freeze," *Electronic Media*, 30 July 2001, p. 2.

35 Merissa Marr, "Magazine Giants Look to Bulk Up With Acquisitions," Reuters dispatch, www.reuters.com, 29 May 2003.

36 "Deal Diary," *Variety*, 8–14 September 2003, p. 1.

37 Joe Flint and Peter Grant, "Comcast: Newfound Clout and Bare-Knuckle Tactics," *Wall Street Journal*, 27 June 2003.

38 To see the holdings of many of the first tier media giants, go to www.pbs.org/wgbh/pages/frontline/shows/cool/giants/index.html.

39 Bill Carter and Geraldine Fabrikant, "Vivendi to Deal With 2 Prospective Suitors," *New York Times*, 27 August 2003.

40 Martin Peers, "How Media Giants Are Reassembling the Old Oligopoly," *Wall Street Journal*, 15 September 2003.

41 "The Corporate Scoreboards," *Broadcasting & Cable*, 12 December 2002, p. 12.

42 David D. Kirkpatrick, "Media Grow, but They Can't Hide," *New York Times*, 8 September 2003.

43 John M. Higgins, "For the Big Fish, the Water's Fine," *Broadcasting & Cable*, 1 December 2003, p. 34.

44 "The Fortune 1,000," *Fortune*, 15 April 2002, pp. F44–F63; "The Fortune Global 500," *Fortune*, 22 July 2002.

45 Martin Peers, "AOL Time Warner Floods Several Units with Ads for Other Parts of the Company," *Wall Street Journal*, 15 November 2001.

46 Daniel Frankel, "Synergy Sings at the WB," *Broadcasting & Cable*, 29 July 2002.

47 Frank Rich, "There's No Exit from the Matrix," *New York Times*, 25 May 2003, section 2.

48 Joe Schlosser, "Synergy Sings Sweetly at CBS," *Broadcasting & Cable*, 19 November 2001.

49 Steve McClellan, "CBS Eyes a $170 Million Sunday," *Broadcasting & Cable*, 3 November 2003, p. 16.

50 Dana Calvo, "Disney Buys the Rights to Miners' Story," www.latimes.com, 3 August 2002.

51 Greg Braxton, "ANC and Disney Turn Park Into Synergyland," www.latimes.com, 23 August 2002; Meg James, "ABC in a Marketing Blitz for Ratings," www.latimes.com, 24 August 2002.

52 Jill Goldsmith, "Pic Licensees Fill Up on Seconds," *Variety*, 16–22 June 2003, p. 5; Sherri Day, "SpongeBob and Pals Provide Licensing Gold for Nickelodeon," *New York Times*, 9 January 2003.

53 Rick Lyman, "Hollywood's Working Title: Harry Potter and the Cash Cow," *New York Times*, 4 November 2001; John Lippman, "Can Harry Revive Warner?" *Wall Street Journal*, 4 October 2001; Anna Wilde Mathews, "Troll Booger—Yes; Candy-Cane Umbrellas—No," *Wall Street Journal*, 4 October 2001; Cathy Dunkley, "Mouse Synergy: A Bear Necessity," *Variety*, 15–21 2002, pp. 9, 13.

54 Michelle Chihara, "When Harry Met Selling," www.alternet.org, 8 November 2001.

55 Richard Verrier, "Movies Imitate Disney's Parks," www.latimes.com, 15 May 2002.

56 Alison Beard, "Rugrats Help Viacom Make a Splash," *Financial Times*, 14–15 June 2003, p. 10.

57 Edward Jay Epstein, "'Final Fantasy' May Lack Plot or Actors, but It Has a Goal: Sell PlayStations," *Wall Street Journal*, 13 July 2001, pp. W1, W11.

58 Jay Sherman, "Character Sale," *Television Week*, 9 June 2003, p. 4.

59 See, for example, Erik Barnouw et. al., eds., *Conglomerates and the Media* (New York: The New Press, 1997).

60 Claudia Eller, "Sony to Launch Feature Animation Unit," www.latimes.com, 9 May 2002.

61 Peter Burrows, "Pixar's Unsung Hero," *Business Week*, 20 June 2003, p. 68.

62 Samar Iskandar, "Vivendi Hopes Deal Will Turn Water into Wine," *Financial Times*, 16 June 2000, p. 21.

63 Peter Bart, "Too Much Togetherness," *Variety*, 4-10 June 2001, p. 4; Bernard Weinraub, "On TV, a Loss of Independents," *New York Times*, 7 May 2000, section 2.

64 Michael Schneider, "TV's Little Guys Stayin' Alive," *Variety*, 19-25 February 2001, pp. 1, 70; "Tangled Webs," *The Economist*, 25 May 2002, p. 69.

65 Martin Peers, "How Media Giants Are Reassembling the Old Oligopoly," *Wall Street Journal*, 15 September 2003.

66 For more information on joint ownership, see Robert W. McChesney, *Rich Media, Poor Democracy* (New York: New Press, 2000), chap. 1.

67 "Malone's Reach," *Variety*, 17-23 March 2003, p. 14.

68 "Gordie's Blues," *Business Week*, 14 October 2003, p. 84.

69 Martin Peers and Julia Angwin, "AOL Time Warner's Steve Case Resigns Amid Intense Pressure," *Wall Street Journal Online*, 13 January 2003.

70 Aaron Moore, "Entangling Alliances," *Columbia Journalism Review*, March-April 2003.

71 David D. Kirkpatrick, "Meeting of Moguls, If Not of Minds," *New York Times*, 14 July 2003.

72 David D. Kirkpatrick, "Media Chieftains Gather for Yearly Retreat in Idaho," *New York Times*, 13 July 2002.

73 John Gorman, "Big Media Lovefest," *Cleveland Free Times*, 16-22 July 2003.

74 Richard Linnett, "Media Rivals Backslap at Cable Conference," www.adage.com, 10 June 2003.

75 David D. Kirkpatrick, "Time Warner Sells Music Unit for $2.6 Billion," *New York Times*, 25 November 2003.

76 Michael A. Hiltzik, "Synergy Proved Their Undoing," www.latimes.com, 4 August 2002; Wayne Friedman, "Vivendi, AOL Valued Scale over Synergy: Ad Buyers," *Advertising Age*, 8 July 2002, pp. 3, 41; Bruce Orwall and Martin Peers, "Media Megamergers Aren't Big Hits as Futuristic Synergies Prove Elusive," *Wall Street Journal Online*, 10 May 2002; Frank Ahrens, "Big Media Mergers Raise Big Doubts," *Washington Post*, 14 May 2002; Tim Rutten, "As All the Buzz Fizzled, Corporate Synergy Died," www.latimes.com, 14 August 2002.

77 "A Media Giant with Giant Problems," *Business Week*, 19 May 2003, pp. 88-89.

78 James Bates, "AOL's $50-Billion Loss Is One from the Books," www.latimes.com, 24 April 2002; Jerry Knight, "AOL Time Warner Merger Adds Up to Less than Sum of Its Parts," *Washington Post*, 1 April 2002; David Henry, Tom Lowry, and Catherine Yang, "AOL, You've Got Misery," *Business Week*, 8 April 2002, pp. 58-59.

79 Mark Landler and Geraldine Fabrikant, "A Tortoise, Many Hares and a Web of Convergence," *New York Times*, 4 August 2002, section 3; Ken Belson, "Sony Looks Golden, by Comparison," *New York Times*, 25 July 2002; Peter Bart, "All Hail Rupert the Reticent," *Variety*, 12-18 August 2002, pp. 1, 3.

80   Paige Albiniak, "The Selling of Prime Time," *Broadcasting & Cable*, 16 September 2002, pp. 18, 20; Geraldine Fabrikant, "Viacom's Profit Increases 21 Percent in Second Quarter," *New York Times*, 25 July 2002.

81   Dianne Brady and Gerry Khermouch, "How to Tickle a Child," *Business Week*, 7 July 2003, p. 48.

82   Josef Adalian, "The Rupe Machine Rocks," *Variety*, 11–17 August 2003, p. 1; David D. Kirkpatrick, "Helped by Fox, News Corp.'s Earnings Soar," *New York Times*, 14 May 2003.

83   "Lizzie's Long Reach," *Fortune*, 29 September 2003, p. 112.

84   "A Cool Half Billion," *Variety*, 13 October 2003, p. 1.

85   Robert Weissman, "Divide and Conquer," *Multinational Monitor*, October/November 2002, p. 16;.

86   John M. Higgins, "Who Says Synergy Is a Bad Word?" *Broadcasting & Cable*, 8 September 2003, p. 44.

87   James Flanigan, "AOL Learns a Hard Lesson on the Internet," www.latimes.com, 21 July 2002; John Motavalli, *Bamboozled at the Revolution: How Big Media Lost Billions in the Battle for the Internet* (New York: Viking, 2002); Seth Schiesel, "News Corp. Posts a Loss, Mostly in Gemstar Mess," *New York Times*, 15 August 2002.

88   See, for example, Stephanie Thompson, "Disappointment for Disney's Extensions," *Advertising Age*, 12 August 2002, p. 12.

89   Bruce Orwall, "Disney Sharpens Stores' Focus, Ending Emporium Approach," *Wall Street Journal Online*, 1 March 2002.

90   Christopher Parkes, "Walt Disney Considers Sale of Its Retail Stores Chain," *Financial Times*, 23 May 2003, p. 18; Richard Verrier, "Disney Puts Its Stores Up for Sale," *Los Angeles Times*, 23 May 2003.

91   Ben Silverman, "Media Owners Foul Out on Pro Teams," www.nypost.com, 17 November 2002.

92   Martin Peers, "Viacom Nears Decision on Divesting Blockbuster," *Wall Street Journal*, 2 December 2003; Geraldine Fabrikant, "A Sale of Blockbuster is Tricky, Both for its Major Stakeholder, Viacom, and for Potential Buyers," *New York Times*, 15 December 2003.

93   PriceWaterhouseCoopers, *Global Entertainment and Media Outlook: 2002–2006, Executive Summary* (PriceWaterhouseCoopers, 2002), p. 7.

94   "What Is the Point?" *The Economist*, 25 May 2002, p. 12.

95   David Croteau and William Hoynes, *The Business of Media: Corporate Media and the Public Interest* (Thousand Oaks, Calif.: Pine Oaks Press, 2001), chap. 1; see also Lawrence Soley, *Censorship, Inc* (New York: Monthly Review Press, 2002).

96   For a nice discussion of this, see Garnham, *Emancipation, the Media, and Modernity*, pp. 57–58.

97   James Bates, "'Die Another Day' Gives MGM a Brighter Outlook," *Los Angeles Times*, 6 February 2003.

98   Tim Burt and Carlos Grande, "Harry Potter Enchants the Book Trade," *Financial Times*," 21–22 September 2002, p. 7.

99   Sathnam Sanghera, "Taking Pleasure from a Titanic Effort," *Financial Times*, 23 August 2002, p. 10.

100   Melissa Grego, "Risk-Averse Syndies Sinking," *Variety*, 24–30 June 2002, p. 19.

101   Garnham, *Emancipation, the Media, and Modernity*, p. 56.

102 See Lois S. Gray and Ronald L. Seeber, eds., *Under the Stars: Essays on Labor Relations in Arts and Entertainment* (Ithaca, N.Y.: ILR Press of Cornell University Press, 1996); Gerald Horne, *Class Struggle in Hollywood, 1930–1950: Moguls, Mobsters, Stars, Reds, and Trade Unionists* (Austin, Tx.: University of Texas Press, 2001).

103 See, for example, John Burman, "Star Power: Setting the Pace," www.hollywoodreporter.com, 5 February 2002; Elizabeth Hackett, "Salary Survey: Hollywood's Quest for the New A-List Actor Means Big Paydays for Virtual Unknowns," www.inside.com, 17 August 2001.

104 Tyler Cowen, *In Praise of Commercial Culture* (Cambridge, Mass.: Harvard University Press, 1998).

105 C. Edwin Baker, *Media, Markets, and Democracy* (New York: Cambridge University Press, 2002), p. 67.

106 John Kay, "Big Media Can Never Be Truly Creative," *Financial Times*, 11 September 2003, p. 13.

107 Nicholas Kraley, "Specs, Fame and Satisfaction," *Financial Times*, 16–17 November 2002, p. III.

108 Michael Schneider, "Fall Pilots Apply Brand-Aid," *Variety*, 1–7 April 2002, p. 23.

109 Joe Flint, "Networks Clone Their Own Shows; Some Even Pay for the Privilege," online.wsj.com, 19 May 2003.

110 "Showbiz Develops Deja View," *Variety*, 4–10 March 2002, p. 1.

111 "Studios Spell Relief S-E-Q-U-E-L," *Advertising Age*, 11 June 2002, p. 16; Dade Hayes, "Sequels Try for Triples," *Variety*, 24–30 July 2002, pp. 1, 70.

112 Claude Brodesser, "Sony's Twice-Told Tales," *Variety*, 27 November–3 December 2000, p. 1; Rick Lyman, "Summer of the Spinoff," *New York Times*, 17 April 2002.

113 Claudia Eller, "Studios Turn to Sequels in a Big Way to Hedge Bets," www.latimes.com, 14 January 2002.

114 Claudia Eller, "Studios Gunshy on Sequels as Franchises Fail to Wow," *Los Angeles Times*, 14 July 2003.

115 Laura M. Holson and Rick Lyman, "In Warner Brothers' Strategy, a Movie Is Now a Product Line," *New York Times*, 11 February 2002.

116 David Hatch, "Study Says TV Getting Smuttier," *Electronic Media*, 3 April 2000. p. 4; Sally Beatty, "What Are Space Aliens and Lingerie Doing on Learning Channel?" *Wall Street Journal*, 27 March 2001; Allison Romano, "Pushing the Raunch Envelope," *Broadcasting & Cable*, 18 March 2002, p. 24; Mark McGuire, "Teen Body Count in May Shows Networks Still Rely on Violence," *Albany Times-Union*, 29 May 2001.

117 Tom Shales, "The Naked Truth about the Fall Season," *Television Week*, 15 September 2003, p. 43.

118 P. J. Bednarski, "Oh, Is TV Naughty," *Broadcasting & Cable*, 29 September 2003, p. 37.

119 Bill Carter, "Survival of the Pushiest," *New York Times Magazine*, 28 January 2001, pp. 22–25.

120 Caryn James, "Reality Shows As Sideshows," *New York Times*, 6 August 2002; Caryn James, "Mixing High Brow and Low, TV Plays to the Bottom Line," *New York Times*, 28 July 2002.

121 Lola Ogunnaike, "No Mealworm Snacks For Late-Night Comic," *New York Times*, 30 June 2003.

122 Bill Carter, "Fox TV Finds Another Way to Sink to Top of the Charts," *New York Times*, 15 March 2002.

123 "Small-Screen Sparkle," *The Economist*, 3 August 2002, pp. 68–69.

124 Tom Shales, "Talking Trash TV," *Electronic Media*, 3 February 2003, p. 31.

125 Jill Goldsmith, "Karmazin Explores Sci-Fi, Regs, Ad Prospects," story.news. yahoo.com/news, 10 December 2002.

126 "Merging Media" segment, *The NewsHour with Jim Lehrer*, PBS television, 25 June 2002.

127 Devin Leonard, "We Know What You're Doing Next Summer," *Fortune*, 1 October 2001, p. 117.

128 Todd McCarthy, "In 2001, It's Quality that Got Fingered," *Variety*, 30 April – 6 May 2001, p. 5.

129 Peter Bart, "Should '10 Best' Be Put to Rest?" *Variety*, 7–13 January 2002, p. 6.

130 Peter Bart, "Shaking Out the Blahs," *Variety*, 2–26 January 2003, p. 8.

131 Peter Bart, "Needed: Some Comic Relief," *Variety*, 6-12 October 2003, p. 5.

132 Dana Harris, "H'Wood Renews Niche Pitch," *Variety*, 7–13 April 2003, pp. 1, 54.

133 Lynn Hirschberg, "Who's that Girl?" *New York Times Magazine*, 4 August 2002, pp. 30–35, 42, 53, 56, 57; see also Joli Jensen, *Nashville Sound: Authenticity, Commercialization, and Country Music* (Nashville, Tenn.: Vanderbilt University Press, 1998).

134 Charles Haddad, "Moanin' the Blues in Nashville," *Business Week*, 11 June 2001, pp. 130, 132.

135 Don Waller, "Epoch of the Rolling Clones," *Variety*, 10–16 April 2000, p. 1.

136 "Britney Spears, AOL Join Up to Promote Music, Tour," Reuters news release, www.aol.com, 18 October 2001; Suzanne Vranica, "Universal Music Seeks Ties to Marketers to Boost Sales," *Wall Street Journal Online*, 8 July 2002.

137 Marc Pollack, "Destined to Duet," *Advertising Age*, 28 July 2003, p. S3.

138 Troy J. Augusto, "Teen Diva Aguilera Makes Her Market," *Variety*, 23–29 October 2000, p. 62.

139 John Leland, "Advertisements for Themselves," *New York Times Magazine*, 11 March 2001, pp. 48, 50–51.

140 See, for example, Paul Buhle and Dave Wagner, *Radical Hollywood: The Untold Story Behind America's Favorite Movies* (New York: The New Press, 2002); Michael Denning, *The Cultural Front* (New York: Verso, 1996).

141 See Aniko Bodroghkozy, *Groove Tube: Sixties Television and the Youth Rebellion* (Durham, N.C.: Duke University Press, 2001). Her discussion of the *Smothers Brothers Comedy Hour* is instructive in this regard.

142 See, for example, Gerald Horne, *Class Struggle in Hollywood, 1930–1950* (Austin, Tx.: University of Texas Press, 2001).

143 See Robert M. Entman and Andrew Rojecki, *The Black Image in the White Mind* (Chicago: University of Chicago Press, 2000); Oscar H. Gandy Jr., *Communication and Race: A Structural Perspective* (New York: Oxford University Press, 1998). Furthermore, successful creative people in the media industry often come from the upper middle class, and certainly end up there or higher, and this class background can manifest itself in elitist media portrayals on issues of class and race.

144 For a superior and detailed critique of how media markets work, see Mark Cooper, *Media Ownership and Democracy in the Digital Information Age* (Stanford: Center for Internet & Society, Stanford University, 2003).

145 Robert W. Welkos and Richard Natale, "Multiethnic Movies Ringing True with Youths," www.latimes.com, 2 July 2001.

146 Owen Gibson, "Murdoch: 'I'm Here to Stay,'" *The Guardian*, 21 June 2002.

147 It is routine to see stories like this: Joe Flint, "NBC Reaps Profits by Shooting for Viewers with More Money," *Wall Street Journal Online*, 20 May 2002. As the airwaves are the collective property of the entire population, this bias becomes more perverse.

148 Garnham, *Emancipation, the Media, and Modernity*, chap. 6.

149 John Kenneth Galbraith, *The Affluent Society* (Boston: Houghton Mifflin, 1958), pp. 158, 167–172.

150 Cited in Robert W. McChesney, *Telecommunications, Mass Media, and Democracy: The Battle for the Control of U.S. Broadcasting, 1928–1935* (New York: Oxford University Press, 1993), p. 97.

151 Steve McClellan, "Big Media Put Money Where Their Mouth Is," *Broadcasting & Cable*, 30 June 2003, p. 12.

152 Charles Lyons, "Disney Preps for PR Blitzkrieg," *Variety*, 30 April–6 May 2001, pp. 1, 87; see also Jonathan Rosenbaum, *Movie Wars: How Hollywood and the Media Conspire to Limit What Films We Can See* (Chicago: A Cappella, 2000).

153 Anthony Kaufman, "Tongue Tied," *Variety*, 8–14 December 2003, p. A3.

154 See McChesney, *Rich Media, Poor Democracy*, pp. 33–34.

155 Claude Brodesser, "Fox: A Brighter Searchlight," *Variety*, 7–13 April 2003, p. 55.

156 Claudia Eller, "Marketing Costs Scale the Heights," *Los Angeles Times*, 20 October 2002.

157 See website of the Recording Industry Association of America: www.riaa.com.

158 Michael Kimmelman, "Lamenting the Fade-Out of Classical Radio," *New York Times*, 17 April 2001.

159 Edward Wong, "Hard Times for TV Documentaries," *New York Times*, 4 January 2001.

160 Baker, *Media, Markets, and Democracy*, pp. 70–71.

161 James Hamilton, *Channeling Violence: The Economic Market for Violent Television Programming* (Princeton, N. J.: Princeton University Press, 1998).

162 See, for example, Jim Rutenberg, "A Wave of Violence Engulfs Children's Cartoon Programs," *New York Times*, 21 January 2001; David E. Rosenbaum, "Violence in Media Is Aimed at Young, F.T.C. Study Says," *New York Times*, 12 September 2000.

163 John Schwartz, "Alcohol Ads on TV Find Their Way to Teenagers, a Study Finds, Despite Industry Guidelines," *New York Times*, 18 December 2002.

164 See James P. Steyer, *The Other Parent: The Inside Story of the Media's Effect on Our Children* (New York: Atria Books, 2002); Edward L. Palmer, *Television and America's Children: A Crisis of Neglect* (New York: Oxford University Press, 1988).

165 Patricia Winters Lauro, "Coaxing the Smile that Sells," *New York Times*, 1 November 1999.

166 *The Kids Market* (Packaged Facts, 2000), executive report, p. 1; Kim Campbell, "How Ads Get Kids to Say, I Want It!" *Christian Science Monitor*, 18 September 2000, pp. 1, 5.

167 Louis Chunovic, "Marketers Turning 'Tween into Green," *Electronic Media*, 5 August 2002, pp. 6, 22; Julie Salamon, "It's Always Saturday on TV," *New York Times*, 2 February 2001; Sally Beatty, "Disney Aims New Cable Network at Preschoolers," *Wall Street Journal*, 21 June 2001; Julie Salamon, "Grabbing Viewers 'Tween 8 and 14," *New York Times*, 15 February 2002.

168 Mercedes M. Cardona, "Young Girls Tar-
geted by Makeup Companies," *Advertising
Age*, 27 November 2000, p. 15; Chuck Ross,
"Kids Have Ad Savvy and Eye for Detail,"
Electronic Media, 18 December 2000, p. 16.

169 Bill McConnell, "Study: Young Kids
'Immersed' in TV," *Broadcasting & Cable*,
3 November 2003, p. 22.

170 See, for example, Thomas Robinson et.
al., "Effects of Reducing Television
Viewing on Children's Requests for
Toys: A Randomized Controlled Trial,"
Developmental and Behavioral Pediatrics 22,
no. 3 (June 2001): 179–84.

171 Marilyn Elias, "Fight for Quality TV Moves
to Pediatrics," *USA Today*, 6 February 2001;
David Heyman, "Too Much Media Harm-
ful: Study," *Calgary Herald*, 20 June 2003.

172 Ruth Gledhill, "Archbishop Fired Opening Shot at Disney," www.timesonline.
co.uk, 23 July 2002; Warren Hoge,
"A Radical Who Backs Gays and Women
as Clerics Will Lead Anglican Church,"
New York Times, 24 July 2002.

173 Cowen, *In Praise of Commercial Culture.*

174 Benjamin M. Compaine and Douglas
Gomery, *Who Owns the Media?*, 3d ed.
(Mahwah, N. J.: Lawrence Erlbaum
Associates, 2000).

175 Tyler Cowen, "Myth of the Media
Giants," *National Post*, 6 January 2003.

176 Benjamin Compaine, "The Myths of
Encroaching Global Media Ownership,"
www.opendemocracy.net, 8 Nov. 2001.

177 C. Edwin Baker, "Media Concentration:
Giving Up on Democracy," *Florida Law
Review* 54, no.5 (December 2002): 883–89.

178 Ibid., p. 884.

179 Daniel Dombey, "Impala Fights for Shelf
Space," *Financial Times*, 24 November
2003, p. 17.

180 I develop this topic further in chapter 6.

CHAPTER 6

1 I was a cofounder of Free Press. The
website is www.mediareform.net.

2 See Eric McLuhan and Frank Zingrone,
editors, *Essential McLuhan* (New York:
Basic Books, 1995); Marshall McLuhan,
*Understanding Media: The Extensions of
Man*, introduction by Lewis H. Lapham
(Cambridge, Mass.: MIT Press, 1999,
first published in 1964).

3 Neil Postman, *Amusing Ourselves to Death*
(New York: Penguin, 1985).

4 Jerry Mander, *Four Arguments for the Elimination of Television* (New York: Quill, 1978).

5 William J. Baumol, *The Free-Market Innovation Machine* (Princeton, N.J.: Princeton
University Press, 2002).

6 See, for an overview of such policy making, Hugh R. Slotten, *Radio and Television
Regulation: Broadcast Technology in the United States, 1920–1960* (Baltimore: Johns
Hopkins University Press, 2000).

7 "Spectrum Issues Key for New NTIA
Chief," *The Washington Post*, 2 September
2003.

8 Quoted in Michael Calabrese, "The Great
Airwaves Robbery," New America Foun-
dation Public Assets Program, Spectrum
Series no. 2, November 2001, p. 1.

9 This point is developed in Joel Brinkley,
*Defining Vision: The Battle for the Future of
Television* (New York: Harcourt Brace, 1997).

10 Dan Careny, "HDTV: Don't Blame the
FCC for Tuning Out," *Business Week*,
5 February 2001, p. 52.

11 Eric A. Taub, "The Big Picture on Digital
TV: It's Still Fuzzy," *New York Times*,
12 September 2002; See Steven Labaton,
"Studies Find Scant Availability of
Spectrum for Wireless Internet,"
New York Times, 31 March 2000.

12   Estimate of Tom Wolzien based on Bern-
     stein research. Cited in "The Third of a
     Trillion Giveaway," Center for Digital
     Democracy, www.democratic media.org,
     18 September 2001.

13   Bill McConnell, "Court Upholds FCC
     Tuner Mandate," *Broadcasting & Cable*, 3
     November 2003, p. 5.

14   See, for example, Stephen Labaton,
     "F.C.C. Acts Against Pirating of TV Broad-
     casts," *New York Times*, 5 November 2003.

15   Shannon Henry, "Clearing a Path for
     Digital Radio," *Washington Post*,
     9 October 2002.

16   David Lieberman, "Radio Close to
     Increased Digital Transmission; IBiquity
     CEO Says Hiss, Static to Go Away,"
     www.usatoday.com, 11 April 2002.

17   Brad King, "Digital Radio: Small Guys'
     Ruin?," www.wired.com, 18 October
     2002; Barnaby J. Feder, "F.C.C. Approves
     a Digital Radio Technology," *New York
     Times*, 11 October 2002,.

18   Jeffrey H. Rohlfs, *Bandwagon Effects in
     High-Technology Industries* (Cambridge,
     Mass.: MIT Press, 2001).

19   See, for example, Howard Rheingold,
     Smart Mobs: The Next Social Revolution
     (Cambridge, Mass.: Perseus, 2003).

20   David Manasian, "Digital Dilemmas,"
     special section on "A Survey of the Inter-
     net Society," *The Economist*, 25 January
     2003, pp. 3-5.

21   See, for example, Doug Halonen, "FCC
     Challenges Open-Access Ruling," *Televi-
     sion Week*, 13 October 2003, pp. 4, 31;
     Richard Waters, "Coming Soon, to a
     Broadband Line Near You," *Financial
     Times*, 20 October 2003, p. 8; Demetri
     Sevastopulo, "Spectrum Lobbyists Cre-
     ate Heat in Halls of Capitol Hill," *Finan-
     cial Times*, 26 September 2003, p. 21.

22   Saul Hansell, "Marketers Adjust as Spam
     Clogs the Arteries of E-Commerce,"
     New York Times, 1 December 2003; Pete
     Blackshaw, "Pull the Plug on Pop-Ups?"
     Advertising Age, 3 November 2003, p. 24;
     Ira Teinowitz, "Calif. Spam Legislation
     to Hurt Marketers," *Advertising Age*,
     3 November 2003, p. 10; Stephen Baker,
     "The Taming of the Internet," *Business
     Week*, 15 December 2003, pp. 78-82.

23   Lawrence Lessig has written indispensa-
     ble work on copyright and the Internet.
     See Lawrence Lessig, *Code and Other Laws
     of Cyberspace* (New York: Basic Books,
     1999); Lawrence Lessig, *The Future of
     Ideas: The Fate of the Commons in a
     Connected World* (New York: Random
     House, 2001).

24   Catherine Yang, "Beyond Wi-Fi: A New
     Wireless Age," *Business Week*, 15 December
     2003, pp. 84-88. For a detailed report
     on this subject, see Kevin Werbach, *Radio
     Revolution: The Coming Age of Unlicensed
     Wireless* (Washington, D.C.: New America
     Foundation, 2003). The report is available
     at http://www.newamerica.net/index.
     cfm?pg=article&pubID=1427.

25   Norman Ornstein and Michael Calabrese,
     "A Private Windfall for Public Property,"
     Washington Post, 12 August 2003; Michael
     H. Rothkopf and Coleman Bazelon,
     "Spectrum Deregulation without
     Confiscation of Giveaways," Spectrum
     Series Working Paper #8, New America
     Foundation Spectrum Policy Program,
     Washington, D.C., August 2003.

26   Michael J. Copps, "Battle to Control
     Internet Threatens Open Access," *San
     Jose Mercury News*, 15 December 2003.

27   For a comprehensive treatment of these
     issues, see Jeff Chester, *Digital Destiny*
     (New York: The New Press, 2004).

28   Demetri Sevastopulo, "Rocky Road to the US's Broadband Future," *Financial Times*, 9 December 2003, p. 10; Matt Richtel, "AT&T Joins Fray for Cheaper Calls through the Web," *New York Times*, 11 December 2003; Geraldine Fabrikant, "In Fight between Cable and Satellite, Customers Gain an Edge," *New York Times*, 1 December 2003.

29   Michael Geist, "Think Web's Virtually Government-Free? Think Again," *Toronto Star*, 1 December 2003.

30   Jennifer L. Schenker, "Nations Chafe at U.S. Influence Over the Internet," *New York Times*, 8 December 2003; Jennifer L. Schenker, "U.N. Agrees to Examine How Internet Is Governed," *New York Times*, 15 December 2003.

31   Dean Baker, "The Artistic Freedom Voucher: An Internet Age Alternative to Copyrights," Briefing Paper, Center for Economic and Policy Research, Washington, D.C., 5 November 2003.

32   See John Motavalli, *Bamboozled at the Revolution* (New York: Viking, 2002); John Cassidy, *Dot.Con: The Greatest Story Ever Sold* (New York: HarperCollins, 2002).

33   I discuss this in considerable detail in Robert W. McChesney, *Rich Media, Poor Democracy* (New York: New Press, 2000), ch. 3.

34   "The Top 20 Internet News Sites," *Columbia Journalism Review*, March/April 2003, p. 28.

35   Tobi Elkin, "Spam: Annoying but Effective," *Advertising Age*, 22 September 2003, p. 40; James Hibbard, " 'ET,' Yahoo! Unite," *Television Week*, 25 August 2003, p. 3; Saul Hansell, "Yahoo's Resurgent Profit Is Led by Strong Advertising," *New York Times*, 9 October 2003; Ben Elgin, "Web Searches: The Fix Is In," www.businessweek.com, 6 October 2003; Tobi Elkin, "Paid Search Appeal Escalates," *Advertising Age*, 13 October 2003, p. 62; Bob Tedeschi, "If You Likes the Web Page, Try the Ad," *New York Times*, 4 August 2003.

36   "Diller's Internet Empire," *Business Week*, 13 October 2003, p. 65.

37   Sue Zeidler, "Tech Group Aims at Profit-Friendly File-Sharing," Reuters, 11 December 2003; Ben Fritz, "Fresh Refrain for Online Biz," *Variety*, 10–16 November 2003, pp. 58.

38   Neil Strauss, "Online Music Business Neither Quick Nor Sure," *New York Times*, 29 October 2003.

39   Tom Lowry, Ronald Grover, and Stephanie Anderson Forest, "Cable Fights for Its Movie Rights," *Business Week*, 27 October 2003, p. 88.

40   Marc Graser, "Movie Downloading Not as Simple as Music Files," *Variety*, 8–14 December 2003, p. 13.

41   Laura M. Olson, "Studios Moving to Block Piracy of Films Online," *New York Times*, 25 September 2003.

42   Chris Nuttall, "Film Industry 'to be Spared Large Losses from Web Piracy'," *Financial Times*, 21 October 2003, p. 9.

43   Bill McConnell, "A Win for Broadcasters, Hollywood," *Broadcasting & Cable*, 10 November 2003, p. 24; Stephen Labaton, "F.C.C. Acts Against Pirating of TV Broadcasts," *New York Times*, 5 November 2003.

44   Paul Majendie, "Bubble Bursts for E-Books," news.yahoo.com/news, 10 October 2003.

45   "The Complete Home Entertainer?" *The Economist*, 1 March 2003, p. 64.

46   Meredith Asmdur, "TV's Rise of the Machines," *Variety*, 8–14 December 2003, p. 28.

47   Scott Donaton, "TiVo's New President Wants to Play Nice with Advertisers, Cable," *Advertising Age*, 6 October 2003, p. 22; Paige Albiniak, "The Incredibly Wired World of Rupert Murdoch's Top Gun," *Broadcasting & Cable*, 6 October 2003, p. 17; Roger Baron, "DVR Threat Real, Growing," *Television Week*, 20 October 2003, p. 11; Diane Mermigas, "Television Ad Model Under Pressure on Two Fronts," *Television Week*, 22 September 2003, p. 28; Seth Schiesel, "Can Cable Fast-Forward Past TiVo?" *New York Times*, 20 October 2003.

48   Maria Matzer Rose and Kathleen Anderson, "News, Studios Tap Ad Power of TiVo," *Hollywood Reporter*, 28 October 2003; Randall Rothenberg, "The Good News about PVRs: Its 'Tough Love' for Marketers," *Advertising Age*, 27 October 2003, p. 26.

49   Peter J. Humphreys, *Media and Media Policy in Germany: The Press and Broadcasting Since 1945* (Oxford, U.K.: Berg, 1990).

50   Antonia Zerbisias, "Venezuelan News Media Dissected," *Toronto Star*, 28 September 2003.

51   Tony Barber, "Defeat of Media Reform Bill Spells Setback for Berlusconi," *Financial Times*, 2 October 2003, p. 4.

52   Dana Rawls, "Minorities and the Media: Little Ownership and Even Less Control," www.alternet.org, 12 December 2002.

53   John C. Busterna and Robert G. Picard, *Joint Operating Agreements: The Newspaper Preservation Act and Its Application* (Norwood, N.J.: Ablex, 1993), p. 122.

54   Keith J. Kelly, "New York Sun Editor Has Ink in His Veins," *New York Post*, 7 April 2002.

55   Ted Peterson, *Magazines in the Twentieth Century* (Urbana, Ill.: University of Illinois Press, 1964).

56   This is a battle still being waged to this day. See Ira Teinowitz and Cara Beardi, "Magazines Go Postal over Rate Hike," *Advertising Age*, 14 May 2001, p. 37.

57   See William L. Rivers and Wilbur Schramm, *Responsibility in Mass Communication* (New York: Harper & Row, 1957), pp. 253-92, for a compendium of the self-regulatory codes of all the major media industries. For a detailed discussion of how this process played out in the comic book publishing industry, see Amy Kiste Nyberg, *Seal of Approval: The History of the Comics Code* (Jackson, Miss.: University Press of Mississippi, 1998).

58   Steven J. Ross, *Working-Class Hollywood: Silent Film and the Shaping of Class in America* (Princeton, N.J.: Princeton University Press, 1998).

59   Gregory D. Black, *Hollywood Censored: Morality Codes, Catholics, and the Movies* (Cambridge: Cambridge University Press, 1994).

60   John Trumpdour, *Selling Hollywood to the World* (Cambridge: Cambridge University Press, 2002).

61   See David Pritchard, ed., *Holding the Media Accountable* (Bloomington, Ind.: Indiana University Press, 1998), p. 191.

62   Angela J. Campbell, "Self-Regulation and the Media," *Federal Communications Law Journal* 51, no. 3 (May 1999), p. 772.

63   Busterna and Picard, *Joint Operating Agreements*, p. ix.

64   Lucas A Powe, Jr., *The Fourth Estate and the Constitution* (Berkeley: University of California Press, 1991), p. 216.

65   Mark Wigifield, "FCC Rebuffs Bid by Producers on Independent TV Programs," online.wsj.com, 13 June 2003; Bill McConnell, "McCain Weighs In for Fin-Syn," *Broadcasting & Cable*, 26 May 2003, p. 2.

66 For an excellent treatment of Clear Channel and radio, see Jeff Sharlet, "Big World: How Clear Channel Programs America," *Harper's Magazine*, December 2003, pp. 37-45.

67 "Tiny to Titan in Six years," *Fortune*, 3 March 2003, p. 120.

68 John Dunbar and Aron Pilhofer, "Big Radio Rules in Small Markets," Center for Public Integrity report, Washington, D.C., www.openairwaves.org, 1 October 2003. The FCC has also been lax with regard to the limits on the number of television stations a single firm can own control in a community. See Floyd Norris, "Making a Mockery of Media Concentration Rules," *New York Times*, 21 November 2003.

69 Anna Wilde Mathews, "Clear Channel Uses High-Tech Gear to Perfect the Art of Sounding Local," *Wall Street Journal Online*, 25 February 2002; David F. Gallagher, "Turning a Digital Database Into Local Radio," *New York Times*, 3 February 2003.

70 Don Waller, "Billions Bet on Car-Tune Rumble," *Variety*, 14–20 August 2000, p. 16.

71 Chuck Philips, "Logs Link Payments with Radio Airplay," www.latimes.com, 29 May 2001; Chuck Philips, "Radio Exec's Claims of Payola Draw Fire," www.latimes.com, 7 March 2002; Greg Kot, "Rocking Radio's World," *Chicago Tribune*, 14 April 2002.

72 Jon Pareles, "It's Radio that Breaks His Heart," *New York Times*, 13 October 2002.

73 *Congressional Record*, 11 September 2003.

74 An excellent discussion of this and much else concerning the development of copyright can be found in: Siva Vaidhyanathan, *Copyrights and Copywrongs:* *The Rise of Intellectual Property and How It Threatens Creativity* (New York: New York University Press, 2002).

75 See Lawrence Lessig, *The Future of Ideas: The Fate of the Commons in a Connected World* (New York: Random House, 2001); Jessica Litman, *Digital Copyright: Protecting Intellectual Property on the Internet* (Amherst, N.Y.: Prometheus Books, 2001).

76 John Kay, "Copyright Law Has a Duty to Creativity," *Financial Times*, 24 October 2002, p. 15.

77 See Kembrew McLeod, *Owning Culture: Authorship, Ownership, and Intellectual Property* (New York: Peter Lang, 2001).

78 Ronald Grover, "Why Is Christopher Robin Sobbing?" *Business Week*, 16 September 2001, p. 51.

79 Meg James, "Big Battle for a Silly Old Bear," www.latimes.com, 5 July 2002.

80 Doug Bedell, "Professor Says Disney, Other Firms Typify What's Wrong with Copyrights," SiliconValley.com, 10 April 2002.

81 Copyright is a crucial battleground concerning the future of the Internet. See Ellen Sheng, "Media, Cable Companies Want Stronger Copyright Protection," online.wsj.com, 9 June 2003.

82 David Carr, "Newsweeklies Agree to Pact on Allegations of Collusion," *New York Times*, 27 January 2003.

83 Powe, *The Fourth Estate and the Constitution*, p. 221.

84 For an overview of mainstream antitrust law, see Keith N. Hylton, *Antitrust Law: Economic Theory and Common Law Evolution* (New York: Cambridge University Press, 2003).

85 See Rudolph J. R. Peritz, *Competition Policy in America* (New York: Oxford University Press, 1996), p. 9.

86   Robert Weissman, "Divide and Conquer: Restraining Vertical Integration and Cross-Industry Ownership," *Multinational Monitor*, October/November 2002, p. 19.

87   Cited in Donald R. Simon, "Big Media: Its Effect on the Marketplace of Ideas and How to Slow the Urge to Merge," *The John Marshall Journal of Computer and Information Law* 20, no. 2 (Winter 2002): 273.

88   Morris L. Ernst, *The First Freedom* (New York: Macmillan, 1946).

89   Simon, "Big Media," p. 273.

90   C. Edwin Baker, "Media Concentration: Giving Up on Democracy," *Florida Law Review* 54, no. 5 (December 2002): 884–91.

91   Simon, "Big Media," p. 276.

92   See, for example, Maurice E. Stuckes and Allen P. Grunes, "Antitrust and the Marketplace of Ideas," *Antitrust Law Journal* 69 (2001): 249–302.

93   Doug Halonen, "Direct Benefit for Murdoch," *Television Week,* 12 May 2003, p. 3; Lauren Weinstein, "Why MS 'Ruling' Is Dangerous," www.wired.com, 11 November 2002.

94   Yochi J. Dreazen, "Senator Examines Lobbyists' Role in Justice, FTC Accord," *Wall Street Journal*, 16 April 2002.

95   See Laura R. Linder, *Public Access Television: America's Electronic Soapbox* (Westport, Conn.: Praeger, 1999).

96   Matthew Lasar, *Pacifica Radio: The Rise of an Alternative Network* (Philadelphia: Temple University Press, 1999).

97   Stephen Frantzich and John Sullivan, *The C-SPAN Revolution* (Norman, Okla.: University of Oklahoma Press, 1996).

98   Aaron Barnhart, "In Public TV We Trust," *Electronic Media*, 22 July 2002, p. 10.

99   See Jean Seaton, "Public Broadcasting: Imperfect but Essential," openDemocracy.net, 2001, p. 3.

100 See Kristin Hohenadel, "Where Television Sponsors the Film Industry," *New York Times*, 11 June 2000.

101 See Carnegie Commission on Public Television, *Public Television: A Program for Action* (New York: Harper & Row, 1967).

102 Roger Smith, "Public Broadcasting as State Television," www.tompaine.com, 11 March 2003.

103 Carnegie Commission, *Public Television*, p. 8.

104 Barnhart, "In Public TV We Trust," p. 10.

105 Linder, *Public Access Television*, p. 2.

106 "Democratic Platform 1968" in Donald Bruce Johnson., compiler, *National Party Platforms, Volume 2 1960–1976* (Chicago: University of Illinois Press), pp. 718–743.

107 Jerry Landay, "Failing the Perception Test," *Current*, June 2001; David Hatch, "PBS Decision Irks Tauzin," *Electronic Media*, 15 May 2000, p. 4.

108 Quotes from Lawrence Jarvik, *PBS: Behind the Screen* (Rocklin, Calif.: Forum, 1997), back cover.

109 Tom McCourt, *Conflicting Communication Interests in America: The Case of National Public Radio* (Westport, Conn.: Praeger, 1999), pp. 2–3.

110 John Nichols, "Here's One Cut NPR Can Afford to Make," *Capital Times* (Madison, Wis.), 23 October 2003.

111 The press teems with stories on this matter. See, for example, Sean Mitchell, "Public Radio, Under the Influence," *Los Angeles Times*, 27 May 2001; Sally Beatty, "Critics Claim PBS Has Gotten Too Close to Its Underwriters," *Wall Street Journal Online*, 11 July 2002; Pamela McClintock, "Blurbs Blur Line between PBS, Nets," *Variety*, 15–21 July 2002, p. 18; Paula Bernstein, "Not Your Parents' PBS," *Variety*, 16–22 April 2001, p. 13; Samuel G.

Freedman, "Public Radio's Private Guru," *New York Times*, 11 November 2001; "Minnesota Grabs the Marketplace," *Brill's Content*, July/August 2002, pp. 106–107.

112 "Myths and Realities," advertising sales pamphlet of the Public Broadcasting Cooperative of Illinois, 2002. Available online at www.pbcionline.org/myths.htm.

113 Elizabeth Jensen, "Corporate Funding Squeezing Public Television," *Los Angeles Times*, 5 February 2003; available online at www.theledger.com.

114 Elizabeth Jensen, "PBS Votes to Accept 30-Second Ad Spots," *Los Angeles Times*, 4 February 2003.

115 Steve Clarke, "Ball Bawls Out Fat Cat BBC," *Variety*, 1–7 September 2003, p. 22.

116 Jennifer Gilbert, "CTW Hunts Eyes, Ads with Sesame Street," *Advertising Age*, 3 January 2000, p. 24; Kimberley Pohlman, "The Commercialization of Children's Television: PBS's Ads Sell Toys, Drugs, and Junk Food to your Kids," *Extra!*, May/June 2000, pp. 13–14.

117 For a few recent titles, and this is just a small sample, see William Hoynes, *Public Television for Sale: Media, the Market, and the Public Sphere* (Boulder, Colo.: Westview Press, 1994); Roger P. Smith, *The Other Face of Public TV: Censoring the American Dream* (New York: Algora, 2002); Tom McCourt, *Conflicting Communication Interests in America* (Westport, Conn.: Praeger, 1999); B. J. Bullert, *Public Television: Politics and the Battle Over Documentary Film* (New Brunswick, N.J.: Rutgers University Press, 1997); James Day, *The Vanishing Vision: The Inside Story of Public Television* (Berkeley: University of California Press, 1995).

118 Joseph Weber, "Public TV's Identity Crisis," *Business Week*, 30 September 2003, pp. 65–66; John Motavalli, "PBS Facing Crisis," *Television Week*, 20 October 2003, pp. 1, 24.

119 Tom Lowry, Joseph Weber, and Catherine Yang, "Can NPR Bear the Burden of Wealth?" *Business Week*, 15 December 2003, p. 77.

120 William Hoynes, "Independent Public Broadcasting for the 21st Century," unpublished paper, November 1998. A summary of the Hoynes proposal is at: www.cipbonline.org/trustmain.htm.

CHAPTER 7

1 Christopher Lasch, *The Revolt of the Elite and the Betrayal of Democracy* (New York: W. W. Norton, 1995), pp. 162–63.

2 David Lieberman, "Media Merger Anxiety," *USA Today*, 9 October 2000.

3 Dhavan Shah, "Mergers and Open Access: Public Concerns and Preferences," report produced for the Digitial Media Forum, 13 September 2000.

4 For an overview of media criticism and activism in the United States over the past century, see Robert W. McChesney and Ben Scott, eds., *Our Unfree Press: 100 Years of Radical Media Criticism* (New York: The New Press, 2004).

5 Part of the deal to include the reduction of LPFM stations from 1,000 to a few hundred in the budget bill was to call for a study of whether, as the NAB claimed, Kennard's plan would have actually led to interference with the existing radio broadcasters. This study was completed in 2003 and it appears to have exonerated Kennard. As we go to press, LPFM advocates are working to

have Congress revisit the issue and implement the Kennard plan.

6   Robert W. McChesney, "Kennard, the Public, and the FCC," *The Nation*, 14 May 2001.

7   John Nichols and Robert W. McChesney, "On the Verge in Vermont: Media Reform Movement Nears Critical Mass," *Extra!*, July/August 2002, p. 26.

8   "FCC Chairman Michael Powell Announces Creation of Media Ownership Working Group," FCC news release., 29 October 2001.

9   Personal communication to author, 30 October 2003.

10 Cherly Arvidson, "FCC's Powell: Time to Give Broadcasters Full First Amendment Rights," www.freedomforum.org, 27 April 1998.

11 Jill Goldsmith and Pamela McClintock, "Powell Eyes Update: Chairman Urges Ownership Rules Changes," *Variety* online, 2 October 2002.

12 Frank Rose, "Big Media or Bust," *Wired*, March 2002.

13 "'The Antithesis of What the Public Interest Demands'," *Broadcasting & Cable*, 14 October 2002, p. 16.

14 Rose, "Big Media or Bust."

15 Dan Roberts, "FCC Chief 'Working Himself Out of a Job'," *Financial Times*, 25 May 2001, p. 3.

16 Bill McConnell, "'A Quiet Warrior for Ownership Deregulation," *Broadcasting & Cable*, 13 October 2003, p. 36.

17 "FCC Approves Digital Radio," online.wsj.com, 10 October 2002.

18 Jube Shiver Jr., "Citizens Knocking on FCC's Door," *Los Angeles Times*, 26 January 2003.

19 Bill McConnell, "Martin Likes the FCC's Measured Pace," *Broadcasting & Cable*, 9 December 2002, p. 26.

20 Dissenting Statement of Commissioner Michael J. Copps, *Re: In the Matter of Applications for Consent to the Transfer of Control of Licenses from Comcast Corporation and AT&T Corp., Transferors, to AT&T Comcast Corporation, Transferee MB Docket No. 02-70*, November 2002.

21 Bill McConnell, "Media Face Grilling From Copps," *Broadcasting & Cable*, 25 November 2002, p. 10.

22 Doug Halonen, "Copps Will Hold Field Hearings on Ownership," *Electronic Media*, 25 November 2002, p. 3.

23 "Commissioner Michael J. Copps Expresses 'Alarm' and 'Disappointment' with FCC's Media Concentration Decision," FCC news release, 5 November 2002.

24 Doug Halonen, "FCC Opens the Door for Broadcast-Cable Combos," *Electronic Media*, 16 September 2002, pp. 1, 18.

25 Pamela McClintock, "Will GOP Change the Rules?" *Variety*, 11-17 November 2002, p. 19.

26 Edward Ericson Jr., "The News from Corporate," *Harper's Magazine*, August 2002, pp. 52-53.

27 Yochi J. Dreazen, "Three Media Firms Ask FCC to Abandon Ownership Rules," *Wall Street Journal*, 3 January 2003.

28 Bill Kovach and Tom Rosenstiel, "All News Media Inc.," *New York Times*, 7 January 2003.

29 Marvin Kalb, "Quality Is No Issue," www.newsday.com, 19 January, 2003.

30 Mark Fitzgerald, "Copps: Media Should Cover FCC Reform," www.editorandpublisher.com, 16 April 2003.

31 Edmund Sanders, "Media Giants at Odds Over FCC Cap on TV Station Ownership," *Los Angeles Times*, 18 February 2003.

32 Mark Wigfield, "FCC Flooded with Letters Opposing Media Consolidation," online.wsj.com, 3 January 2003.

33 "A Call for Media Democracy," letter to FCC organized by Fairness & Accuracy in Reporting, December 2002.

34 "Statement of Commissioner Jonathan S. Adelstein, Dissenting," FCC release, 2 June 2003, p. 5.

35 Doug Halonen, "FCC's Deregulation Proposals Hit Hurdle," *Electronic Media*, 20 January 2003, p. 4.

36 Robert W. McChesney and John Nichols, "Holding the Line at the FCC," *The Progressive*, April 2003.

37 Pamela McClintock, "FCC to Tackle Ownership Rules," *Variety*, 20-26 January 2003, p. A11.

38 Bill McConnell, "Powell Grants Dereg Hearing in Richmond," *Broadcasting & Cable*, 9 December 2002, p. 8.

39 "Onward to Richmond," *Broadcasting & Cable*, 9 December 2002, p. 40.

40 Catherine Yang, "The FCC's Loner Is No Longer So Lonely," *Business Week*, 24 March 2003, p. 78; "Ownership Hearings Added," *Electronic Media*, 10 February 2003, p. 6.

41 Peter Thal Larsen, "Viacom to Seek More US Acquisitions," *Financial Times*, 12 February 2003.

42 Edmund Sanders, "Reflecting on Media Ownership Debate," www.newsday.com, 2 June 2003.

43 Doug Halonen, "Michael Copps," *Electronic Media*, 20 January 2003, p. 52.

44 Andrew Ratner, "FCC Is Assailed on Plan Aiding Big Media Firms," *Baltimore Sun*, 25 May 2003.

45 Mark Jurkowitz, "FCC Chairman: Consolidation Hasn't Inhibited Variety, Fairness," *Boston Globe*, 17 April 2003.

46 Goldsmith and McClintock, "Powell Eyes Update," 2 October 2002.

47 Demetri Sevastopulo, "Vote to Relax Media Rules Sparks Protest," *Financial Times*, 3 June 2003, p. 1.

48 Dan Fost, "FCC Media Rules Up for Revision," *San Francisco Chronicle*, 13 Feb. 2003.

49 "Remarks of Michael J. Powell, Chairman, Federal Communications Commission," The Media Institute, 27 March 2003.

50 Robert W. McChesney and John Nichols, "Holding the Line at the FCC," *The Progressive*, April 2003.

51 Patricia Aufderheide, *Communications in the Public Interest* (New York: The Guilford Press, 1999), p. 168.

52 Stephen Labaton, "Senators Move to Restore F.C.C. Limits on the Media," *New York Times*, 5 June 2003.

53 Fost, "FCC Media Rules Up for Revision."

54 Jon Fine, "FCC Chief: Media Consolidation Serves Public," www.adage.com, 28 April 2003.

55 "Remarks of Michael J. Powell," Media Institute, Peter Thal Larsen and Demetri Sevastopulo, "Powell Under Pressure: As the US Prepares to Relax Its Laws on Media Ownership, a Political Battle Brews," *Financial Times*, 30 April 2003, p. 13.

56 Al Tompkins, "Powell: 'Rising Anxiety Over Radio Ownership'," www.poynter.org, 9 April 2003.

57 Michael K Powell, "New Rules, Old Rhetoric," *New York Times*, 28 July 2003.

58 "Remarks of Michael J. Powell," Media Institute.

59 Staci D. Kramer, "FCC Chairman Michael Powell Sees Bright Future for Online Media," *Online Journalism Review*, www.ojr.org, 4 September 2003.

60 Michael K. Powell, "Should Limits on Broadcast Ownership Change?" *USA Today*, 21 January 2003.

61 Todd Bishop, "FCC May Drop Rules Limiting Media Ownership in a Single Market," *Seattle Post-Intelligencer*, 29 April 2003.

62 "Dialogue with NBC Chairman Bob
    Wright," *Hollywood Reporter*,
    18 February 2003.

63 Michael Powell, comments to National
    Association of Broadcasters Convention,
    Las Vegas, Nevada, April 2003.

64 Joanna Glasner, "Media More Diverse? Not
    Really," www.wired.com, 30 May 2003.

65 Peter Thal Larsen and Demetri
    Sevastopulo, "Free-to-Air TV is Under
    Threat, Warns FCC Chief," *Financial
    Times*, 30 April 2003, p. 1.

66 Associated Press, "FCC Chief Wants
    Ownership Rules Eased," 27 May 2003.

67 Comments of Michael K. Powell, John
    McLaughlin's *One on One* television
    program, taped 4 September 2003.

68 Joe Flint, "Loosening Media Regulations
    Risks Thwarting Innovation," *Wall Street
    Journal Online*, online.wsj.com, 2 June 2003.

69 Edmund Sanders and Jube Shiver Jr.,
    "FCC Relaxes Limits on Media Owner-
    ship," *Los Angeles Times*, 3 June 2003.

70 Brooks Boliek, "FCC Majority Set on Rules
    Rewrite," *Hollywood Reporter*, 9 May 2003.

71 Tom Shales, "Michael Powell and the
    FCC: Giving Away the Marketplace of
    Ideas," *Washington Post*, 2 June 2003.

72 Stuart Elliott, "Early Ad Sales for the
    2003-4 TV Season Turn Into a 'Runaway
    Sellers' Market'," *New York Times*,
    23 May 2003.

73 Steve McClellan, "Broadcast Nets Hit the
    Jackpot," *Broadcasting & Cable*, 2 June
    2003, p. 24.

74 "It's Way Upfront," *Broadcasting & Cable*,
    2 June 2003, p. 1.

75 Jay Sherman, "Study: Broadcast Ad Cash
    on the Rise," *Television Week*, 11 August
    2003, p. 6; Diane Mermigas, "Broadcast
    Growth Projected," *Television Week*,
    16 June 2003, p. 3.

76 Jube Shiver Jr., "Senate Committee to
    Take On FCC Rules," *Los Angeles Times*,
    5 June 2003.

77 Michael K. Powell, "New Rules, Old
    Rhetoric," *New York Times*, 28 July 2003.

78 Catherine Yang and Joseph Weber,
    "Where Media Merger Mania Could Strike
    First," *Business Week*, 9 June 2003, p. 96.

79 For a very small sampling, see Ira Tein-
    owitz and Jon Fine, "Media Giants Gird
    for Merger Mania," *Advertising Age*, 19 May
    2003, pp. 3, 142; Jay Sherman, "Station
    Deals Wait in the Wings," *Television Week*,
    19 May 2003, pp. 1, 62; Mark Fitzgerald
    and Todd Shields, "After June 2, Papers
    May Make Broadcast News," *Editor &
    Publisher*, 26 May 2003, pp. 3-4; Lucia
    Moses, "On the Road to Freedom," *Editor
    & Publisher*, 24 March 2003, pp. 14-19, 29.

80 Louis Aguilar, "Post Publisher: FCC to
    Lift Bans," *Denver Post*, 23 February 2003.

81 Catherine Yang and Joseph Weber,
    "Media Merger Mania: The First Wave,"
    www.businessweek.com, 30 May 2003.

82 Alec Klein and David A. Vise, "Media
    Giants Hint They Might Be Expanding,"
    Washington Post, 3 June 2003.

83 Dominic Timms, "US Media Bill Faces
    Further Revolt," media.guardian.co.uk,
    16 July 2003.

84 "Statement of Commissioner Jonathan
    S. Adelstein, Dissenting," FCC news
    release, 2 June 2003.

85 "Statement of Commissioner Michael J.
    Copps, Dissenting," FCC news release,
    2 June 2003.

86 Michael Copps, "Crunch Time at the
    FCC," *The Nation*, 3 February 2003, p. 5.

87 Powell, "New Rules, Old Rhetoric";
    Comments of Michael K. Powell.

88 Mark Wigfield, "Bear Stearns Analyst
    Helps FCC Reshape Ownership Rules,"

Dow Jones Newswires, 2 June 2003.

89 Dean Baker, "Democracy Unhinged: More Concentration Means Less Public Discourse—A Critique of the FCC Studies on Media Ownership" (Washington, D.C.: Department for Professional Employees, AFL-CIO, 2003), p. 23. http://www.dpeaflcio.org/pdf/FCC_Critique.pdf

90 Jennifer 8. Lee, "Musicians Protest Monopoly in Media," New York Times, 18 December 2003.

91 Martin Kaplan, "The 'Local' in Local TV Is in Danger," Christian Science Monitor, 2 June 2003.

92 Baker, "Democracy Unhinged," p. 22.

93 Robert W. McChesney interview of Michael Copps, 20 February 2003.

94 Bill McConnell, "Critics: FCC Stacks Dereg Deck," Broadcasting & Cable, 7 Oct. 2002.

95 McChesney, "Holding the Line at the FCC."

96 Edmund Sanders, "FCC Takes Debate on the Road," Los Angeles Times, 28 February 2003.

97 David Ho, "Media Ownership Review to Finish in May," Associated Press dispatch, 26 February 2003.

98 Keri Brenner, "FCC Member Warns about Consolidation," Marin Independent Journal, 26 April 2003.

99 "The Arizona Forum on Media Ownership," www.Benton.org, 7 April 2003, Alwyn Scott, "Move to Ease Media-Ownership Rules Given a Cool Reception in Seattle," Seattle Times, 8 March 2003; Hunter Lewis, "FCC Gets an Earful at Hearing," Herald-Sun, 31 March 2003, Suzanne Bohan, "Huge Turnout at FCC Meeting," Argus, www.theargusonline.com, 3 April 2003.

100 Jonathan S. Adelstein, "Big Macs and Big Media: The Decision to Supersize," Remarks at the Media Institute, 20 May 2003.

101 Steven T. Jones, "The Democracy Disaster," www.sfbg.com, 6 May 2003, Karen Young, "The Midwest Public Forum on Media Ownership," CMW Report, Spring 2003, pp. 6-7.

102 John Sugg, "You Say You Wanna Bigger Cox?" Atlanta.creativeloafing.com, 29 May 2003.

103 Charles Layton, "News Blackout," American Journalism Review, December/January 2004. Available online at www.ajr.org.

104 See, for example, Jennifer Lee, " On Minot, N.D., Radio, a Single Corporate Voice," New York Times, 31 March 2003; Joanne Ostrow, "Musicians Blast FCC Plan," Denver Post, 23 May 2003.

105 Tom Shales, "Dialing In a Bland TV Landscape," Television Week, 2 June 2003, p. 53.

106 Craig Linder, "FCC Dems Hear from Deregulation Opponents," Hollywood Reporter, 28 May 2003.

107 "Time for Congress to Save the Media," Seattle Times, 3 June 2003.

108 George F. Curry, "FCC Decision Curbs Dissent," Final Call.com News, 22 June 2003; "Who Killed Black Radio News?" The Black Commentator, issue no. 44, www.blackcommentator.com, May 2003.

109 Eric Boehlert, "Clear Channel's Big, Stinking Deregulation Mess," www.salon.com, 19 February 2003.

110 Mark Cooper, "Mass Deregulation of Media Threatens to Undermine Democracy," news release of Consumer Federation of America, 3 June 2003; "Key Facts about Media Markets in America," report of Consumers Union and the Consumer Federation of America, Washington, D.C., May 2003.

111 Catherine Yang, "The News Biz: Is Bigger Better?" Business Week, 3 March 2003, p. 97.

112 "Powell Remarks," Media Institute.

113 "The Silence of the Lambs: Who Speaks for Journalists Before the FCC?" *Columbia Journalism Review*, January/February 2003; P. J. Bednarski, "Losing Our Voices," *Broadcasting & Cable*, 9 June 2003, p. 67.

114 "Pushing Back at the FCC," *The Guild Reporter*, 24 January 2003, pp. 1–2.

115 "IFJ Criticises Proposed Changes in Media Ownership Rules," IFJ news release, May 2003.

116 John Eggerton, "Unions Fight Urge to Merge," *Broadcasting & Cable*, 30 December 2002, p. 12.

117 Edmund Sanders, "Hollywood Guilds Band Together to Defend Media Ownership," *Los Angeles Times*, 13 January 2003.

118 "Union Movement Says Media Monopolies Threaten Democracy," AFL-CIO news release, 5 March 2003.

119 "PR Society Seeks More Transparency in FCC Broadcast Ownership review," www.businesswire.com, 27 May 2003, Ira Teinowitz, "4A's to Dispute FCC Findings on Media Industry Mergers," *Advertising Age*, 21 October 2002, p. 8; David Verklin, "Go Slow on FCC Rule Change," *Advertising Age*, 19 May 2003, p. 22.

120 Pamela McClintock, "Sony, Ad Firm Say Consolidation Leads to Bland TV," *Variety* news dispatch, 2 February 2003.

121 Ted Turner, "Monopoly or Democracy?" *Washington Post*, 30 May 2003.

122 Tom Shales, "Michael Powell and the FCC: Giving Away the Marketplace of Ideas," *Washington Post*, 2 June 2003.

123 Frank Ahrens, "FCC Bid to Alter Media Rules Spurs Free-Speech Debate," *Washington Post*, 28 May 2003.

124 Rick Ellis, "Commentary: The Surrender of MSNBC," www.allyourtv.com, 25 February 2003.

125 Ira Teinowitz, "FCC Chairman Ho-Hums Anti-War Ad Controversy," www.adage.com, 29 January 2003.

126 Brent Staples, "The Trouble with Corporate Radio: The Day the Protest Music Died," *New York Times*, 20 February 2003.

127 Andy Paras, "Morning Radio Co-Host Sues Station That Fired Her," greenvilleonline.com, 7 July 2003; Paul Schmelzer, "The Death of Local News," AlterNet.com, 22 April 2003; Tom Shales, "Michael Powell and the FCC: Giving Away the Marketplace of Ideas," *Washington Post*, 2 June 2003.

128 "Powell Remarks," Media Institute; Andrew Ratner, "War Coverage Could Alter U.S. Media Policy," *Baltimore Sun*, 30 March 2003.

129 Ted Hearn, "Commish: Media Copping Out on Coverage," *Multichannel News*, 29 April 2003.

130 See Gal Beckerman, "Tripping Up Big Media," *Columbia Journalism Review*, November/December 2003, pp. 15–20.

131 Marc Fisher, "FCC Tests Reception for Lifting Ownership Limits," *Washington Post*, 28 February 2003.

132 Statement of Richard Burr, Hearing on Media Ownership, Duke University, Durham, N.C., 31 March 2003.

133 Wayne LaPierre, "Speak Out vs. FCC While You Can," New York *Daily News*, 18 July 2003.

134 Richard Burr and Jesse Helms, "Keep Control of TV Local," *Charlotte Observer*, 19 October 2003.

135 "Statement of Michael Copps," 2 June 2003.

136 William Safire, "On Media Giantism," *New York Times*, 20 January 2003; William Safire, "Big Media's Silence," *New York Times*, 17 July 2003; William Safire,

"Localism's Last Stand," *New York Times*, 24 July 2003; William Safire, "Bush's Four Horsemen," *New York Times*, 20 January 2003; William Safire, "The Senate Says No," *New York Times*, 17 September 2003.

137 William Safire, "The Great Media Gulp," *New York Times*, 22 May 2003.

138 William Safire, "The Russian Reversion," *New York Times*, 10 December 2003.

139 William Safire, "Regulate the F.C.C.," *New York Times*, 16 June 2003.

140 Mark Wigfield, "FCC's Powell Urges Divided Media Industry to Back Dereg," Dow Jones Business News dispatch, 7 April 2003.

141 Lucia Moses, "Powell to NAA: Expect Ownership Reform," *Editor and Publisher Online*, 28 April 2003.

142 John Nichols, "The FCC Rejects Public Interest," www.thenation.com, 2 June 2003; Bob Williams, "Behind Closed Doors," Center for Public Integrity, 29 May 2003.

143 Bob Williams and Morgan Jindrich, "On the Road Again—and Again," *The Public I*, July 2003, pp. 1, 4.

144 Mark Wigfield, "Bear Stearns Analyst Helps FCC Reshape Ownership Rules," Dow Jones Newswires, 2 June 2003.

145 Mark Wigfield, "Top FCC Aide to Become Lobbyist for Broadcasters' Assoc.," Dow Jones Newswires, 8 December 2003.

146 Nichols, "The FCC Rejects Public Interest."

147 Thane Peterson, "Why the FCC Needs a New Chief," *Business Week Online*, 9 September 2003.

148 "Statement of Michael Copps," 2 June 2003.

149 "Adelstein remarks," Media Institute.

150 "Chicago Says No to Dereg," *Broadcasting & Cable*, 19 May 2003, p. 12.

151 Dante Chinni, "Media Drop Ball on FCC Rules Changes," *Christian Science Monitor*, 10 June 2003.

152 "FCC Chairman Defends Position Ahead of Media Rules Vote," www.cnn.com, 28 May 2003; "Powell remarks," Media Institute.

153 David Ho, "U.S. Pushes FCC on Media Ownership Review," Associated Press, 24 April 2003.

154 Annie Lawson, "US Media Dig Deep for Politicians," *The Guardian*, 7 April 2003.

155 Tim Grieve, "Fox News: The Inside Story," www.salon.com, 31 October 2003.

156 Alex Ben Block, "FCC: The Fix Was In," *Television Week*, 9 June 2003, p. 8.

157 Bernard Weinraub, "CBS Is Reconsidering Mini-Series on Reagan," *New York Times*, 4 November 2003.

158 James Harding, "CBS Pulls Reagan Biopic after Lobbying," *Financial Times*, 5 November 2003, p. 1

159 "The New Fairness Doctrine," *Broadcasting & Cable*, 3 November 2003, p. 40.

160 Ron Orol, "FCC to Vote on Media Rules," www.thedeal.com, 15 April 2003.

161 "FCC, Powell Must Bring the Public into the Process," *Television Week*, 21 April 2003, p. 8.

162 David Ho, "FCC Democrats Frustrated on Media Review," Associated Press dispatch, 10 May 2003.

163 Stephen Labaton, "F.C.C. Vote on Media Ownership Unlikely to Be Delayed," *New York Times*, 14 May 2003.

164 "Ownership Protestors March in 14 Cities," *Hollywood Reporter*, 30 May 2003.

165 "Consumer Groups Charge FCC Analysis Supporting Media Ownership Rules Is Fundamentally Flawed," news release of Consumers Union and Consumer Federation of America, 21 July 2003.

The full report is Mark Cooper, "Abracadabra! Hocus-Pocus! Making Media Market Power Disappear with the FCC's Diversity Index," issued by Consumer Federation of America and Consumers Union, July 2003.

166 "Statement of Michael Copps," 2 June 2003.

167 "Adelstein Statement," 2 June 2003.

168 Bill McConnell, "Tauzin's Heir Apparent Seen as Cable's Friend," *Broadcasting & Cable*, 17 November 2003, p. 8.

169 Demetri Sevastopulo, "Senators Deploy Veto to Attack Media Rules," *Financial Times*, 16 July 2003, p. 3.

170 Dominic Timms, "US Media Bill Faces Further Revolt," media.guardian.co.uk, 16 July 2003.

171 William Safire, "Regulate the Media," *New York Times*, 16 June 2003, p. 23.

172 Brooks Boliek, "House Panel Votes to Roll Back Ownership Cap," *Hollywood Reporter*, 16 July 2003. See also: http://www.cbc-raleigh.com/capcom/news/2003/corporate_03/fcc_congress/fcc_congress.htm.

173 Jube Shiver Jr., Richard Simon, and Edmund Sanders, "FCC Ruling Puts Rivals on the Same Wavelength," *Los Angeles Times*, 9 June 2003.

174 Richard Simon and Janet Hook, "FCC Rule May Bring a Veto Standoff," *Los Angeles Times*, 25 July 2003.

175 Yochi J. Dreazen, "Democrats Seize on FCC Role," online.wsj.com, 4 June 2003.

176 Pew Research Center for the People and rhe Press, "Strong Opposition to Media Cross-Ownership Emerges," A Survey Conducted in Association with the Project for Excellence in Journalism, 13 July 2003; see also Dan Trigoboff, "New FCC Rules Get Thumbs Down," *Broadcasting & Cable*, 21 July 2003, p. 22.

177 "[Industry-Sponsored] Survey Finds Public Tuning Out FCC Debate," *Hollywood Reporter*, 3 September 2003.

178 Peter J. Howe, "FCC Chief Defends Changes in Media Ownership Rules," *Boston Globe*, 11 June 2003; Mark Jurkowitz, "FCC Chairman: Consolidation Hasn't Inhibited Variety, Fairness," *Boston Globe*, 17 April 2003.

179 Stephen Labaton, "F.C.C. Chief Talks of Frustration and Surprise," *New York Times*, 22 September 2003.

180 Craig Rimlinger, "Feingold Leads Charge Against New FCC Rules," *Capital Times* (Madison, Wis.), 16 July 2003.

181 Author conversation with Rep. David Price, Washington, D.C., 25 September 2003.

182 Brooks Boliek, "FCC Hill-Bent for Grilling," *Hollywood Reporter*, 4 June 2003.

183 Susan Crabtree, "Networks Move to Foil Pols on FCC Regs," *Daily Variety*, 14 July 2003, p. 35.

184 Memo to NAA Publishers from John F. Sturm, president and CEO, MAA, 4 August 2003.

185 "NAB About-Face on FCC Ownership Rules," TV Week E-mail Alert, 9 July 2003.

186 Richard Simon and Janet Hook, "FCC Rule May Bring a Veto Standoff," *Los Angeles Times*, 25 July 2003.

187 "Powell Fights Back," www.TVtechnology.com, 7 July 2003.

188 "FCC Sets June 2 Ownership Hearing," *Television Week*, 31 March 2003, p. 4; "MMTC Endorses FCC Diversity Advisory Committee," Minority Media and Telecommunications Council news release, 27 May 2003.

189 Brian Lowry, "Powell's Doomed Power Play," *Variety*, 29 September–5 October 2003, p. 22.

190 David Ho, "FCC to Study Industry-Sponsored Trips," Associated Press dispatch, 2 September 2003.

191 Mark Wigfield, "FCC Suffers Court Setback on Media Ownership Rules," Wall Street Journal, 4 September 2003.

192 "FCC's Powell Seeks to Counter Criticism with New Initiatives," Wall Street Journal, 20 August 2003; Jacques Steinberg, "Facing Criticism, F.C.C. Is Thinking Local," New York Times, 21 August 2003.

193 "Statement of James F. Goodmon, President and CEO, Capitol Broadcasting Co., Inc., following FCC Michael Powell's News Conference," Raleigh, N.C., 21 August 2003.

194 "Copps Criticizes Willingness to Let Media Consolidation Continue," FCC news release, 20 August 2003.

195 Ted Hearn, "Tauzin, Upton Warn Money Panel on FCC," Multichannel News, 14 July 2003.

196 Bill McConnell, "Ready, Aim, Re-Reg," Broadcasting & Cable, 21 July 2003, pp. 1, 48.

197 Frank James, "Battle over FCC Rules on Media Ownership," Seattle Times, 10 August 2003, p. E1.

198 Simon and Hook, "FCC Rule May Bring Veto Standoff."

199 "House Republicans Fail to Rally Media Bill Opposition," Bloomberg dispatch, 31 July 2003.

200 Statement of Senator Fritz Hollings, released by his office, 25 November 2003.

201 Doug Halonen, "Ownership Cap Deal Angers Some Lawmakers," Television Week, 1 December 2003, p. 77.

202 David Firestone, "Senate Won't Vote on Spending Until 2004," New York Times, 10 December 2003.

203 Stephen Labaton, "F.C.C. Plan to Ease Curbs on Big Media Hits Senate Snag," New York Times, 17 September 2003.

204 Bill McConnell, "Ownership Reg Faces Murky Outcome," Broadcasting & Cable, 22 September 2003, p. 3.

205 Ibid.

206 Mark Wigfield, "FCC Suffers Court Setback on Media Ownership Rules," Wall Street Journal, 4 September 2003.

207 Stephen Labaton, "U.S. Court Blocks Plan to Ease Rule on Media Owners," New York Times, 4 September 2003.

208 Lou Dobb's Tonight, 2 December 2003. www.cnn.com/CNN/Programs/lou.dobbs.tonight/

209 Bill McConnell, "Dean Takes a Shot at Media Concentration," Broadcasting & Cable, 8 December 2003, p. 10; John Nichols, "Kucinich Makes Media an Issue," The Nation Online, 14 December 2003. http://thenation.com/thebeat/index.mhtml?bid=1&pid=1128

INDEX

Amendment and, 225–26, 228; Internet campaign and, 217; new media industries and, 227–28; newspaper industry, 226, 227, 228, 229–30; radio broadcasting, 230–32; self-regulatory codes, 228–29. *See also* copyright

Pacifica (broadcasting) system, 242
Paine, Thomas, 22
Palast, Greg, 81
partisanship, 58–60, 102, 108–9, 116, 118–23, 133; professionalism and, 66, 68, 71. *See also specific political party*
Pataki, George, 129
Patterson, Thomas, 125
payola (bribes), in radio, 231–32. *See also* corruption
PBS (Public Broadcasting System), 91, 244, 245, 247, 248, 250
Pearl Harbor (film), 85
Pennsylvania, property rights in, 22
Pentagon Papers case, 75
Pepsico, 155
Perot, Ross, 52
Petty, Tom, 232
Pew Research Center, 83, 288
Philadelphia Inquirer (newspaper), 77
Philips Electronics, 154
Phillips, Kevin, 125
Pickard, Victor, 14
Pingree, Chellie, 277
Pirates of the Caribbean (film), 185
Pittstown sit-down strike (1998), 76
Pixar (animation studio), 185
policy debates, 24, 38, 63
policy issues, 173, 209, 216, 251, 295–96; advertising and, 168–72; *See also* media reform movement. *See* policy making
policy making, 10–12, 47–48, 51, 205, 210–24; communication technology and, 211–16; corruption in, 56; democratic, 7, 207, 296–97; digital broadcasting, 213–16;

Internet and, 217–24; journalism and Internet, 216–17; nonprofit subsidies, 211, 220–21; process of, 37–38, 210–11; public participation in, 12, 38, 202, 252–53, 296–97. *See also* ownership policy; regulation
political activism, Internet and, 216–17
political culture, 70, 99, 125–26, 133–34, 220; depoliticization and, 72, 95, 126
political ideology, 71, 118–19. *See also* conservatism; liberalism
populist movement, 112–13
Posner, Richard, 124
postal subsidies, 32–33, 62–63
Postman, Neil, 211
Post Office Act of 1792, 33
Powe, Lucas, 235
Powell, Colin, 121
Powell, Michael, 13, 254, 258–65, 276, 283, 290; activist pressure on, 258–59, 284–85; on benefits of media concentration, 277, 280; Congress and, 266; corporate lobbies and, 46, 259–60; deregulation arguments of, 268–73, 281; FCC public hearings and, 261–62, 263–64, 265, 290; media mogul critique of, 278–79
power: of journalists, 99–102, 108–9; market, 221, 238. *See also* corporate power
Pravda (newspaper), 99, 100
Premier Retail Networks, 160
presidency, coverage of, 69. *See also specific president*
press: alternative, 90; as fourth estate, 28, 36, 81. *See also* free press; newspaper publishing
Price, David, 289
price, rationing by, 190–91
price competition, 139–40, 177
Princeton Video Image, 147
privacy rights, 218
product information, 169–70, 172